100 *Best*
Golf Resorts
of the
World

Packed with Solid Advice on the
Best Places to Play and Stay

KAREN MISURACA

The
Globe
Pequot
Press

GUILFORD, CONNECTICUT

TO MY GOLF GURU, MICHAEL, AND TO
MY GOLF BUDDIES, BARBARA AND LYNDA—
MAY THE EAGLES FLY! (OR, AT LEAST THE BIRDIES)

Text design: Nancy Freeborn

ISBN 0-7627-2222-3

Manufactured in Korea
First Edition/First Printing

CONTENTS

Introduction vi

NORTH AMERICA

United States

Arizona

The Boulders 2
Fairmont Scottsdale Princess 4
Four Seasons Resort Scottsdale at Troon North 6
Hyatt Regency Scottsdale Resort at Gainey Ranch 8
The Lodge at Ventana Canyon 10
The Phoenician 12
The Westin La Paloma Resort and Spa 14

California

Four Seasons Resort Aviara 16
The Inn and Links at Spanish Bay 18
La Quinta Resort and Club 20
Marriott Desert Springs Resort and Spa 22
Ojai Valley Inn and Spa 24
Pebble Beach Resorts .26
Quail Lodge Resort and Golf Club 28
The Ritz-Carlton, Half Moon Bay 30
Silverado Resort 32
St. Regis Monarch Beach Resort and Spa 34
Westin Mission Hills Resort 36

Colorado

The Broadmoor 38
The Lodge and Spa at Cordillera 40

Florida

Amelia Island Plantation 42
Doral Golf Resort and Spa 44
Grand Cypress Resort .46
Hyatt Regency Coconut Point Resort and Spa 48
Palm Coast Golf Resort 50
The Ritz-Carlton Golf Resort, Naples 52
Sawgrass Marriott Resort and Beach Club 54

Turnberry Isle Resort and Club 56
Westin Innisbrook Resort 58
World Golf Village 60

Georgia

Callaway Gardens Resort 62
The Cloister at Sea Island 64

Hawaii

Four Seasons Resort Maui at Wailea 66
Hilton Waikoloa Village 68
Hyatt Regency Kauai Resort and Spa 70
Kapalua Bay Hotel 72
The Lodge at Koele 74
The Manele Bay Hotel .76
Mauna Kea Beach Hotel 78
Mauna Lani Bay Hotel .80
Princeville Resort 82

Idaho

The Coeur d'Alene Resort 84

Michigan

Grand Traverse Resort and Spa 86

Nevada

Hyatt Regency Lake Las Vegas Resort 88

New York

The Otesaga 90

The Sagamore 92

North Carolina

Pinehurst Resort 94

Oregon

Sunriver Resort 96

Westin Salishan Lodge and Golf Resort 98

Pennsylvania

Nemacolin Woodlands Resort and Spa 100

South Carolina

Hilton Head Resorts 102

Kiawah Island Resorts 104

Wild Dunes Resort 106

Texas

Barton Creek 108

The Westin La Cantera Resort 110

Vermont

The Equinox 112

Virginia

Williamsburg Inn 114

The Homestead Resort .116

Kingsmill Resort 118

Washington

Resort Semiahmoo 120

West Virginia

The Greenbrier 122

Wisconsin

The American Club 124

Canada

The Fairmont Banff Springs 126

Fairmont Château Whistler 128

Fairmont Le Château Montebello 130

Mexico

Four Seasons Resort Punta Mita 132

Grand Bay Hotel Isla Navidad 134

Meliá Cabo Real Beach and Golf Resort 136

Palmilla Resort and Golf Club 138

Westin Regina Golf and Beach Resort Los Cabos . . .140

EUROPE

France

Dolce Chantilly 144

Dolce Frégate 146

Royal Parc Evian 148

Ireland

Adare Manor Hotel and Golf Resort 150

The Kildare Hotel and Golf Club 152

Portmarnock Hotel and Golf Links 154

Italy

Palazzo Arzaga Hotel Spa and Golf Resort 156

Scotland

Carnoustie Hotel Golf Resort and Spa 158

The Gleneagles Hotel 160

Old Course Hotel Golf Resort and Spa 162

Westin Turnberry Resort 164

Spain

The San Roque Club 166

Westin La Quinta Golf Resort 168

CARIBBEAN ISLANDS
& THE BAHAMAS

The Bahamas

Ocean Club 172

Our Lucaya Beach and Golf Resort 174

Barbados

Sandy Lane Hotel and Golf Club 176

Dominican Republic

Casa de Campo 178
Punta Cana Resort and Club 180

Jamaica

Ritz-Carlton Golf and Spa Resort, Rose Hall 182
Wyndham Rose Hall Resort and Country Club 184

Nevis

Four Seasons Resort Nevis 186

Puerto Rico

Hyatt Regency Cerromar Beach 188
Westin Rio Mar Beach Resort and Golf Club 190
Wyndham El Conquistador Resort 192

AFRICA

South Africa

Sun City Resort 196

PACIFIC RIM

Australia

Hyatt Regency Sanctuary Cove 200

Indonesia

Amanusa 202
Le Meridien Nirwana Golf and Spa Resort 204

Thailand

Amanpuri 206

CENTRAL AMERICA

Costa Rica

Meliá Playa Conchal All-Suites Beach
    and Golf Resort 210

About the Author 212

The information listed in this guidebook was confirmed at press time but under no circumstances are they guaranteed. We recommend that you call establishments before traveling to obtain current information.

INTRODUCTION

You love to play golf. You love to travel. The perfect vacation combines both in a splendid location that has a fabulous hotel with great personal service, good food, and, above all, a challenging and visually spectacular golf course.

Within this guide are resorts to make a golfer's dreams come true. Imagine arriving at a world-famous hotel, being greeted by name, and being relieved of all your bags and all your cares. Imagine setting off on the first tee of a course where legendary players have trod and golf history has been made.

Besides beauty and tradition, great course condition, and practice venues, what should we expect of the world's best golf resorts?

The Setting

The resorts in this book are located in unique surroundings, from the stunning river valley of the Canadian Rockies at the Fairmont Banff Springs to the vibrant color and drama of The Boulders in the Sonoran Desert of Arizona. Each one has a sense of place that distinguishes it from all others.

Perhaps more than at any other site on the planet, the spirit and tradition of the game is palpable at St.

Andrews in Scotland. Against a backdrop of the ancient stone buildings of the town, an audience of locals, caddies, and golfers is omnipresent on the first tee. They listen raptly as the starter calls, "Gentlemen, hit away." Nary a golfer drives his first shot into the swirling mists off the North Sea without a catch in the throat.

In California the pulse of the sea comes into play at Pebble Beach, where the wind-battered finishing hole comes to a smashing conclusion on a rocky point above a boiling cauldron of waves. Barking harbor seals seem to laugh while you struggle to keep the ball from flying off the skinny fairway into the Pacific as you approach the green, menaced by Monterey pines and a quartet of bunkers, and backed by one of the world's great hostelries, the Lodge at Pebble Beach.

At Nicklaus North in British Columbia, the famous River of Golden Dreams meanders through the fairways, and feisty Fitzsimmons Creek creates havoc for golfers where it fronts the eighteenth green. Water lilies bloom on the pond near the fifth hole, where blue-winged teal chatter and hide in the bulrushes. Great blue herons stalk about, fishing in the tall reeds and rising on 6-foot wingspans to fly off when golf balls land in the water.

Attitude and Special Services

From the bellmen and the front desk clerks, to the golf starter, the concierge, and the housekeepers, staff members at top resorts are unfailingly helpful and watchful for your every desire. You know you are in the right place when your golf bags and shoes are whisked away, only to reappear in your cart at tee time; and, the doorman and receptionist call you by name.

Four- and five-star hotels are expert at providing discrete, personal assistance. A twenty-four-hour butler is not uncommon. How about an impromptu cocktail party in your suite, a housecall from a doctor, a bonded baby-sitter, special dietary items, gifts and flowers, golf balls, or even a helicopter or a Rolls Royce? Just ask!

At the Mauna Lani Bay Hotel in Hawaii, you are met at the airport, greeted with an "Aloha!" and a lei, and entertained with a run-down on local history on the way to the resort. Everyone knows your name when you step out of the shuttle, or the limo. You are escorted to a comfortable armchair in the flower-filled atrium, handed a cold fruit drink—or a Mai Tai, if you prefer—and encouraged to relax before the formalities of registration. Next day your clubs and shoes are waiting on your solar-powered golf cart, along with a cooler of iced, bottled water. Turn on the GPS, and the fun begins.

The Golf

Designed by the masters—Alister MacKenzie, Donald Ross, Robert Trent Jones Sr., Pete Dye, and others—or inspired by them, these courses combine classic style with a modern focus on the wide range of playing abilities on the part of resort guests. The architects strive to entertain and sternly test low-handicappers, while presenting average golfers with a relaxing, scenic experience from the less-intimidating forward tees.

The genius architects who manage to pull that off gracefully wield their magic, in part, by exaggerating differences between tee boxes; five or six tees are not unusual nowadays. Coeur d'Alene's floating island green is moved to a different anchoring in the lake every day, about 100 to 175 yards from the back tees.

Landing zones and putting surfaces are often

Ready, Set, Go! Packing Tips

When packing your car, lay your clubs width-wise to protect them from bending against the front or back of the trunk. To gain more space, lay the longer clubs on top of the bag.

When traveling by air with your clubs, use a hard travel case or wrap them with clothing before zipping them up in a soft travel bag. Position a golf umbrella above the longest club as protection against over-enthusiastic baggage handlers. Consider using one of the smaller, hard, round cases that accommodate about seven to eight clubs (they are much lighter, can be carried with a shoulder strap, and set right on the golf cart). Your shoes and accessories should be packed in your main suitcase.

If you're on a budget, bring golf balls and tees from home. Resort pro shops charge sky-high retail prices.

Always pack a lightweight, waterproof jacket with a hood, and a small plastic bag in which to rest club handles on wet grass. And, wet weather golf gloves are good to pack, too. They work great if you soak them first.

scraps of grass between wild places. Forced carries as long as 200 yards over a patch of cacti, a creek, or a rocky canyon are reserved for those who drive from the tips. You must carry at least 250 yards for a comfortable

Fast Pass

A yardage booklet, describing each hole in detail and offering strategic tips, may cost several dollars in a pro shop. By all means, invest in the yardage books to make the most of your golfing experience at these world-class courses. When you can, check out the resorts' Web sites in advance; you will often find in-depth hole descriptions. Many resorts now offer a free, daily pin placement sheet, which comes in handy as you approach a green for the first time in your life.

The best golf resorts of the world are so popular that tee times may be booked only nine or ten minutes apart. Vacationing golfers often find this stressful, particularly at a pricey resort. Course marshals, sometimes called "Guest Assistants," inform golfers verbally or by colored flags if their group is not maintaining an acceptable pace, and gently but firmly encourage them to forge speedily ahead.

For maximum enjoyment of these formidable courses, definitely hire a caddie when available. Caddies save time by locating errant balls, pointing out hidden hazards, figuring distance, and suggesting the most efficient approach techniques. They also read the greens. All of this helps to hasten play and lower your score.

Another way to defend against the press of golfers and marshals is to invite the foursome behind to play through, giving you and your companions a chance to relax, snap a few photos, and just enjoy. In fact, my buddies and I often wave several foursomes through during a single round. Do take care to discuss the "play-through" with your fellow players, and make a mutual decision.

approach to "Wee Burn," number sixteen on the Alisa Course at the renowned Turnberry Resort in Scotland. The green is surrounded by Wilson's Burn (a burn is a creek or stream), and anything short of the putting surface rolls down into the dark waters. Long-handled ball retrievers are provided for those who end up in the burn. (Host to the British Open in 1884, 1977, and 1986, the Alisa will be the site of the 2007 Open.)

Older courses, almost without exception at the resorts herein, have been updated, and many lengthened, according to the greater distances gained by today's high-tech clubs and balls. Turnberry's Kintyre course, formerly called the Arran, reopened in 2001 after a comprehensive redesign by Donald Steel. Greens were elevated, enlarged, reshaped, and bunkered, and tees were enlarged, elevated, and moved back. Also, a nine-hole practice course was built at the new Colin Montgomerie Links Golf Academy at Turnberry.

Today more than ever golf courses are skillfully united with the natural landscape, and are meant to look as if they just grew up where they lie. The edges of fairways, lakes, and ponds are left to grow knee-high with native flora. Golf legend and course designer, Jack Nicklaus, said, "When I first look at designing a hole, I consider what Mother Nature has already created on that property. . . . I don't believe in forcing an idea on a piece of land, but rather, I blend my ideas with the natural environment and let it help me shape the design. I guess you could say that Mother Nature is a co-designer of each of my courses."

At the La Quinta PGA West complex in Southern California, Aussie golf great Greg Norman severely limited turf and merged native grasses and wildflowers into a dramatic, low-desert setting. Indigenous mesquite, paloverde, and acacia trees, and goldeneye, desert marigold, and white brittle brush bloom along the fairways.

Facilities

The world-wide boom in golf in the 1990s powered the growth of elaborate practice venues and golf academies. Also, eighteen-hole putting and chipping

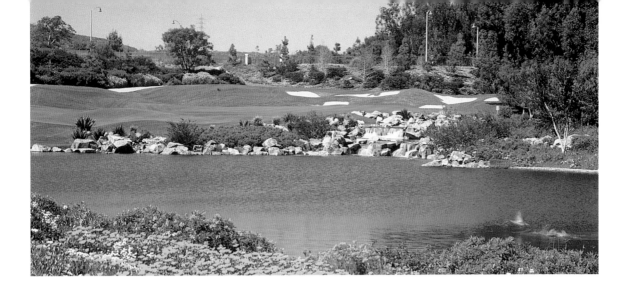

courses are sprouting up everywhere:

At the new Seve Ballesteros Natural Golf School at the San Roque Club in southern Spain, touring pros train in the wintertime in the covered driving bays and on the two eighteen-hole and the nine-hole putting and chipping courses.

Tiger Woods' coach opened his second Butch Harmon School of Golf at Our Lucaya Resort on Grand Bahama Island, complete with indoor, four-camera video analysis—some golf schools have six or seven stationary cameras.

At the World Golf Village in Florida, one of the Top 100 American golf teachers, Scott Sackett, and resident instructor and former PGA star, Calvin Peete, lead schools and clinics at the first ever PGA TOUR Golf Academy.

At Sunriver, Oregon, budding golfers and their parents putt around a course on the banks of the Sun River, where aspens and maple trees glow gold and red in the fall.

Designed by the "King of Waterscapes," Ted Robinson, The Greens at the Desert Springs Resort in Palm Desert, California, is a 1,435-foot-long, eighteen-hole pitching and putting course with rolling fairways, landscaped rough, and plenty of water.

Guest Amenities

Each of the resorts included here provide thoughtful, even luxurious, amenities. Many have received five-diamond ratings from the Automobile Association of America (AAA), and four- and five-star ratings from Mobile Travel Guide. All accommodations have desks or work surfaces, and dual phone lines with data ports. Most will provide a laser printer, fax, surge protector, an ergonomic chair, and a task light. Plush robes, hair dryers, mini-bars, iron and board, in-room movies and music are always available. DVD, flat-screen TV, Nintendo, and wireless keyboards can often be found too.

At the Westin resorts, the all-white "Heavenly Bed" features pillowtop mattresses, down comforters, a pile of plush pillows, and smooth-as-silk linens.

At Sandy Lane in Barbados, a beach attendant cleans the saltwater off your sunglasses and mists your face with iced Evian water. Chilled, moist towels are handed to golfers as they return to the clubhouse at Wailea, on the island of Maui. Belgian chocolate-covered strawberries are delivered to your room every evening at the Ocean Club in the Bahamas.

Tariffs and Bookings

Price guidelines used in this book are based on a typical, three-day package, including room and golf:

$$$$ Ultra-luxurious . . . .$2,000 and up per couple

$$$ Superior . . . .$1,000 and up per couple

$$ Value . . . .$800 and up per couple

Golf package descriptions and rates are subject to change and blackout periods, and seasonal discounts may not apply year-round. Some rates apply to specific room location and standards, and a minimum stay may be required. Take care to request current rates and conditions when making your reservations.

These are not only the best golf resorts, they are also the most popular. Off-season, shoulder season, and midweek are often the best times to visit, when tee times are most available and stay-and-play rates are lower. In any case, take care to reserve well in advance. For the grand old estates to which every avid golfer makes a pilgrimage at least once in a lifetime—such as St. Andrews, Pinehurst, or the Broadmoor—reserve your tee times months ahead. As a resort guest you may enjoy special access to courses not open to the general public. The more exclusive the course, however, the more chance that tee times will be booked up.

Spas for Golfers

Without exception, each of the world's top golf resorts offers massage and other treatments to rejuvenate the body and spirit after grueling days on the fairways. In fact, most resorts added opulent spa facilities or expanded and glamorized their existing spas around the turn of the twenty-first century, in response to guests who desire a comforting, healing element to their stay. You can expect treatments specifically designed for men, for golfers, and for couples.

At La Quinta Resort and Club in Southern California, the "Just for Guys Facial"—a deep cleansing followed by a lesson in proper shaving techniques to reduce skin sensitivity—and the "Sports Pack Body Wrap" are popular. The wrap involves warm mud sensuously applied and wrapped over the hands, arms, lower back, and shoulders. Protecting their skin for movie screen close-ups, some of the celebrities who frequent La Quinta finish their spa experiences with the "Solar Body Bronzer," emerging (artificially) tanned and relaxed.

Available at several European spas, Sports Hydrotherapy combines underwater compression techniques with pressurized jet massage, toning and restoring energy to tired muscles. At the new Anara Spa at the Hyatt Regency Kauai, a refreshing outdoor shower and lava rock sauna precedes the unique "Jet Lag Facial," an exfoliating, rehydrating masque combined with neck and shoulder massage, perfect for the traveling golfer.

Apuane Spa at Punta Mita, near Puerto Vallarta in Mexico, really caters to golfers, with a "Golfer's Massage," and a "Refresher Facial" to hydrate and heal the face after a day in the sun. The venerable Gleneagles Hotel in Scotland has an entire program called "Mainly for Men," including the "Laird's Remedy" aromatherapy massage and the "Gentleman's Stress Curative," the perfect ending to a bracing day on the moorlands of the King's Course.

You and your favorite golfing companion can walk off the eighteenth hole at one of Asia's top courses, the Bali Golf and Country Club, take a dip in your own swimming pool at Amanusa, and lie down for a couple's Balinese massage in the private garden of your thatched-roof suite overlooking the Indian Ocean. A golf vacation has never felt so good.

Carry Your Card and Your Raincoat

At most European golf clubs, you will be expected to have a membership card from a golf club, and possibly a letter of introduction from the pro at your home club, too. Proof of handicap of about 25 or lower may also be required; check before leaving home.

You should also be prepared to walk. In Europe only the infirm ride carts. Cart paths are generally absent, except on the Costa del Sol, where some American-style, paved cart paths have been built.

Bring foul weather gear even in summer. The weather in northern Europe is unpredictable, and that is an understatement.

Finding Your Best Game

By Scott Sackett, a *Golf Magazine* Top-100 Teacher and Director of Instruction,
PGA TOUR Golf Academy at World Golf Village, St. Augustine, Florida

If you want to play golf and take some instruction on your next trip, here are a few tips to keep in mind.

At most resorts, you have the option of taking one-on-one private lessons or group lessons such as clinics or golf schools. There are pros and cons to each. Private lessons offer a more individualized approach, and are also more expensive. Rates will average $75 to $150 or more an hour, depending on the instructor's experience and reputation. While most teachers have varying philosophies and lessons, you will receive great instruction at a well-known resort.

Golf School

If you are looking for dramatic improvement in your game in the short run, try a golf school vacation. Most top resorts offer two-, three-, and five-day golf schools, which are usually packaged with accommodations, instruction, daily golf, and sometimes meals. Packages offer great value, versus buying everything individually.

While a private lesson will give you enough to think about and practice, the experience of a golf school will allow more time to break old habits in the presence of a qualified instructor. A low student-to-teacher ratio, use of video analysis, and overall reputation of the program are indicators to watch for.

Look for a school with a good reputation. Spend time researching on the Internet. Or, choose one from *Golf Magazine*'s list of the top twenty-five golf schools. A few national companies, such as Resort Golf, offer numerous options, where the student can rest assured they will have a first-rate learning experience at each location. However, this does not mean that students should automatically discount a golf school that does not have multiple outlets. Some schools offer free follow-up advice to alumni, as well as alumni discounts.

Credentials and Awards

In choosing an instructor, look for PGA or LPGA members. Also, being a full-time teacher is important. The best instructors receive PGA Section awards and are named to *Golf Magazine*'s list of the country's Top 100 Teachers. Beyond that, the number of years of teaching experience is a good gauge as well.

High-Tech Help

Video analysis is an integral part of instruction these days. The top teachers and the best schools use it. Look for a video system that allows you to take home a tape or CD of your swing and/or your lesson.

Facilities

The best golf schools and resorts have their own private short-game and full-swing practice areas within the resorts, although these are not absolutely essential. All-weather hitting bays are ideal for the inclement weather that is part of the golfing experience. However, there are probably fewer than twenty of these bays in operation across the United States, so they may be hard to find. Eighteen-hole putting courses, and putting-and-chipping courses, are opening at many resorts.

Traveling with Clubs

If you can bring along only two or three clubs, I would recommend the driver, the putter, and your favorite rescue iron. While it is always preferable to play with your own golf clubs, since you are comfortable with them, most resorts and instruction centers rent brand-name golf clubs. Keep in mind that rental clubs can average $40 to $75 per day, per person.

Finally, if your budget or time frame does match with a private lesson or golf school, inquire at the pro shop as to whether or not they have daily clinics for resort guests. If offered, these complimentary or inexpensive clinics are fun and informative, and usually focus on the basics.

NORTH AMERICA

THE BOULDERS
Carefree, Arizona

Appearing like a mirage in the Sonoran Desert foothills, the contemporary, Southwestern-style lodge at The Boulders is a collection of low-rise, russet- and ochre-toned buildings, situated against a dramatic landscape of giant granite boulders and century-old saguaro cacti. Hand-rubbed woods, massive timbers, Native American–design art and fabrics, terra cotta floors, and stone fireplaces are warm and welcoming in the public spaces.

New owners have refurbished the adobe-style guest casitas and villas, which are arranged in villagelike clusters. Each has timber-beamed ceilings, wood-burning fireplaces, private patios or decks in desert settings, and earth-toned tile, fabrics, and wood furnishings.

At 2,500 feet in elevation, the climate here is 10 degrees cooler than metropolitan Phoenix, 30 miles away. The air is clean and crystal clear—perfect for exploring the desert by jeep, glider, hot-air balloon, or on foot. You can get close to the unique ecosystem by taking a rock-climbing clinic, a guided hike to ancient cliff dwellings, or a nighttime nature tour, where night-vision equipment illuminates coyotes, owls, and night-blooming cacti.

At the sumptuous new Golden Door Spa, guests calm their spirits in the meditation labyrinth and enjoy waterfall and nature-oriented treatment rooms with rounded edges—a Native American element believed to foster the flow of energy. In addition to traditional health and beauty therapies, signature treatments include the "Turquoise Wrap," which features a smudging ceremony, dry-brush massage, ionized turquoise clay, and indigenous herbs such as aloe, yucca, and sage.

Two quintessential, target-style desert golf courses are rotated daily between club members and resort guests. Legendary for their rugged beauty and forced carries over groves of cacti and beautiful rock formations, the North and South Courses are Jay Morrish designs. Golfers share the rocky canyons and granite monuments with cooing doves and quail, roadrunners, fat gila monsters, deer, and the occasional bobcat and coyote. (The "coyote rule" allows you to replay a shot without penalty when a coyote grabs your ball.)

Now 7,007 yards from the tips, the South Course received a million-dollar face-lift—with tees added and bunkers rebuilt—resulting in a bracing 73.3/146 rating and slope. The precariously balanced boulders and ancient saguaros, dry washes, and vast, sandy waste areas are visually stunning along the narrow fairways. On the signature "Boulder Pile" fifth hole, the green lies below a tremendous and beautiful ochre-colored bastion of boulders.

On a plethora of doglegs careening across the desert landscape, the fairways on the North Course are generous. Towering cacti and giant boulders are so distinctive and sizable that they show up in the yardage booklet. On sizzling summer days, a misting system cools the air by nearly 30 degrees in and around the golf carts.

Big Saguaro, Little Turf

Long, forced carries over dry riverbeds and arroyos, around giant boulders and cacti, and across sandy, rocky wastelands to minuscule patches of turf are typical of the type of "target golf" most often encountered on desert courses throughout the Southwest. Pioneered in Arizona due to water conservation and wildlife issues, target golf allows the flora, the fauna, and the natural landscape to remain intact.

A prime example is Troon North Golf Club. Tom Weiskopf, PGA pro and architect of the course, said, "We disturbed very little of the natural desert, limited the amount of irrigated land, and used the desert creatively. We did some fun things such as splitting the fairway on Number Three instead of moving a huge boulder."

A "neo-classic" style has emerged as recent adaptation of the often penal target golf concept. Outstanding examples are Talking Stick, designed by Ben Crenshaw and Bill Grove, the track at Camelback, and Legend Trail Golf Club. Not as punishing as the truly target layouts, these courses feature shorter carries and larger landing zones, with a little more grass between tee and green.

After a day of desert golf, couples in the mood for romance arrange for a private, candlelit "Tee Box" dinner on the South Course, complete with music, flowers, champagne, and starlight.

The Boulders
34631 North Tom Darlington Drive
Carefree, AZ 85377
Phone: (480) 488–9009, reservations (800) 488–4118
Fax: (480) 488–4118
Web site: www.wyndham.com
General Manager: Mark Vinciguerra
Accommodations: Five-diamond rated, 160 adobe-style casitas and 50 one-, two- and three-bedroom pueblo villas, each with fireplace, private patio, large dressing and bath areas, elegant Southwestern-style decor, leather armchairs.
Meals: American regional cuisine served in cozy booths or on an outdoor patio with fireplace at Latilla; seafood, Southwestern specialties, and an exhibition kitchen at Palo Verde; panoramic views and hearty American food on the terrace at the Boulders Club; healthy fare in the spa.
Facilities: Eight plexi-paved tennis courts; pro shop; lessons and clinics; resident teaching pros; three swimming pools; full-service health and beauty spa; Watsu pools; salon; fitness center.
Services and Special Programs: Women To The Fore helps women learn the game of golf. Guided mountain-biking and hiking tours; rock climbing and tennis clinics; yoga, Pilates, kick-boxing, and aerobics classes; art classes, nutrition and cooking classes.
Rates: $$$–$$$$
Golf Packages: Gold Medal Golf, a four-night vacation package, includes accommodations, a daily round of golf and cart, and daily breakfast. $986–$3,410 for two, double occupancy.
Getting There: Located 33 miles from Phoenix Sky Harbor International Airport and 13 miles from Scottsdale Airport. Private planes land at the Carefree Airport, 5 miles away; a heli-pad is available at the resort.
What's Nearby: Gallery hopping for cowboy and Native American art and Western Americana in Scottsdale's trendy Arts District; ArtWalk is Thursday nights. Shopping at Moroccan-themed El Pedregal Festival Marketplace and at Borgata with upscale shops reminiscent of the Italian village of San Gimignano.

FAIRMONT SCOTTSDALE PRINCESS

Scottsdale, Arizona

Surrounded by the majestic McDowell Mountains, the Spanish Colonial–style complex of the Princess resembles a gracious hacienda in an oasis-like, desert setting—the jagged silhouette of the mountains looms on one side while the starkly beautiful Sonoran Desert stretches into the distance on the other. Just outside the terra-cotta-toned, low-rise buildings there are garden courtyards shaded by cottonwood and palm trees, cooling fountains and lakes, and distinctive bell towers reminiscent of bygone days in the Southwest.

The Tournament Players Club at Scottsdale (TPC) consists of two courses—the Weiskopf-Morrish–designed Stadium Course, which was built to host the PGA Tour's Phoenix Open, and the Desert Course, a shorter, less demanding, and quite pretty resort course.

Along the 7,089-yard length of the Stadium Course are innumerable mounds and seventy-two bunkers—some 7 feet deep. Add to this a half-dozen water hazards, what seems like endless desert scrub, and large, multitiered bermuda grass greens in amphitheater settings, and you have some of the toughest holes on the Tour.

Century-old saguaro cacti and mesquite trees are much in evidence. The largest paloverde tree in the state stands on the fifteenth hole, which has an island green. On the 332-yard seventeenth, Andrew Magee drove the green during the 2001 Phoenix Open for the only par-4 double eagle in the history of the PGA Tour. His tee shot bounced off Tom Byrum's putter, rolling into the hole.

The eighteenth hole, 438 yards, par-4, is the most dramatic hole with a large lake along the left and desert sand on the right.

You get a break on the Desert Course, a par-70, which is rather flat, and with larger, bent grass greens. Do not underestimate the track, as prevailing winds

and contiguous desert wilderness come into play.

The ultimate in after-golf relaxation may be a refreshing coast down the two longest resort water slides in the state at the brand new Sonoran Splash water play area. Little kids like the graduated deck entry into the swimming pool, while teens enjoy water basketball and volleyball. Those hoping for quiet and seclusion can head for the rooftop, adults-only swimming pool at the new Willow Stream Spa. This spa is a three-level, Colonial-style complex with twenty-five lovely treatment rooms, fireplaces, shady garden courtyards, waterfalls, and a fitness center and salon. The "Golf Performance Treatment" is a unique combination of massage, stretching, and acupressure, designed to lower your score and avoid injury.

The prestigious Nicklaus/Flick Golf School offers three-day instruction programs using the state-of-the-art Jack Nicklaus Coaching Studio. Golfers can choose from Playing and Scoring School, the Resort School, For Women Only program, or the one-day Faults and Cures.

The Phoenix Open

Attracting the largest crowds of any golf event in the world, the Phoenix Open involves four pro-am tournaments, a skills challenge, a pro-celebrity shoot-out, a Special Olympics putting contest, and golf clinics for juniors and ladies, among other activities during the week (www.phoenixopen.com).

First played in 1935 and traditionally played on Super Bowl weekend in January, this PGA event boasts winners that include Byron Nelson, Ben Hogan, Billy Casper, Arnold Palmer, Jack Nicklaus, Johnny Miller, and Ben Crenshaw. Mark Calcavecchia, a winner in 1989 and 1992, won again in 2001 with a 28-under-par 256, breaking the 72-hole scoring record held for forty-six years by Mike Souchak. He also set a record for most birdies in 72 holes. Tiger Woods made more history when he made a hole in one on sixteen at the 1997 Open.

Fairmont Scottsdale Princess
7575 East Princess Drive
Scottsdale, AZ 85255
Phone: (480) 585–4848, reservations (800) 344–4758
Fax: (480) 585–0086
Web site: www.fairmont.com
General Manager: John Pye
Accommodations: Five-diamond rated, 650 large rooms and suites, each with private terrace or balcony, sitting area and work space, plus casitas at the tennis center, and golf villas. Casitas and villas have living rooms, fireplaces, and huge, luxurious bathrooms.
Meals: La Hacienda, in a lively nineteenth-century ranch house setting with strolling mariachis, is the only four-diamond Mexican restaurant in North America. Mediterranean cuisine in the elegant Marquesa, with garden patio and fireplace. Award-winning steak and seafood at the Grill in the golf clubhouse. Light fare at the poolside Las Ventanas and at Cazadores in the plaza.
Facilities: Seven tennis courts with pro shop, clinics, and resident teaching staff; the stadium court hosts ATP and WTA events. Racquetball, squash, mountain bikes, three swimming pools, waterslides, private cabanas. Full-service health and beauty spa, fitness center. Catch-and-release fishing lagoon, Nicklaus/Flick Golf School.
Services and Special Programs: Exercise classes; guided fitness walks; Kid's Club supervised play for ages 5–12. The golf concierge will book tee times at more than one hundred courses in the area.
Rates: $$$–$$$$
Golf Packages: Royal Tee includes standard room for two nights' accommodations, two rounds of golf and cart at the TPC or partner courses, and daily breakfast. Rates start at $522–$779 for two, double occupancy.
Getting There: A thirty-minute drive from Phoenix Sky Harbor International Airport. Private aircraft land at Scottsdale Municipal Airport, ten minutes away.
What's Nearby: Adjacent to the resort is Westworld, a large equestrian center with polo fields and a cross-country course. Tours of Frank Lloyd Wright's western studio, Taliesin West. World-renowned Native American artifacts and fine art at the Heard Museum North.

FOUR SEASONS RESORT SCOTTSDALE
AT TROON NORTH

Scottsdale, Arizona

Above the desert highlands of northern Scottsdale, within an amphitheater of granite boulders and tall saguaro cacti, lies the city's newest luxury resort—an intimate hideaway of territorial-style casitas with lovely mountain and city views from private terraces, and each luxuriously appointed with kiva fireplaces, deep soaking tubs, walk-in closets, and comfy sitting areas with armchairs and ottomans. Some suites have outdoor plunge pools and garden showers. Huge, bi-level swimming pools are connected by waterfalls, and there is a separate kid's pool with kid-size chaises. After dark, telescopes on the lobby terrace scan a dome of sparkling stars over the pitch-black desert.

Built in the 1990s, the two Weiskopf-Morrish–designed courses at Troon North Golf Club lie in a stunning setting at the foot of Pinnacle Peak. They are among the top public courses in the western states, alternating daily for public use.

With an ominous rating of 73.3 and a 147 slope, the Pinnacle is true desert target golf with landing zones between massive boulders and granite outcroppings, established mesquite and ironwood trees, and carries over yawning arroyos and canyons. Multitiered, sometimes blind, greens merit twelve or more on the stimpmeter. From mountainside to low desert, the track leaps up cliffs and down valleys, all the while providing dazzling natural landscape and mountain views. Fortunately for mere mortals, the 7,044-yard course has five sets of tees.

Rated "#1 in the State," the Monument is no slouch at 7,028 yards. Scattered with piles of gigantic granite boulders and seventy-nine bunkers, the layout has tight fairways and a plethora of dry washes, saguaros, and mesquite and paloverde trees.

Looking to improve your golf skills? Check in for the Four Seasons' new sport-specific training for golf (also for tennis and running), involving workouts, cardiovascular endurance, muscular strength, body composition and flexibility, and dietary consulting.

Other Places to Play

Wide fairways and open approaches to big, firm greens are characteristic of Legend Trail Golf Club above Phoenix. Views of Pinnacle Peak, the McDowell Mountains, the Mummy Mountains, and Camelback are distractions from the challenging Rees Jones–designed track. Jones integrated his traditional bunkering and wide approaches to the greens into routing crossed by dry arroyos. Legend Trail is managed by the excellent Troon Golf (480–488–7434, www.legendtrailgc.com).

Unlike typical desert courses, the three Wigwam Resort championship tracks are green and parklike. Laid down in the 1960s on flattish terrain, Wigwam Gold is a vintage Robert Trent Jones Sr. design, 7,200 yards long with a hefty 74.1 rating and 133 slope. Long, tight fairways with small landing zones, eight ponds, and elevated greens are bordered by hundreds of date palms and nearly 100 traps. The Blue Course gives an appealing option for older and higher-handicap players, while the very pretty Red Course has several lakes, dry streambeds, and large greens (800–327–0396).

Four Seasons Resort Scottsdale at Troon North
10600 East Crescent Moon Drive
Scottsdale, AZ 85262
Phone: (480) 515–5700, reservations (888) 207–9696
Fax: (480) 515–5599
Web site: www.fourseasons.com/scottsdale
General Manager: Chris Hart
Accommodations: 210 rooms and suites in one-, two-, and three-story, territorial-style buildings. Each has a landscaped terrace or balcony with mountain, desert, or cityscape views, spacious bathrooms, weathered local materials, and fine, desert-toned linens, fabrics, and upholstery.
Meals: Alfresco dining at all restaurants, including contemporary American cuisine at Acacia, with seafood flown in daily. All-day informality at Crescent Moon; light fare at Saguaro Blossom. Cocktails and snacks by the fireplace overlooking Pinnacle Peak in the Lobby Lounge.
Facilities: Four Supercushion tennis courts at the Peter Burwash tennis complex with clinics, lessons, and matching. Three swimming pools, full-service health and beauty spa, complimentary bicycles. Complete golf practice venues with lessons and clinics.
Services and Special Programs: Kids For All Seasons offers supervision of children ages 5–12 for arts and crafts, games, nature hikes, and meals. Separate teen program available. The Kids Concierge arranges activities from "Pee Wee Golf" to "Tennis for Tykes." Complimentary yoga and aerobics classes. Twenty-four-hour business center.
Rates: $$$–$$$$
Golf Packages: For a one-night stay the Monument Gold Package includes deluxe casita room, one round of golf, golf amenities, and breakfast. $400–$1,000 for two, double occupancy.
Getting There: Phoenix Sky Harbor International Airport is a thirty-five-minute drive away. By arrangement, a driver will meet you at the gate and provide sedan or limousine transportation.
What's Nearby: Guided backcountry tour by Hummer or on horseback. Hot-air ballooning, and day trips to the Desert Botanical Gardens, Out of Africa Wildlife Park, the Phoenix Art Museum, and Frank Lloyd Wright's Taliesin West.

HYATT REGENCY SCOTTSDALE RESORT AT GAINEY RANCH

Scottsdale, Arizona

A flat plain surrounded by mountains, the Phoenix/Scottsdale "Valley of the Sun" enjoys three hundred dry, sunny days a year. It rains less than 8 inches a year and although temperatures may exceed 100 degrees in the summertime, from November through April the climate is near perfect, attracting almost seven million vacationers annually.

The setting sun washes red across the valley and the McDowell Mountains behind this striking, contemporary-designed resort that was inspired by the architecture of Frank Lloyd Wright. Surrounded by five courtyards, the heart of the place is a water playground composed of a white sand beach, waterslides, the "Big Gun" waterfall, fountains, cold plunges, poolside bars, and ten swimming pools connected by an elevated aqueduct. Cascades fall from a Grecian-style "Water Temple" and the Fountain Court, illuminated in the evening, is a place to stroll in the fragrant gardens or sit by an outdoor fireplace.

The open-air, three-story atrium lobby is a perfect vantage point from which to enjoy views of the mountains, golf courses, a lake, and the abundant water features. Wall sconces light a multimillion-dollar collection of ethnic art and sculpture, including pre-Columbian artifacts, Thai masks, stone carvings, and paintings. The resident flamenco guitarist, Estéban, plays in the evenings while guests glide about a landscaped lake on Venetian-style gondolas.

Rooms, suites, and casitas are decorated subtly in pale copper, eggplant, and sand tones, with bleached oak, brass, and marble accents. Glorious views from private balconies and patios are the focus of these accommodations.

Designed by architects Benz and Poellot, the three nines at Gainey Ranch Golf Club are the Dunes, Arroyo, and the Lakes. Sluggish Bermuda grass greens are balanced by the demanding nature of the target-style layouts.

Arroyo is Spanish for "dry river," and, indeed, a dry, grassy gully winds throughout the longest, most open, and most difficult of the three nines. Surrounded by palms, four traps, and a lake, the skinny ninth green appears as a serene island across from the main swimming pool terrace. On the Dunes, greens are scattered throughout rolling sand dunes in a semi-Scottish links–style arrangement of ridges, knolls, and moguls. Five lakes on the Lakes, plus ponds, streams, and waterfalls, create a lovely track.

Within the resort, the Native American Learning Center brings local Hopi artists and educators together to showcase their art and culture with exhibits, talks, and tours.

At the Sonwai Spa, ancient traditions of the Hopi peoples and other Native American tribes are the basis for signature treatments, including a therapeutic massage targeting muscles used in the game of golf, incorporating long-flowing, kneading strokes and stretches with pressure applied to relieve muscle fatigue.

Cacti and Claws

A public-fee club in Scottsdale with an upscale-members club feeling, the Grayhawk Golf Club offers special amenities such as private lockers, copies of *The Legend of Bagger Vance,* and personal services, plus two outstanding golf courses, the Raptor and the Talon, within walking distance.

A Tom Fazio design, the 7,108-yard Raptor has gentle fairways, plenty of mounding, and seventy bunkers. Pinnacle Peak is the backdrop for several hundred tall saguaros, thousands of native plants, a winding creek, and a forty-foot-deep box canyon.

With a 74.3 rating and 141 slope, the Talon was designed by the Gary Panks/David Graham duo, who created a wide variety of challenges. The "Three Sisters" par-5 third hole, a dogleg left, sports deep, wood-plank-walled bunkers. A massive bunker follows the fifth from tee to green. "Devil's Drink" is the island hole (602–502–1800, www.grayhawk.com).

The Kostis McCord Learning Center here is directed by PGA Senior Tour pro Gary McCord and CBS commentator Peter Kostis, with classes and clinics by one of *Golf Magazine*'s "Top 100" instructors, Peter Trittler.

After golf, stop in for a meal at Phil's Grill named for Grayhawk's resident ambassador, PGA star Phil Mickelson.

Hyatt Regency Scottsdale Resort at Gainey Ranch
7500 East Doubletree Ranch Road
Scottsdale, AZ 85258
Phone: (480) 991–3388, reservations 800–554–9288
Fax: (480) 483–5550
Web site: www.hyatt.com

General Manager: Bill Eider-Orley

Accommodations: 493 rooms, suites in a four-story hotel, and one- and two-story casitas with sitting areas, private balconies, or patios. Fine fabrics, linens, and furnishings are in subtle desert tones. Casitas have fireplaces and Jacuzzi tubs.

Meals: Southwest cuisine by the lagoon at the Golden Swan or interact with the chefs here at the Sunday brunch kitchen marketplace. Take a gondola ride to the intimate bistro, Ristorante Sandolo, complete with singing servers. Casual Southwestern style at Squash Blossom in the Fountain Court.

Facilities: Eight tennis courts, clinics, and lessons; jogging and bicycle paths with free bikes; full-service health and beauty spa; fitness center; croquet court; boutiques and galleries.

Services and Special Programs: A large selection of adult and Family Camp activities including Camp Hyatt Kachina for ages 3–12. Themes are Native American culture and local flora and fauna. Free aqua aerobics and fitness classes. Regency Club guests merit special privileges, including a private club, complimentary food service, and personal concierge. The Four World program explores the people, food, and environment of the Sonoran southwest.

Rates: $$$–$$$$

Golf Packages: Gainey Ranch Golf Package includes one night accommodations, one round of golf and cart, golf shop, and lesson discounts. Children ages 8–17 can play free with an adult from the end of May through early September. $410–$659 for two, double occupancy.

Getting There: A twenty-five-minute drive from Phoenix Sky Harbor International Airport. Shuttle and limousine service is available.

What's Nearby: Opportunities to explore the desert and centuries-old Native American cliff dwellings and ruins by ATV or jeep; hike the Apache Trail; take a biplane flight; visit the Desert Botanical Gardens or the Rawhide 1880s Old West theme town; browse at the Borgata of Scottsdale Farmer's Market on Friday afternoon.

THE LODGE AT VENTANA CANYON

Tucson, Arizona

In the foothills of the Santa Catalina Mountains north of Tucson, bordered by the Coronado National Forest, The Lodge at Ventana Canyon lies within a 1,100-acre nature preserve watered by freshwater springs and is a cactus and canyon haven for desert wildlife such as bobcats, coyotes, and birds, including a dozen kind of hummingbirds.

Renovated extensively in the late 1990s, the luxurious residential-style accommodations are a mere fifty suites, each private and quiet, with no convention-oriented activity to mar the serene desert vistas. Pale pine, dark mahogany, fieldstone, and slate create a natural look accented by iron chandeliers and timber-beamed, vaulted ceilings. The heart of the exclusive resort is a three-story fireplace made of Anasazi-style, hand-stacked stones anchored by an ancient rock from the Grand Canyon.

Each suite has a kitchen, dining and living room areas, one or two bedrooms, and large baths with clawfoot tubs. Private balconies or patios provide dazzling views of city lights and desert vistas.

The 3,000-foot elevation is helpful for long wilderness carries on the Mountain and Canyon Courses—both Tom Fazio designs—in spectacular canyons below the mountains.

Built in 1984 and costing more than one million dollars to construct, the Mountain Course is believed to be the first environmentally sensitive desert course ever built. Now Audubon Cooperative Sanctuary certified, the Mountain Course is also said to be the most difficult track in the Southwest with a 73.6 rating and 149 slope from the tips. Narrow fairways, several blind shots, and small, hard, fast, bent grass greens are to be confronted. The third hole is notorious but photogenic. Golfers ride a cart up to a high promontory and tee off over a yawning ravine 107 yards above a tiny putting surface that is surrounded by giant boulders. (During a

Merrill Lynch Shoot-out, Tom Watson four-putted the hole, thereby losing the tournament to Fuzzy Zoeller.) A view to the south from eighteen is your reward—the Mexican border is 100 miles away in the distance.

Slightly more forgiving than its sister course, with a 73.6 rating and 137 slope, the Canyon winds in target-golf style through the beautiful Esperrero Canyon, incorporating the massive rock formation known as Whaleback Rock. Greens tend to be firm and slope away, hard to hold.

The Tucson Open

Ten lakes and 188 sand bunkers decorate the three nines at the Omni Tucson National Resort. The PGA Tour Touchstone Energy Tucson Open in February is played on the Orange and Gold nines: 7,108 yards liberally scattered with deep grass bunkers and hundreds of mature pines, magnolias, and willows. The traditional layout is demanding with wide landing areas and large, elevated, well-defended Bermuda grass greens (520–575–7540, www.tucsonnational.com). The shorter Von Hagge-and-Devlin-designed Green nine has tighter landing zones, several blind shots, and steep elevation changes. The resort is home base for the John Jacobs School of Golf (www.johnjacobs.com).

The Lodge at Ventana Canyon
6200 North Clubhouse Lane
Tucson, AZ 85750
Phone: (520) 577–1400, reservations (800) 828–5701
Fax: (520) 577–4065
Web site: www.wyndham.com
General Manager: George White
Accommodations: 50 one- and two-bedroom luxury suites with private balconies or patios, mission-style furniture, Southwestern art, complete kitchens with stocked refrigerators, clawfoot bathtubs, vaulted ceilings, and living and dining areas.
Meals: Floor-to-ceiling windows reveal mountain vistas at the Hearthstone where Southwestern and all-American cuisine is on the menu. Alfresco dining is on the Sabino Terrace; snacks and light meals at the Sierra Bar by the fireplace. At the eighteenth green, the Bar V Bar and Grill, taste test one or more of thirty varieties of tequila.
Facilities: Twelve lighted, hard-surface tennis courts, clinics, and lessons by USPTA teaching staff; 2.5-mile par course trail; twenty-four-hour fitness center; junior Olympic-size swimming pool; salon; complete golf practice facility, lessons, and clinics.
Services and Special Programs: The Ventana Aquatics Program includes swim instruction for all ages and skill levels in a 25-meter, heated pool. Women to the Fore helps new women golfers learn the game. Daily aerobics and exercise classes.
Rates: $$$–$$$$
Golf Packages: Suite accommodations, breakfast, unlimited golf, golf balls, and free rental clubs. $239–$589 per person per night, double occupancy.
Getting There: A thirty-five-minute drive from Tucson International Airport with transportation available.
What's Nearby: Day trips to Arizona-Sonora Desert Museum, Biosphere II, Kitt Peak Observatory, San Xavier Mission, and Saguaro National Monument. Hiking in Sabino Canyon and on Ventana Canyon nature trails.

THE PHOENICIAN
Scottsdale, Arizona

Sprawled across the rugged southern slope of Camelback Mountain, The Phoenician is a glamorous resort as flamboyant as an Italian palazzo. It is shaded with thousands of palms and gleams with acres of polished marble and gold leaf reflected in lagoons and pools draped with blooming vines and flowerbeds. Public spaces are galleries for a multimillion-dollar art collection, from Allan Houser's life-size bronzes to European antiques, Persian and Navajo rugs, and French tapestries and paintings. Music wafts from eleven Steinway grand pianos. A recent expansion of the water recreation area added a 165-foot water slide, a huge zero-entry pool lined with mother-of-pearl, and a tiered series of waterfalls, creating a refreshing paradise in the desert.

Guest rooms and private villas were refurbished at

the turn of the twenty-first century and outfitted with elegant new furnishings, original artwork, Berber carpeting, flat-screen TVs, and Italian marble bathrooms.

Three nines comprise the golf complex. The original nines, the Oasis and the Desert, were entirely rejuvenated and a gorgeous new nine, Canyon, was added. The courses are lush with natural Sonoran Desert flora and introduced flowers, palms, and shrubs. Wide vistas of the nearby metropolis and a vast desert panorama are viewed from elevated tees. Picturesque waterfalls, tall saguaro cacti, steep drops from the mountainside, and some wilderness carries give the twenty-seven holes drama and challenge.

Wrapping around the foot of the mountain, the Desert has fountains, lakes, and expansive waste areas studded with tall cacti. The 120-yard eighth is a roaring downhill par-3 demanding accuracy to make the napkin-size, bent grass green. Ponds, lakes, and waterfalls cool golfers' heels on the Oasis, a traditional layout.

The Canyon has the greatest elevation change, moving between immense sandy tracks, rocks, and boulders to small greens with stunning city views. Expect a smashing finish on the eighth—with a carry over water to a sand- and palm-fringed putting surface—and ninth, a severe dogleg menaced by water along the entire 525 yards and fronting the green.

Spirituality and tranquillity are emphasized at the Centre for Well-Being health and beauty spa, one of the largest and most elaborate in the region. The spa has two dozen treatment rooms and special offerings for the sportsminded, such as miniback massages for golfers before they hit the greens to loosen and stretch muscles for enhanced performance. Among unique treatments are "Table Thai," a clothed massage involving slow, deep pulls and stretches and using yogic positions; "Kachina Aromatherapy;" and "Traveler's Exercise Programs." There are even Tarot readings and chakra balancing.

Talking about It

With a nod to Native American heritage and indigenous grasslands, the Talking Stick Golf Club architects, Bill Coore and Ben Crenshaw, directed the replanting of native plants that once were abundant here. On the Salt River Pima-Maricopa Indian Community, with a backdrop of Camelback Mountain, the McDowell Mountains, and Pinnacle Peak, Talking Stick is a superior example of target golf on a flat desert site. Wild horses are not an unusual sight near the links-style, 7,133-yard North Course where wide fairways are devoid of trees, threatened by rough-edged bunkers, and bordered by sky-high grasses. Greens are crowned with wavering rims. The South Course is lush and parklike with thousands of sycamores, cottonwoods, and eucalyptus.

The prestigious Golf Digest Learning Center here is directed by Tim Mahoney, one of the "Top 50 Instructors in the World." Outstanding facilities at the twenty-five-acre school include space for one hundred hitting stations, including those for inclement weather; a 170-yard practice hole; and the latest high-tech, multi-camera swing analysis programs (602–860–2221, www.talkingstickgolfclub.com).

The Phoenician
6000 East Camelback Road
Scottsdale, AZ 85251
Phone: (480) 941–8200, reservations (800) 888–8234
Fax: (480) 947–4311
Web site: www.thephoenician.com
General Manager: Bunty Ahamed
Accommodations: Five-star rated, 654 enormous rooms, suites, and villas with private balconies or patios, rattan furnishings, original art, large Italian marble baths, Frette linens, flat-screen TVs. Casitas and villas have fireplaces, kitchens, butler service, and privacy.
Meals: *Gourmet* magazine names Mary Elaine's as the best restaurant in Scottsdale, with live music, a huge wine cellar, and Arizona's sole master sommelier; James Boyce, mastermind of French cuisine, holds a single-digit handicap. Regional fare in the formal Terrace Dining Room. Southwest-grill menu at five-star rated Windows on the Green, a casual and fun eatery at the golf course. Elaborate English tea service in the Lobby Tea Court.
Facilities: Twelve tennis courts with four surfaces including grass, automated practice court, USPTA-certified staff, clinics, and lessons; croquet court, lawn bowling, bicycles, nine swimming pools, and water play area; comprehensive golf practice center, lessons, clinics, and golf schools; full-service health and beauty spa, fitness center, and salon; business center; boutiques and galleries.
Services and Special Programs: Games and outdoor recreation at Funician, a children's program for ages 5–12; also teen activities. Meditation, yoga, and Pilates classes; guided tours of the world-class cactus garden and art collection; stargazing parties.
Rates: $$$$
Golf Packages: Masters Package includes accommodations for three nights, unlimited golf and cart, daily breakfast, and a one-hour private lesson with video analysis. $2,360–$4,360 for two, double occupancy.
Getting There: Limousine or shuttle from Phoenix Sky Harbor International Airport, 9 miles away.
What's Nearby: In Scottsdale the Heard Museum of Native American artifacts, the Scottsdale Center for Performing Arts, and more than one hundred Western and Southwestern art galleries. Scottsdale Fashion Square has five major department stores and more than 200 specialty shops.

THE WESTIN LA PALOMA RESORT AND SPA

Tucson, Arizona

The deep, reddish color—La Paloma Rose—of the wide-open, mission-revival-style, low-rise hotel blends right into the rugged landscape in the high Sonoran Desert foothills. Dramatic rock formations are softened by waterfalls, blooming gardens, and a swimming pool terrace with the 177-foot-long waterslide called the "Slidewinder." More than seven thousand stately saguaro cacti live on the property, along with hundreds of barrel, hedgehog, pincushion, prickly pear, cholla, and ocotillo cacti and mesquite trees, creating a veritable Southwestern botanical garden.

Guest rooms and suites are in several complexes in a charming village setting, each with their own landscaped courtyard. The oversized accommodations were redecorated at the turn of the twenty-first century in golden tones, with new cherry-wood furnishings, granite countertops, and Westin's signature "Heavenly Beds," plush with pillow-top mattresses, down comforters, and platoons of king and queen-size pillows. Each accommodation has a private exterior entrance, private patio or balcony, and separate sitting room area. Some have wood-burning fireplaces and spa tubs. With Spanish arches, two- and three-story windows, wing chairs, elaborate iron sconces, and other elegant accents, public spaces have a more formal look than at other Southwestern hostelries.

The prestigious Elizabeth Arden Red Door Spa and salon offers traditional beauty treatments and special therapies for golfers, such as sports massage, the fitness facial for men, and the "Body Bronzer," for guests who wish to have a smooth, deep tan without skin damage from the relentless desert sun.

Bleached cattle skulls, quail, and the occasional bobcat or puma show up on the Jack Nicklaus Signature course at La Paloma, three nines of target golf—the Hill, the Ridge, and the Canyon. One of Nicklaus's early designs, the layout is characterized by formidable, deep trapping of the greens, which tend to drop off to an alarming degree. Fairways are generally lined

with mounds that help direct your ball toward safety. You will encounter hundreds of grassy hollows, swales and mounds, numerous canyon crossings, elevation changes of up to 100 feet, and dry washes that meander across the twenty-seven holes. The services of a forecaddie will save golf balls.

Golf for Women magazine recognized La Paloma Country Club as one of America's most women-friendly courses, based on such services and amenities as top notch staff attitude, multiple tee boxes, and female-friendly golf instruction.

Other Places to Play

The new Raven at Sabino Springs in eastern Tucson is a stunner in the foothills of the Santa Catalina Mountains. Robert Trent Jones Jr. left great stretches of a saguaro cactus forest untouched, angling his layout around and between broad, mesquite-filled arroyos and stark rock outcroppings. Thousands of the cacti and paloverde trees were moved from the sites of fairways and greens to the hillsides, and literally tens of thousands of other native trees, including pines, sumacs, and oleander, were added.

Steep, uphill holes, inescapable carries, a tangle of scratchy shrubs, pine needle thatch, and cacti bordering the fairways make the track formidable from the back tees. The par-3 twelfth gives you options with nine tee boxes, six of them above a one-thousand-year-old spring-fed pond, one of several natural desert springs on the course. Fasten your seat belts for the seventeenth where eight tees are scattered among tall cacti leading to a smallish, uplifted, rolling green fiercely protected by bunkers. Two hundred feet above the fairway on the spectacular eighteenth tee, golfers ponder their plight as they gaze 100 miles into Mexico. Bunkers line up on both sides of the first landing zone, while a lake, more sand, and battalions of saguaros round the curve up to a small green (520–749–3636, www.ravengolf.com).

The Westin La Paloma Resort and Spa
3800 East Sunrise Drive
Tucson, AZ 85718
Phone: (520) 742–6000, reservations (800) 937–8461
Fax: (520) 577–5878
Web site: www.westinlapalomaresort.com
General Manager: Steve Shalit
Accommodations: 487 spacious rooms and suites with private balconies or patios in low-rise, village-style complexes, each with sitting areas, luxurious cherry-wood furnishings and "Heavenly Beds."
Meals: On the garden patio or indoors with mountain views through 30-foot windows, the Desert Garden Bistro is a light-flooded space where all-American food, Southwestern food, and the legendary Sunday brunch are served. Four-star, French-inspired Southwestern cuisine at the elegant Janos. Snacks and light meals at Sabinos (poolside), at J Bar, and at the Courtside cafe at the Tennis Center.
Facilities: Elizabeth Arden Red Door full-service health and beauty spa; Tennis and Health Center with fitness equipment, exercise classes, and ten tennis courts, including clay and hard surface; racquetball; children's lounge and play yard; large swimming pool with waterslide; children-only and adults-only pools; sand volleyball; croquet; jogging and cycling trails; upscale boutiques.
Services and Special Programs: At the Westin Kids' Club, children ages 6–12 enjoy indoor and outdoor games, a play yard, and crafts.
Rates: $$$$
Golf Packages: Two Player Package includes traditional or deluxe room, a round of golf and cart, golf clinic, and breakfast. $485–$655 per couple, depending on season.
Getting There: Tucson International Airport is 18 miles from the resort.
What's Nearby: History and culture at the Arizona-Sonora Desert Museum and Mission San Xavier del Bac. Antiques, art, and movie sets in Old Tucson. The shops and sights of Mexico are an hour away.

FOUR SEASONS RESORT AVIARA

Carlsbad, California

Imagine a villa high above the Mediterranean with white marble floors, exotic woods, plantation-style furnishings, huge potted palms, and blooming orchids. Gardens are awash in bougainvillea, bright bird-of-paradise, and citrus trees heavy with fruit. Beside an "edgeless" swimming pool that seems to flow into the distant sea, pampered guests lounge in their green-and-white striped private cabanas. The blue water in view is actually the Pacific, although the warm, dry climate, the flora, and the casually elegant atmosphere are pure Southern Italy.

The Four Seasons Resort Aviara appears to float above beautiful Batiquitos Lagoon, a saltwater estuary habitat for more than one hundred species of waterfowl and shorebirds. Waterfalls and wildflowers cascade down the hillsides from the hotel to fairways that tilt and roll like the ocean surf. Arnold Palmer and Ed Seay's 74.2 rated, 137 slope course is built on a bed of peat. It wanders more than 7,000 yards along the lagoon through three coastal valleys, where wild vegetation, legions of boulders, and streams encroach upon the fairways. Flattish bunkers, few in number and cleverly placed, lie in wait by fairways heaving in waves of moguls, mounds, and hollows. Poa Annua greens are large—some as long as 50 and 60 yards. Club up on the short sixth hole to reach the raffish green sitting 30 feet above; weaken and your approach will roll back off the steep face.

Bordered by tall eucalyptus, the eighth hole sports terraced pools connected by a stream flowing downhill across the front of the green to a lower pool and large beach bunkers. Arnie calls this one "a heroic par five reachable in two, but water and bunkers demand accuracy." Bird-of-paradise blooms all year on the eleventh, where cascading pools and a lake are decorated in the springtime with the pur-

ple spikes of the "Port of Madeira" plant.

The eighteenth starts wide, doglegging downhill between wetlands and a large lake to a huge, undulating green guarded by a phalanx of boulders and a monster bunker. Sated golfers trudge past bubbling fountains into the courtly Spanish colonial-style clubhouse, where a PGA-award-winning pro shop and the clubby Argyle restaurant are welcome retreats. Warm with walnut paneling and antiques, and containing gorgeous locker rooms, this is one of the largest and most elegant clubhouses in the world of golf.

Deep soaking tubs and sunsets over the Pacific await guests in their spacious hotel rooms, each with balcony or landscaped terrace and most with ocean views. Each of five restaurants has alfresco dining, the better to enjoy the mild Southern California climate. Burnt orange walls, eggplant-colored carpets, and a magnificent stone fireplace create a rich backdrop for Tuscan cuisine at Vivace restaurant. Families gather in the California Bistro for the French Buffet, the Seafood Buffet, and the unforgettable Sunday Brunch. Children have their own buffet complete with stuffed animals, sandwiches with crusts cut off, fruit and cheese cubes, and colorful plastic dishes. Reminiscent of grand hotels of decades past, the Lobby Lounge serves an elaborate afternoon tea as the sun sets over the ocean.

Children have their own water playground and guests sip refreshments at the Ocean Pool Bar and Grill on the lush tropical grounds with splashing fountains. Beside the new "Tranquility" swimming pool, private cabanas with dazzling views are equipped with phones, TV, and Internet access. Cabanas in a zen garden at the new spa make outdoor massage a private affair, while indoor treatment rooms are cozy with fireplaces.

Other Places to Play

Two Tom Fazio courses at Pelican Hill Golf Club, about forty-five minutes from Aviara on the "Orange Riviera," opened in the 1990s to rave reviews by every major golf magazine. The Pacific Ocean can be seen from every hole on both tracks and stout sea breezes are a given. Ocean South has dramatic, deep canyon crossings, pine trees in maddening locations, and steep breaks toward the ocean. Equally as stunning, the links-style Ocean North is narrower, flatter, and 200 yards longer (714–760–0707, www.pelicanhill.com).

A PGA "Teacher of the Year" and his staff offer VIP schools and state-of-the-art facilities. Callaway Big Bertha woods and irons await the clubless.

The luxurious Four Seasons Newport Beach at swanky Fashion Island and the Ritz Carlton at Laguna Niguel are favorite resting spots for many Pelican Hill golfers.

Four Seasons Resort Aviara
7100 Four Seasons Point
Carlsbad, CA 92009
Phone: (760) 603–6800, reservations (800) 332–3442
Fax: (760) 603–6801
Web site: www.fourseasons.com/aviara
General Manager: Brian Parmelee
Accommodations: 329 rooms and suites in a Spanish Colonial–style building wrapped in glorious gardens. Exceptionally spacious, each has a private balcony or terrace, a deep tub, a comfy sitting area, and original art.
Meals: Elegant Tuscan cuisine at Vivace; elaborate buffets and casual meals at California Bistro; hearty fare at the clubhouse restaurant.
Facilities: Kip Puterbaugh's Aviara Golf Academy attracts golfers from across the country for three-day schools with video analysis. Swimming pools; two clay and four hard-surface tennis courts; a gallery of upscale shops; and the José Eber Salon. A large, contemporary-design spa offers fitness classes, Pilates, and yoga; indoor/outdoor treatment rooms; private couple's suites; and a solarium. Signature treatments include underwater Watsu massage, Batiquitos Sage Scrub, and after-sun avocado wraps and aloe masks.
Services and Special Programs: Kids for All Seasons is popular with children ages 4–12 for games, stories, field trips, crafts, and games.
Rates: $$$$
Golf and Spa Packages: $650 per room, per night, includes a choice of one round of golf for two, two spa treatments, or one of each.
Getting There: Major airline service at Lindbergh Field International Airport in San Diego, thirty minutes south. Private aircraft are accommodated at Palomar Airport in Carlsbad. Chauffeured airport transfer can be arranged.
What's Nearby: Sunning, surfing, and strolling on miles of Southern California beaches. Tours to Callaway, Taylor-Made, Founder's Cup, and Cobra golf club production facilities. Tours to vast fields of commercially grown flowers. Shopping at a menagerie of antiques shops in the charming seaside village of Carlsbad.

THE INN AND LINKS AT SPANISH BAY

Pebble Beach, California

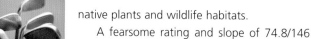

Tom Watson, co-architect of the golf course, said, "Spanish Bay is so much like Scotland, you can almost hear the bagpipes." In fact, you can hear them every night at dusk. In tribute to the spiritual home of golf by the Scottish sea, a lone, kilted bagpiper skirls an eerie tune at sunset from the inn's stone terrace and around the grounds.

A Robert Trent Jones Jr. and Tom Watson design, the Links at Spanish Bay roll in low, sandy mounds on fescue grass fairways and billow into sand dunes up to twenty-four feet high. Just a few Monterey pines and cypress trees frame platoons of merciless pot bunkers. Blue and yellow lupine, gray-green sage, and thistle supply soft color against the dazzling, often turbulent, blue Pacific, bordering all but four holes. Dunes and wetlands are fringed with sedge and native plants, which act as natural water filters and protect the fragile dunes from golfers' footsteps. The first course in California to be awarded Audubon Cooperative Sanctuary status, Spanish Bay carefully protects the native sand dunes—which are actually endangered geologic phenomena along the California coast—and the native plants and wildlife habitats.

A fearsome rating and slope of 74.8/146 and a true Scottish links climate of damp, cool, breezy weather test the golfer's mettle. Each hole has a quaint name, as on Scottish tracks. "Shepherd's Haven" is a 190-yard, par-3 enclosed by dunes, with a multitiered green. Aim for the island landing zone on the fifteenth—"Missing Link"—then clear the gorse and dunes, setting down on a seriously undulating green completely surrounded by marsh and tall reeds, where a heron or an egret may hide. Sea otters float on their backs offshore, seeming to watch as golfers drive over the long dunescape.

In the lee of the brooding Del Monte forest, the luxurious Inn at Spanish Bay lies a few hundred feet from the rocky shoreline on the world-famous 17-Mile Drive. The hotel, with its low-rise, ivory-colored, stucco exterior topped by a red-tile roof and washed in subtle sand and sage tones, rests quietly in the lovely, seacoast setting. Indoors, simple elegance and a warm, intimate atmosphere combine with superb Pebble Beach–style personal service.

Decorated in soothing earth tones and furnished with overstuffed sofas and armchairs, guest rooms and suites have gas fireplaces, pouffy comforters, large marble baths with oversized tubs, and private balconies or patios. Seclusion and views of the stunning ocean and shore are the orders of the day. A stroll on seafront and forest footpaths around the resort rewards you with glimpses of shorebirds, seals, deer, and the occasional fox.

Spanish Bay is one of a trio of luxurious resort hotels that share guest facilities; the others are the Lodge at Pebble Beach and Casa Palmero, both 3 miles south, and accessible by hotel shuttle.

Other Places to Play

Nearly two dozen golf courses lie on or near the shores of Monterey Bay Peninsula, where daytime temperatures range from 50 to 75 degrees year-round. Mornings are often foggy and afternoons usually sunny and breezy. Golfers in the know dress in layers and carry water-resistant jackets.

The damp weather and Poa Annua greens produce listless putts at Poppy Hills Golf Course, located inland of the bay. Owned by the Northern California Golf Association, this is one of three tough courses used in the annual AT&T Pebble Beach National Pro-Am. The oversized, rolling, rather slow greens designed by Robert Trent Jones Jr. are balanced by deep rough and dense stands of mature trees that line and droop over the fairways, which are criss-crossed by deep barrancas. Five par-3s, five par-5s, and an austere rating from the tips—74.6/144—distinguish this hilly track (831–625–2035).

The oldest course in continuous operation west of the Mississippi, the Del Monte Golf Course is located in the city of Monterey. Reasonably priced, Del Monte is rather flat and easy to walk. Accuracy is required on narrow fairways bordered by beautiful Monterey pines, mossy oaks, and cypress trees (831–373–2700).

The Inn and Links at Spanish Bay
2700 17-Mile Drive
Pebble Beach, CA 93953
Phone: (831) 647–7500, reservations (800) 654–9300
Fax: (831) 644–7960
Web site: www.pebblebeach.com
General Manager: David Oliver
Accommodations: Five-star rated, 254 rooms and 16 suites with fireplaces, private patios or balconies, oversize tubs, delightful sea views, roomy armchairs, and sofas.
Meals: Exhibition kitchen, Euro-Asian cuisine, and wood-fired pizza at the casually elegant Roy's at Pebble Beach. Tuscan-style dishes, rotisserie meats, and a focus on fine wines at Pèppoli. Hearty golfer's fare at the Clubhouse Bar and Grill. Appetizers, drinks, sports TV, and a fireplace at Traps.
Facilities: At the Spanish Bay Club, fitness equipment, gym, heated outdoor swimming pool, and massage studio. Eight-court Tennis Pavilion, private lessons and clinics, full-time staff, pro shop. Guests are welcome to use the elegant Spa at Pebble Beach and all guest facilities at the sister resort.
Services and Special Programs: Shuttle to sister resort hotels, golf courses, and downtown Carmel. Horseback riding and guided nature and photography walks.
Rates: $$$$
Golf Packages: None available.
Getting There: Monterey Airport, served by major airlines, is ten minutes away; complimentary transportation available.
What's Nearby: 17-Mile Drive, Monterey Bay Aquarium; shopping and art galleries in quaint Carmel-by-the-Sea and on Cannery Row in Monterey; historic sights and museums on the "Path of History" in old Monterey; coastal drives to Big Sur and the Point Lobos State Reserve.

LA QUINTA RESORT AND CLUB
La Quinta, California

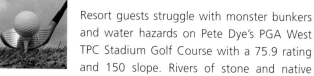

In the glamorous Hollywood heyday of the 1920s and 1930s, Errol Flynn, Ginger Rogers, and their movie star cohorts made the 100-mile drive over the mountains to the desert to relax at the tiny, Spanish-style La Quinta Hotel and play on the nine-hole golf course—the first in the Coachella Valley—for a green fee of one dollar. More than one hundred golf courses later, there are now seven glittering resort cities and more than 30,000 swimming pools. And the original twenty casitas at La Quinta Resort and Club are now 750 luxurious rooms, suites, and villas in lush tropical gardens. A stroll around the gardens and grounds turns up forty-two swimming pools and forty-nine whirlpool spas. Oceans of magenta-colored bougainvillea cascade over the walls of private patios, and you can pick oranges and lemons every month of the year. It's hard to beat the weather here, with an average year-round temperature of 88 degrees. Seclusion, spa treatments, and golf remain the order of the day at La Quinta, called the "Western Home of Golf."

No other resort property in Southern California offers ninety holes of top-rated golf, including Jack Nicklaus's PGA West Tournament Course, where tour players test their mettle in PGA Qualifying School.

Resort guests struggle with monster bunkers and water hazards on Pete Dye's PGA West TPC Stadium Golf Course with a 75.9 rating and 150 slope. Rivers of stone and native grasses stream across Dye's Mountain and the Dunes layouts. A Scottish links layout, the Dunes rolls like a stormy green sea across the desert floor, scattered with large bunkers and abundant water on eight holes. Rimmed by a lake, guarded by sand at the curve of a dogleg, and with a severely sloping green, the seventeenth on the Dunes was rated as one of the toughest holes in the country.

On the sixth hole of the Mountain Course, rocky foothills descend to the edge of the fairway and the two-level green, which is ferociously guarded by sand and grass bunkers. A deep ravine and a desert wilderness border the fourteenth fairway, leading to an elevated green graced by yet another ravine and waves of sand. On the sixteenth, you get turf on the tee and the green, and 167 yards of rocks between.

On his new PGA West Greg Norman Course, the Aussie golf great touched the terrain lightly with wildflowers and indigenous paloverde and acacia trees in a spectacular, low-desert setting. More than

one hundred "Great White Shark" bunkers are filled with brilliant-white, crushed-marble sand.

After a rigorous day on the fairways, golfers head for Spa La Quinta for a "Just for Guys Facial" or the "Sports Pack Body Wrap," where warm mud is wrapped over hands, arms, lower back, and shoulders. Health and beauty treatment rooms are open to garden patios with close-up views of the sheer Santa Rosa Mountains. The hacienda-style spa is a perfect match for the 1920s-style, tile-roofed resort, where bubbling Talavera-tile fountains soothe golfers' spirits at day's end as they relax by aromatic mesquite-burning fireplaces in 1- or 2-story casitas. Mediterranean cuisine awaits in the historic Montañas dining room. Hand-blown, flickering lanterns glow like jewels in the Adobe Grill, overlooking gardens and waterfalls.

Wandering beneath towering palms and shaded archways in the oasis-like resort, guests venture out to shop in the boutiques or play tennis at the state-of-the-art complex of grass, clay, and hard-surfaced courts. *Tennis* magazine ranks this one of the "Top 10 Greatest U.S. Tennis Resorts."

Making Fun While the Sun Shines

Snowbirds flock to the Coachella Valley to play on more than one hundred golf courses under a clear, azure desert sky. The average year-round temperature is 88 degrees. The eight Palm Springs Desert Resort cities are famous for golf and tennis resorts, palm-fringed boulevards lined with exclusive shops, and wilderness adventures in the Sonoran Desert. When visitors tire of lolling at the natural hot springs spas and swimming in the 30,000 pools in the valley, they head out on horseback or by jeep to explore shady streams in the Indian Canyons, to search for petroglyphs at Joshua Tree National Park, and to glide in the Palm Springs Aerial Tram to the top of 10,000-foot-high Mount San Jacinto for hiking or sunset cocktails.

La Quinta Resort and Club
49–499 Eisenhower Drive
La Quinta, CA 92253
Phone: (760) 564–4111, reservations (800) 598–3828
Fax: 760–564–5768
Web site: www.laquintaresort.com
General Manager: Larry Scheerer
Accommodations: 750 rooms (averaging 500 square feet), suites, and villas in Spanish-style casitas with adobe walls and red tile roofs, garden or mountain views, wood-burning fireplaces (even in some bedrooms and bathrooms), private patios, and huge tubs.
Meals: Mediterranean cuisine in the historic Montañas dining room. Authentic Mexican food in the colorful indoor/outdoor Adobe Grill. California cuisine at Morgans. Acclaimed seafood at Azur by Le Bernardin. Spanish-style afternoon tea in the art- and antiques-filled lobby; casual meals in the stylish golf and tennis clubhouses.
Facilities: Golf instruction by three of America's top teaching pros—David Leadbetter, Dave Pelz, and Jim McLean. Spa La Quinta offers signature health and beauty treatments, healing inhalation, Celestial Showers, and private outdoor patios. Also here: twenty-three tennis courts, forty-one private swimming pools, an Olympic-size pool, and thirty-eight whirlpool spas; shopping plaza in a lush garden setting; and an executive business center and fitness center.
Services and Special Programs: Diagnostic services and preventive treatments at the new Cosgrove WellMax Clinic, from MRI to colonoscopy, CT scans and personal evaluations. Camp La Quinta for children, including pool play, crafts, and games.
Rates: $$$–$$$$
Golf and Spa Package: Master's Package includes unlimited golf on any of the five courses and casita accommodations for one night. Starting at $400–640 per couple, double occupancy.
Getting There: Major carriers service Palm Springs Regional Airport, 19 miles from the resort; private aircraft are accommodated there and at nearby Indio and Thermal Airports. Ontario International Airport is a ninety-minute drive away. Chauffeured airport transfer can be arranged.
What's Nearby: Explore the stunning Sonoran desert by horseback, four-wheel-drive vehicles, hot-air balloon, or camel. Visit Joshua Tree National Park and the Indian Canyons. Take in outstanding local theater, top-name performers in concert, film and art festivals, polo matches, and PGA golf tournaments. Shop in upscale El Paseo boutiques in Palm Springs.

MARRIOTT DESERT SPRINGS RESORT AND SPA
Palm Desert, California

An exotic hanging garden with running streams, waterfalls, and chattering tropical birds, the eight-story atrium lobby at the Marriott overlooks a large lake, where gondolas ferry guests around Venetian-style canals. One of the largest resorts in the Coachella Valley, Desert Springs is a favorite with sports-oriented families. Besides thirty-six holes of championship golf, there are five swimming pools, a tournament tennis complex, one of the largest spas and gyms in California, jogging trails, and even a rock-climbing wall.

The "King of Waterscapes," Ted Robinson liberally watered his Palm and Valley golf courses with lakes, ponds, and falls, adding 5,000 trees—mostly palms—for good measure. The two courses are gently undulating, with medium-size greens and fiendishly located banks of flowers at every turn. On the third hole of the Palm, which wraps completely around the

hotel, there are waterfalls to the left, islands in a stream on the right, a line-up of palms, and a giant bunker backing the deep green.

Gondolas cruise around the four finishing holes of the Valley course. The seventeenth tees off above cascading falls and flowerbeds over a pool where a flock of pink flamingos pose, to a small island green rimmed with palms. The players go back across the footbridge to be greeted on the eighteenth by five giant bunkers on each side of a narrow fairway. A lake with swans and the inevitable waterfalls guard a three-tiered, sunken green backed by a platoon of palms—a scene reminiscent of a 1940s Busby Berkeley movie set.

Another fanciful Ted Robinson creation, "The Greens," is a 1,435-foot-long, eighteen-hole pitching and putting course with rolling fairways, doglegs upon doglegs, nasty bits of beautifully landscaped rough, and plenty of water.

Exhusted golfers retire to the spa, where windows and skylights are open to the dramatic Santa Rosa Mountain range and lush gardens. Here is one of the largest free-weight and cardio-gym fitness facilities in the country. Also included are an adults-only lap pool, hot and cold plunge pools, and a private, clothing-optional sun deck. One of many health and beauty treatments is Ayurvedic Shirodhara Therapy: A stream of warm oil is poured on the "Third Eye"—the center of the forehead—while hands and feet are soothingly massaged. Après spa, adults head for The Retreat, a quiet pool with private cabanas.

Top-40 DJs and well-known dance bands play at Costa's nightclub, where a huge dance floor is encircled by cushy, upholstered seating and contemporary artwork. One of the nicest amenities here is the adjacent terrace, where you can have a cocktail by a bubbling fountain beside the lake, puff a cigar if you wish, and watch the moon come up over the snow-capped mountains.

Other Places to Play

Desert Willow Golf Resort in Palm Desert has the look, the personal service, and the atmosphere of a private country club. It is perhaps the most impressive city-owned golf facility in the country, with a luxurious clubhouse and a golf academy operated by one of the world's top instructors, David Leadbetter.

Skillfully integrated into the natural landscape, with fewer acres of the perfect turf typical of most Southern California courses, both Firecliff and Mountain View at Desert Willow have vast stretches of natural vegetation. Huge sand and crushed granite waste bunkers are fringed with magnificent groves of palms and red and golden barrel cactus. While Mountain View is user-friendly for the high handicapper, elevation changes and more than one hundred bunkers make Firecliff a stern test. Unique features behind the eighth and seventeenth holes are replicas of striking stone formations found in the mysterious Indian Canyons, the ancestral home of the Agua Caliente Cahuilla Indians (www.desertwillow.com).

The Golf Resort at Indian Wells is a masterpiece of architect Ted Robinson, who integrated nine lakes and a flurry of waterfalls into the East and West courses. The West is infamous for elevation changes of up to 60 feet, wildly undulating pedestal greens, and a lively collection of 120 sand traps and pot bunkers. Short but deadly, the thirteenth hole carries from an elevated tee to an island green, with a distracting view of the Santa Rosa Mountains. Holes one and two surround ancient Indian burial grounds, now covered by rampant flower gardens.

Although rolling and hilly with some steep slopes, the East is a little easier. Just don't be fooled by the dogleg island fairway on the 370-yard thirteenth—use a long iron instead of a wood if you plan to stay dry (760–346–4653).

The 1995 Bob Hope Pro-Am at Indian Wells was one for the history books when three presidents—Clinton, Bush, Ford—teamed up with then ninety-two-year-old Bob Hope, Palm Springs' most beloved permanent resident. The First Players' scores were Clinton 95, Bush 93, and Ford 103.

Marriott Desert Springs Resort and Spa
74855 Country Club Drive
Palm Desert, CA 92260
Phone: (760) 341–2211, reservations (800) 331–3112
Web site: www.marriotthotels.com

General Manager: Tim Sullivan

Accommodations: Four-star rated, 884 rooms and suites, newly redecorated in desert tones with private balconies, separate sitting areas, luxurious baths with granite vanities, and limestone floors.

Meals: Twelve restaurants including Northern Italian cuisine at the elegant Ristorante Tuscany; a huge saltwater aquarium and Pan-Asian seafood at Sea Grille Restaurant; wine country cuisine at LakeView; regional Mexican food at Colibri Grille; all-American menu at the Oasis; healthy fare at the Spa Bistro; and the Mikado Japanese Steak House.

Facilities: John Jacobs Golf School, GPS golf carts, private golf lessons; twenty hard-surfaced, clay, and grass tennis courts, private lessons, clinics, tournaments, 4.+ drill sessions; eighteen upscale boutiques; five swimming pools; sand volleyball; basketball; croquet; 3.5-mile jogging trail; full-service spa; gym; José Eber Salon.

Services and Special Programs: Kid's Club for ages 4 and up with games, swimming, mini-golf, meals, and arts and crafts.

Rates: $$$

Golf Packages: One-night golf package includes resort view room, a round of golf, golf valet services, and breakfast. $499 per couple, double occupancy.

Getting There: Palm Springs Airport is 11 miles from the resort and served by major airlines. Limousine service is available.

What's Nearby: Joshua Tree National Park; birdwatching in the Big Morongo Canyon Preserve; looking for lizards at the Coachella Valley Preserve; Living Desert wild animal and botanical park; history at the Palm Springs Desert Museum and the Palm Springs Air Museum.

OJAI VALLEY INN AND SPA

Ojai, California

High above the haze of Southern California cities lies a magical green valley, shaded by ancient oaks and warmed by perpetually sunny skies. Since 1923 celebrities and weekenders have hidden away here at the rambling, Spanish colonial-style Ojai Valley Inn at the foot of the Topa Topa Mountains, playing golf and tennis, horseback riding and biking on wooded trails, and, nowadays, luxuriating at a sumptuous new spa.

The site of Senior PGA tour events, the golf course is a Billy Bell and George C. Thomas Jr. original, updated by Jay Morrish in the 1980s. Laid out among wild stream canyons, the fairways are lined with thousands of mature oaks and eucalyptus trees, some 150 feet tall with branches as thick as truck tires.

Mowed everywhere, even under the trees, wide, unfeatured fairways on the front nine tilt softly toward the valley floor, with undulating greens in absolutely perfect condition. Just when you think you can handle this 70.76-rated course, the back nine ambushes you like a tiger, surprising golfers with hidden ravines and creekbeds, gaping barrancas, massive overhanging oaks, and greens that slope sharply off on the sides. In the light rough, a herd of deer or a steely-eyed coyote may silently observe.

Built in the Roaring Twenties, Ojai Valley is the only George C. Thomas Jr. design course open to the public. He designed the Los Angeles North, Bel Air, and Riviera country clubs—three, notorious old beauties that are aging with style.

Rugged mountains encircle the resort, creating a "Shangri-la" atmosphere as gossamer mists from the coast, only 14 miles away as the crow flies, hang on the ridges at

dawn and melt in a blaze of warmth at midday. At sunset, the legendary "pink moment" occurs, when a rosy glow washes across the peaks. The inn has the look of an old Spanish hacienda, with tiled floors and walls, intricate iron work, and breezy, arched loggias lined with art and antiques. Lounges are cozy with big fireplaces and oversized sofas. Bougainvillea cascades over thick garden walls. Feathery pepper trees, fragrant Ojai tangerines, and century-old olive trees shade the lawns and walkways, secret teahouses, and herb gardens.

Spreading oaks and the ever-present mountains are a backdrop for glorious Sunday brunches on the Oak Cafe terrace, overlooking the first tee. A guitarist plays softly and the scent of jasmine is heavy as diners partake of Pacific Coast seafood and locally grown fruits and vegetables.

While horseback riding through wildflower meadows and up rocky hillsides on the inn's 800-acre ranch, guests get an idea of what California looked like when Spanish conquistadors first saw the countryside in the 1700s. The big red barn is the scene of hoe-downs and Western-style parties. For those who favor biking and hiking, a 9-mile, paved trail starts at the inn and winds through the valley and into charming Ojai village.

The Spa Ojai, one of the largest and most commodious in California, is an Andalusian-themed village with bubbling fountains, a bell tower, a leafy garden terrace, mosaics, and painted tiles. Lovely treatment rooms have fireplaces, as do lobbies and lounges, which are outfitted with deep armchairs and sofas. A lap pool and sun deck for adults only and the Acorn Cafe—

serving light meals, healthy snacks, juices, and smoothies—make this a true oasis.

Site of the oldest amateur tennis tournament in the United States, held continuously since 1895, the tennis complex includes four hard-surface and four cushioned courts.

Other Places to Play

Guests at the glamorous new Bacara Resort and Spa on the Santa Barbara "Riviera" get preferred tee times at the adjacent Sandpiper Golf Course, one of the top public courses in the country. A rolling links-style track is laid on 1 mile of rolling seaside terrain (877–422–3533, www.bacararesort.com). About an hour's drive from Ojai at the Alisal Guest Ranch and Resort in Solvang, the newly renovated, Billy Bell–designed course meanders through historic, rolling ranchlands (800–425–4725, www.alisal.com).

Ojai Valley Inn and Spa
905 Country Club Road
Ojai, CA 93023
Phone: (805) 646–5511, reservations (800) 422–6524
Fax: (805) 646–7969
Web site: www.ojairesort.com
General Manager: Thad Hyland
Accommodations: Over 200 spacious rooms and suites with private balconies or patios in two-story, Spanish-hacienda-style buildings, with valley or mountain views, in forest and garden settings. Rooms in the original buildings are updated 1920s California mission-style, some with fireplaces. Shangri-La and Vista rooms have valley, golf course, or garden views, and private balconies.
Meals: Hearty bistro menu at the Oak Cafe; California French cuisine and Pacific Coast seafood at Maravilla. At the spa's Acorn Cafe, light meals, snacks, and freshly extracted juices are served on the patio or poolside.
Facilities: Eight tournament tennis courts; stable and horseback riding on a private ranch; two large swimming pools and 60-foot lap pool; full-service spa village.
Services and Special Programs: At the spa, complimentary daily fitness, health, and art classes—yoga, salsa dancing, water aerobics, power walks; the "Golfer's Massage" or "Sports Massage," hydrotherapy; and anti-stress facials. Customized health evaluation at the "Destination Health" clinic. Camp Ojai for kids offers scavenger hunts, games, pony rides, meals, playground, and volleyball. Private golf instruction and "total immersion" lessons at the Academy of Golf, and daily golf clinics with PGA pros.
Rates: $$$–$$$$
Golf Packages: The "Classic Golf Package" includes unlimited golf with cart during the week or one round per day on weekends; one night's accommodations and golf services is $379 for two. The "Best of Ojai" includes room and choice of golf, tennis, horseback riding, Camp Ojai, dinner plan, fishing, golf lesson, jeep tour, massage, or facial at $430 per couple.
Getting There: Santa Barbara Airport is forty-five minutes away, and Los Angeles Airport is ninety minutes away. Chauffeured airport transfer can be arranged.
What's Nearby: Ride complimentary bikes on a beautiful paved bike trail starting from the inn; explore hiking trails in the Los Padres National Forest and at Lake Casitas. Galleries, shops, and gourmet restaurants are within walking distance in the village of Ojai; legendary beaches in Santa Barbara; museums and historic districts; an original Spanish mission; upscale shopping, restaurants, and cultural events.

PEBBLE BEACH RESORTS

Pebble Beach, California

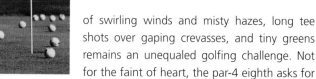

Grassy dunes above the rocky shores of Stillwater Cove on the Monterey coastline are reminiscent of Scottish links. Here lies Pebble Beach Golf Links, the dream course of every American golfer. This is where Nicklaus, Watson, and Kite won the U.S. Open, and where Tiger roared at the AT&T Pebble Beach National Pro-Am.

In 1919, Jack Neville laid down a rippling figure-eight track along a series of jagged palisades and sandy moors, placing a miraculous series of holes on windy headlands within sight and sound of the pounding surf. There is plenty of sand; knee-high rough; several lakes, creeks, and gullies; and groves of mature pines and cypress. The notorious combination of swirling winds and misty hazes, long tee shots over gaping crevasses, and tiny greens remains an unequaled golfing challenge. Not for the faint of heart, the par-4 eighth asks for a blind tee shot to the cliff's edge. Then it's 190 yards over the beach, 100 feet below, to a little bitty green encircled by traps.

The experience of Pebble Beach is brought to a smashing conclusion on the eighteenth, situated on a rocky point above a boiling cauldron of waves—a ghostly, isolated place when enveloped in fog. Barking harbor seals seem to laugh while gangs of sweet-faced sea otters float, unconcerned, in their kelp beds. One of the world's great hostelries—The Lodge at Pebble Beach—is in sight as you tee off. You hope the headwind doesn't blow you off the narrow fairway before arriving at the final green, menaced by trees and a quartet of bunkers. It was this hole at the 1976 and 1984 Open, respectively, that Nicklaus's ball ended up in the drink and Hale Irwin's tee shot smacked into the rocks only to arch gracefully back onto the fairway. Nonetheless, Jack Nicklaus holds to the statement: "If I had only one more round of golf to play, I would play it at Pebble Beach."

In preparation for the 100th U.S. Open in 2000, course conditioning was greatly improved. Nicklaus designed a new fifth hole, a stunning par-3, and extended the spectacular, unbroken string of waterfront holes on the bluffs.

Plan your pilgrimage to Pebble Beach well in advance—even as much as a year or more—since tee times are difficult to secure; March through November are the busiest months.

The Lodge at Pebble Beach, formal in atmosphere and California rustic in low-rise buildings in the trees, caters to an international clientele of golfers who expect, and receive, perfect personal service and luxurious accommodations. A former mansion on the

resort property is now the small, very private, very grand Casa Palmero, a Spanish Mediterranean–style villa adjacent to the lodge and the first hole. You might catch a glimpse of a movie star or a golf hero in the billiards room or by the pool. These rooms have fireplaces, oversized tubs, and private garden spas. Adjacent is the new Spa at Pebble Beach, where post-sports revitalizers, complete with aromatherapy massage and warm seaweed packs on tired back muscles, are a fitting reward for hard-won fortunes on the links of the California coast. Stillwater Cove seaweed masques and wraps are popular, as well as the "Cypress Pine Exfoliation."

The Golf Academy, one of the top rated in the country, has exceptional teaching pros led by Laird Small, one of America's fifty greatest golf teachers as named by *Golf Digest*.

Other Places to Stay

Guests at the Lodge at Pebble Beach share guest facilities at the Inn at Spanish Bay, accessible by hotel shuttle, and may book tee times at the Links at Spanish Bay, Del Monte Golf Course, and Spyglass Hill Golf Course. Spyglass Hill is a long, super-difficult Robert Trent Jones Sr. design and one of his greatest masterpieces. Views of the Pacific are magnificent. Sand dunes, dense stands of Monterey pine and cypress, stiff sea breezes, and very well-bunkered, large greens are elements that result in the intimidating 74.3/148 rating and slope. Inspired by the novel *Treasure Island,* Spyglass Hill is the toughest golf course in Northern California.

Pebble Beach Resorts
1700 17-Mile Drive
Pebble Beach, CA 93953
Phone: (831) 624–3811, reservations (800) 654–9300
Fax: (831) 644–7960
Web site: www.pebblebeach.com
General Manager: Janine Chicourrat
Accommodations: The four-star rated Lodge at Pebble Beach has 161 elegant rooms in a main lodge and in low-rise annexes, most with fireplaces and balconies or patios with views of the golf course and the coast. Casa Palmero is a Spanish-style, twenty-four-room estate with a large garden courtyard, private living room, library, billiard room, and swimming pool; some suites have fireplaces and private patios.
Meals: At Stillwater Bar and Grill, fresh seafood is served in a contemporary, casual setting with golf course views. With a view of the eighteenth hole, the casual Tap Room serves seafood, grilled steaks, and chops, and features a museum-like collection of golf memorabilia. Club XIX serves prix-fixe gourmet French cuisine in an elegant indoor setting or out on the cozy patio with a fireplace and ocean view. The Gallery, with sweeping views of Stillwater Cove, specializes in rotisserie specialties and American food.
Facilities: Outdoor pool; ten hard-surface and two clay tennis courts; pro shop; equestrian center with extensive bridle trails; private, oceanside Beach and Tennis Club; exercise classes; fitness center; several upscale boutiques and galleries.
Services and Special Programs: At the Golf Academy, top teaching pros, golf schools, video analysis, two driving ranges and caddie service; access to Peter Hay Golf Course, a nine-hole, par-3 course.
Rates: $$$$
Golf Packages: None available.
Getting There: Monterey Peninsula Airport, served by major airlines, is 7 miles away; complimentary transportation available. San Jose International Airport is one-and-one-half hours north and San Francisco International Airport is about two hours north.
What's Nearby: Walking and jogging trails in the Del Monte Forest and on the surrounding bluffs and beaches; Monterey Bay Aquarium; shopping and gallery hopping in Carmel and on Cannery Row in Monterey; historic sights and museums on the "Path of History" in old Monterey; coastal drives to Big Sur and the Point Lobos State Reserve.

QUAIL LODGE RESORT AND GOLF CLUB

Carmel Valley, California

The Carmel River ambles between two mountain ranges through a picturesque valley with horse farms, ranch resorts, and tawny meadows liberally sprinkled with spreading oaks. About 4 miles inland from the often fogbound Monterey Peninsula on the Pacific Coast, the Carmel Valley is warm and dry, perfect for horseback riding, hiking, biking, tennis, and golf.

Quail Lodge, a quiet hideaway in mid-valley, was named one of the "Best Small Hotels in the World," and is one of the prestigious Peninsula Group properties that includes the Peninsula Hotels in Hong Kong and Beverly Hills. With cedar siding and heavy shake roofs, the complex of low-profile buildings lies under the spreading branches of ancient oaks, cypress, eucalyptus, and pines. Indoors the rustic charm of Spanish tile, redwood, and cedar accents set a casual California scene. French doors open to private balconies and patios in the guest rooms and villas, and lead to luxuriant gardens and views of forested hillsides. Recently redecorated in autumn tones, warm woods, and rattan, some of the accommodations have fireplaces and oversize tubs.

A new European-style spa offers signature treatments using Carmel Valley and marine botanicals. The popular "19th Hole Gentlemen's Facial" includes face, neck, and shoulder massage. You can take a Pilates or yoga class with other guests or privately. Or, take a hike

or bike ride in nearly 600 acres of private resort property.

The elegant Covey restaurant, one of the best on the peninsula, overlooks Mallard Lake, gardens, and the hills. Sunday brunch and some evenings feature live "Jazz on the Deck." Pacific sea bass, abalone, and Sonoma squab are a few of the California cuisine specialties.

The lovely Robert Muir Graves golf course is draped on gently rolling countryside and watered by ten lakes. Carts are not required, giving the opportunity to walk this heavily wooded course, which is surrounded by a nature preserve. Swans and ducks glide on willow-shaded lakes. Coveys of California quail skitter across the fairways to their brambly nests beneath the cottonwoods. Deer and wild turkeys amble along the steep-sided Carmel River, which borders several holes. The front nine is rather level, with spacious landing zones and well-bunkered greens; while the back nine closes in, requiring greater accuracy. Driving from the tips involves a few carries over deep, rocky gullies.

Noted by *Golf for Women* as a top track for female golfers, the Graves design has no forced carries from the forward tees and has generally large, level greens. The two- and three-day golf schools here are exceptional, with instructors such as former LPGA touring pro, Janet Coles, and Ben Doyle, named one of *Golf Digest*'s fifty greatest golf teachers in 2002

Pete Dye in Carmel

One of the most challenging on the Monterey Peninsula, the Pete Dye Golf Course at the Wyndham Carmel Valley Ranch follows the Carmel River on the front nine before heading up into the oak-studded hills and descending headlong in changing elevations of up to 350 feet. Little bitty greens and the ubiquitous Dye railroad ties, plus three lakes, provide a lively golfing experience. The sprawling, 1,700-acre, luxury resort offers 144 oversized, secluded suites with fireplaces and private decks (831–625–9500, www.wyndham.com).

Quail Lodge Resort and Golf Club
8205 Valley Greens Drive
Carmel, CA 93923
Phone: (831) 624–2888, (888) 828–8787
Fax: (831) 624–3726
Web site: www.peninsula.com
General Manager: James Cecil
Accommodations: Four-diamond, four-star-rated, in two-story buildings; 97 rooms, suites, and villas with private decks or patios; some with fireplaces.
Meals: California cuisine in The Covey. Hearty breakfasts and lunches at the Country Club at the golf course. Continental breakfast is complimentary to lodge guests.
Facilities: Golf practice range, putting and chipping greens, golf school; four hard-surface tennis courts; two outdoor swimming pools; full-service health and beauty spa; twenty-four-hour fitness center.
Services and Special Programs: Guided tours to local wineries. Pets welcome, for a fee.
Rates: $$$
Golf Packages: Accommodations for two nights, three days unlimited golf with cart, and continental breakfast $985 for two, double occupancy.
Getting There: A twenty-minute drive from Monterey Peninsula Airport, served by major airlines. Ninety minutes from San Jose International Airport.
What's Nearby: Hundreds of boutique shops and art galleries in the village of Carmel, horseback riding and hiking in the Carmel Valley, expeditions to historic Monterey for sightseeing, the 17-Mile Drive, and Big Sur.

THE RITZ-CARLTON, HALF MOON BAY

Half Moon Bay, California

On the rugged, western edge of California the sun chases away fingers of morning fog, glimmers across wildflower-covered bluffs, and turns fiery red as it sinks into the horizon beyond rocky sea stacks offshore. This daily performance of weather and landscape is unmatched in its drama anywhere else on earth.

Over the hills from Silicon Valley and San Francisco, nature and the sea take the lead on the Half Moon Bay Ocean Course, a Scottish links–style layout with spectacular ocean views from every hole. The architect, Arthur Hills, took a traditional approach by providing unobstructed views of most holes from the tee, avoiding earth moving, keeping turf to a minimum, uniting each hole with the original native grasses, retaining low hollows and mounds, and adding no trees. Only eleven cypress trees grace the course, where constant sea breezes, and sometimes gales, call for the irons.

Walking is the best way to enjoy the 6,732 yards of gently rolling links. The seventh is one of the prettiest holes and a short test of true target golf with a 155-yard carry over a large pond, a 30-foot-high grassy bank on the right, and a domed, lightning-fast green.

Crashing waves create a soft curtain of sound on the finishing holes. Sixteen plays along the shore, down a 350-yard slope, and levels off for a view of miles of coastline. The short seventeenth has no fairway, carrying over a yawning crevasse and plunging waterfall to a putting surface with sound effects—barking sea lions. The boomerang-shaped, par-4 eighteenth is right on the edge of the cliff. You shoot uphill, then down a fairway liberally dotted with bunkers and grassy knobs to a huge green laid on a windy plateau. This hole requires dead aim if you plan to avoid the sucking gorse.

The Half Moon Bay Old Course, lined with Monterey pine and cypress trees, has a longer, yet less demanding layout. It is an Arnold Palmer-Frank

Duane–designed beauty built in 1973 and updated at the turn of the twenty-first century. Bound by some narrow chutes, the fairways are gently mounded and crossed by natural wetlands, riparian areas, and small lakes. Ever-present sea breezes up the ante. The beach is a lateral hazard on the eighteenth, which glides to a graceful conclusion just below the terraces of the hotel.

Fortunately you can walk these beautiful courses and a public walking trail winds along the edge of the cliffs. From November through March, pods of whales are often seen spouting and rolling offshore on their way to and from Baja, California, where they spend the winter.

The Ritz-Carlton rides imposingly on the bluff above the Pacific—a rambling, shingle-style lodge reminiscent of the grand seaside hostelries of the nineteenth century. Big stone fireplaces are often ablaze in the rather formal public rooms, all with stunning ocean views. English antiques, Portuguese ceramics and tapestries, and a notable collection of oil paintings and watercolors recall the 1800s, when the seacoast was settled by European shipbuilders. Tea is taken among the potted palms in the light-filled conservatory. A warm, Roman mineral bath awaits in the secluded spa. Most guest rooms have fireplaces and comfy window seats.

Catering to a toney clientele from nearby Silicon Valley, the Ritz offers the unique services of a Technology Butler, high-speed Internet access, full-size work areas, and complete executive business services. Stress reduction exercise classes and anti-tension massages are popular, along with traditional health and beauty treatments. Golfers go for the "Sport Treatment," where feet are laved in aromatic oils, exfoliated, masked, coated with soothing wax, and massaged.

The gourmet restaurant, Navio, attracts diners from throughout the San Francisco Bay Area for the freshest seafood caught in nearby Princeton Harbor.

Locally produced herbs, greens, poultry, and cheeses are incorporated into inventive California cuisine. With high windows looking onto the ocean, Navio looks like the wood-lined, candlelit interior of a yacht on the Mediterranean. Special features are the raw bar and large display kitchen.

Old Beauty Is New Again

Hundreds of buildings and relics in San Francisco's Presidio are the remnants of more than 200 years of occupation by Spanish, Mexican, and American military. Among the treasures are seventeenth-century bronze cannons, Civil War barracks, pre-earthquake Victorian houses, and adobe walls built by the conquistadors.

Built in 1895, the Presidio Golf Course was the much-coveted private sanctuary of the U.S. Army until the army base became a national park. A multimillion dollar upgrade by Arnold Palmer Golf Management Company added bent grass greens, a glitzy new clubhouse, and the Presidio Cafe on the eighteenth green, where golfers enjoy live jazz and California cuisine on the heated terrace.

On a peninsula of woodlands and bluffs above the Golden Gate Bridge, the Presidio layout winds among stands of towering cypress, eucalyptus, and pine trees. Peregrine falcons and eagles circle above. Wild rhododendrons explode into clouds of red and white blooms from January through April. Sidehill, uphill, and downhill lies are the order of the day, plus erratic winds off San Francisco Bay.

The Ritz-Carlton, Half Moon Bay
One Miramontes Point Road
Half Moon Bay, CA 94019
Phone: (650) 712–7000, reservations (800) 241–3333
Fax: (650) 712–7070
Web site: www.ritzcarlton.com
General Manager: John Berndt
Accommodations: 262 luxurious, traditionally decorated guest rooms and suites in the main lodge and private guesthouses with Frette linens, oversized baths, fine fabrics, and fabulous ocean, mountain, and golf course views. Most have fireplaces and window seats; some have patios. Club-level rooms enjoy a private lounge and concierge. Five complimentary food and beverage presentations daily and more.
Meals: Fine dining in Navio, specializing in California cuisine and Pacific Coast seafood. Light meals, snacks, drinks, and afternoon tea in the Conservatory. Hearty lunches and dinners at Caddy's in the golf clubhouse.
Facilities: Six lighted, oceanside tennis courts; outdoor fireplace; hot tubs on the clifftop; executive business center; "Technology" Butler; full-service spa, salon, and fitness center.
Services and Special Programs: Valet service; Ritz Kids program for ages 5–12, with supervised games, hikes, cooking lessons, meals, and more.
Rates: $$$–$$$$
Golf Packages: Tee for Two includes one night deluxe accommodations and a round of golf for two at $595 per couple. Golf and Spa Package includes overnight accommodations, a round of golf for two, and two sixty-minute Swedish massages at $795 per couple.
Getting There: A forty-five-minute drive from San Francisco International Airport; airport transport can arranged.
What's Nearby: Beautiful beaches on the San Mateo Coast; hiking trails in Purissima Creek Redwood Park; tidepools at Fitzgerald Marine Reserve; scenic vistas at Pigeon Point Lighthouse; antiques shopping and gallery hopping in Half Moon Bay; deep-sea fishing, sea kayaking, and windsurfing; garden and nursery tours.

SILVERADO RESORT

Napa, California

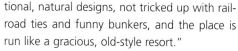

Spring arrives in the Napa Valley on 2-foot-high waves of wild golden mustard, vivid yellow rivers beneath the grapevines blanketing the valley floor. The grapes ripen all summer, and in the fall when the leaves turn red and gold, open bins of harvested grapes are ferried to the wineries for the crush, a busy, celebratory time of year in the Wine Country.

In the heart of the valley on a quiet country road stands a white-pillared, antebellum-style mansion reminiscent of a southern plantation. Anchoring the 1,200-acre grounds of Silverado Resort, this building was built for a Civil War general on a Spanish land grant circa 1870. The rambling grounds are shaded by towering eucalyptus, palms, oaks, and magnolias whose creamy white, dinner-plate-size blooms are seductively fragrant in the summertime.

More than 2,000 overhanging trees—oaks, willows, redwoods, eucalyptus, and pines—that are more than a century old line the fairways of the two Robert Trent Jones Jr. layouts built in the 1960s. A new grounds maintenance program has raised course conditions to near perfect, creating a stiff challenge, especially on the greens. Johnny Miller, Silverado Country Club member and U.S. Open winner, said of the courses: "They are so popular because they are tradi-

tional, natural designs, not tricked up with railroad ties and funny bunkers, and the place is run like a gracious, old-style resort."

Surrounded by vineyards and wooded hills, the 6,896-yard North Course is wide, with very little water and acres and acres of sand. Greens are big, flat, slanted, and as slick as plate glass.

Ducks and birds inhabit the creeks and ponds that cross or border eleven holes of the South Course. Greens are elevated, large, super fast, and softly tiered—the architect's trademark. The great arms of the valley oaks loom over the edges of wide, seriously undulating fairways; sidehill lies are the order of the day. A 500-yard, par-5 dogleg obstructed by towering pines, the eighteenth ends in a picturesque garden setting below the verandah of the mansion on a green guarded by yawning bunkers. Arnold Palmer thrilled Senior Tour crowds in the 1990s when he eagled the eighteenth on the first and final rounds; and David Duval nearly gave his father, Bob Duval, heart failure when he made a surprise appearance as his dad's caddie on the first tee at the 1999 tournament. Big crowds turn out for the annual Senior PGA Napa Valley Championship in October, a 1.3-million-dollar event sponsored by Beringer Vineyards.

Low-rise condominium and cottage accommodations are clustered in intimate courtyards, each with gardens and a swimming pool. There are nine pools in all, with a long, lap pool at the glamorous new spa. Privately owned and managed by the resort, each unit is quite spacious with a fully equipped kitchen, dining/living area, wood-burning fireplace, and private patio or balcony.

Daily clinics for adults and juniors are scheduled at the largest tennis complex in Northern California. One of the largest, newest, and most commodious spas in a valley known for spa resorts, the Spa at Silverado has enough attendants for an army of sybarites. Complementing a menu of traditional and exotic treatments, Tui-Na is an ancient Chinese combination of vigorous massage, acupressure, and stretching. Popular with non-golfers is the "Golf Widow," a four-hour treatment including massage, facial, manicure, and pedicure. Couples are pampered together in a private two-story, skylit pavilion with a fireplace, while sunseekers relax in the private men's and women's sundecks and whirlpools. Guests enjoy light meals by the fireplace in the tiny cafe or beneath a vine-covered arbor in the spa gardens.

Other Places to Play

The new Yountville Golf Course, a walkable nine-holer at the foot of Mount Veeder, is dotted with young trees, bordered by giant redwoods, and crisscrossed by a small creek and ponds (707–944–1992, www.YountvilleGC.com).

At the south end of Napa Valley, Chardonnay Golf Club is an anomaly—a links course surrounded not by the ocean but by a sea of vineyards (800–788–0136, www.chardonnaygolfclub.com). Draped gracefully on low hills where the valley sweeps toward the top of San Pablo Bay, the two courses here are dependably breezy and often cooled by fog. The Vineyards Course is rugged with deep gullies, cliff-top tees, and rocky outcroppings. The sleek, 7,001-yard Club Shakespeare Course, with a demanding 74.4 course rating, is open for reciprocal play.

Silverado Resort
1600 Atlas Peak Road
Napa, CA 94558
Phone: (707) 257–0200, reservations (800) 532–0500
Fax: (707) 257–2867
Web site: www.silveradoresort.com
General Manager: Kirk Candland
Accommodations: 280 one-, two-, and three-bedroom, low-rise cottage suites and condominiums located around garden courtyards with swimming pools; each with equipped kitchens, living/dining rooms, private balconies or patios.
Meals: Old oak trees, gardens, and a glimpse of the North Course comprise the setting at the Royal Oak, where steak, seafood, and Wine Country cuisine are among the best in a valley famous for its restaurants—prime beef, double-cut lamb chops, and fresh fish are grilled over hardwood charcoal. The wine list is legendary here. The Friday night seafood buffet is a tradition in the Vintner's Court. Hearty breakfast buffet and lunches at the Bar and Grill at the golf club. Light appetizers in the Main Lounge. Light fare at the Spa Cafe.
Facilities: Seventeen tennis courts, pro shop, and professional staff; full-service spa, salon, and fitness center with new CYBEX equipment, lap pool, and cafe; exercise, yoga, and aqua-aerobics classes; volleyball and basketball courts; jogging and bike trails; business center.
Services and Special Programs: Exclusive to the resort, the Napa Valley Experience includes two nights in a junior suite; dinner and wines; daily breakfast; spa treatments; entrance to COPIA; a private lunch at the Hess Collection winery; and private, VIP tours and tastings at Groth Vineyards and Pine Ridge Winery: $999 per couple.
Rates: $$$
Golf Package: The Silverado Classic includes one night accommodations in a standard room, a round of golf, and unlimited tennis. $310 per couple, double occupancy.
Getting There: A 1.5-hour drive from San Francisco International and Oakland International Airports; one hour from Sacramento International. Private aircraft land at Napa Airport, fifteen minutes away.
What's Nearby: Wine tours abound at more than 240 wineries; the concierge will make arrangements for you. Browse art galleries, shops, and restaurants in the historic villages of Yountville and St. Helena. Float in a hot-air balloon; visit the Culinary Institute of America at Greystone; and visit COPIA, a cultural center for wine, food, and the arts. COPIA has extensive gardens, exhibits, Julia's Kitchen restaurant (named for co-founder, Julia Child), food and lifestyle seminars, events, and classes.

ST. REGIS MONARCH BEACH RESORT AND SPA
Dana Point, California

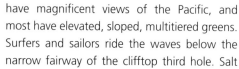

The architecture, landscape, climate, and ocean view of the St. Regis Monarch Beach Resort are pure Mediterranean. The location just south of Los Angeles at Dana Point, on a cliff overlooking the Pacific, is pure Southern California. The opening of its five-star hotel in 2001 coincided with the complete renovation of the adjacent Robert Trent Jones Jr.–designed Links at Monarch Beach, bringing the twenty-year-old layout up to contemporary standards.

Ninety-eight bunkers were refilled with crushed Augusta white marble, one of the most playable and beautiful bunker materials. Rock walls were installed around the lake edges and putting surfaces were improved. Three hundred yards in length were added, for a total of 6,601. Sea breezes and plenty of sand and water hazards create a links-type design with a parkland look.

Always breezy, sometimes gusty, thirteen holes have magnificent views of the Pacific, and most have elevated, sloped, multitiered greens. Surfers and sailors ride the waves below the narrow fairway of the clifftop third hole. Salt Creek ambles along the entire sixth to the two-tiered green, while on the 602-yard seventh, a 230-yard tee shot must carry the riverbed to reach a narrow fairway, to a sloping, severely elevated green only 26 yards deep. Twelve, the signature hole, runs along the ocean to a large green with undulations as high as stormy ocean waves. December through February, golfers can stand on the green and watch gray whales cruise by on their migration to and from Mexico.

Jones's course became world-famous in a hurry after the televised Hyundai Team Matches were played here by top pros on the PGA, Senior PGA, and LPGA tours.

Golfers linger by the fireplace and enjoy California cuisine and weekend brunches on the seaview terrace at Club 19, the gracious, Tuscan-themed clubhouse.

Palms, white columns, garden courtyards, fountains, and arched loggias draped with bougainvillea create a formal Mediterranean setting for the Tuscan-style hotel, one of the prestigious St. Regis hotel group. Wander the olive, pine, and cypress groves to the white marble gazebo for a quiet moment overlooking the golf course and the sea. Linger by one of ten elaborate fountains depicting Greek gods and ocean themes.

Inside, public spaces are exquisite with marble floors and vibrant contemporary art such as Dale Chihuly's radiant glassworks, and a magnificent reproduction of Maxfield Parrish's *Garden of Allah*.

At the luxurious Gaucin Spa, couples' rooms with fireplaces and whirlpools are a divine retreat after a day of golf. Natural skylights filter the sunlight in serene venues with bamboo floors, botanical theme decor, and blooming orchids. Try the invigorating "Orange Sugar Scrub" or the soothing "Avocado Cream Wrap." Take a dip in the lap pool, which has a sound system. Or, if business summons your attention, retreat to a private poolside cabana equipped with phone, fax, Internet access, music, ceiling fan, and butler.

Twenty-two Miles across the Sea

An hour's ride on a passenger ferry, the island of Santa Catalina is a world away from the bustle of Southern California. Avalon, a harborfront town, looks much as it did when the Art Deco landmark "Casino" was erected in 1929. Autos have long been off-limits here. Golf carts, bikes, and touring vans are the way to go, and there is much to see in the wildlife-rich outback. There are beaches to explore, river rafting, buffalo, horseback riding, snorkeling, boating, and golf at the Catalina Island Golf Course.

The oldest course in Southern California, built in 1892, it was formerly owned by the Wrigley family of chewing gum fame and underwent a complete renovation in 1993. The annoying kikuya grass has been tamed and greens are much improved. Not a championship course by any means, Catalina is nicely maintained and promises a refreshing nine, or double nine, on a ruggedly beautiful site.

With no par-5s, holes are generally short, narrow runways between hillsides dense with natural vegetation and bordered by eucalyptus trees, with an occasional giant fig tree loaded with fruit in the summertime.

Number eight begins on a high hillock above a ravine, dropping 100 feet to the landing zone. From here, you have a sweeping view of Avalon Bay, the channel, and, on a clear day, Monarch Beach on the mainland.

St. Regis Monarch Beach Resort and Spa
One Monarch Beach Resort
Dana Point, CA 92629
Phone: (949) 234–3200, reservations (800) 722–1543
Fax: (949) 234–3333
Web site: www.stregismonarchbeach.com
General Manager: Ulrich Krauer
Accommodations: Five-diamond, five-star rated, 400 large, elegant guest rooms and suites in warm earth tones with contemporary decor, private balconies and ocean views, flat-screen TV, CD and DVD library, down comforters and large, lavish bathrooms.
Meals: Six dining venues include sensational seafood at Aqua; Italian bistro fare at Chianti; tea service, cocktails, and snacks in the Lobby Lounge by the fireplace; all with ocean-view terraces. A light, ethnic menu at the pool Bar and Grill.
Facilities: Upscale shops and galleries; twenty-four-hour business center; full-service health and beauty spa; salon; aerobics and yoga classes; three swimming pools; private poolside cabanas; private beach club; tennis courts; nature trails.
Services and Special Programs: At all St. Regis hostelries, the legendary twenty-four-hour, Maître D'Etage butler service is part of the exceptional Old World, European-style personal service.
Rates: $$$$
Golf Package: Tee Times in Paradise includes one night deluxe accommodations, a round of golf, golf gifts and services, and breakfast. $675–$1,373 for two, double occupancy.
Getting There: Twenty-five minutes from John Wayne International Airport and one hour Los Angeles International and San Diego International Airports.
What's Nearby: Beaches; shopping; museums; and the sights of La Jolla, San Diego, Newport Beach, and Laguna Beach. At the Dana Point harbor, sailing, whale watching, and shopping.

WESTIN MISSION HILLS RESORT

Rancho Mirage, California

A green mosaic on the edge of the vast, arid spaces of the Mojave Desert, the Coachella Valley is the golf capitol of Southern California with more than one hundred courses that thrive in perfect, dry, clear weather from November through April.

Mission Hills, a tile-roofed, royal-blue-domed, Spanish-Moroccan-style extravaganza, is one of the most luxurious golf resorts in the valley. It is a complex of low-rise buildings, with two golf courses and luxuriant garden terraces graced by water channels, arched loggias, fountains, and pools. Stunning views of the San Jacinto Mountains surround the resort. Bright quatrefoil tile ornamentation and elaborate wrought iron combine with vivid coral tones to create an opulent atmosphere. In two-story pavilions, guest rooms have private patios or balconies, perfect vantage points for watching pink and gold dawns streak across the jagged mountain peaks. At sunset, the sun drops behind the ridges, turning them into a serrated black wall against a fading curtain of sky.

Newly redecorated guest rooms are comfy retreats, with all-white "Heavenly Beds" consisting of pillowtop mattresses, down comforters, plush pillows, and luxurious linens.

At the heart of the resort, the Las Brisas pool was built to recall the nearby Indian Canyons. A sixty-foot water slide that spills into a lagoon-style pool is surrounded by explosions of bougainvillea, bird-of-paradise, and hibiscus flowers. Enclosed within lush landscaping are two more pool terraces with private cabanas.

At the new spa at Mission Hills, the "Executive Escape for Men" is popular, comprising a mini-facial, manicure and pedicure, and Swedish massage. Women seeking wrinkle-free skin choose the "Buff and Bronzer," a treatment involving a sea-salt exfoliation and sunless-tanner application. Guests stay clothed for the unique golf massage—a sequence of pre-sport stretches and massage with golf balls. "The Tennis Tune-up," also a clothed massage, involves stretches and the use of tennis balls to increase blood flow.

Managed by the excellent Troon Golf company, the golf courses are among the top rated in the Palm Springs area. In true Pete Dye fashion, railroad ties are ubiquitous on the Resort Course, along with long lakes, waterfalls, rolling fairways, and deep pot bunkers. Added to this are elevated tees, obscure pin placements, and hundreds of trees—olive, eucalyptus, California pepper trees, date palms, and fan palms.

Mission Hills North is a Gary Player original, reflecting the natural contours and flora of desert arroyos with boulder-strewn lakes and sloped fairways. No residential development mars the feeling of isolation. Waterscapes, falls, and craggy rock formations decorate wide, gently rolling fairways and fast putting surfaces. The golfer's task is to brave the 7,062-yard length of the course and the seasonal winds.

Practice facilities are expansive with a multitiered, two-sided driving range, three putting greens, chipping green, and bunkers at the North Course. Another driving range, putting and chipping greens, bunkers, and a nice clubhouse are at the Resort Course.

Palm Springs Spas

Since before the turn of the nineteenth century, healthseekers have flocked to the Palm Springs area to "take the waters" at the natural thermal springs. Bubbling up out of the ground at hundreds of sites in the Coachella Valley, at a temperature of more than 100 degrees, the pure, mineral-rich waters of the desert are legendary for their restorative and healing powers.

The Spa Hotel and Casino Resort and Mineral Springs rests on the site of the original hot mineral springs and palm grove for which the town of Palm Springs is named. Cahuilla Indian–owned, the hotel is one of forty in the valley with direct access to the waters believed by the local Native Americans to have magical attributes.

The Givenchy Hotel and Spa, a white-columned mansion in a rose garden, is a bastion of French elegance master-minded by the couturier, Hubert de Givenchy. White orchids and bowls of fresh roses soften a formal atmosphere in the Kingdom of Beauty spa. Only here will you enjoy the glorious, very private indoor swimming pool and beauty products from the Givenchy Spa in Versailles. In addition to traditional European-style treatments, guests slip into hydrotherapy tubs to be blasted by forty-seven jets of water, with therapeutic seaweed and oils added for skin softening.

Hidden in a palm and willow grove overlooking the valley and the mountains, Two Bunch Palms has been frequented since the 1930s by celebrities seeking complete privacy and rejuvenation. Hot mineral waters fill a large swimming pool, which is surrounded by tropical greenery and a waterfall. A signature treatment here is the "Watsu Massage," where the lucky patron receives a slow, yoga-like underwater massage.

Westin Mission Hills Resort
71333 Dinah Shore Drive
Rancho Mirage, CA 92270
Phone: (760) 328–5955, reservations (800) 937–8461
Fax: (760) 770–2199
Web site: www.westin.com
General Manager: Bill Feather
Accommodations: Four-diamond-rated, 512 newly redecorated rooms and suites in low-rise buildings with private balconies or patios, "Heavenly Beds," soft desert colors and fine fabrics.
Meals: California cuisine in Spanish-mission environment at Bella Vista served in the atrium or on the patio. Seafood and Black Angus beef at La Concha. Snacks and light meals at the Cafe and Ice Cream Parlor, and in the Lobby Lounge.
Facilities: Extensive golf practice facilities, PGA Instruction, John Jacobs Golf School; five-star-rated Reed Anderson Tennis School, seven lighted courts, instruction, and pro shop; bike rentals and bike trails; full-service health and beauty spa with life enrichment classes, massage, facials, and peels; business center.
Services and Special Programs: Children ages 4–12 love nature walks, crafts, games, swimming, and sports at Cactus Kids.
Rates: $$$
Golf Packages: Golf Replay Package includes one night standard room and unlimited golf for two, starting at $439. The Golf Replay and Spa Package allows for unlimited golf for one, and a sixty-minute spa treatment for one, starting at $439.
Getting There: 5 miles from Palm Springs Airport, served by major airlines.
What's Nearby: Agua Caliente Casino, Children's Discovery Musuem of the Desert, Knott's Oasis Water Park, boutique and gallery shopping in Palm Springs, McCallum Theatre for the Performing Arts.

More than one hundred LPGA pros compete at the adjacent Mission Hills Country Club in the annual Dinah Shore LPGA Classic—an event that fills the valley with golf fans. The 1996 champ, Patty Sheehan, waded into the lake on the eighteenth fairway with her trophy, continuing a tradition started when Amy Alcott jumped in the lake after her 1988 win, along with Dinah herself. The 2002 winner, Carrie Webb, jumped feet first into the murky water, joined by her caddie and singer Celine Dion, an avid golfer.

THE BROADMOOR

Colorado Springs, Colorado

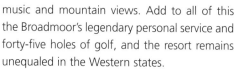

Like a pink mirage at 6,500 feet in the Rocky Mountains, the Italian Renaissance–style Broadmoor is a grand old resort hotel and the longest-running winner of the Mobil Five-Star and AAA Five-Diamond awards. At the turn of the twenty-first century, this aging beauty received a marvelous facelift, with all guest rooms completely redecorated and updated with high-tech amenities, bathrooms with soaking tubs, and lovely, period furnishings, fabrics, and linens.

In a spectacular setting on Cheyenne Lake, a huge swimming pool was built with a unique Infinity Edge, making pool waters seem to flow into the sparkling lake. The monumental new Spa, Golf, and Tennis Club is headquarters for active sports, with a whopping fifty-five spa treatment rooms decorated with gilt, brass, alabaster, and warm Colorado sandstone accents. Additional features include luxurious locker rooms, three dining options, pro shops, a spring-loaded aerobics floor, daily sports specific training and classes—and a glorious, glassed-in swimming pool with underwater

music and mountain views. Add to all of this the Broadmoor's legendary personal service and forty-five holes of golf, and the resort remains unequaled in the Western states.

Each of the three golf courses here have an Audubon Cooperative Sanctuary System certification for environmental excellence. All have huge greens, some more than 120 feet across. Your ball will definitely break away from the surrounding, snowcapped mountains and fly farther in the thin air. Donald Ross, the renowned Scot, designed the first nine of the East Course in the shadow of Cheyenne Mountain in 1918. Tall blue spruce, Siberian elms, and Douglas firs loom above wide fairways. Super-slick, crowned, quiet elevated greens, and a waterfall or two are here too. Robert Trent Jones Sr. added the second nine and updated the Ross design. In the 1990s *Golf Digest* named it the number one resort course in the state.

In the 1960s Jones laid out the resort's least forgiving track, the rolling, narrow, 7,340-yard West Course, with multilevel, steeply angled greens framed by white pines and maples. Running up onto the flanks of Cheyenne Mountain, the West sports absolutely stupendous mountain and city views.

A Palmer-Seay design of the 1970s, the nine-hole Mountain Course is narrow and often windy, with many blind tee shots. Bordered by scrub oaks and roughed up by barrancas, it calls for near-perfect accuracy.

Rocco Mediate, the Broadmoor's touring pro, is often seen about the new sports center. Tennis Hall of Famer and Wimbledon champ, Dennis Ralston, heads the resort's pro tennis staff, rated number one in the country according to *Tennis* magazine.

Enjoying about 300 days of sunshine annually, resort guests pedal around the lake on paddle-boats and lounge in private poolside cabanas, which are complete with ceiling fans and patios. They repair to the elaborate spa for yoga and massage, and for swimming in the

indoor atrium pool. Anglers enjoy the Fly-Fishing School.

Guest rooms, suites, and public areas are spacious, glowing retreats, ornately decorated with Asian artifacts and seventeenth century paintings, traditional fabrics and furnishings, frescoes, and bas reliefs. In addition to all the finery and formality, the superbly trained staff and the glorious mountain setting contribute to a relaxed, comfortable atmosphere.

High Altitude Flyers

At 8,000 feet in the Colorado Rockies near the world-famous ski resort at Vail, golf balls seem to hang in the thin air forever. Climbing high up into a spectacular mountain setting, the Jay Morrish/Bob Cupp–designed Sonnenalp Golf Club drops down from elevated tees to tiny greens far below. The Beaver Creek Golf Club hangs on the mountainside with narrow, steep fairways bordered by mega-mansions and a pine and aspen forest—a neon-yellow tableau when the trees turn in the fall. Situated just beneath the ski slope chair lifts, the towering Hyatt Regency Beaver Creek makes both courses available to guests (800–233–1234).

The Broadmoor
1 Lake Avenue
Colorado Springs, CO 80906
Phone: (719) 634–7711, reservations (800) 634–7711
Fax: (719) 577–5700
Web site: www.broadmoor.com
General Manager: Stephen Barolin Jr.
Accommodations: Five-star and four-diamond rated, the Broadmoor Main, the new West tower, and the South and West buildings contain 593 rooms and 107 suites, each with elegant, reproduction period furnishings and spacious baths, and most with beautiful views. The Lakeside Suites are four stories of new, luxurious accommodations with lake views, fireplaces, private patios or balconies.
Meals: Among eleven restaurants and lounges, the Penrose Room is an opulent salon serving contemporary French cuisine, with live music and dancing. Wood-fire grilled steaks and chops, and nightly music and dancing at the Tavern. American regional dishes and lakeside alfresco dining at the Charles Court. An authentic nineteenth-century London pub, the Golden Bee, is a cozy spot for yards of ale, steak and potato pie, and ragtime piano. Stars' Club and Cigar Bar is a lively nightclub dedicated to the big band, jazz, and rock eras. Enjoy big-screen TV and hearty meals at the Grill at the Golf Club.
Facilities: Various treatments at the lavish spa include the "Abayanga Massage," an Ayurvedic therapy. The tennis center is one of the tops in the country, with twelve plexi-cushion courts and full-time staff. Nineteen upscale boutiques and pro shops; a large outdoor swimming pool, one indoor pool, and one lap pool; waterslides and a children's pool with bubble jets; riding stables; first-run movie theater; a walking path circling the lake.
Services and Special Programs: An award-winning tennis program, cooking classes, skeet and trap shooting, bike rentals, boating. Bee Bunch Children's program for ages 4–12, with field trips, zoo visits, hiking, boating, golf, and tennis clinics.
Rates: $$$–$$$$
Golf Packages: Deluxe accommodations, one round of golf, cart, and golf services. $314–$650 per couple, double occupancy.
Getting There: A twenty-minute drive from Colorado Springs Airport, which is served by nine major airlines; sedan and shuttle transfer available.
What's Nearby: The scenic Pikes Peak Road and the cog railway rise to 14,110 feet. Hiking, llama trekking, four-wheeling, mountain biking, river rafting, and fly-fishing in the surrounding mountains. In Colorado Springs, tours of the Cave of the Winds, the Cheyenne Mountain Zoo, the Pro Rodeo Hall of Fame, and the U.S. Air Force Academy.

THE LODGE AND SPA AT CORDILLERA
Edwards, Colorado

Looking like a Belgian château, the white stucco and stone Cordillera lodge clings to a mountainside high above the Vail Valley on 6,500 acres of wilderness at the edge of the White River National Forest. The intimate, fifty-six room lodge is a grand country house with a superbly trained, international staff, a four-star restaurant, and four top-notch golf courses.

Rooms are spacious and most have fireplaces, vaulted ceilings, and private balconies from which to contemplate the astounding views of the New York Mountains, Bellyache Ridge, and the Gore Range.

When not golfing in the high altitude and clear, dry climate, guests hike, mountain bike, and fish for trout on a private stretch of the Eagle River. You can go river rafting; horseback riding; and cross-country skiing and snowshoeing on 5 kilometers of groomed trails.

Each of four golf courses comes with its own architecturally dramatic clubhouse complete with pro shop, locker rooms, and a restaurant.

The new Summit Course, a whopping 7,596-yards long, opened in 2001. It is a Jack Nicklaus Signature design on a mountaintop at 9,000 feet. Only three American golf courses are at a higher elevation and few take the natural landscape into account to the extent that Nicklaus has done. The course has only eighty acres of irrigated turf in wildly rolling terrain dense with an aspen forest, towering firs and spruce, and aromatic sage in pristine alpine meadows. Rock encroachments, narrow, tree-lined chutes, "punchbowl" greens, and wetland carries are

among the distractions from the awesome views of mountains and valley. You may be sharing the fairways with local inhabitants—over a hundred species including elk, deer, black bears (usually from a distance), coyotes, rabbits, and foxes.

A monumental, territorial-style clubhouse of stone and timber, with a three-story river-rock fireplace, anchors the Hale Irwin–designed Mountain Course. A Colorado native, Irwin worked around aspen groves and pines on undulating terrain that was once a working ranch. Natural mounds and swales, ridges, meadows, and forests add to the beauty and the challenge.

At the foot of the Gore Mountain Range, Tom Fazio laid the Valley Course around plunging ravines, creeks, and clusters of sagebrush and native juniper. On south-facing slopes at 6,500 feet, the course plays into the fall season, when aspens turn vibrant gold and are reflected in the Eagle River. Vail's premier resident, former President Gerald Ford, is a member at Cordillera and is occasionally seen playing the Valley.

The only one of its kind in the United States is the ten-hole, par-3 Dave Pelz Short Course. Located on a high plateau with panoramic views, it has an exceptional teaching facility, including four chipping and putting areas. As Pelz says, "Over 50 percent of all golf shots occur in the short game. The better your short game, the more you enjoy golf."

The elegant, European-style spa offers a lively schedule of classes in Pilates, yoga, cardio-kickboxing, and sports strengthening; the latest workout equipment; as well as traditional and New Age beauty and health treatments. The atmosphere at the spa and throughout the resort is one of pampered seclusion and privacy.

Restaurant Picasso in the lodge is renowned throughout the region for light, Continental cuisine and an astounding French and Californian wine list. Hand-hewn timbers, a fireplace, and the sophisticated accents of Picasso etchings create an enchanting ambience reminiscent of a château in the Pyrenees. For those craving hearty dishes, Irish stew, fish and chips, and homemade sausages are on the menu at Grouse-on-the-Green, a pub built in Ireland and erected within the Short Course clubhouse.

Golf and Ski

Nearly all of Colorado's major ski resorts sprouted new golf courses around the turn of the twenty-first century. The newest at Steamboat Springs—the Haymaker Golf Course—is a real beauty. It is a treeless, Scottish-links-style course with rolling fairways, steep bunkers, crisscrossing streams, and native grasses. Robert Trent Jones Jr.'s Steamboat Springs Golf Course at the Sheraton's Resort meanders alongside a rushing river and evergreen forests, from elevated tees to big and bigger greens.

Jones's original Ranch Course at Keystone Resort has been updated and joined by the new River Course, a Michael Hurdzan design of considerable variation in elevation. Tom Fazio laid out Red Sky Ranch near Vail; it will soon be partnered by a Greg Norman design. Jack Nicklaus added nine holes to the city-owned Breckenridge Golf Club. At Copper Mountain, Pete Dye's masterpiece is touted to be the highest eighteen-hole course in North America.

Guests at Wyndham Peaks Resort in the picturesque old mining town of Telluride play golf at 9,300 feet, just below the Sneffel Mountain Range. Then they repair to the Golden Door Spa for "Yoga for Golfers," and warm herbal packs on their arms and shoulders (www.rockiesgolf.com).

The Lodge and Spa at Cordillera
2205 Cordillera Way
Edwards, CO 81632
Phone: (970) 926–2200, reservations (800) 877–3529
Fax: (970) 926–2486
Web site: www.cordillera-vail.com
General Manager: Tom Zeisel
Accommodations: Frette linens, bath sheets, and fully supplied cocktail bars (rather than mini-bars) are among the exceptional amenities in each of the 56 spacious rooms. The casually-elegant, mountain-lodge-style furnishings, art, and fabrics create a luscious aerie from which to enjoy dazzling views. Luxurious homes are also available to rent.
Meals: Grouse-on-the-Green serves substantial pub food. Formal and elegant, Restaurant Picasso features light Continental fare. At the Mountain Course, it's Southwestern cuisine at the Timber Hearth Grille. The Chaparral Steakhouse serves grilled meats at the Valley Course.
Facilities: The Trailhead is a ten-acre family recreation center with a pool, play fort, lawns, and teepee village. Trail rides and lessons at the equestrian center. Fishing in stocked trout ponds and a private section of the Eagle River. Five kilometers of groomed cross-country ski and snowshoe trails, rentals, and lessons; biking and hiking trails.
Services and Special Programs: Shuttle service to downhill skiing at nearby Vail and Beaver Creek. Guided flyfishing, cattle drives, field trips; plus supervised play for children at Club Cordy.
Rates: $$$$
Golf Packages: Three nights deluxe accommodations, daily breakfast, one daily round of golf per person, and a one-hour massage per person, $2,249 for two.
Getting There: A 20-mile drive from the Vail/Eagle Airport, with limousine, shuttle, and helicopter service available to and from the resort.
What's Nearby: Hiking and recreational access to three million acres of the neighboring National Forest; hot-air ballooning; dog-sledding; shuttle service to Vail and Beaver Creek for skiing, shopping, sightseeing, and outdoor recreation.

AMELIA ISLAND PLANTATION
Amelia Island, Florida

Just across the St. Mary's River from Georgia, the scenic barrier island of Amelia Island lies between Atlantic Coast beaches and the Intracoastal Waterway. Unlike most destination resorts in the state, the island is privately owned, secluded, and protected by a gated entry. Lush, green marshlands and low marine forests cover the island—and one is never far from the sight and sound of the ocean. Condominiums, two large hotels, and residential areas are scattered on narrow roads beneath a canopy of oaks, palms, Southern pines, and tropical vegetation along 3 miles of beaches with high, rolling dunes.

The resort's Nature Center offers guided wildlife and birding tours on the island, which is threaded with quiet walking and bicycling paths, and a boardwalk meandering through the mysterious Sunken Forest. If pedal power is not your choice, rent a gas-powered Island Hopper, which transports up to four adults around the island.

Tom Fazio, Pete Dye, and Bobby Weed laid the Long Point, Ocean Links, and Oak Marsh courses within the maritime forest and the marshlands. Each course is designated an Audubon Cooperative Sanctuary.

At the new Amelia Inn, guest rooms open to balconies overlooking the beach. Gracious Southern hospitality is the order of the day in the lobby lounge, where floral armchairs, comfy sofas, potted palms, a fireplace, and a nice bar comprise a popular gathering place.

Nestled on the banks of Red Maple Lake in a picturesque marsh and garden setting is a new spa with private balconies overlooking the greenery. Among unique treatments are the Watsu (water shiatsu) massage in a private, indoor, heated pool, followed by a soothing "Cocoon Hydra-Aroma Wrap;" the deep-tissue "Sports Massage;" and the "Sun Lover's Facial," to reverse the damaging effects of UV rays.

Site of the WTA Bausch and Lomb Championships, Racquet Park is a gorgeous tennis complex in the shade of ancient oak trees, with twenty-three Har-Tru clay courts where USPTR certified teaching pros conduct lessons and clinics. *Tennis* magazine says it's one of the top fifty tennis resorts in the country—Navratilova, Hingis, and Agassi have trained and competed here.

Wrapped like a green velvet shawl around primal marshlands, Long Point is Tom Fazio's inspired plan for a truly magnificent setting of tidal marshes, sand dunes, and a dense pine and oak forest. Natural waste bunkers, grass basins, and deep pot bunkers guard rolling fairways and large, elevated greens. Mounds and moguls along the fairways help to prevent balls from flying into the impenetrable tree barrier and water hazards. Among several long carries, the second hole requires a 230-yard fly over wetlands to a wide zone that gradually narrows between savannah and the water to an almost blind putting surface surrounded by deep hollows. The Amelia River and the salt marshes are rich wildlife habitats, where great egrets, wood storks, kingfishers, killdeer, and gulls are beautiful distractions. A private club except for resort guests, Long Point is set serenely apart with its own clubhouse, restaurant, and the golf school.

Salt marshes and creeks come into play on many holes of Pete Dye–designed Oak Marsh. Accurate shot placement is necessary on narrow fairways and small, bulkheaded greens bordered closely by hammock groves and moss-draped cypress and oak trees. It was an understatement when Dye uttered about Oak Marsh: "We've left the rough in its natural state. Only the areas of play are manicured."

A good short game and efficient approach shots are called for on Ocean Links, a Dye/Weed track just 6,108 yards from the back tees. Seven seaside holes are unpredictably breezy, while ten holes are menaced by marshy wetlands and lagoons. Greens are small and cleverly dipped, swaled, and tilted.

The director of the Golf School, Ron Philo Sr., is the father of LPGA star Laura Diaz and has coached such luminaries as David Duval. Private lessons, clinics, and schools are conducted in a lovely, oak-studded environment with private practice venues.

A Good Walking Course

Among six golf courses on Amelia Island, Royal Amelia Golf Links is a parkland layout designed around small lakes, a creek, and a forest of palmettos, myrtles, Southern pine, and oak, with no residential development to mar its natural loveliness. Fairways and greens are gigantic on this 6,850-yard track. A few surprises include a palm tree smack in the middle of the second hole and a peninsula green on seventeen.

The clubhouse verandah is a good perch from which to contemplate the sunset over the tidal marsh and Intracoastal Waterway (904–491–8500, www.royalamelia.com).

Amelia Island Plantation
P.O. Box 3000
Amelia Island, FL 32035–3000
Phone: (904) 261–6161, reservations (800) 874–6878
Fax: (904) 277–5945
Web site: www.aipfl.com

General Manager: Walther M. Vliegen

Accommodations: Four-diamond rated, 660 guest rooms and one-, two-, and three-bedroom villas. Large, luxurious rooms at the Amelia Inn have private, ocean-view balconies, spacious sitting areas, and large baths. Ocean- and resort-view hotel rooms and condos at Villas of Amelia are elegantly decorated and fully equipped for longer visits.

Meals: Panoramic ocean views from the elegant Amelia Inn Dining Room where Sunday brunch is served. The casual Golf Shop Restaurant serves American food. The Verandah at the Raquet Club specializes in seafood, such as mango chutney shrimp, caught daily by Mayport fishermen. Come as you are to the Beach Club Grill.

Facilities: Twenty-three clay tennis courts, pro shop, and resident pros offering lessons and daily clinics; two swimming pools at oceanside; playground; bicycles. At the Nature Center, buy binoculars and field guides, and sign up for tours.

Services and Special Programs: Just For Kids and Kids' Camp for ages 3–10, with hayrides, treasure hunts, pool parties, golf and tennis clinics, games, and art. Teen Explorers offers field trips and sports for ages 11–19. Aqua aerobics, yoga, and other exercise classes.

Rates: $$$

Golf Packages: Golf Amelia includes a luxury hotel room, a round of golf and cart, full breakfast, and discount coupons. $386–$526 for two, double occupancy.

Getting There: Jacksonville International Airport is thirty minutes from the island, with hotel shuttle available. Private aircraft land at Fernandina Beach Municipal Airport, 4 miles north.

What's Nearby: Sightseeing in the 1880s fishing village of Fernandina with 50 blocks of Victorian buildings, galleries and antiques shops, and waterfront cafes. Visit the Amelia Island Museum of History, Kingsley Plantation, and Fort Clinch State Park to see 1880s military reenactments.

DORAL GOLF RESORT AND SPA

Miami, Florida

An aerial view of the ninety-nine golf holes at Doral reveals a watery scene of lakes, ponds, and island greens on the Great White, Silver, Gold, and Red Courses—and the famous Blue Monster. A recent 50-million-dollar update transformed and expanded the entire resort and all five golf courses. A glitzy new clubhouse was built and the spa was renovated with glamorous new spa suites added. The splashy new Blue Lagoon water park at Doral is now a popular Miami tourist attraction.

The Blue Monster is 7,125 yards of water, water, everywhere. Notorious since 1962, it has been the site of the PGA Genuity Doral Championship and the LPGA Office Depot Tournament. Trees have been added, vistas opened up, and bunkers redefined. The third hole is now the most difficult to drive since the driving area was narrowed to 25 yards. Between the lake and deep Bermuda rough, you approach the green, hoping to avoid a steep drop-off on the left. No greenside bunkers here—it's tough enough.

Some call the eighteenth the toughest hole on the PGA tour. Wind and water are factors, along with a flattish, sandy beach that stretches around the lake, into the palm trees, and approaches a long, narrow, fearsome green. The monumental effect of the wind is evidenced by the wildly variant scores at the Doral-Ryder Open—4-under 288 by Mark McCumber in a 1985 gale, and the 23-under 265 by Greg Norman on a dead calm day in 1993.

Golfers get an easier challenge on the Red Course. Lake views and pretty landscaping are on this relatively short track, although water is an issue on twelve holes and on the two island greens.

Raymond Floyd restored the traditional Florida layout of the Gold Course, redefining strategic bunkers and adding a tier or two to the undulating greens. Water comes into play on every hole, notably on the eighteenth island green.

Jerry Pate enhanced the Devlin/Von Hagge design of the Silver Course with new greens, new tees, and better drainage. Narrow fairways are mounded and moguled, leading to elevated target greens. You will find water on sixteen holes and an island green.

Home of the Franklin Templeton Shootout, the Great White is Greg Norman's new desert-scape with 222 coquina sand pot bunkers, natural marshes, lakes and wetlands on fourteen holes, and a unique triple green of 25,000 feet—all resulting in a sizzling 75.1 course rating.

Coach of top tour professionals, Jim McLean directs the Golf Learning Center, which focuses on course management and a winning frame of mind. The center offers video analysis, swing computers, motion trainers, a huge lighted driving range, three putting greens, and one of the largest pros shops on the planet.

Home of the Pros

In Palm Beach Gardens, the PGA National Resort and Spa is the home of the PGA of America. It is also the site of the PGA Seniors' Championship and other tournaments on its five golf courses. Jack Nicklaus reworked the Tom Fazio–designed Champion Course, a long track brushed by steady winds with water on seventeen holes, over one hundred sand bunkers, and concave catchments on the fairways and greens. The tough finishing holes are called "The Bear Trap," contributing to the course rating and slope of 74.7/142.

Arnold Palmer laid out the Scottish links–style General Course with undulating fairways, numerous grass bunkers, fifty sand bunkers, and lots of water. High handicappers favor the Fazio-designed Haig and Squire Courses, and the Karl Litten Estate Course.

More than a dozen instructors conduct daily clinics, private lessons, and schools at the Academy of Golf, a huge complex with five practice ranges and a three to one student/instructor ratio. Among unique programs that match golfers' swings to their body type is the Ladies Only Golf School.

Worth a visit in itself, the Bear Trap Bar and Grille is a golf-themed sports bar with a historic photo gallery and eleven TVs showing sporting events. The resort, home to the largest croquet club in the Western Hemisphere, hosts international tournaments on five USCA courts. The tennis club features nineteen Har-Tru tennis courts.

A multimillion-dollar renovation and expansion at the end of 2001 upgraded the entire resort, including the decor of guest rooms, suites, and cottages (www.pga-resorts.com, 800–633–9150).

Doral Golf Resort and Spa
4400 Northwest 87th Avenue
Miami, FL 33178
Phone: (305) 592–2000, reservations (800) 713–6725
Fax: (305) 594–4682
Web site: www.doralresort.com
General Manager: Joel Paige
Accommodations: 694 rooms and suites in three- and four-story lodges in tropical settings, with plantation shutters, wicker and wood furnishings, and fine fabrics in seafoam, sandalwood, and golden tones; plus 48 Tuscan-style suites at the spa, with curving staircases, fountains, private balconies or terraces, separate dressing areas, Jacuzzis, and views of formal gardens.
Meals: Popular for the luncheon buffet and the sushi bar, the flower-filled terrace of Windows on the Green overlooks the Blue Monster. Serene with live piano music, healthy meals with Caribbean and Asian accents at the elegant Atrium. Casual indoor or terrace dining at the Terrazza Restaurant, featuring seafood and Caribbean cuisine. Burgers, appetizers, and big-screen TV at Champions sports bar. Drinks, sandwiches, and snacks poolside at Bungalou's Bar & Grill.
Facilities: Nine-hole, par-3 course, superior Jim McLean Golf Learning Center, and extensive practice facilities. The new Mediterranean-style spa is a self-contained resort with luxurious new suites; among one hundred treatments are the Blue Monster Massage, "Sports Recovery" jet hydrotherapy, and stress management. Indoor and outdoor swimming pools; cold plunge pools; indoor running track; private men's and women's sundecks. The Arthur Ashe Tennis Center has eleven hard-surface and clay courts, resident pros, and pro shop. Equipment and courts for volleyball, softball, and basketball; biking; jogging; fly-fishing.
Services and Special Programs: Synergy Golf Conditioning classes use miniclubs to practice swing techniques and improve posture, weight shift, and rotation. Supervised fun for children ages 5–12 at Camp Doral, with swimming, fishing, tennis, golf, soccer, softball, and art.
Rates: $$$
Golf Packages: One night in a garden room, breakfast, golf clinic, round of golf, and golf services. $125–$299 per person, double occupancy.
Getting There: Fifteen minutes from Miami International Airport and 30 miles from Fort Lauderdale/Hollywood International Airport.
What's Nearby: The beautiful beaches and the fabulous restaurants, shops, and nightclubs of South Beach. Yachting on 300 miles of inland waterways; island hopping in Key West; chic shopping in Palm Beach.

GRAND CYPRESS RESORT

Orlando, Florida

Tens of thousands of flowers are planted annually on 1,500 acres of gardens at Grand Cypress Resort, which comprises forty-five holes of Jack Nicklaus–designed golf; a Hyatt Regency hotel; a complex of elegant, condominium-style villas; an equestrian center; and a tennis complex. Set apart in their own quiet, landscaped environment, the tile-roofed, Mediterranean-style villas are huge, ranging from 650 square feet to 3,100 square feet (for Club Suites). Each has private, gated entries and private patios overlooking a lake and the golf courses.

Twelve-foot-tall, sod-wall pot bunkers, seven double greens, a snaking, rather deep burn (stream), and a familiar-looking stone bridge on the New Course are Jack's tribute to the Old Course at St. Andrews. Even the famous "Road Hole" is replicated. You can walk the wide, wide fairways—the better to smell the grapefruit and orange blossoms and hear the colorful birds sing. One-hundred-fifty bunkers are to be avoided.

Super challenging, the original North-South Tournament Course is unique for distinctive, multilevel, "ledged" fairways, which improve the golfer's visual perspective while adding to the difficulty. Expect a demanding, target-style game (75.1 rating, 137 slope), tall, grassy mounds; small, platform greens with easy approaches; and water on thirteen holes. The East Nine is a low-country track with generous fairways and manageable bunkers.

The excellent Academy of Golf, directed by famous golfers and teachers (including LPGA Hall of Famer, Kathy Whitworth; PGA champ, Phil Rogers; and Top

100 teacher, Fred Griffin), is unique for its trio of Nicklaus-designed holes, for on-course instruction, and for the use of CompuSport technology. At the huge practice and learning complex are special schools for women, advanced golfers, and juniors, plus mini-schools and short game schools.

A plethora of outdoor recreational facilities includes the Equestrian Center. Approved by the British Horse Society for livery and training, this is the headquarters for trail rides, riding lessons, and a schedule of dressage and jumping shows and clinics. You can rent running gear for the 4.7-mile jogging course and the par course. A mile of raised boardwalks meanders through an idyllic nature preserve. You can fish on Lake Windsong, paddle a canoe, sail, or loll on the sandy beach.

For the vacationer who enjoys superior personal service, upscale accommodations, and a feeling of seclusion, Grand Cypress Resort is a good alternative to the larger, busier, nearby Disney World hotels. You can, however, hop a shuttle to Disney World, EPCOT Center, and other Orlando area amusements.

Grand Cypress Resort
One North Jacaranda
Orlando, FL 32836
Phone: (407) 239–4700, reservations (800) 835–7377
Fax: (407) 239–7219
Web site: www.grandcypress.com
General Manager: David Kochi
Accommodations: Four-star, four-diamond rated, one-, two-, three-, and four-bedroom villas are elegantly appointed, private retreats with spacious living areas including fireplaces, full kitchens, large whirlpool tubs, sofabeds, valet service, gated entry, and private patios. Club Suites are huge, with sunken sitting areas.
Meals: A Continental menu at the four-diamond-rated Black Swan, which overlooks the golf course. All-day dining in a casual country club setting at Fairways. New World and French cuisine with a lake view at La Coquina. Seafood and steaks at Key West–themed Hemingways, located above the pool and gardens. Prime rib and barbecue at the Western-style, White Horse Saloon. The Cascade, named for its indoor waterfall, serves all-American food.
Facilities: Fitness center with sauna, steam, and exercise classes; salon; swimming pool with waterfall; racquetball; bicycles; eight clay and four hard-surface tennis courts with daily clinics, private lessons, and matching; pro shop; equestrian center and tack shop; nine-hole, pitch-and-putt course, nine-hole putting green; electronic games room.
Services and Special Programs: Children ages 3–12 like supervised play and games at Camp Hyatt. At the equestrian center, lessons in dressage, hunt seat, jumping, and Western. Shuttles to nearby theme parks. Golf caddy service and valet service.
Rates: $$$–$$$$
Golf Packages: One night accommodations in a Club Suite, one round of golf, golf services, additional same-day round for reduced fee. $195–$355 per person, double occupancy.
Getting There: A half-hour drive from Orlando International Airport; on-site helipad.
What's Nearby: Take the hotel shuttle to the adjacent Disney's Magic Kingdom, EPCOT Center, Sea World, and Universal Studios.

Arnie's Favorite

Arnold Palmer has seriously tweaked the original Dick Wilson design of the Challenger, the Champion, and the Charger nines at Bay Hill Club and Lodge, which Arnie now owns (888–422–9445, www.bayhill.com). Definition was added to the flattish terrain with mounds, grassy hummocks, and all kinds of bunkers. Water comes into play on ten holes, fairways are generous, and greens are supershort and superfast—10.5 or higher on the Stimpmeter. Perfect course conditions and high rough are maintained year-round in preparation for the prestigious PGA Tour Bay Hill Invitational. Some say Bayhill has the toughest first and last holes on the tour.

The tournament is held on the Challenger/ Champion combination, a 7,204-yard track with a 75.1 rating and 139 slope, and alligators in the ponds, which don't seem to bother two-time defending champion, Tiger Woods. The club is open to members and guests at the cozy, fifty-nine-room lodge.

HYATT REGENCY COCONUT POINT RESORT AND SPA

Bonita Springs, Florida

World Golf Hall of Famer, Raymond Floyd, designed the new, twenty-seven-hole Raptor Bay Golf Club on the southwest Florida coast, the first American resort course to receive Audubon International's Gold Signature Certification for environmental stewardship and sustainable practices. Hundreds of acres of native vegetation were retained along the Aquatic Preserve of Estero Bay, while artificial mounding was minimized. There are no sand bunkers; instead, acres of crushed coquina shell waste areas. Amid the lush native forest of mangroves, cabbage palms, pines, live oaks, and palmettos are a lively population of egrets, herons, and other water birds; tortoises; fiddler crabs; and white-tailed deer. Alligator sightings are not uncommon.

Fairways are wide, elevated greens are large and sloped, and there are five tees, the better to manage the challenge of the surrounding hammocks and wetlands. A superior pitcher and chipper himself, Floyd makes short club play the top issue. Devilish approaches and grassy swales make accuracy a must on bump-and-runs and flop shots. *Sports Illustrated* named Raptor Bay one of the Top Ten New Public Courses in 2001.

A series of cart bridges allow players to tread lightly on the land while enjoying the course's natural features. Walking trails are a prominent feature throughout the resort in the adjacent "Eco-Park," a 144-acre

preserve traversed by Halfway Creek.

In a tropical setting on Estero Bay, the new Hyatt Regency Coconut Point Resort has an old Florida-style, Ernest Hemingway–era feel to it, with a metal roof and thick walls punctuated by large openings and Bahama shutters. Rich, dark mahogany paneling and glowing, golden-toned chandeliers and sconces are accents found inside, while beautiful gardens and grounds that are watered by fountains and shaded by palms draw you outside.

A huge lagoon swimming pool with a giant corkscrew water slide and lap pools, and a waterfall pool with a parade of fountains comprise a true oasis. Active guests take the short boat ride to a private beach island for watersports and beachcombing.

At the golf clubhouse, mahogany floors, exposed wood and sisal ceilings, palm tree chandeliers, and sconces create a sultry, West Indies look at Braxton's, where diners relax on the verandah overlooking the eighteenth green and the practice area. The Raptor Bay Golf Academy provides hi-tech swing analysis and a variety of multiday and minischools.

At the sumptuous Stillwater Spa, the Watsu pool is the private venue for "Aqua Massage," a deeply relaxing, tension-relieving treatment that combines the buoyancy of water with a Shiatsu-style massage and is particularly beneficial for fatigue and insomnia.

The Keys to Florida Golf

Warm up your putter for the big putting surfaces at the Resort at Longboat Key Club. Aim high over water hazards on every hole of the Islandside Course, a Billy Mitchell design graced with thousands of palms. Lakes and canals meander through the layout, while winds off the adjacent Gulf of Mexico add to the fun. Bring your binoculars, as the course is located in a bird sanctuary.

Three nines comprise the Harbourside Course on Sarasota Bay, where old-growth stands of live oaks, pines, palms, and massive fig trees are hazards in themselves. Look for plenty of water on this track, too.

On a long stretch of white sand on a barrier island off Longboat Key near Sarasota, the resort consists of four- to ten-story buildings, upscale garden apartments, condos, and rental homes (800–237–8821, www.longboatkeyclub.com).

Hyatt Regency Coconut Point Resort and Spa
5001 Coconut Road
Bonita Springs, FL 34134
Phone: (239) 444–1234, reservations (800) 233–1234
Web site: www.coconutpoint.hyatt.com
Fax: (239) 390–4277
General Manager: Carlos Cabrera
Accommodations: In a nineteen-story tower, 450 rooms and suites in soothing tans and light greens with mahogany armoires, ceiling fans and private balconies, plus oversize bathrooms decorated with handmade tiles. Regency Club guests have a concierge, a private lounge, and food and beverage presentations.
Meals: Fine international cuisine is on the menu at Tanglewood and served on two outdoor terraces. Casual, oak-paneled Tarpon Bay specializes in fresh Florida seafood including oysters, stone crab claws, mussels, and clams served indoors or on the patio; wood-fired pizza also served. Live entertainment, snacks, and formal afternoon tea at Mangroves in the lobby lounge. Sandwiches, desserts, and snacks in the Kofe Nut cafe. Caviar and exotic martinis in the Belvedere Lounge.
Facilities: Huge swimming pool, children's lagoon with waterslide, lap pools, waterfall pool; fitness center; full-service European-style spa and salon; upscale shops; four Har-Tru tennis courts; marina, private island beach, and water sports.
Services and Special Programs: Camp Hyatt, for children ages 3–12, offers supervised activities, a playground, and special programs that focus on the Lee Island Coast environment. Private, guided ecotours on Estero Bay.
Rates: $$$$
Golf Packages: Raptor Bay Rapture includes one night accommodations, breakfast, one round of golf, and golf amenities. $280–$710 for two, double occupancy.
Getting There: Fifteen minutes from Southwest Florida International Airport. Miami and Tampa are approximately two hours away.
What's Nearby: Fly-fishing, bird-watching, walking tours, and ecotours.

PALM COAST GOLF RESORT

Palm Coast, Florida

Between St. Augustine and Daytona Beach, the look and feel of Old Florida is apparent in the ancient, Spanish moss-draped oaks and the slow parade of boats along the Intracoastal Waterway. Miles of tree-lined, walking and biking trails contribute to a relaxed, outdoorsy atmosphere. And golfers have the pleasure of plying the fairways of five championship golf courses designed by Palmer, Player, and Nicklaus—Cypress Knoll, Matanzas Woods, Palm Harbor, Pine Lakes, and Ocean Hammock.

The Palm Coast Golf Resort, adjacent to the Waterway, is a headquarters for visitors. It is an oasis of low hotel buildings surrounded by overhanging oaks, palms, and sweeping lawns. A landscaped recreation area has a swimming pool, indoor and outdoor games, waterfalls, and fountains. Moving water masks the sounds of kids having fun. On your explorations, bike rides, and strolls, you are likely to see dolphins, manatees, turtles, osprey, and many other birds.

The eighteen-court Players Racquet Club is one of the premier tennis centers in the country. Directed by Peter Burwash International, the club offers clinics, lessons, and USTA events.

The first oceanfront golf course built in Florida since the 1920s, Ocean Hammock is a stunning Jack Nicklaus Signature design meandering through natural dunes, lakes, ravines, and a scrubby oak and pine forest. The six holes along the Atlantic are named "The Bear Claw" for the challenge of the stiff winds, deep bunkers, high native grasses, and distracting sea views. One of the most beautiful golf courses in the Southeast, the track runs 7,201 yards, with a daunting 77 rating and 147 slope. When Ocean Hammock opened in 2000, *Golf Magazine* named it one of the "Top Ten Places You Can Play."

Site of a PGA Qualifying School and masterminded by Arnold Palmer and Ed Seay, the Matanzas Woods Golf Club has wide, flat, breezy fairways on the front nine, and tighter holes on the back with lively elevation changes, water hazards, and fast greens. Three holes play around and over the Waterway and Lake Success, with water carries. On eighteen, the green awaits you in the middle of the lake.

A little inland, Pine Lakes Country Club, another Arnold Palmer/Ed Seay original, is wide open and mainly unfettered by trees—and therefore rather windy. This is 7,074 yards of doglegs—eleven of them, short and long, right and left—with water on more than half of

the course and large greens; blissfully, no forced carries.

In an oak and pine forest and wetlands setting, Cypress Knoll Golf Club is inhabited by hundreds of tropical birds who flit amid marshes, streams, and lakes. The length of 6,591 yards from the back tees belies the 130 slope. With not much rough, narrow, rolling fairways are cut through the dense cypress forest, making this Gary

Player design seem delightfully isolated.

The oldest of the group, opened in 1972, Palm Harbor Golf Club features thirteen doglegs closely framed by live oaks, tall pines, and sabel palms— a Bill Amick design with elevated greens requiring accuracy with the irons. Nancy Lopez honed her game on this course.

Golf Daytona

Twenty-three miles of sandy beaches and motorsports action at Daytona USA draw vacationers to Daytona Beach. Golfers know it's the ultimate for golf, too (Golf Daytona Beach, 800–881–7065). Among more than fifteen courses on this coast, Indigo Lakes Golf Club is a charmer, its wide fairways lined with pines, with sloped, elevated greens, and ten holes menaced by water.

In a gorgeous setting between Bulow and Tomoka State Parks on Old Dixie Highway, Halifax Plantation Golf Club caters to players who love the beautiful, plantation-style layout decorated with century-old oaks, water lilies, and wild azalea. Dramatic coquina stone monuments mark the tees, and delicious meals are enjoyed on the clubhouse verandah.

Rees Jones designed the Champions Course at LPGA International, a 7,088-yard beauty in a flat, marshy nature preserve. This course boasts a zippy 74.6 rating and 137 slope, with large, terraced greens and generous fairways bordered by huge mounds that help collect flying balls. Keep your eyes peeled for resident alligators in the lake on the seventeenth.

The more difficult, target-golf-style Legends Course at the LPGA complex was laid out by Arthur Hills in lovely, pine-studded wetlands with narrow greens and plenty of water. You may see LPGA and PGA pros at the excellent practice facilities—a multi-ended driving range, several putting and chipping greens, and three superb practice holes. Knickers Bar and Grill is a top spot for lunch, even if you don't play golf (www.lpgainternational.com).

Palm Coast Golf Resort
300 Clubhouse Drive
Palm Coast, FL 32137
Phone: (386) 445–3000, reservations (800) 654–6538
Fax: (386) 445–2947
Web site: www.palmcoastresort.com
General Manager: Brad Shreiber
Accommodations: Newly renovated, 154 spacious rooms with Waterway or marina views from private French balconies; one king or two double beds, and sofabeds; attractive, not fancy, furnishings; oversize baths with Roman spa tubs.
Meals: Buffets and regional cuisine at airy, waterfront Flagler's Restaurant. Henry's Sports Bar and Grill for big-screen TV sports, live weekend entertainment, cigar nights, lunches, and snacks.
Facilities: Full-service Academy of Golf, eighty-slip marina, three swimming pools, and a private beach nearby. At the tennis center: twelve clay courts, four hard-surface courts, and two grass courts, racquetball, pro shop, lounge, snack bar, clinics, lessons, matching, and swimming pool.
Services and Special Programs: Rental boats, bikes and kayaks, fishing charters, and golf concierge. Guided boat tours of the Waterway, local canals, and the region.
Rates: $$–$$$
Golf Packages: Deluxe accommodations, discount on breakfast buffet, unlimited golf on four courses and cart, and merchandise discount. $59–$79 per person, double occupancy. A service charge will be added to play a round at Ocean Hammock.
Getting There: Thirty minutes from Daytona International Airport and seventy minutes from Jacksonville International Airport.
What's Nearby: The antiques shops of St. George Street; museums and romantic neighborhoods of old St. Augustine, a half-hour's drive up the coast highway; St. Augustine Outlet Center; fresh- and saltwater fishing and boating; Cape Kennedy Space Center.

THE RITZ-CARLTON GOLF RESORT, NAPLES
Naples, Florida

From late November through May, perfect weather attracts "snowbirds" to Florida's chic southwest coast. They come for the sugar-white beaches on the Gulf of Mexico, for shopping and cafe sitting on palmy boulevards, and for golf all winter long on more than one hundred courses, most of them private.

Tiburón is the Spanish word for shark, hence the name of Greg Norman's thirty-six-hole design for the Tiburón Golf Club, the site of the Franklin Templeton Shootout. Norman avoided adding rough around the greens or the fairways. He said, "Rough makes a course easier because it will stop balls from rolling off the green." And away they do roll, over putting surface perimeters mowed to a half-inch or less, toward the natural wetlands. The firm, fast, links-style design is expressed in boundless, rose-pink, coquina shell waste bunkers and stacked-sod wall bunkers, with unpredictable wind conditions and short game options. Norman said, "The first time people play the course, they hate it, but the second time they play, they understand the course better and tend to really love it."

Phil Mickelson, Ray Floyd, Jack Nicklaus, and other PGA stars have benefited from the teaching talents of Rick Smith at the Golf Academy. At half-day and multiday schools, the teacher-student ratio is a favorable 2 to 1.

Offering preferred tee times to guests, the new Ritz-Carlton Golf Resort has a clubby, British colonial atmosphere, complete with platoons of lazily twirling ceiling fans, potted palms, and the look of a luxury safari. Sink into a deep leather chair at a candlelit table in the cigar bar, where you can play billiards or card games, and sip rare scotches while listening to live jazz and blues. Sumptuously furnished, semitropical-themed public and private spaces; extraordinary dining; and the Ritz's legendary personal service combine to make this one of the top resort hotels in the state.

The spa is pure Mediterranean-style opulence, with thirty treatment rooms, a flower-filled conservatory, hot and cold plunge pools and a mineral pool. Traditional therapies are offered as well as unique experiences such as "Liquid Yoga," which combines water with body movement in a sea-view pool. A boon for the overworked individual, the buoyancy helps relieve tension and stress.

Après golf, guests may enjoy the "Cigar and Cognac Bath," complete with a fine cigar, a cigar magazine, bath salts and oils, a loofah sponge, and bath pillow.

A Grande Design

Characteristic of Rees Jones's world-famous design style, five sets of tees on Naples Grande Golf Club are elevated to give golfers a clear view of the layout. No houses loom to distract from a large lake, a wandering creek, a variety of terrain changes, and mature live oaks, pine hammocks, and cypress trees. This track runs from 5,210 to 7,102 yards, depending on the tee (941–659–3700, www.naplesgrande.com).

Behind the seventeenth tee is a helipad for course developer Wayne Huizenga, owner of the Miami Dolphins. A comprehensive professional practice facility has bunkered target greens, a chipping area, and multiple putting surfaces. Tom Patri, one of America's top one hundred golf instructors, is Director of Instruction at the Golf School.

A private club, Naples Grande is available to guests at the Registry Resort (800–247–9810) and The Edgewater Beach Hotel (800–821–0196).

The Ritz-Carlton Golf Resort, Naples
2600 Tiburon Drive
Naples, FL 34109
Phone: (239) 593–2000, reservations (800) 241–3333
Fax: (239) 254–3300
Web site: www.ritzcarlton.com
General Manager: Bradley Cance
Accommodations: Four-star, four-diamond rated, 295 guest rooms and suites with private balconies overlooking the golf course and luxurious amenities, such as feather beds, Frette linens, and oversize marble bathrooms. Club level guests have private lounge and concierge, food and beverage presentations. (This resort is not to be confused with the new Ritz-Carlton, Naples).
Meals: Tuscan cuisine in a light, airy environment at Lemonia. Snacks, light meals, and formal afternoon tea in the lobby lounge, Bella Vista. Australian specialties at Sydney's Grill at the golf clubhouse.
Facilities: Four Har-tru tennis courts; elaborate 18-hole putting green, excellent golf practice facilities and school; business center; full-service spa.
Services and Special Programs: Ritz Kids provides supervised play and child care. Animal-friendly rooms, pet concierge, technology butler. Guest privileges at the restaurants, spa, and beach of the nearby, five-star Ritz-Carlton, Naples.
Rates: $$$$
Golf Packages: One night luxury accommodations, one round of golf and cart, Continental breakfast, and welcome gift. $379–$699 for two, double occupancy.
Getting There: Sedans, luxury coaches, and limousines available for the 9-mile drive from Naples Airport; 29 miles from Southwest Florida International Airport at Fort Myers.
What's Nearby: Upscale shopping at the Waterside and Venetian Village centers. Wildlife viewing at Corkscrew Swamp Sanctuary, Babcock Wilderness, and the Everglades, less than an hour away.

SAWGRASS MARRIOTT RESORT AND BEACH CLUB

Ponte Vedra Beach, Florida

The official home of the PGA and site of The Player's Championship, this is the second largest golf resort in the country, with ninety-nine holes of some of the best golf in the Southeast. Here on the sunny Atlantic Coast between Jacksonville and St. Augustine, golfers make their pilgrimages to the notorious TPC at Sawgrass Stadium Course, while enjoying four more courses and a stupendous golf practice facility—all of these are private, with access provided to Marriott Resort guests.

Pete Dye pioneered the concept of bleacher mounds for spectators on the TPC Stadium Course, while integrating vast sandy wastes, water on every hole, dangerous, links-style pot bunkers, narrow landing zones, high rough (Johnny Miller calls it "cabbage"), and small, tough greens. When it's windy and dry, the greens are dry and almost impossible to hold. One of the most photographed holes in the world, the 132-yard seventeenth sports an island green swirled with wind. It has had a major role in The Player's Championship, which is played in the windy month of March. When the pin is in the back right corner, you face a postage stamp landing spot.

Three of the Stadium's holes are said to be the most difficult on the PGA Tour. If you are not up to it, it's still worth a visit here just to see the huge pro shop filled with trophies, photos, and other golf memorabilia.

There's not much rough on the TPC at Sawgrass Valley Course, a Dye/Weed/Pate design, although severely sloping hills and swales, water, trees, and wavery greens take their toll.

Watch out for water on twenty-four of the twenty-seven holes on the Sawgrass Country Club Course, Ed Seay's layout of windy, oceanside fairways. The fifth hole on the East nine drops ninety feet while the ninth ends on a triple-tiered green brushed by vigorous breezes. Greens are small and surrounded by sand, landing areas are narrow, and the native forest impinges closely on the fairways.

Marsh Landing Country Club Course, another Seay original, is a nature preserve winding through Intracoastal tidal marshes and lagoons dotted with tall pines. A perfect postcard, the third hole begins on the elevated tee box looming over 173 yards of underwater fairway, heading toward a green pitch sharply forward, and grazed by stiff crosswinds.

Oak Bridge Club Course is a short, tight Seay creation in an old-growth forest in marshy swampland. With water on every hole, it asks for accurate irons. This course will be less crowded than the others.

If and when your score rises, repair to one of four driving ranges and six putting greens, or to the miniature golf course, followed by a "trigger point" massage at the spa.

As emerald green and gleaming as the land of Oz, the Marriott is a favorite with families who love the 2.5-mile beach, hiking and biking nature trails, horseback riding, fishing, and mini golf. Tennis players head for the multisurfaced court complex. Directed by Wimbledon champ, Brian Gottfried, it is the site of the ATP Tour International Headquarters.

Between the Intracoastal Waterway and the Atlantic Ocean, the hotel is wrapped with picturesque lagoons—inhabited by alligators—and mossy oaks, tall palms, and spreading magnolias. It comprises an oasis of hundreds of acres of tropical vegetation, lakes, and lagoons. The seventy-foot-tall garden atrium lobby and public spaces are decorated with waterfalls, towering palms, and stone carvings. A luxurious tone is set with antique furnishings and Oriental rugs.

A Donald Ross Original

Henry Flagler, Standard Oil tycoon, commissioned renowned architect Donald Ross to design Ponce de Leon Golf Club, which opened in 1916. A private sanctuary of the St. Augustine Country Club for years, it became part of the Radisson Ponce de Leon Golf and Conference Resort in 1997, finally giving golfers the chance to play one of America's earliest and loveliest layouts.

Idyllic marshlands border the open front nine, while ancient magnolia, oaks, palms, and pine trees overhang the narrower fairways of the back nine. A nine-hole pitch-and-putt and an eighteen-hole putting course make this a great practice venue (800–351–9575, www.radisson.com/staugustinefl).

Sawgrass Marriott Resort and Beach Club
1000 PGA TOUR Boulevard
Ponte Vedra Beach, FL 32082
Phone: (904) 285–7777, reservations (800) 228–9290
Fax: (904) 285–0906
Web site: www.marriotthotels.com/jaxsw
General Manager: George Fetherson
Accommodations: 508 rooms, suites, and villas with private balconies or patios; attractive, understated furnishings and decor.
Meals: A clubby atmosphere, golf memorabilia, signature Crab Cake Porcupine, and grilled specialties at the Augustine Grill. Casual dining, buffets, and views of the thirteenth hole at Cafe on the Green. Seafood at the beachfront Cabana Club. Snacks and light meals poolside at the 100th Hole. The Sea Porch is a casual bar and grill.
Facilities: Seventeen tennis courts—red clay, Har-Tru, and cushioned hard courts; pro shop; restaurant; clinics; lessons and camps; three swimming pools and two children's pools; 2.5 miles of beach with Hobie cats, boogie boards, beach bikes; full-service health club and spa; business center; guest laundry; stables with quarter horses, ponies, and Appaloosas for riding and hayrides.
Services and Special Programs: The Grasshopper Gang children's program for ages 3–12 features beach activities, evening pizza-pool parties, games, and movies.
Rates: $$$
Golf Packages: TPC Deluxe Golf Package includes luxury accommodations, a round of golf and cart, and breakfast. $185–$250 per person, double occupancy, with surcharges for some courses.
Getting There: Thirty-five-minute drive from Jacksonville International Airport. Private plane access at Craig Airport and St. Augustine Airport.
What's Nearby: Lake and pond freshwater fishing, and deep-sea charters. Shopping and sightseeing in St. Augustine; Alligator Farm; ancient fort of Castillo de San Marcos; boutiques in Sawgrass Village.

TURNBERRY ISLE RESORT AND CLUB
Aventura, Florida

In a lush, tropical area in North Miami on the Intracoastal Waterway, you'll discover a Mediterranean-style resort on 300 secluded acres, along with two Robert Trent Jones Sr.–designed golf courses, two tennis clubs, a marina, and a private Ocean Club.

Managed by Mandarin Oriental International since 2000, the hotel has been rated number one in the Miami area by Zagat guidebooks. The European-trained staff (averaging three per guest) speaks twenty-one languages and is as welcoming, discrete, and helpful as any at top hotels, worldwide.

Everything in the oversized guest rooms is aimed at luxury and comfort, from sunken whirlpool tubs and TVs in the bathrooms to plush Oriental rugs, gleaming terra-cotta tile floors, oceans of blooming orchids, and French doors opening onto private terraces or balconies with garden views.

The private Ocean Club on the Atlantic is on a beautiful beach with a swimming pool and cabanas. Guests enjoy ocean swimming, windsurfing, and Hobie-cat sailing. Two tennis complexes make this "One of the 50 Greatest U.S. Tennis Resorts," according to *Tennis* magazine. Former Wimbledon champ, Fred Stolle, is resident pro, directing a lively schedule of match-making play, daily drills and clinics, and junior programs.

The new European Spa and Fitness Center is highlighted by a domed skylight and has a grand spiral staircase, waterfalls, and fountains. In twenty-six treatment rooms, among traditional beauty and health therapies, are lavish experiences such as "Javanese Lulur," involving jasmine-frangipani-scented massage and exfoliation; the "Shea Butter" French skin process; and Ayurvedic therapies to restore inner calm, which may come in handy after a day of golf.

Built in the 1970s, both courses were recently renovated. At 7,003 yards, the South Course plays to the longer hitter, while the North is narrower. Water, sea breezes, and Jones's sprawling putting surfaces are major issues on both tracks. You will encounter lakes and other water hazards on fourteen holes of the South, which rates 73.7 with a 136 slope. Look for the world's largest triple green—about 150 yards long—and the famous island green on the par-5 eighteenth.

On the shorter North Course, perpetual winds blow across the lagoons and the densely wooded fairways. The golf courses and grounds of the resort are virtual botanical gardens inhabited by exotic birds, including pink flamingos, snowy egrets, white ibis, blue and green parakeets, swans, herons, and colorful ducks. Tropical plants and trees are fragrant and blooming, from bird-of-paradise, jasmine, and gardenia, to tree ferns, weeping banyans, plumeria, and the pendulous, creamy-white bells of the Angel's Trumpet. Guided botanical tours are offered daily.

The golf clubhouse restaurant and bar are lavishly decorated in pale peach and alabaster, with Carrara marble floors, Oriental rugs, and fine oil paintings.

One of the most highly rated restaurants in southern Florida, the Veranda is romantic and elegant in brocades and Asian accents, overlooking the starlit pool gardens. On the menu are creative combinations of Cuban, Caribbean, and Latin American cuisines. Lights are low in the Veranda bar and reflect on the dark woods and soft, forest green leather armchairs and sofas.

Homage to Doral

On the edge of the Everglades between Sarasota and Fort Myers in Coral Springs, the Tournament Players Club at Heron Bay was designed by Floridian and PGA pro, Mark McCumber. He claims that the layout of Doral's Blue Monster course was a strong influence. Fairways are open and wind-strafed, devoid of landmarks, and defined primarily by 109 shallow, quite large bunkers. Approaches generally range from wide to big, gently undulating greens (954–796–2000). Site of the PGA Tour Honda Classic, Heron Bay was named as one of America's 10 best new public clubs by *Golf Digest*.

Lessons and clinics are among the best in the southeast at the Nicklaus/Flick Game Improvement golf school.

Turnberry Isle Resort and Club
19999 West Country Club Drive
Aventura, FL 33180
Phone: (305) 932–6200, reservations (800) 327–7028
Fax: (305) 933–6560
Web site: www.turnberryisle.com
General Manager: Jens Grafe
Accommodations: 395 guest rooms (averaging 800 square feet) and suites, with private balconies or patios, pale peach and terra-cotta tones in fine draperies and bedding, separate sitting areas, and large baths with TVs and whirlpool tubs.
Meals: New World specialties are on the menu at the five-star-rated Veranda. An upbeat bistro, with a presentation kitchen, The Grill overlooks the golf course. Pacific-rim cuisine and sushi are served indoors or on the patio in a clubby atmosphere at The Signature. The Ocean Club Grill is a seaside eatery with indoor/outdoor dining. Hearty meals after golf in the elegant Clubhouse.
Facilities: Nineteen clay and plexi-pave tennis courts; health and beauty spa; salon; business center; private beach and Ocean Club with cabanas and watersports; four swimming pools; 3-mile jogging path; 117-slip marina for boats up to 200 feet.
Services and Special Programs: Complimentary shuttle service throughout the resort and to the Aventura Mall. Spa cooking classes, exercises classes, guided botanical garden tours.
Rates: $$$
Golf Packages: Turnberry's Tee Time includes two nights in a Deluxe Country Club room, unlimited golf and cart, breakfast daily, golf gifts, and golf clinic. $278–$438 per person, double occupancy.
Getting There: Limousine service available for the 12-mile drive to Fort Lauderdale International Airport and for the 18 miles to Miami International. Helipad on property.
What's Nearby: 250 shops and stores at Aventura Mall; upscale boutiques at Bal Harbour Shops; Pro Player Stadium, home of the Miami Dolphins and Florida Marlins; Hialeah and Calder Race Courses.

WESTIN INNISBROOK RESORT

Palm Harbor, Florida

In the rolling hills of Florida's central Gulf Coast in Pinellas County, the Westin Innisbrook is near the Greek sponge-diving and fishing community of Tarpon Springs, and a few minutes from beautiful Gulf beaches. Seventy-two holes of championship golf are laid on hilly terrain and in pine and oak woodlands with several natural lakes.

Golf Digest called the Copperhead Golf Course one of "America's Greatest." Home of the PGA's Tampa Bay Classic and host to PGA and LPGA stars at the JC Penney Classic, Copperhead was refurbished in 1999, bringing greenside bunker complexes back into play, opening up views, and adding length. Now 7,280 yards, it rates a sizzling 75.6/134. Rolling fairways wind through pines, palms, and oaks, while seventy-two bunkers, ten water hazards, and at least one 225-yard carry over water will

get your attention. PGA pro Billy Andrade calls the dogleg sixth hole "a monster." The 590-yard fourteenth is the signature hole, a double dogleg with a huge bunker. Armadillos, swans, and turtles are some of the wildlife often seen around the lakes.

Also a stiff challenge, the Island Golf Course stretches along tight fairways over 7,000 yards with the first six holes dominated by lateral water hazards and with cypress and pine trees on rolling hills on the back nine. Save some energy for the tenth hole, running 440 yards, with a water carry and a long, uphill approach to a sloping green.

The very pretty Highlands North Golf Course is a traditional layout, rolling and shifting between tall pines, with a playable rating of 70.5/125. Elevation changes on Highlands South, plus prevailing winds,

thirteen water hazards, an island green, and the longest hole in Florida—650 yards—create an exciting challenge. Recent improvements resulted in longer, more difficult par-4s and 5s, plus additional bunkers and waste areas, creating greater penalties. The new Highlands Clubhouse has a lively Caribbean restaurant.

Head of the PGA instructors at the Innisbrook Troon Golf School, Lew Smither was named one of Florida's Top Teachers. A variety of multiday schools, daily clinics, a summer junior's program, and women's programs are among the offerings. Three complete practice facilities are an advantage in the high winter season.

Set among tall pines, magnolias, and blooming gardens, guest suites are in low-rise lodges, each with a swimming pool. Distractions for the kids include the new, 3.5-million-dollar Loch Ness pool, a giant water playground with waterslides, two sandy beaches, pop-up bubble jets, and a waterfall, against a backdrop of lush woods and landscaping.

You can stroll and bike on trails in the nature preserve, or spend a few hours in historic Tarpon Springs, exploring the saltwater bayous and the antiques shops. Take a sight-seeing cruise on the Anclote River, tour the sponge museum, or go deep-sea fishing.

Westin Innisbrook Resort
36750 U.S. Highway 19 North
Palm Harbor, FL 34684
Phone: (727) 942–2000, reservations (800) 456–2000
Fax: (727) 942–5576
Web site: www.westin-innisbrook.com
General Manager: Ian Baxter
Accommodations: 700 spacious rooms and condo-style suites in 28 lodges, with kitchens, private balconies or patios; upscale, plantation-style furnishings, tropical-theme fabrics, spacious bathrooms.
Meals: Seven restaurants, including hearty fare at the Turnberry Pub; Angus beef and lobster at DY's Steak House at the golf course; casual meals at the Grill at Loch Ness; a festive Caribbean menu at Bamboo's.
Facilities: Eleven Har-tru tennis courts and pro shop; three racquetball courts; fitness center; six swimming pools; recreation center with playground, basketball, volleyball, mini-golf, and sports equipment.
Services and Special Programs: Complimentary resort shuttle. Children ages 5–12 enjoy supervised swimming, games, and play at Camp Innisbrook; special activities for teens, too.
Rates: $$$
Golf Packages: Preferred Golf includes a round of golf, cart, and breakfast. $149–$269 per person, double occupancy.
Getting There: Shuttle service to Tampa International Airport, 23 miles away.
What's Nearby: See thoroughbred racing at Tampa Bay Downs; visit Busch Gardens, Walt Disney World, and Sea World; explore the historic village of Tarpon Springs; go to the beach or deep-sea fishing.

Practice Arnie's Way

The Arnold Palmer Golf Academy, two Palmer-designed golf courses, and a whopping forty-five tennis courts are located a few miles north of Tampa at Saddlebrook Resort (800–729–8383, www.saddlebrookresort.com). The Saddlebrook Course navigates through cypress-, pine-, and palm-lined fairways and around meandering lagoons, while the Palmer Course has larger landing zones and greens. A unique "Scoring Zone" area consists of a variety of terrains and grass surfaces for the short game.

Junior players can enroll in the Saddlebrook Preparatory School, an accredited college prep program offering a combination of academics and intense golf instruction.

WORLD GOLF VILLAGE
St. Augustine, Florida

The World Golf Village is the center of golf-dom, it seems. You need a map to navigate the sprawling complex of two golf courses designed by golf legends; three hotels; the World Golf Hall of Fame; an IMAX theater; the one-and-only PGA Tour Golf Academy; one of the largest golf emporiums in the world; and fifteen restaurants—and homes to buy if you care to stay forever. Around a central lagoon, herons hide in the reeds and bubbling fountains mask the sounds of the outside world. Who needs the outside world?

Shopping at the two-story Tour Stop, mother-of-all-golf-stores, can be hazardous to your credit cards. Look for David Duval's cool shades, Greg Norman's signature straw hats, signed memorabilia, books, videos, and logo apparel. Only here can you get custom laser-fitting for shoes, gloves, and clubs. While your golfing buddy shops, take a break on the indoor putting green and driving ranges.

Andy Hird is the St. Andrews-born popular player assistant who greets you on the first tee of The King and The Bear. He is full of stories of when Arnold Palmer and Jack Nicklaus co-designed the course, which is lush with loblolly pine hammocks carpeted with needle thatch. There are 200-year-old oak trees that overhang ponds, creeks, and marshlands, and the course is awash with natural sandy waste areas. Jack and Arnie don't fool around: Check out the 141 slope and 75.2 rating.

The Slammer and The Squire is a whisper easier, although you might watch for the alligator on the ninth hole. Named for Sam Snead and Gene Sarazen, "S&S," the site of the PGA Senior Tour Liberty Mutual Legends of Golf, winds among wetlands and an ancient pine forest—called flatwoods. In the fall red berries decorate the hollies, and native grasses turn bright purple. The entire area is a former private game reserve and remains a habitat for foxes, wood storks, osprey, eagles, deer, and tortoises who lay eggs in the bunkers.

One of the country's top golf teachers, Scott Sackett, directs the new PGA Tour Golf Academy. In the state-of-the-art practice center are seven fixed cameras for in-depth swing analysis, eight practice bays under roof, and the revolutionary "Model Golf" software program that compares your swing to tour players. As a student you get a written, personalized training and practice plan and a video of your progress to take home. Don't be surprised if you recognize the resident instructor, PGA Tour winner, Calvin Peete. In April, thirty of America's top one hundred teachers come together to offer a week of clinics, demonstrations, and classes—a rare opportunity for golfers.

Streams run beneath a canopy of tropical vegetation in the atrium lobby of the World Golf Village Renaissance Hotel overlooking the lagoon, where guest rooms have bird's-eye views of the entire village and the golf courses. Look for the giant golf ball embedded in the wall at Murray Brothers Caddyshack, a lively, fun restaurant and watering hole loaded with golf memorabilia and serving Chicago Blues Burgers and ribs.

The World Golf Hall of Fame

Plan at least two hours or more to make your pilgrimage to the Hall of Fame, where the game's history and the greatest players, courses, and architects are honored in interactive exhibits in an expansive, light-filled building with views of the golf courses and the surrounding landscape (800–WGV–GOLF). Find your favorite player in an interactive scrapbook with sound and video; listen to Lee Trevino joke as he caddies for Arnie. Stand under a parabolic sphere for your own personal showing of four decades of Shell's Wonderful World of Golf. Immerse yourself in golf history, from Mary Queen of Scots in 1567 to Old Tom Morris, a visit to St. Andrews, and a fabulous museum of clubs—from Massie nibliks to baffie spoons; Bing's driver to President Ike's Cushman golf car. It is fun to see Jack Nicklaus's fishing rod, Gary Player's black cowboy hat, and Chi Chi's signature white Panama.

Golf's greatest moments are on screen, including the Zinger's chip out of the sand in 1998, Nick Price's double eagle to win the 1998 British Open, and Alan Shepard's "Moon Shot" drive on the moon. Today's top players and current tournaments are live on monitors and an actual leaderboard. The most popular venue in the museum is the golf simulator, where you can hit the ball on forty-eight famous courses. On the indoor green, you can have a putting contest with your friends complete with a virtual audience that claps and yells, sighs and roars, as you sink 'em, or you don't.

As Arnold Palmer said, "Golf is deceptively simple and endlessly complicated . . . it satisfies the soul and frustrates the intellect. It is at the same time rewarding and maddening—and it is without a doubt the greatest game mankind has ever invented."

World Golf Village
500 South Legacy Trail
St. Augustine, FL 32092
Phone: (904) 940–8000, reservations (888) 740–7020
Fax: (800) 940–8008
Web site: www.wgv.com
General Manager: Jeff Johnsen
Accommodations: In a twelve-story World Golf Village Renaissance Hotel atrium tower, 300 spacious rooms and suites furnished in traditional, European style with large desks and ergometric chairs, wet bars and refrigerators, and sitting areas.
Meals: Hearty American food at Murray Brothers Caddyshack. An all-American menu in a tropical setting at the Cypress Point Restaurant in the hotel atrium. Pub food and TV at Sam Snead's Tavern. Deli sandwiches, salads, and snacks at the Hall of Fame Cafe. Two clubhouse restaurants and BBQ at Marvin's.
Facilities: GPS, comprehensive golf practice facilities, and one of the top rated golf schools in the country; elaborate eighteen-hole, natural grass putting course around the lagoon; beach club, twenty-four-hour fitness venue and sauna; twenty-four-hour business center; cigar club; billiard room; swimming pool; tennis courts; golf simulator; shopping arcade.
Services and Special Programs: Little Legends Club offers supervised play and games for kids.
Rates: $$$
Golf Packages: Two nights accommodations; two rounds of golf; and tickets to the Hall of Fame, the IMAX theater, and the putting course. $357–$555 per person, double occupancy. Discounted extra nights.
Getting There: Fifty minutes to Jacksonville International Airport. Private aircraft land at the St. Johns County Municipal Airport.
What's Nearby: Historic St. Augustine, twenty minutes away, offers sightseeing, shopping in boutiques and galleries, and famous beaches. One-hundred-eighty outlet stores are within 5 miles.

CALLAWAY GARDENS RESORT
Pine Mountain, Georgia

The charming little town of Pine Mountain, in the foothills of the Appalachians in Georgia's southern Piedmont, is the gateway to Callaway Gardens. The resort sprawls over thousands of acres and is a vacation wonderland beloved by families, garden lovers, and golfers. The indoor and outdoor horticultural displays are world famous. Sixty-three holes of golf are decorated by a dozen lakes, pine woods, and elaborate landscaping.

At the 2001 PGA Buick Challenge held annually in October on the Mountain View Golf Course, Chris Dimarco used his unique claw grip to beat defending champion David Duval on the first hole of the playoff. The 7,057-yard layout is tight and tree lined, a beautiful ramble in pine forests and hills, with six doglegs, high rough, and no development to mar the natural beauty. With a 73.9 course rating and slope of 136, and small, very well protected greens, the track requires near-perfect accuracy off the tee. The complicated fifteenth hole has an elevated tee box and is menaced by dense vegetation and a lake jutting twice into the fairway.

Both Mountain and Lake View Courses were recently renovated and improved. Lakes and streams raise the bar on Lake View Golf Course, where masses of azaleas, dogwoods, and seasonal flowers create a spectacular backdrop. Generous, open holes on hilly terrain skirt the lakes, situated throughout the woodlands.

Wide fairways on rolling land are bordered by orchards and vineyards on the Gardens View Golf Course. Sky View is a sweet nine-holer that families and high-handicappers like to play. Davis Love III is scheduled to redesign Gardens View and Sky View in the near future.

Among a wide variety of accommodations, the recently renovated Callaway Gardens Inn is an upscale, motel-like lodge comprising restaurants, shops, and an outdoor swimming pool. Scattered in a tall pine forest, Southern Pine Cottages are decorated with country furnishings, fireplaces, living/dining areas, screened porches, and equipped kitchens. Each of the spacious Mountain Creek Villas has a large living/dining area, tall stone fireplace, equipped kitchen, laundry, screened porch, patio, sundeck, and one to four bedrooms.

Beautiful Mountain Creek Lake and several smaller lakes are stocked with trout and other fish. Fly-fishing lessons are available. Summer sunseekers swim, water ski, go boating on the lakes, and bask on the largest inland, man-made sandy beach in the world, Robin Lake Beach. Kids love the mini-golf, the minitrain, paddle boats, and "Flying High" circus performances.

The Gardens

Superlatives are hard to avoid when describing Callaway Gardens, the nonprofit horticultural fantasy that twenty million people have visited since the 1950s—14,000 acres of indoor and outdoor gardens and wildlife displays. The world's largest azalea cultivation, comprising forty acres of 5,000 varieties, explodes into oceans of bloom in shades of vivid red, magenta, pink, and white. Wildflowers are on display year-round. Hundreds of types of vegetables, fruit, and herbs grow on the site of the television show, "The Victory Garden." One of the largest glass-enclosed tropical butterfly conservatories in North America shelters more than one thousand free-flying butterflies, hummingbirds, and other birds, which flutter around a waterfall and stream. Visitors see hawks, owls, eagles, and peregrine falcons exhibit their natural behaviors at the dramatic Birds of Prey show.

Guests on foot and on bikes, on miles of trails through the gardens, on lake ferries and trams, find quiet hideaways to enjoy the stupendous flower and plant displays. Seminars, talks, guided walks, and other educational events are held daily.

Callaway Gardens Resort
P.O. Box 2000
Pine Mountain, GA 31822–2000
Phone: (706) 663–2281, reservations (800) 225–5292
Fax: (706) 663–5068
Web site: www.callawaygardens.com
General Manager: Joe Henry
Accommodations: 349 inn rooms and suites with country decor; 155 two-bedroom cottages, and two- and four-bedroom villas.
Meals: Among seven restaurants, nouveau southern cuisine in the Georgia Room; steak and seafood overlooking the lake at the Gardens Restaurant; the casual Veranda for Italian cuisine; buffets and brunches at the Plantation Room; casual meals and pizza at the Flower Mill; American food at the Country Kitchen; cafeteria fare at the Mountain Creek Cafe.
Facilities: Ten hard- and soft-surfaced tennis courts; racquetball; pro shop; par course; skeet, trap, and sporting clay gun club and shop; fishing and boating on thirteen private lakes; resort shuttles; gift, garden, and outdoor recreation stores.
Services and Special Programs: Supervised Summer Adventure for kids, a day camp including circus activities, golf clinics, theater, outdoor fun, and more. Annual events include a water-ski tournament, circus performances, concerts, and a hot-air balloon festival.
Rates: $$–$$$
Golf Packages: The Champion includes one night accommodations, a round of golf and cart, breakfast and dinner at the Plantation Room, and admission to the Gardens. $249–$398 for two, double occupancy.
Getting There: Major airlines serve Hartsfield Atlanta International Airport, a one-hour drive away, and Columbus Metropolitan Airport, a half-hour drive away. Private aircraft land at nearby Harris County Airport.
What's Nearby: In Pine Mountain, visit FDR's Little White House. Take a hike at F.D. Roosevelt State Park. Go fishing and boating on Lake Delano. See wildebeests, camels, giraffes, rhinos, water buffalo, and antelopes at the drive-through Wild Animal Safari.

THE CLOISTER AT SEA ISLAND

Sea Island, Georgia

Since 1928 Southern families have returned year after year for summer vacations on Sea Island—for the tennis and golf, for the 5 miles of private beach, for the shooting school, for the horseback riding, fishing, and biking, to explore the salt marshes, and to sightsee along the Georgia coastline. Cherished traditions include shrimp boils at the beach, and black tie dinners and dancing in the hotel dining room—live orchestra included.

The Beach Club restaurants, wrap-around terrace, Ocean Houses, and additions to the Terrace Houses are new or refurbished. Recently opened is the impressive, stone-and-shingle Lodge at Sea Island Golf Club, reminiscent of classic northeastern clubs of the 1920s and 1930s, with luxurious guest rooms, restaurant, and a wood-paneled trophy room displaying local golf history.

Only members or guests of resort accommodations may play the three courses at the Golf Club, which is approached on the Avenue of the Oaks, a rambling roadway gloriously lined with mossy oaks and weeping willows. With lovely panoramas of the island, salt marshes, creeks, the ocean and St. Simons Sound, all three have been recently updated and improved. Rees Jones, the genius of golf course renovations, who is called "the U.S. Open Doctor," turned vintage Walter Travis and Dick Wilson nines into eighteen stunning parkland holes, retitled the Plantation Course. Many trees were removed to open up long views, although plenty of gigantic, overhanging oaks remain. Golfers contend with two new lakes, flower-filled landscaping on tight, winding holes, and winds off the ocean.

Tom Fazio rearranged the Seaside and Marshside nines into the gorgeous, new Seaside Course, a symphony of tidal inlets, dunes, and salt marshes, playing fast and firm in semi-Scottish-links style. Deteriorated and lost over time, giant bunkers and sandy waste areas have reappeared, to balance steep-banked greens, wide landing zones, and steady sea breezes.

Opening in time to host the 2001 Walker Cup, the Retreat Course was redesigned and expanded from an older course by resident pro, Davis Love III. Love's father, Davis Love Jr., was a longtime, much-beloved teaching pro at the golf academy here.

Champions of the LPGA and PGA tours, including Louise Suggs, Jack Lumpkin, and Mike Cook, lead the staff at the Golf Learning Center, which is operated jointly with *Golf Digest* magazine. Lessons, clinics, and schools take place on superb practice venues—two short game courses, indoor and outdoor swing areas, putting greens, bunkers, mounds, rough, and fairways. A large selection of videos and books is available in the golf school library.

Southern hospitality is top priority at The Cloister, the red-tile-roofed, traditional, Spanish-Mediterranean-style hotel surrounded by sunny patios and quiet garden terraces. Always owned and operated by the

Jones family, the hotel is at once laid-back and sultry, yet formal in an Old World way. Personal service is exemplary. Suites located near the beach and throughout the landscaped grounds, in the Terrace and Ocean Houses, and in the glamorous new lodge are newer accommodations.

Voted the top spa in North America by *Travel & Leisure,* the Sea Island Spa features traditional treatments and unique offerings such as "Beach Tai Chi," "Fairway Flexibility" (incorporating golf specific warm-ups and stretches), and classic Hatha and Kundalini yoga. Available outdoor recreation includes archery; skeet and five-stand sporting clays; and horseback riding—trail, marsh, ring, and bareback on the beach—with English and Western lessons offered.

Jekyll Island High Jinks

The Vanderbilts, the Rockefellers, J.P. Morgan, and Joseph Pulitzer built a hunting club on Jekyll Island in 1886, where lawn and beach parties, carriage rides, and yachting filled summer days for their families and friends. Much of the island became a state park in 1947. The rest comprises the Jekyll Island Club Hotel (a National Historic Landmark, recently restored to its former glory), a quaint old town of shops and galleries, and four beautiful, long-established golf courses offering the advantage of reasonable green fees (800–535–9547).

The longest and narrowest, Pine Lakes Golf Club is a Dick Wilson design, densely tree-lined and doglegging across the island. Wilson also created the Oleander Golf Course here. Oversize greens and generous fairways help along the high handicapper through the woods on the Indian Mound course.

A real treat is the Historic Oceanside 9 (also called Great Dunes), a breezy 1920s-era, Walter J. Travis, links-style layout with elevated tees—the better to see the tiny greens and deep bunkers.

Best not to search for your ball too long in the lakes and ponds, unless you carry 'gator repellent.

The Cloister at Sea Island
100 First Street
Sea Island, GA 31561
Phone: (912) 638–3611, reservations (800) 732–4752
Fax: (912) 638–5159
Web site: www.seaisland.com
General Manager: Tom Wicky
Accommodations: 269 rooms and suites in the resort, including those with traditional decor in The Cloister; luxurious, spacious rooms and suites in the Lodge and the Houses, some with private pool, terrace, and fireplace; and larger cottages. Full American plan available.
Meals: At the Lodge, Colt and Alison serves steaks, chops, and hearty fare, and the Terrace Room is open for Continental and Southern regional cuisine. An international menu is offered in the Main Dining Room, with live music and formal attire required some nights. Alfresco dining, and famous seafood buffets, at the Beach Club.
Facilities: Two swimming pools; full-service health and beauty spa; fleet of vessels from vintage yachts to fishing charters and speedboats; saltwater fishing school; twenty-five Har-tru clay tennis courts, pro shop, practice court, professional staff, and tournaments.
Services and Special Programs: Bridge schools; ballroom and contemporary-style dancing instruction; Big Band Festival; junior tennis and golf programs; garden and food and wine events. Supervised play and storytelling, plus dinner-and-a-movie evenings for ages 3–12 with the Junior Staff. Golf and tennis for children under 19 is free. Individually designed Golf Fitness Program.
Rates: $$$$
Golf Packages: Sea Island Golf Package includes accommodations, unlimited golf, cart and forecaddie, and golf services. $484–$1,240 for two, double occupancy.
Getting There: One-hour drive from Savannah and Jacksonville International Airports. Private aircraft land at McKinnon Airport on the island.
What's Nearby: Cruises on the Intracoastal Waterway and offshore fishing charters. Guided off-island tours to the Museum of Coastal History, Slave Cabins of Hamilton Plantation, Cumberland Island, and other plantations and islands.

FOUR SEASONS RESORT MAUI AT WAILEA

Wailea, Maui, Hawaii

Wailea, a huge resort on the south Maui coast, consists of six large hotel complexes; an upscale shopping center; five white, sandy beaches; and ninety holes of championship golf. In gleaming splendor in a magical garden above Wailea Beach, the Four Seasons Resort Maui is an oasis of white fountains, white columns, white limestone and marble floors, white cabanas, and oceans of white orchids. In the sultry evenings, candles and torchlight glow around the gardens and the regal pool terrace.

Oversize guest rooms come with pale-toned teak, rattan, and wicker furnishings, and champagne-colored marble baths with soaking tubs. Fine fabrics, original artwork, and lots of orchids create a smooth, tropical elegance. Unequaled for personal service, the members of the Four Seasons staff are extraordinary in their charming attitudes and discrete attention to detail.

A top gathering place for the beautiful people, Wolfgang Puck's newly opened Spago's restaurant serves a blend of Pacific Rim cuisines, from Thai coconut soup with lobster, chili, and Indonesian galangal to fresh *opakapaka* and Chinois lamb chops with Hunan eggplant and chili-mint vinaigrette. The luscious and romantic open-air setting has island decor that is sleek and contemporary, enriched with vibrant artworks.

Under the stars, *cucina rustica* is on the menu while violins play at Ferraro's, Wailea's only oceanfront restaurant.

Shoppers can walk a shoreline path or take the hotel shuttle to the Shops at Wailea, a glitzy retail complex with Tommy Bahama, Louis Vuitton, and more trendy retail.

Starting with an ocean view on the first hole beside a bubbling stream and red-blooming Royal Poinciana trees, Wailea's Gold Course begins a steady upward climb over 7,000 yards into the foothills of Healeakala. Rated 73/139, the track is a Robert Trent Jones Jr. design, tilted and terraced alongside historic rock walls with well-protected, super-fast greens and high, dense fairway shoulders. Like bits of torn white paper, herons fly above the ponds and lakes, and you can hear the sound of the surf on the back nine. In 2002 Palmer, Nicklaus, Irwin, and Floyd battled it out at the Senior Skins Game on the Gold, managing to avoid most of the fearsome lava outcroppings and ninety-three bunkers filled with dazzling-white Idahoan sand.

Gently stepping up the hillsides, the Blue Course, host to the LPGA Kemper Open, is a riot of hibiscus, great banks of bougainvillea, fragrant plumeria, and just a few of the fearsome lava rocks. Only slightly marred by street traffic and some prettily landscaped residential development, the Blue ascends the lower foothills of Healeakala with wide fairways and generous approaches. The fourth hole does seem less than charitable, with a blind tee shot below a mountainous fairway that drops off toward the green—views of Maalaea Bay and Molokini Crater are the rewards. Cameras usually come out on the fourteenth, where oceans of blooming flowers and trees crowd the deep green, which has a mercifully open approach.

Explosions of brilliant flowers and trees line gentle fairways that funnel drives toward the center on the Emerald Course, which has an ocean view from every hole and four to six sets of tees. *Golf for Women* magazine has awarded the Emerald the title, "Most Women-Friendly Club," due to its kinder, gentler fairways and few forced carries; top-notch pro shop staff; and the natural beauty of the course, which is a botanical garden of bird-of-paradise, orange-blossoming wiliwili trees, sky-blue beach morning glory, and blazing-red firecracker plants. Ten and seventeen share a huge double green fronted by a large, landscaped lake.

The Gold and the Emerald are topped by a luxurious clubhouse and an open-air restaurant, the Sea-Watch, which is one of Wailea's best eateries, specializing in fresh Hawaiian fish.

Golfers retreat to the spa for deep tissue sports massage, "Sunburn Relief Wraps," or the "Lomi Pohaku Therapy," which combines heated and frozen stones to relax muscles and open energy centers.

South Maui Breezes

Tradewinds head in a west-northwest-erly direction on South Maui courses, and greens usually break toward the setting sun. Just up the road from Wailea, the Makena South course at Makena Resort earns a 138 slope rating with lightning fast, tifdwarf greens, ocean hazards, and sloping, hillside fairways. The track dips to the seashore at a bay called Turtle Town, where giant sea turtles often linger.

Makena North beats that at 139. Carved from craggy lava beds on the upcountry flank of Healeakala, the North is a wild ride up, down, and around ancient Hawaiian rock walls, gullies, streams, and ravines. An array of big lava boulders and forced carries, and glimpses of wild boar, deer, and pheasant add to the excitement (808–879–3344).

Four Seasons Maui at Wailea
3900 Wailea Alanui
Wailea, Maui, HI 96753
Phone: (808) 874–8000, reservations (800) 819–5053
Fax: (808) 874–2222
Web site: www.fourseasons.com/maui
General Manager: Radha Arora
Accommodations: 380 five-diamond, award-winning rooms and suites, the largest in the islands, with Venetian marble tubs, private balconies, sitting areas with sofas and armchairs in tropical fabrics, and wall-size mirrors to reflect the tropical landscape or the sea views.
Meals: Spago's elegant Pacific-Asian cuisine is served in a contemporary, open-air setting. Oceanside, Ferraro's features a Mediterranean menu. Fabulous breakfast buffets, Asian wok, grill, and rotisserie specialties; and slack key guitar, on the patio at the Pacific Grill. On the fifteenth fairway of the Blue Course, Harry's Sushi Bar and seafood at Lobster Cove.
Facilities: Full-time trainers and Cybex equipment in the Health Centre; sea views and your own TV on the outdoor ProCor elliptical trainers; exercise classes, yoga, and massage on the beach. The spa offers mango salt glows, orchid aromatherapy baths, and traditional treatments. Putting and croquet greens; two large swimming pools; on the sixth floor, two synthetic grass, lighted tennis courts, with lessons, clinics, ball machines, and matching.
Services and Special Programs: Demonstrations by local fine artists on weekday mornings; scuba diving and certification; snorkel and kayak tours. Kids for All Seasons for ages 5–12 includes storytelling, hula dancing, computers, games, beach play, and meals.
Rates: $$$$
Golf Packages: Golf for Two features a round of golf with cart on the Gold or Emerald Courses, a full-size rental car, and oceanview accommodations, from $740 per couple, per night. Ask about the romantic Deluxe Bougainvillea Trail package for spouses and newlyweds.
Getting There: Airport limousine and sedan transfers are available to Kahului Airport, a thirty-minute drive away and served by interisland airlines.
What's Nearby: Take the short beachside path to the Grand Wailea Resort for a tour of glorious tropical gardens and waterfalls, and to see the monumental, bronze sculptures of bodacious Hawaiians. The Spa Grande here is one of the largest luxury spas in the world. Continue walking to The Shops at Wailea. The entire shoreline path is 1.5 miles long. Daytrips to Healeakala National Park; helicopter tours, upcountry horseback riding and hiking; museums and shopping in Lahaina; and the Maui Ocean Center. Snorkeling and diving trips to Molokini Crater.

HILTON WAIKOLOA VILLAGE
Waikoloa, Hawaii

As surreal and fantastic as a Hollywood set, this Kohala Coast resort is sometimes called the "Disneyland of Hawaii." Mahogany boats cruise along canals throughout the tropical grounds, while guests stroll on a ¾-mile garden path past waterfalls and fine Asian and Oceanic sculpture and artwork. Included in the multimillion dollar collection of 1,700 objects are a life-size bronze cart with six horses from Thailand, two-ton marble urns, ceremonial crocodiles, and bronze Buddhas. Among several swimming areas are dolphin interaction pools; a 175-foot, twisting waterslide; a river pool; an adult pool; a snorkeling lagoon; and the main beach. Guests go kayaking, paddle boating, snorkeling, and water cycling from the beautiful palm-fringed lagoon and the beach, or they settle into two-person hammocks under the coconut palms.

Troon Golf manages the Kings' and Beach golf courses here. The Robert Trent Jones Jr.–designed Beach Course is menaced by oceans of black lava fields, four water holes, and seventy-four sand traps on narrow fairways lush with vivid banks of bougainvillea and fragrant plumeria trees. Beautiful Anaeho'omalu Bay looms along the entire twelfth hole, with lava leading the way to a green elevated above the sea and backed by waving coconut trees. Jones added bunkers and lakes, expanding the course in 1989. Look for the fascinating petroglyph fields near the sixth, seventh, and eighth holes. Isao Aoki, a PGA star, holds the course record of 63.

The Kings' Course, a strategic Tom Weiskopf/Jay Morrish layout, is reminiscent of Scottish links. Inland from the Pacific, it runs 7,064 yards around huge lava formations, with wide fairways, high grasses, six lakes, and bunkers as deep as 5 feet.

Ocean breezes definitely come into play.

Both courses have open-air clubhouse restaurants, pro shops, driving ranges, and putting greens. The most popular offering at the Waikoloa Golf Academy is the one-day school, which includes a lesson, lunch, and a nine-hole scramble with the pro. Open to all ages, the elaborate, oceanside, eighteen-hole Seaside Putting Course is dotted with sand traps, water hazards, waterfalls, and ponds swimming with koi.

At one of the largest and most comprehensive spas in Hawaii, guests relax with Lomi Lomi massage and Tai Chi classes. After a day of golf, choose from exotic, moisturizing wraps such as coco-mango, rare orchid oil, and the "Kilauea Herbal Heat Wrap" with acupressure facial and foot massage. The "Ultimate Self-Tanner" exfoliates and gives your skin a healthy, tanlike glow without sun damage.

A unique program here is Dolphin Quest, where guests—after winning a dolphin lottery—can touch and play with dolphins in a warm water lagoon. Teens and youngsters also get the chance to learn about dolphin and pet training.

Maui Linksland

Opened in 1999 the Dunes at Maui Lani is said to be the only true links track in Hawaii. On sloping terrain created by massive, ancient sand dunes, the routing is out-and-back, into the trades on the front nine, and downwind on the back. Partial blind shots, dramatic elevation changes, and gigantic, undulating greens surrounded by deep, turf-sided bunkers make this a challenge. The rewards are views of the Iao Valley, the West Maui Mountains, and the deep blue Pacific. Conveniently located near Kahului International Airport, the Dunes has a lighted practice range with Bermuda grass tees and target greens with bunkers. The Golf College here offers day and nighttime instruction and schools (808–873–0422, www.mauilani.com). The Dunes Restaurant is a nice retreat, serving Asian-Hawaiian regional cuisine.

Hilton Waikoloa Village
425 Waikoloa Beach Drive
Waikoloa, HI 96738
Phone: (808) 886–1234, reservations (800) 445–8667
Fax: (808) 886–2900
Web site: www.hiltonwaikoloavillage.com
General Manager: Dieter Seeger
Accommodations: 1,240 rooms and suites in low-rise towers with private lanais or balconies, sofas and sitting areas, pale, soothing tropical colors, walk-in closets, original art, and antiques. Executive Level rooms have a concierge and food and beverage presentations.
Meals: Seven restaurants, including Northern Italian cuisine on the waterfront at Donatoni's; traditional Japanese food in a Zen garden at Imari; pupus on the sunset lanai, and seafood and Angus beef at the Kamuela Provision Company; buffets on the Palm Terrace; sophisticated Chinese food and ancient art at Kirin; snacks and small meals at Hang Ten, the Orchid Cafe, and the Boat Landing Pavilion Food Court; healthy fare at the Spa Cafe.
Facilities: Seven plexi-cushion tennis courts, pro shop, and teaching pros; the "Legends of the Pacific" dinner show featuring exotic dancing and music, and a luau; full-service spa, salon, and fitness center with sports performance evaluation, training, and treatments.
Services and Special Programs: Guided botanical garden and art collection tours. Supervised play at Camp Menehune for ages 5–12, with water activities, cooking, computers, and games. Dolphin Quest encounters with bottlenose dolphins; and Dolphin Discovery for ages 5–12. Astronomy program; scuba lessons.
Rates: $$$
Golf Packages: Endless Fairway includes a garden or golf view room and unlimited golf with second round on the same course. $419 for two, double occupancy.
Getting There: Eighteen miles from Kona International Airport, with shuttle available.
What's Nearby: Within the Waikoloa Beach Resort, the Kings' Shops is a gigantic complex of stores, restaurants, and entertainment venues; there are condominiums to rent as well as other hotels. Expeditions to the Waipio Valley, Kona Town, the Parker Ranch, and the old town of Hilo.

HYATT REGENCY KAUAI RESORT AND SPA

Koloa, Kauai, Hawaii

Set against a serene backdrop of silken-green mountains above a series of idyllic, crescent-shaped beaches, the Poipu Beach Resort area has long been the main attraction for vacationers on Kauai due to dependably warm weather, the beautiful beaches, and championship golf courses near one of Hawaii's loveliest resorts, the Hyatt Regency Kauai.

The 1920s-inspired, plantation-style, low-rise architecture of the resort, which is nestled in glorious, tropical gardens, has gracious verandahs and public spaces open to the salt air. No building stands taller than the tallest coconut tree. Guest rooms with large, private balconies are perfect perches from which to contemplate the sunset on Keoneloa Bay and watch the action in the myriad of water features, from landscaped saltwater lagoons to two large swimming pools and a 150-foot water slide.

The atmosphere is romantic and seductive. Passionate Samoan and Tahitian performers spin torches and dance to stirring drums at twice-weekly luaus under the stars. Children are happy at "night camp" in the evenings, while parents listen to Hawaiian musicians on the Seaview Terrace. Stargazing through telescopes in the gardens and walking barefoot on the white sand beach complete the fantasy.

Soothing New Age treatments at the Anara Spa range from lava rock showers to the healing properties of volcanic ash and kukui nut oil. Rejuvenate your face with a "Jet Lag Facial," an exfoliating, rehydrating masque combined with neck and shoulder massage. Men like the "Sportsman's Facial," which relieves shaving irritation and massages chest, neck, shoulders, and face.

The links-style Poipu Bay Golf Course, site of the one-million-dollar PGA Grand Slam of Golf, was designed to be 7,034 yards long by Robert Trent Jones Jr. in the early 1990s. The course is situated between the mountain peaks and jagged bluffs a hundred feet above the surf. On the shoreline holes during the winter, you can watch humpback whales rolling and spouting offshore. On the beach below fifteen and sixteen, green sea turtles and monk seals are often seen sunbathing.

Tiger Woods held forth here in 2001 to win his fourth straight Grand Slam of Golf with a record twelve-under 132, and a three-stroke victory over David Toms. GPS on the carts will be a help as you navigate the rolling terrain and wildly undulating fairways that failed to faze Tiger. Fairway bunkers lurk on nearly every hole, and when breezes blow in the afternoons, headwinds and crosswinds are a given. And, when your ball lands in the stony ruins of ancient places of worship, called *heiaus,* there it must stay, as the ruins are off-limits.

On the final four holes, the sound of the surf will be in your ears and the tradewinds in your hair as you play along the oceanfront. In the beautiful clubhouse restaurant, enjoy the sea view, the mango pancakes at breakfast and the Dungeness crab hash at lunch.

Lovely Lagoons and Kiahuna

Five minutes from Lihue Airport on the island of Kauai, Jack Nicklaus created two tropical beauties, the Kiele and Mokihana Courses at Kauai Lagoons, both with lovely views of the Pacific and Nawiliwili Bay. A blooming paradise of tropical flowers softens the challenge on Kiele, stretched along high cliffs over the sea and the harbor. Drives carry over verdant jungle canopies to putting surfaces on surf-splashed peninsulas. Forty acres of freshwater lagoons come into play. Getting off the tees accurately is the primary issue—over streams, wetlands, and gorges dense with tropical vegetation.

Equally as lush and beautiful, Mokihana plays shorter, in rolling links style, with wide fairways, sensuous, undulating greens, and the lagoons. The backdrop is green and gorgeous Mount Waialeale (www.kauailagoonsgolf.com). A recent "soft" renovation added landscaping, coconut palms, and coral rock hazards.

Guests at the newly renovated Kauai Marriott Resort and Beach Club get preferred tee times at Kauai Lagoons. Draped along a .25-mile stretch of white sand on Kalapaki Beach, the resort is wrapped around one of the largest swimming pools in Hawaii and acres of opulent tropical gardens (www.marriotthotels.com).

The Kiahuna Golf Club in the heart of Poipu is a 6,353-yard, par-70 track adorned with landscaping, water features, and the rocky remnants of an old Hawaiian village. Numerous water hazards, wavering, multitiered greens and prevailing trade winds have created a reputation for Kiahuna as "the longest short golf course you'll ever play" (www.kiahunagolf.com).

Hyatt Regency Kauai Resort and Spa

1571 Poipu Road
Koloa, Kauai, HI 96756
Phone: (808) 742–1234, reservations (800) 554–9288
Fax: (808) 742–1557
Web site: www.kauai-hyatt.com
General Manager: Gerald C. Gibson
Accommodations: 602 rooms and suites, averaging 600 square feet, with private balconies, sitting areas, and sea, lagoon, or mountain views; luxurious, island-style, earth-toned decor, rattan and koa wood furnishings. Ground-floor rooms have lovely garden lanais. Regency Club rooms offer private lounge and concierge, complimentary breakfast, beverages, food service, and extras.
Meals: A Pacific Islands menu at Tidepools, under a thatched roof by the koi pond, overlooking Keoeloa Bay. An award-winning wine list and contemporary Italian fare, plus Franciscan murals and a Romanesque courtyard, at Dondero's. Luscious buffets on the open-air Iilima Terrace. Healthy food at Kupono Cafe in the spa. Hearty lunches and dinners at the Poipu Bay Grill at the golf clubhouse.
Facilities: Four plexi-paved tennis courts, daily clinics, round robins, lessons, and pro shop; mountain bikes, snorkeling, and watersports equipment; two swimming pools; swimming and paddling in the saltwater lagoon; full-service spa with health and beauty treatments, daily fitness classes, lap pool, weight room, salon; upscale shopping arcade.
Services and Special Programs: Daily golf clinics and private lessons. Camp Hyatt for ages 5–12 features Hawaiian crafts and games, swimming, computer fun, tennis, tidepool exploration, and nature hikes. Traditional Polynesian arts and crafts are demonstrated daily. "Talk Story" sessions focus on the legends of Kauai. Scuba diving lessons.
Rates: $$$–$$$$
Golf Packages: Golf Is Suite includes seven nights accommodations in Ocean Suite, unlimited golf, and one private lesson per stay. $3,950 per person, double occupancy.
Getting There: Thirty minute drive from Lihue Airport, which is served by major airlines.
What's Nearby: Kayak a jungle river, horseback ride on the beach, or take a sailing cruise or helicopter tour. Take the dune walk on the beach and in the sand dunes to see excavations of prehistoric Hawaiian sites.

KAPALUA BAY HOTEL

Kapalua, Maui, Hawaii

In Hawaiian Kapalua means "arms embracing the sea," referring to the black lava peninsulas that enclose five beautiful bays lined with white sand beaches. Consisting of two luxury hotels, luxurious rental villas, and thirty-six holes of championship golf, Kapalua Resort seems to rise from this splendid shoreline and into the mists of the West Maui Mountains.

Situated on a bluff over Kapalua Beach are the terraced gardens and grounds of the gracious, plantation-style, Kapalua Bay Hotel, which recently underwent a multimillion-dollar enhancement. Guest room decor is sleek and contemporary island style, with handsome, pale fabrics and light wood furnishings that create serene frames for stunning oceanfront views.

The average high temperature is 80 degrees in January, when humpback whales patrol the shore and the PGA Mercedes Championship is played on the Plantation Course, a semi-links-style layout by Ben Crenshaw and Bill Coore. This course plays 7,263 yards up and down rolling foothills, across jungly ravines and tradewind-swept ridges. Fairways and greens are massive, bunkers are gigantic, and pili grass is high.

At 663 yards from the back tees, the eighteenth is the longest hole on the PGA tour. With Pacific Ocean and island views, the fairway drops 170 feet from the tee and narrows toward the green, playing down-wind—and the wind can be treacherous. The 16,000-square-foot green roils and rolls, tilting toward a ravine. Andy Bean double-eagled it with a 6-iron in 1991. Sergio Garcia made a pair of 10-foot birdie putts on the eighteenth in 2002 at the Mercedes—one to get into the sudden-death playoff with David Toms, and the other to win.

Designed by Arnold Palmer and Ed Seay in 1980 and updated in 2001, the Village Course climbs 800 feet up the mountain slopes through a Cook pine and eucalyptus forest, tall grasses, and pineapple fields. It

emerges at its apex on the sixth hole a hundred feet above the landing zone, with pines on the left and a lake on the right, approaching a shallow green. Skinny fairways, deep gulches and valleys, wind-washed, firm greens, and lovely cross channel views of Molokai and Lanai make this one of Maui's most satisfying tracks.

The first in the country to be certified as an Audubon International Cooperative Sanctuary, the Bay Course offers a creative program called "Birdies and Eagles," which acquaints players with the twenty-three species of birds seen on Kapalua's courses. The most traditional of the three at Kapalua, the Bay Course was designed by Arnold Palmer and Francis Duane, opening in 1975. Greens are generous and fairways generally wide. The signature fifth hole calls for a long tee shot over the crashing surf of Onelua Bay.

The high-tech Kapalua Golf Academy, which opened in the new millennium, was designed by Hale Irwin, the resort's Senior PGA Tour professional. Private lessons and one- and two-day, all-weather golf schools are available with a 4-to-1 student-teacher ratio; daily clinics are open to all. An eighteen-hole putting course, outstanding grass teeing areas and target greens, greenside and fairway bunkers, a specialty short game area, indoor hitting bays, and thirty-five PGA teaching pros make this academy unmatched in Hawaii.

Snorkeling, swimming, and kayaking are excellent in the crystal-clear, azure waters off the gorgeous, golden sand beaches, which are fringed with palms, landscaping, and greenswards. Protected by offshore reefs and rocky peninsulas, Kapalua Bay has one of the safest beaches on the island. (A university study of 650 beaches across the country named Kapalua Beach the "Best Beach in America.")

Guided tours are offered in the private forest preserve, home of rare, colorful Hawaiian birds and a veritable botanical garden of native plants and trees.

Other Places to Play

Over the sixteen golf courses on Maui the prevailing trade winds blow about 300 days a year and are generally northeasterly, and livelier in summer than in winter, and stronger in the afternoons.

Maui's first resort course, Robert Trent Jones Sr.'s Kaanapali North begins at the shoreline and climbs high into the hills before it drops back to the ocean for three stunning finishing holes. Bermuda grass greens are large, fairways are wide, the elevation dips and rises, and a ball-drowning lake comes into play on the first and last holes. Kaanapali South is a traditional, 1970s era layout favored by high handicappers. Watch out for the fairway bunkers fiendishly placed on the low side of the fairways (808–661–3691).

At 1,200 feet on the cool slopes of the volcano, Healeakala, thick-bladed kukuya grass hides golf balls at the public Pukalani Country Club in West Maui. Look for left-turning doglegs, wide fairways, and Norfolk pines. The third hole features two greens, which you may choose from (808–572–1314).

Kapalua Bay Hotel
One Bay Drive
Kapalua, Maui, HI 96761
Phone: (808) 669–5656, reservations (800) 367–8000
Fax: (808) 669–4649
Web site: www.kapaluabayhotel.com
General Manager: Jon Gersonde
Accommodations: At the Kapalua Bay Hotel, 210 oversize rooms and suites with private balconies or lanais in three low-rise wings, with "Tea for Two" tubs and sumptuous amenities. Also within the resort is a Ritz-Carlton Hotel, and luxurious rental villas and homes.
Meals: Eighteen restaurants and lounges are available. Above the sea, dine on Pacific/Asian cuisine in the elegant Bay Club; lavish buffets and views of neighboring islands at the Gardenia Court; crab cakes, BBQ, buffets, and hula shows at the Plumeria Terrace; creative Pacific Rim cuisine at Fleming's on the Greens at the new Village Clubhouse; Hawaiian and Mediterranean food at the Plantation Course Clubhouse; steak and seafood at Jameson's Grill; innovative Japanese cuisine at Sansei Restaurant and Sushi Bar; light meals and snacks at the Honolua Store.
Facilities: Two beautifully landscaped tennis complexes include twenty plexi-pave courts and Hawaii's largest USPTA staff, with instruction, daily clinics, junior and adult tennis camps, and matching; 10,000-square-foot, triple-tiered, cascading swimming pool; twenty upscale boutique shops; twenty-four-hour fitness center; three white sand beaches with equipment for snorkeling, kayaking, and boogie boarding.
Services and Special Programs: Guided nature and historic walks in the private forest preserve; Hawaiian cultural talks; stargazing; hula shows and lessons; lei making; slack key guitar demos. Hawaiian artisans illustrate their talents daily on the lobby terrace. Supervised Kamp Kapalua for ages 5–12.
Rates: $$$–$$$$
Golf Packages: Unlimited Golf Package includes garden view room, one round of golf per person (unlimited golf on some dates), and golf services. $450–$670 per room, per night, double occupancy, depending on the season.
Getting There: A ten-minute trip via airport shuttle to the Kapalua West Maui airport, which is served by inter-island airlines. A fifty-minute drive from Kahului Airport, served by major airlines.
What's Nearby: Parasailing; deep-sea fishing; helicopter tours; sightseeing in historic Lahaina; Pineapple Tour takes guests to harvest fields and to the only pineapple cannery in the United States; classes for visual and performing arts, dance, and yoga at the Art School at Kapalua; hiking and guided tours in the Maunalei Arboretum and the Pu'u Kukui Preserve.

THE LODGE AT KOELE

Lanai City, Hawaii

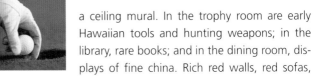

Imagine the estate of a wealthy plantation owner: a manor house with two-story-tall stone fireplaces, Hawaiian-themed carpets, deep, cushy sofas and armchairs, and a valuable Asian-African art collection gathered from world travels. Rare bronze Tibetan horses guard the entry hall. Beveled glass windows light the game room, where leather club chairs and felt-topped tables are inviting. In the mists of the 1,600-foot elevation, the grounds are shaded by giant Cook and Norfolk pines, and ancient banyan trees. Sleek horses graze in emerald-green pastures.

On the grand porches are wicker lounge chairs placed to take in sunsets and distant ocean views. An English bowling green, a croquet court, a sheltered swimming pool, tennis courts, and a greenhouse full of orchids are found on a ramble around the gardens, where sculptures, streams, ponds, and gazebos are reasons to linger. Musical interludes take place under a ceiling mural. In the trophy room are early Hawaiian tools and hunting weapons; in the library, rare books; and in the dining room, displays of fine china. Rich red walls, red sofas, and low lamplight make for romantic evenings in the lounge. Every public room and some guest rooms have fireplaces for cool evenings—rare occurrences in the islands but commonplace here.

Add a Greg Norman/Ted Robinson golf course to this dream and the Lodge at Koele becomes a reality. Hanging on steep hillsides and freshened with seven lakes, rushing streams, and double waterfalls, fairways and bent grass greens are the lushest in the islands due to the moisture-laden climate and fewer rounds of golf than at most resorts. Inspired by the magical setting, Robinson called it ". . . reminiscent of Shangri-La," while Norman said, it was " . . . created by the gods of Hawaii."

Wild turkeys and pheasant prattle in the brush. Axis deer wander on the upper nine, hide in the dense forest, leap over gullies, and drink from the lily ponds. On seventeen, you abruptly lose the altitude you gained, teeing off over a precipitous drop to a narrow landing zone with a lake on the right and wilderness all around the tiny green. When playing with Norman in an exhibition match, Jack Nicklaus hit eight tee shots before he landed on this fairway. The rush of a waterfall is in your ears on eighteen, which skirts 100 yards of lake and plays briskly downwind.

Shooting enthusiasts enjoy the only resort sporting clay range in the islands, with equipment and instruction for trap, skeet, compact sport-

ing, and sporting clay shooting. An elaborate, professional archery range attracts all ages. Jet lag recovery massage and deep tissue sports massage are popular in the spa, which even offers children's massages and poolside chair massage.

Guests rest from the day's activities in rooms outfitted with window seats and four-poster beds, and decorated with provincial-print fabrics and locally created artwork depicting Hawaiian flora and history. Private balconies and patios look onto the gardens and over the treetops.

The Koele Collection

On display throughout the lodge, the collection of art, crafts, antiques, and artifacts is a wonder. Many of the pieces are museum quality—some were commissioned from Lanai artists. Of particular note are the Tibetan horses, Chinese altar tables and ceremonial weapons; armoires, chests, and chairs from the eighteenth and nineteenth centuries; and traditional Hawaiian quilted pillows. Local artisans have painted intricate details on the door surrounds, the ceilings, and the floors.

The Great Hall is filled with interesting accessories, including a nineteenth-century Chinese enamel figure, Burmese candlesticks, an Islamic trunk, Thai rain drums, and a seven-panel screen painted with tumbling acrobats. The subtly colored rugs and carpets were inspired by Tibetan symbols, and Hawaiian fruits and flowers. Floors are of exotic woods such as chocolate heart eucalyptus. Hand-painted ceilings and walls depict local flora, faux woven cane, Hawaiian and European themes, and a reproduction of Captain Cook's 1779 map of the Sandwich Isles.

Watercolor botanical and animal paintings are in every hallway, and each guest-room door is adorned with a miniature painting of a Lanai flower. A booklet locating and describing the collection is available.

The Lodge at Koele
P.O. Box 630310
Lanai City, HI 96763
Phone: (808) 565–7300, reservations (800) 321–4666
Fax: (808) 565–4561
Web site: www.lanai-resorts.com
General Manager: Paul Horner
Accommodations: 106 rooms with four-poster beds, window seats, wicker furnishings, luxurious country-style fabrics, private balconies, and spacious baths. Each building has a living room and hallways lined with original art and historic artifacts.
Meals: Formal dining in the main house with a view of the grounds. Breakfast and casual meals on the terrace; lunch on the deck at the Koele Clubhouse.
Facilities: Archery range and lessons; equestrian stables with Western and English lessons, carriage tours, and private riding; elaborate eighteen-hole putting course; croquet; lawn bowling; mountain bikes; tennis courts; sporting clays.
Services and Special Programs: Shuttle to Manele Bay Hotel for restaurants, golf, use of the beach and watersports, the spa, and all guest facilities; yoga classes and instruction in all the sports available at the lodge; guided hikes and horseback rides; Pilialoha Children's Program for ages 5–17, with hikes, astronomy, beach safaris, and games; visiting artist program with filmmakers, musicians, chefs, and visual artists.
Rates: $$$–$$$$
Golf Packages: Tee Time package includes deluxe room for three nights, unlimited golf, $50 gift credit, and gifts. $1,503–$2,121 per couple.
Getting There: Aloha Airlines, Hawaiian Air, and Pacific Wings fly into the small Lanai Airport; transport to the two resort hotels is complimentary. There's a day trip ferry from Lahaina, Maui.
What's Nearby: Four-wheel driving, mountain biking, horseback riding, and hiking on 100 miles of dirt roads and on footpaths in the highlands; hunting for wild pig and feral goats; sunning at the beach and water sports at Manele Bay; gallery hopping in the tiny village of Lanai City.

THE MANELE BAY HOTEL
Lanai City, Hawaii

The privately owned, small island of Lanai, just 13 miles wide and 18 miles long, is unique among the Hawaiian Islands for a lack of development and wild, deserted highlands. Two very different resorts, and two very different golf courses—one upcountry, one at the shoreline—are all you will find on Lanai, plus a charming, little town that once housed pineapple plantation workers.

The Manele Bay Hotel, located on the edge of deep-blue Manele Bay, where whales and spinner dolphins are often seen playing, has the look of a tile-roofed villa on the Mediterranean—at least on the outside. An exotic palace awaits indoors—glazed marble floors, Chinese ceramic dogs, carved elephant tusks, vibrant rugs, exotic fabrics, Fijian cannibal forks, and spectacular, painted murals depicting historic events in Hawaii and Asia. The Great Room, open-air restaurants, lounge, and library are museum-like, filled with Asian antiques and artifacts.

Joined by breezeways and flower-draped trellises and bridges, two-story wings of guest rooms are set within lush, terraced gardens with waterfalls and lily ponds, fragrant with jasmine and gardenia. Light-filled and breezy with openings to private patios or balconies, nearly every room has a sea view. A recent, multimillion dollar makeover of the accommodations has raised the standard of comfort and luxury.

Often 15 degrees or more warmer in temperature than its sister golf course in the highlands, the Challenge at Manele seems to ride steep, volcanic hillsides and high cliffs above the sea. Every hole has wide ocean views and ocean breezes—there is a reason why the flags are wind socks. Jack Nicklaus fiercely protects the greens on his courses. In this case, well-guarded greens are an understatement. Approaches are narrow, and legions of high-sided, pink sand

bunkers closely encircle most greens. Five choices of tees save the day for the high handicapper, who may be taken aback by seriously sloping fairways, blind tee shots, and carries over gullies and the ocean. At the top of the course on five, views of Maui, Kahoolawe, and spouting whales are distractions from the second shot, which drops 60 feet. The dogleg left on sixteen drops 100 feet from tee to green onto a clifftop. Seventeen is famous for a 200-foot carry over crashing surf from the black tees. Your second shot is downhill to a cliffside, kidney-shaped green defended by a large mound and a front bunker.

Some of the most perfectly maintained in the islands, the greens and fairways are bounded by native shrubs and lava rock—no fancy landscaping here to compete with the jawdropping vistas. In years to come, the wild look of the place will be tempered by new fairwayside homes and condominiums.

After golf, stop in at the oceanfront clubhouse restaurant to see the vibrantly painted undersea murals and have some fresh ahi or spicy grilled prawns.

Snorkeling, tidepool exploration, and swimming are popular at Hulopo'e Beach, just below the hotel. Large pods of dolphins are common and can be seen close to shore all year. A catamaran takes guests on snorkeling, sailing, and scuba-diving day trips. At day's end, sunset cocktails in the open-air Hale Aheahe lounge is idyllic before dinner at open-air restaurants with equally wonderful views.

Fly to Lanai

Visitors wishing to spend a whole or a half day golfing can arrange for a small plane flight with Paragon Air, Inc. (800–428–1231) or AirLinks (808–871–PLAY). Arrangements also include ground transportation and prearranged tee times on Lanai and on the other Hawaiian Islands. Golfers staying on the island of Maui can also take the early morning passenger ferry to Lanai for a round of golf, departing in the late afternoon (808–661–3756).

The Manele Bay Hotel
P.O. Box 630310
Lanai City, Hawaii 96763
Phone: (808) 565–7700, reservations (800) 321–4666
Fax: (808) 565–2483
Web site: www.lanai-resorts.com
General Manager: Mark Vinsko
Accommodations: 250 spacious rooms and suites in garden settings, most with ocean views. Decor is a sophisticated, tropical mix of light woods and fine fabrics, blooming plants, original floral artwork and Asian artifacts, and spacious bathrooms with huge tubs. British-style butler service is available.
Meals: Sashimi, Hawaiian bouillabaisse, luau for two, and more island cuisine at Hulopo'e Court restaurant on the seaview terrace. In a formal Monarchy setting, French Mediterranean and Asian cuisine in the intimate Ihilani dining room. Salads and fresh fish at the clubhouse.
Facilities: Six plexi-paved tennis courts, with daily clinics and professional lessons; health and beauty spa and salon with traditional and Hawaiian treatments; beautiful swimming pool terrace with cabanas; a curve of sandy beach with water-sports equipment available; shuttle to the Lodge at Koele for restaurants, golf, and use of all guest facilities.
Services and Special Programs: Pilialoha children's activities for ages 5–17 including art, swimming, and beach play; scuba and yoga classes; instruction in all the sports available at the resort; visiting artist program with filmmakers, musicians, chefs, and visual artists.
Rates: $$$–$$$$
Golf Packages: Tee Time package includes deluxe room for three nights, unlimited golf, $50 gift credit, and gifts. $1,545–$2,190 per couple.
Getting There: Aloha Airlines, Hawaiian Air, and Pacific Wings fly into small Lanai Airport; transport to the two resort hotels is complimentary. Passenger ferry from Lahaina, Maui.
What's Nearby: Deep sea fishing; jeep and limousine safaris; whale watching; scuba and snorkeling cruises; daytripping to Lahaina by ferry; shuttle to the Lodge at Koele for hiking, horseback riding, golf, and restaurants.

MAUNA KEA BEACH HOTEL

Kohala Coast, Hawaii

Walk out of the lobby of Mauna Kea Hotel and find yourself on the first tee of the Robert Trent Jones Sr. course. On the first hole and on most of the rest, be prepared to club up one and sometimes two clubs for the dramatically elevated greens. Be sure to bring your camera for dazzling ocean vistas from the front nine. On the third hole from the back tee, drink in the sound of crashing surf and look from the clifftop to see colorful fish in the tidepools. Then follow your drive all the way through to make the nearly 200-yard carry over the water to a huge green guarded by seven bunkers. Jones designed a wide variety of exciting features into this classic Hawaiian track, opened in 1964. It is still as gorgeous and as tough as when both Palmer and Nicklaus set the back nine record with 31s.

Hundreds of coconut palms, mature wili-wili trees, monkey pods, and banyans create a postcard setting. On the front nine, wide fairways and wide approaches are countered by super-fast greens and the ubiquitous elevated tees and greens. By nine, you will be on the top of the world, looking across miles of ocean and a string of volcanic cinder cones in the distance. Fasten your seat belt as fairways turn into hills and dales, swales and gullies, and you encounter even more of those outrageously high tees and greens. Eleven drops from the tee more than 100 feet toward the water to a green guarded by four steep bunkers. Trade winds keep the large greens dry and slick. Four tees make the course playable for (nearly) everyone, even though it's 7,114 yards and a formidable 73.6/143 rating from the tips.

Built by Laurance Rockefeller in the mid-1960s as the first major hotel on the Kohala Coast, Mauna Kea set the standard for luxury resorts throughout the islands for decades. The tropical setting is unequaled. Located on a powdery-white, palm-fringed crescent of sand on Kauna'oa Bay, where waters are calm—perfect for good swimming, snorkeling, and kayaking. The Travel Channel called it "America's Best Beach," while *Gourmet* magazine named it the "World's Top Beach." At night torches light the footpaths and floodlights illuminate shallow coves where giant manta rays glide. A narrow trail wanders along the wild shoreline and through lava fields about a mile to Hapuna Beach, another of the most beautiful beaches on the Pacific Rim.

Nearly half of the hotel staff has been here over a decade, and more than two dozen were here when the hotel opened. Making Mauna Kea world famous for island hospitality, they continue a tradition of exceptional personal service and discretion.

Rooms are generally small and nicely done up with teak paneling, furnishings, and built-ins. Original Hawaiian floral prints are the theme for subtle, tropical color schemes in the fine fabrics. Guests in ocean-view rooms loll on their private balconies over the idyllic beachfront or sway on hammocks between the coconut palms, watching the sun set.

The fabulous Rockefeller collection of Asian, African, and Pacific Islands art and artifacts (more than one thousand pieces), is displayed in the public areas. The collection includes golden buddhas, masks from New Guinea, Maori war canoes, ceremonial drums, Hawaiian tapa cloth and quilts, Japanese screens, and bronze guardian dogs from Thailand. Ask for a free booklet, and spend an hour or so following the self-guided art tour.

Sister Resort

Owned by the same company, the Hapuna Beach Prince Hotel and its wonderful Palmer-Seay–designed golf course opened in 1992, is just next-door to the Mauna Kea. With an ocean view from every hole, the course rises from the shoreline to 700 feet. This is a links-style, target golfing experience in a lush, tropical landscape maintained as wildlife habitat for birds, including the rare Pu'eo, or Hawaiian owl. Your main challenge here is to get off the tee over forced carries to exceedingly narrow landing zones. Then you have it made, with generous approaches and greens.

Guests at one hotel are treated as honored guests at the other and are welcome at all of the restaurants, lounges, swimming pools, beaches, golf courses, and spa; a shuttle makes the five-minute trip back and forth between the resorts and golf courses.

A huge central lobby, terraced restaurants, and public spaces are open to the sea view and breezes. The sprawling hotel complex of 350 rooms and suites is dazzling white against the blue waters and the blooming, landscaped grounds (800–880-3112).

Hapuna Beach has been named the number one beach in the country for its scenic beauty and superlative sand and swimming conditions.

Mauna Kea Beach Hotel
62-100 Mauna Kea Beach Drive
Kohala Coast, HI 96743
Phone: (808) 882-7222, reservations (800) 882-6060
Fax: (808) 880-3112
Web site: www.maunakeabeachhotel.com
General Manager: Charles Park
Accommodations: 310 rooms, suites, and bungalows, each with private balconies or lanais, and separate dressing areas. Most have sea views—some look onto the mountains. Plantation-style shutters open to sea breezes on both sides of the rooms, creating a tropical atmosphere.
Meals: Asian and Continental cuisine, curries, and Thai delicacies at the exotic Batik restaurant. Breakfast buffet and casual meals in the oceanfront Pavilion—Sunday brunch here is legendary; luau on Tuesday night; clambake seafood buffet on Saturday; light meals and snacks at the beach bar/cafe.
Facilities: Swimming pool terrace; kayaks and water-sports equipment at the beach; new business center; thirteen plexi-pave tennis courts with video training, pro shop, ball machine, and matching. At the sister hotel, a large pool complex, full spa facilities, the Paul Brown Salon, and a stunning beach.
Services and Special Programs: Scuba classes in the swimming pool. Daily golf clinics and demonstrations, private lessons, and PGA golf schools. Oriental medicine, acupuncture, and acupressure, plus traditional and Hawaiian beauty and health treatments. All day Keiki Club for ages 5–12, with beach and pool play, art, Hawaiian crafts, games, and movies. Horseback riding at the hotel's stables on Parker Ranch.
Rates: $$$
Golf Packages: Deluxe room and unlimited golf. $449–$615 per night for two, double occupancy.
Getting There: Major airlines serve Kona International Airport, a thirty-minute drive away. Helicopter transport can be arranged.
What's Nearby: The concierge will book scuba, snorkel, kayak, helicopter, sunset sail, and whale-watching expeditions. Day trips to the black-sand beach, to Kailua-Kona for shopping, and four-wheel driving in the Waipio Valley.

MAUNA LANI BAY HOTEL

Kohala Coast, Hawaii

A walking path meanders among ancient, spring-fed fish ponds and shallow lagoons at the edge of the wide curve of Makaiwa Bay on the Kohala Coast. Palms and low-lying kiawe trees shade sunbathers on four perfect beaches. Protected from the surf by coral and lava reefs, the azure bay waters are calm, just right for swimming. Close to the bay, the Mauna Lani is a secluded oasis that seems a world away from tourist-packed Kailua-Kona, enclosed in an enchanted garden of blooming Hawaiian flowers and trees and freshened by streams alive with tropical fish.

As hidden floodlights blink on to illuminate the rolling waves after dark, guests in oceanfront rooms in the understated, international-style hotel linger on their private balconies, in blue cabanas, and on hammocks between the palms. Gleaming, exotic woods are used throughout the spacious accommodations, which are enhanced by subtle, tropical-print fabrics and original art. Leaving glitz and noise to more touristy properties, the focus at Mauna Lani is on the magnificent shoreline and floral setting, and discrete, gracious personal attention—a sense of quiet seclusion prevails. Red-headed birds flutter in the lush greenery of the six-story atrium lobby, where, in the evenings, hula dancers and musicians entertain by the waterfall.

There is a historic cottage museum to explore, paddle boats and swimming at the beach club, and golf on the two Francis H. I'i Brown courses—one inland, one oceanfront. Quiet, solar-powered carts cruise the wide fairways on the South Course, site of the Senior Skins Game. With few bunkers, it looks easier than it is. Menacing black lava outcroppings provide plenty of hazards, along with sticky, Velcro-like kukuya grass on the shoulders. The jagged lava eats balls, although lucky players often get great bounces off the rocks. The greens are huge. A lake begins the water hazards on the fifth hole and the ocean comes into view on the seventh. On fifteen, you shoot over the roiling sea to a large landing zone backed by a stunning view of the coastline and the West Maui Mountains.

Expect to add a couple of strokes on the inland North Course, particularly on the seventeenth, a par-3 with the green set in a lava pit 50 feet deep. Wild goats frequent the track, nipping the turf and become living, moving hazards.

Unique to the resort is its spa and sports center. Tucked away in a leafy bower are beautiful tennis courts, a lap pool, and a spacious venue for exercise classes and workout equipment. Hidden behind the elegant, new Asian-Pacific-style "Fire and Ice" spa is a tiny village of thatched *hales* (huts). Each *hale* is completely private and silent, except for birdsong, and surrounded by lava rock and a riot of aromatic greenery. This is the "Fragrance Garden" where guests and couples indulge in "Cocanilla Experience," "Ginger Honey" massages, and other spa treatments while enjoying the outdoor lava rock sauna, outdoor "rainfall" showers, and the scent of ginger, pikake, and gardenia.

Renowned in Hawaii for contemporary Asian and Pacific Islands cuisine, the palm-shaded deck of the Canoe House is cantilevered out over the sea. In the Honu Bar, it's sushi (the California handroll with fresh crab is a favorite), pool tables, board games, televised sports, and dancing to live music. Brilliant tangs, stingrays, green sea turtles, and other sea creatures frolic in the stream alongside the outdoor dining patio of the Gallery. The mahogany-paneled, open-air clubhouse restaurant is a good spot for fresh ono sandwiches.

Playing the Hawaiian Trade Winds

By Ron Castillo, Jr., P.G.A., Director of Golf, Hapuna Golf Club, Island of Hawaii

- **When playing in the wind, keep it simple. Wayward drives too often come from overcorrecting or overcompensating for a strong crosswind or headwind. Try not to fight the conditions, rather play a shot that rides the wind. For example, on a strong crosswind from right to left, aim right of the fairway and surf the wind back to the center of the fairway. Understand that the ball will roll more once it hits the ground, so allow for more roll.**

- **Playing directly into the wind, try not to hit the super-low shot. Concentrate on hitting the ball solidly, rather than swinging extra hard. Focus on making a slow, unhurried backswing and a smooth transition back to the ball on the downswing.**

- **Putting may be the most difficult aspect of playing golf in the wind. Try widening your stance; keep your head steady and over the ball. Time your stroke between the gusts of wind.**

- **Most important, par is just a number! When it is windy, some holes will play difficult and some holes downwind will make you feel like Tiger Woods. Don't worry if the best score you can make is a six on a par 3. You will have an equal amount of holes that play downwind. The downwind holes are where you can pick up a couple of lost strokes.**

Mauna Lani Bay Hotel
68-1400 Mauna Lani Drive
Kohala Coast, HI 96743
Phone: (808) 885–6622, reservations (800) 367–2323
Web site: www.maunalani.com
General Manager: Kurt Matsumoto
Accommodations: 350 spacious, airy, plantation-style rooms with tranquil island decor, nearly all with fabulous ocean views. 4,000-square-foot bungalows have private swimming pools, whirlpools, steam showers, two master bedrooms, plush silk fabrics, and butler service. 29 condominium units in garden settings near waterfront are also managed by the hotel.
Meals: Sophisticated Asian and Pacific cuisine at the elegant Canoe House; an Italian-Mediterranean menu at the Bay Terrace; fresh fish and pizza at the Ocean Grill; American food and buffets at the Gallery Restaurant.
Facilities: Lomilomi massage, Cocanilla wraps, and more Hawaiian-style and traditional treatments at the new spa; ten plexi-paved tennis courts and pro shop; a museum of Hawaiian history; beach club with water toys.
Services and Special Programs: Golf training and conditioning; free golf clinics; yoga, aerobics, and hula. Camp Mauna Lani for ages 5–12, with fishing, Hawaiian crafts, historical tours, and special menus; junior sports camps for ages 7–16. Kids golf free in the summer. Annual multiday "Cuisine of the Sun" culinary event with noted chefs, seminars, and wine tastings. On-staff historian conducts guided tours.
Rates: $$$–$$$$
Golf Packages: Deluxe guest room, one round of golf per person, golf services, and gift. $445–$565 per couple, per night (minimum of three nights).
Getting There: A twenty-minute drive north of Kona International Airport; hotel provides greeter and shuttle transport.
What's Nearby: The hotel will arrange scuba diving, sailing, fishing and snorkeling, bicycling, and sunset cruises.

PRINCEVILLE RESORT

Princeville, Kauai, Hawaii

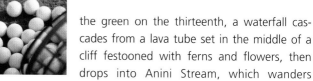

Countless waterfalls rush through the rainforest and down the steep mountainsides on the north coast of Kauai, the Garden Island. Princeville Resort sprawls on a terraced cliff above Hanalei Bay, below the spectacular peak of Bali Hai. The film, *South Pacific,* was shot in this gorgeous setting of velvet green mountains and sugar-white beaches.

Located in three buildings situated like a giant stairway down Pu'u Poa Ridge, guest rooms and restaurants are anchored at the bottom by the oceanfront, infinity edge swimming pool, which appears to merge with the azure sea. Two-story-tall windows in the stunning lobby show off the breathtaking Shangri-la-like panorama across the water. Indoor waterfalls and rivulets meander through the public spaces, green and gorgeous with trees and flowers, and decorated with lacy ironwork, Hawaiian art, and historic artifacts.

The recently redecorated guest rooms are lavish, private, tropical retreats with original artwork; vibrant colors of Hawaiian flora against sand-colored, silken fabrics, eighteenth- and nineteenth-century antiques and reproduction furnishings; and oversized tubs and gold-plated fixtures in the green marble baths. Unique windows can be turned from marvelous sea views to opaque for privacy.

Integrated into a glorious rainforest located on rolling tableland and along the oceanfront are forty-five holes of golf designed by Robert Trent Jones Jr. Awarded the title of number one course in Hawaii by *Golf Digest,* the Prince Course is waterfalls and streams, jungly ravines, and thousands of trees and blooming shrubs—paradise with a formidable 75.3/145 rating and slope earned by forced carries, stiff trade winds, and a clever dearth of bailout areas. Fairways careen downhill and over gorges, as on the seventh, which reminds golfers of the famous sixteenth at Cypress Point. With the Pacific all along the left, a 180-yard carry against the wind heads toward waves breaking on the reef off Anini Beach. Behind

the green on the thirteenth, a waterfall cascades from a lava tube set in the middle of a cliff festooned with ferns and flowers, then drops into Anini Stream, which wanders around the green and dissects the fairway landing zone, 200 yards from the back tees.

The three nines of the Makai resort course—the Lakes, the Ocean, and the Woods—range from the seaside to the hillsides, with generous fairways and distracting views. An Audubon Cooperative Sanctuary, the Makai is habitat for the endangered 'alaie and 'ae'o birds. Rock-garden-style bunkers encroach pine-bordered fairways on the Woods.

On the Ocean's seventh hole, a 200-yard tee shot is required over the surf to a green fronted by a cliff, in sight of miles of shoreline. Take extra clubs for steady trade winds on the Lakes' four, toward the Kilauea Lighthouse. And, on the Lakes' nine, be ready for successive shots over two large lakes to the green.

The Princeville practice facility is one of the largest and most elaborate in the islands, with huge putting and chipping greens, and three separate teeing venues allowing for different wind direction. Named number one in Hawaii by *Golf Digest,* the clubhouse is multifaceted, with grand locker rooms, a health club and spa, and a nice restaurant and lounge with dazzling mountain and sea views. A Hawaiian Salt Glow and a sports massage in the spa are the perfect ending to a day of golf.

As the sun sets behind Mount Makana and its fiery rays beam into the Living Room cocktail lounge, the hula is performed to passionate drumming and chanting—a moving, never-to-be-forgotten experience for guests. Luaus with Polynesian-style entertainment are held on the beach three nights a week. Romantic, private, candle- and torch-lit dining can be arranged on the beach, poolside, and in the gardens.

On Kauai's lush north shore, the beach at Anini is ideal for windsurfing and the resort offers lessons and

Princeville Resort

5520 Ka Haku Road
Princeville, Kauai, HI 96722
Phone: (808) 826–9644, reservations (800) 826–4400
Fax: (808) 826–1166
Web site: www.princeville.com
General Manager: Kelly Hoen
Accommodations: 252 rooms and larger suites with ocean, bay, or mountain views, averaging 547 square feet; furnished with deluxe, understated, tropical-European interiors, fine linens, original artwork and antiques, and over-size tubs.
Meals: Friday buffets and Sunday brunch at the Hanalei Cafe are legendary; daily menu is Asian-Pacific with open-air dining and views of Bali Hai. Cuisine from northern Italy at the elegant La Casata; decor is warm with terra-cotta floors and trompe l'oeil paintings.
Facilities: Spa with exercise venue, personal training, aerobic dance floor, 25-meter lap pool, and a wide variety of health and beauty treatments; six plexi-pave tennis courts, pro shop, and teaching staff; upscale boutiques at the Princeville Shopping Center.
Services and Special Programs: Keiki Aloha program for ages 5–12, with Hawaiian music, dance, and crafts; games, movies, and storytelling. Visiting artisans program includes hula, quilt making, weaving, carving, painting, and more.
Rates: $$$–$$$$
Golf Packages: Princeville Unlimited Golf Package includes one night in an Ocean View or Prince Junior Suite, full buffet breakfast, and golf 'til you drop. $415–$515 for two, double occupancy.
Getting There: 32 miles from Lihue Airport, served by inter-island airlines and by United Airlines from the mainland; a few minutes from Princeville Airport, where commuter flights and private aircraft are accommodated.
What's Nearby: Cruising, kayaking, and helicopter tours along the famed Na Pali Coast; horseback riding; mountain biking in Waimea Canyon; hiking on the Kalalau Trail; and deep-sea fishing. Go sightseeing in the charming town of Hanalei and visit the National Wildlife Sanctuary at Kilauea.

rentals. Along the coast of Haena, surfers from around the world congregate for the big waves. The concierge will arrange royak (a cross between a kayak and a canoe) excursions in the lush Hanalei River Valley, and cruising, sailing, and helicopter tours along the famed Na Pali Coast, where spectacular green valleys cut through folds in the mountains and open out to the sea.

Stopover in Honolulu

The only Waikiki hotel with its own golf course, the Hawaii Prince Hotel Waikiki and Golf Club shuttles guests to the Hawaii Prince Golf Club at Ewa, about a half hour away. Waianae and Koolau Mountains are the dramatic backdrop for Palmer-Seay's relatively flat twenty-seven holes overlooking the lively Ala Wai Yacht Harbor. Ten lakes, ninety bunkers, and some of the fastest putting surfaces in the islands make for exciting rounds of golf. The A Course and C Course combination yields a formidable 74.4/134 rating and slope. You can walk the track, a pleasant experience at twilight when rare and endangered Hawaiian birds alight in the trees. The plantation-style clubhouse has a fine restaurant (www.princeresortshawaii.com).

THE COEUR D'ALENE RESORT
Coeur d'Alene, Idaho

In northern Idaho on the shores of Lake Coeur d'Alene stands a sleek, eighteen-story hotel—not so genteel as Greenbrier and not as quaint as St. Andrews. Nonetheless, it is a resort beloved by those who seek a pampered Rocky Mountain golfing experience.

You will seldom catch sight of others on the Coeur d'Alene track due to the unique, contoured Scott Miller design that subtly shields each foursome from the next. On what *Golf Magazine* calls "the best maintained course in America," golfers enjoy four distinct and beautiful environments, blissfully free of residential development: the lakeshore, a forested ridge, gently rolling woodlands, and the banks of a rushing trout stream, Fernan Creek.

The parklike front nine is forgiving, with fairways slanted to corral runaway drives. Rising into the hills, the back nine is abloom in spring and summer with thousands of azaleas and native shrubs under a canopy of tall Douglas firs. (The most luxurious rest rooms in golfdom are hidden underground beneath the turf and trees of holes seven and ten.) The course is famous for the world's first floating island green on the fearsome par-3 fourteenth. A gimmick, and great fun, the 15,000-square-foot target, comprising pine trees, bunkers, beds of red geraniums, petunias, and a big green, is moved to a different anchoring every day about 100 to 175 yards offshore. Club up one, to account for breezes off the lake. A photographer will await your group to record the event.

A mahogany speedboat ferries golfers to the first tee, an invigorating seven-minute cruise across the lake. Each foursome is accompanied by a forecaddy who measures distances with a laser-gun and performs other thoughtful tasks, such as cleaning balls, raking bunkers, and offering local knowledge. If, in spite of the personal support, scores are high and shoulders ache, repair to the driving range for a complimentary upper-body massage. At the over-the-water practice range, balls float on the lake; and there are lessons, clinics, and frequent demo-days.

Full-body sports massage is available at the Resort

Eurospa, where wildflower facials and medicinal muds are among the signature treatments.

Guests are drawn to the waterfront and the 372-slip marina for a variety of activities, from strolling the world's longest floating boardwalk (three-quarters of a mile) to sight-seeing cruises, fishing, sailing, jet skiing, and parasailing. Horseback riding, hiking, and mountain biking trails are abundant. Live entertainment and music on the Floating Stage lights up summer evenings under the stars. The "Fun Fleet" of lake cruisers offers sunset dinner and Sunday brunch tours on the lake.

A year-round destination, the resort is headquarters for cross-country and downhill skiing at Schweitzer Mountain and Silver Mountains; and for ice skating, sleigh rides, and snowmobiling.

From late November to New Year's Day, brisk nights are warmed by the annual "Fantasy In Lights," when more than a million lights blaze in the biggest light show in America. Over two hundred displays sparkle along the boardwalk, at Santa's North Pole Workshop, and around the resort.

Apple Island

Southwest of Coeur d'Alene floats another island green, this one shaped like a Washington delicious apple. Nine elevated tees give every player a chance to hit 90 to 180 yards over the water and the leaf-shaped bunker onto a silky-smooth green; regardless of flag placement, aim for the center to avoid sliding off the diabolically shaped edge of the island.

Rated one of the top ten public courses in the state, the Apple Tree Golf Course in Yakima, Washington, was built in an apple orchard. In the springtime, hundreds of the trees burst into clouds of white blossoms. Come late summer, apples are ready to pick for a fairway snack. Sixty pure white bunkers and six lakes create enough provocation to merit a 124 slope rating from the middle tees (509–966–5877).

The Coeur d'Alene Resort
On the Lake, 115 South Second Street
Coeur d'Alene, ID 83816–1941
Phone: (208) 765–4000, reservations (800) 688–5253
Fax: (208) 664–7276
Web site: www.cdaresort.com
General Manager: Stephen T. Wilson
Accommodations: 337 rooms and suites, many with lakefront patios or balconies; lake, city or mountain views; best rooms are above the seventh floor. Premier suites are extra large with sunken living area, separate dressing and bath areas, and private balcony. Recently renovated rooms feature contemporary Italian furnishings, mirrors, and glass.
Meals: With glorious lake views, Beverly's serves Northwest cuisine, including such specialties as Atlantic salmon, Dungeness crab, red trout, and huckleberry pie (ask for a comfy booth or a window table). Families favor sunset dinners and monumental Sunday brunches at Dockside, a casual dining room with water and mountain views, and featuring an 18-foot-long salad bar. At Tito Macaroni's, kids make their own pizzas while parents dig into pasta and steak. The Beachhouse on Silver Beach is famous for cedar-plank roasted seafood and barbecued ribs.
Facilities: Four tennis courts; outdoor and indoor swimming pools; racquetball; fitness center; bowling; Par-T Golf; private beach. Among signature treatments at the Eurospa are wildflower facials, medicinal muds, and sports massage. Guests relax in the lakeside meditation room and the junior-Olympic pool. Boutiques and galleries are within the resort; antiques shops nearby.
Services and Special Programs: Games and crafts, swimming, outdoor play, movies, and meals at Very Important Kid Camps for ages 4–14.
Rates: $$$–$$$$
Golf Packages: Gold Medal Golf Package includes one night deluxe accommodations, golf, dinner, breakfast, and services of Concierge Club. $749–$999 for two, double occupancy.
Getting There: Transportation available to Spokane International Airport, served by major airlines and a forty-five-minute drive away. Private aircraft arrive at Coeur d'Alene Airport, 15 miles away.
What's Nearby: Take a 3-mile nature hike around the peninsula, or trod the Route of the Hiawatha on 13 miles of historic railbed, tunnels, and trestles. Ride the Silver Mountain Gondola up and bike back down. Wild rides at Silverwood, the northwest's largest theme park. Fly-fishing and white-water rafting in pristine mountain rivers.

GRAND TRAVERSE RESORT AND SPA

Traverse City, Michigan

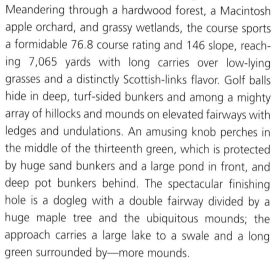

Seen from the top floors of the high-rise hotel, the morning sun glints on Lake Michigan and streaks across the eighteenth hole on The Bear, one of Jack Nicklaus's most intriguing tracks. Meandering through a hardwood forest, a Macintosh apple orchard, and grassy wetlands, the course sports a formidable 76.8 course rating and 146 slope, reaching 7,065 yards with long carries over low-lying grasses and a distinctly Scottish-links flavor. Golf balls hide in deep, turf-sided bunkers and among a mighty array of hillocks and mounds on elevated fairways with ledges and undulations. An amusing knob perches in the middle of the thirteenth green, which is protected by huge sand bunkers and a large pond in front, and deep pot bunkers behind. The spectacular finishing hole is a dogleg with a double fairway divided by a huge maple tree and the ubiquitous mounds; the approach carries a large lake to a swale and a long green surrounded by—more mounds.

Muskrats play on the banks of the lakes, ponds, and streams, sharing their habitat with ducks and other wild birds, including swans, herons, and red-winged blackbirds—even deer and the occasional fox can be seen. Bluebird and purple martin houses were installed as part of Audubon certification, as were thick buffers of native grasses, cattails, and reeds.

The original resort course, Spruce Run, is a relaxing counterpoint to Nicklaus's demanding design. Gary Player's Wolverine is equally as scenic and slightly less intimidating than the bite of The Bear, with wide open fairways tilted toward the center—the better to corral hooks and slices—and zippy greens. Backing the first tee boxes and the eighteenth green is a magnificent grove of 100-foot-tall, deciduous trees. Fall burnishes the maples, oaks, poplars, birches, and beeches, turning the golf courses and the surrounding forested hills into molten gold and flaming red. Country roads dotted with old barns make pleasant walking and biking routes.

A premier golf academy, the Jim McLean Golf School offers indoor/outdoor hitting bays, video and computer analysis, and programs taught by some of the Top 100 PGA teaching pros in the country. A top notch junior tennis program attracts hundreds of little swingers in the summertime, when there is daylight sixteen hours a day.

On the shores of East Grand Traverse Bay, the resort is the largest full-service, year-round destination resort in the Midwest, and anchors a popular northern Michigan golf region with fifty-four holes of tournament-level golf.

Northern Michigan cuisine is interpreted with panache in the sky-high Trillium restaurant, where views of sunsets over the lake are legendary. Menus reflect the bounty of the local region: cherries (this is the nation's cherry capital), stone fruits, and apples, and wild game and beef. On the award-winning wine list are hard-to-get California labels and some surprisingly good Michigan wines, including Black Star Farms.

Guests hop the hotel shuttle to the lakeside for sunning, boating, and jet skiing at the Shores Beach Club. Bonfires and special live entertainment lure them back to the beach on summer evenings. Families favor the resort's lakeside condominium complex in a forest glade, where shady walking paths wind beside a creek. Fly-fishing is popular, as is mountain biking and hiking. Stop in at the Orvis shop in the lobby to sign up for a fly-fishing lesson with an on-site guide.

A small town of fancifully painted Victorian mansions, Traverse City is chockful of quaint shops and galleries. In fall visitors flock to the region for several weeks of bright color. And when snow blankets The Bear, Nordic skiing and snowmobile trails lead right from the hotel into the countryside and the adjacent State Forest. The resort opens two ice-skating rinks and keeps guests busy in the gigantic spa and indoor recreation complex, complete with tennis courts and swimming pools, aerobics classes, and the comforts of a

new spa facility, where a "Cherry Essence Massage" or the "Cherry Honey Glow" are a golfer's sweet reward.

Other Places to Play

Thirty miles north of Traverse City, take the chair lift up to see a quartet of golf courses at Shanty Creek Resort (800–678–4111). The newest, Cedar River, is a beauty by Tom Weiskopf. Palmer and Seay laid out The Legend in the late 1970s.

With 153 holes at the northern tip of the state, Boyne USA is a major golf destination, ninety minutes north of Traverse City (800–462–6963). A mile-long cart ride brings you to the first tee of the Monument on Boyne Mountain, where the "Sam Snead" hole finishes with a beautiful island green. Three nines at Bar Harbor Golf Club are laid above Lake Michigan along bluffs and dunes, among hardwood forests, ponds, and waterfalls. Robert Trent Jones Sr. created a blockbuster at Treetops Links, where the signature hole drops 120 feet over the Pigeon River Valley.

Grand Traverse Resort and Spa
100 Grand Traverse Village Boulevard
Acme, MI 49610
Phone: (231) 938–2100, reservations (800) 748–0303
Fax: (231) 938–2399
Web site: www. grandtraverseresort.com
General Manager: Paul McCormick
Accommodations: 424 spacious rooms and suites with lake, golf course or garden views; oversize whirlpool tubs; bathroom TVs; deluxe rooms in the tower. 236 lakeside condos have one, two, or three bedrooms.
Meals: Fine dining with lake views on the sixteenth floor at Trillium restaurant; hearty meals in the Grille at the golf clubhouse; and a casual cafe off the lobby. Guests dance to live music in the Trillium nightclub.
Facilities: Private beach; indoor/outdoor swimming pools; game arcade; water sports; cross-country ski trails, downhill skiing, and snowboarding nearby; snowshoeing; horse-drawn sleigh rides; ice-skating; biking and hiking trails; upscale lobby shops. The 100,000-square-foot spa boasts cardio-theater and aerobics studio; thermal therapies; traditional and unique treatments such as the Legends facial for men; and mind/body fitness consulting. Indoor/outdoor tennis courts with full-time pros.
Services and Special Programs: Kids of all ages like Camp Traverse and the Cub House, with field trips, evening parties, and licensed daycare; exercise and yoga classes; Orvis Fly Fishing School, guided stream fishing, and charter boat expeditions.
Rates: $$$–$$$$
Golf and Spa Packages: Three-Night Weekend Package offers deluxe room, golf and breakfast daily, discount on replay and golf clinic, and extras. About $560 per person. Deluxe Spa Package includes deluxe room, daily breakfast, four signature spa treatments, hair styling, fitness classes, and extras. About $600 per person.
Getting There: Major airlines service Traverse City Cherry Capital Airport, 6 miles from the resort. Airport shuttle is free.
What's Nearby: Idyllic countryside drives; farm stands; fall color tours; day cruises to historic Mackinac Island; The Old Mission Peninsula; Interlochen Center for the Arts; casinos; and summer recreation on the lakeshore.

HYATT REGENCY LAKE LAS VEGAS RESORT

Henderson, Nevada

Within thirty minutes of the neon-glitzed, twenty-four-hour playground of the Vegas Strip are seven golf complexes—and forty more courses a few minutes farther away. East of the city, the Jack Nicklaus Signature Course at Reflection Bay Golf Club wraps around the Hyatt Regency and along the northern shore of the resort's private Lake Las Vegas.

Waterfalls lead to the first tee and stream into a pond, setting the scene for target golf in rolling desert terrain, through canyons, across landscaped water features, beaches and arroyos, and along a mile and a half of the lakeshore. One of the West's most spectacular layouts, the parkland-desert course is characterized by Nicklaus's favorite design principles—wide fairways, daunting approaches, and seriously guarded and undulating putting surfaces. The peninsula greens jutting into the lake recall his Cabo de Sol tracks. Huge beach bunkers are cleverly situated in landing zones and fronting greens. On fifteen, a 544-yard par-5, you cross the 75-foot-deep "Grand Canyon" twice. Save some energy for the finishing hole, which is adorned with mid-fairway bunkers and watery hazards on the entire right side and behind the green.

In November Wendy's Three-Tour Challenge brings in stars from the PGA, the Senior PGA, and the LPGA.

Jack and Jim will personally sign your diploma when you graduate from the prestigious Nicklaus/Flick Golf School, based in the state-of-the-art, high-tech Jack Nicklaus Coaching Studio, where multiple camera angles provide personalized videotape analysis. On-course practice follows daily instruction, which culminates in an exciting skills contest with the PGA pro staff. Putting and chipping greens, bunkers, and a double-sided grass-tee driving range are among the best in the state.

At the elegant clubhouse, golfers relax on the terrace of La Chandele, enjoying California and Continental cuisine and an award-winning wine list.

On a terraced hillside above the lake, the Hyatt is a sprawling Mediterranean oasis with Moorish accents—a vibrantly colored, palm-fringed, royal enclosure in the desert. Gondolas glide beneath a covered bridge on a cerulean lagoon. Tall, arched windows and deep loggias, ornamental ironwork, and lush landscaping with hundreds of waving palms create an exotic backdrop for white tents around the stunning swimming pool terraces and white sand beaches.

After desert golf, the pools are refreshing—one with a fifty-yard waterslide and playground, the other an adult affair with private cabanas. Families wishing to avoid the gaming-oriented atmosphere of the city find the Hyatt resort a welcome alternative.

The European-style Casino Baraka, as impressive as the hotel, is flooded with light from two-story windows with views of the lake and surrounding mountains. Compared to the mammoth gaming palaces in the city, this is a small casino, very fresh and appealing, with a romantic, "Casablanca" atmosphere and top-notch, live entertainment in the lounge.

The resort's postcard-perfect North African–Mediterranean setting, with its misty mountain backdrop, was the location for the filming of *America's Sweethearts*, a movie starring Julia Roberts and Billy Crystal. No doubt, they retreated to Spa Moulay for a "Raindrop Massage" (a Native American–inspired treatment using nine essential oils dropped along the spine in a crosswise motion), a "Moroccan Rhassoul Clay Wrap," or the "Harem's Blend" of spices, citrus, and rose petals.

Other Places to Play

October through May are the prime months in the clear, dry, warm desert climate of Las Vegas, home to more than fifty courses. A faux medieval-castle clubhouse sets the scene at Royal Links Golf Club, where Perry Dye created linkslike golf holes inspired by legendary British Open courses such as St. Andrews, Royal Troon, Turnberry, and Carnoustie. These holes are guarded by plenty of those Scottish sod-walled bunkers (888–397–2499). A life-size bronze of Old Tom Morris stands out front, along with a sculpture of the Claret Jug awarded to British Open winners.

Thousands of palm trees, gleaming blue ponds, jet-black coral, and dazzling white, crushed granite beaches—instead of rough— resemble an island in the South Pacific at Bali Hai Golf Club, right on the Vegas strip next to the Mandalay Bay Hotel (888–397–2499).

You can try eighteen of Jack Nicklaus's favorite golf holes from his courses worldwide, at Bear's Best in Summerlin, site of the PGA Invensys Classic. On display at the clubhouse, called Jack's Place, are photos and memorabilia from his unequaled career (702–804–8500).

Pete Dye designed three courses for the Las Vegas Paiute Resort. Nu-Wai Kaiv (Snow Mountain) has elevated tees, pot bunkers, lake and mountain views, and wind-brushed, zippy greens. Tav-Ai Kai (Sun Mountain) features railroad ties and more pot bunkers below the dramatic Sheep Mountains. The newest course, the Wolf, is 7,500 yards of ups-and-downs. Anchored by a huge, luxurious clubhouse and golf school, two more golf courses are on the way at Paiute, as well as a spa, casino, tennis complex, and equestrian center (888–966–2833).

No greenhorns need tee up at the Rees Jones–designed Rio Secco Course at the Rio All Suite Hotel. He laid out 7,332 yards of target golf on rugged desert landscape with forced carries over a dry riverbed, through steep canyons, and along high ridges and mesas overlooking the city skyline (888–396–2483). Tiger Woods's coach, Butch Harmon, headquarters his only U.S.-based golf school here.

Hyatt Regency Lake Las Vegas Resort

101 Montelago Boulevard
Henderson, NV 89011
Phone: (702) 567–1234, reservations (800) 554–9288
Fax: (702) 567–6067
Web site: www.lakelasvegas.hyatt.com

General Manager: Daniel Amato

Accommodations: 496 rooms, including 47 luxurious suites and 10 Casbah units, all with lake or mountain views. Rich desert colors, hand-painted armoires and headboards, arched windows with stunning views.

Meals: Pacific Rim cuisine and sushi above the lake at Japengo, with a presentation kitchen; casual dining alfresco or indoors at Cafe Tajine; sandwiches and salads at Sandsa Bar and Grill.

Facilities: Pedal and electric boats; kayaks; bicycles; full-service Moroccan-themed spa and fitness center; two swimming pools and swimming lagoon; wading pool; waterslide; beaches; fishing; windsurfing.

Services and Special Programs: Supervised play, fishing, stargazing, swimming, meals and educational activities for ages 3–12 at Camp Hyatt.

Rates: $$$

Golf Packages: One night deluxe accommodations, a round of golf and cart, starting at $499 for two players.

Getting There: Major airlines serve McCarran International Airport, a 14-mile drive away. Daily shuttle service to the Las Vegas Strip.

What's Nearby: Helicopter tours to the Grand Canyon; four-wheel-drive and Hummer desert tours; water sports at Lake Mead; tours of Hoover Dam. In Las Vegas the Guggenheim Las Vegas Museum at the Venetian Resort; Speed, The Ride at the NASCAR Cafe in the Sahara Hotel; Wet 'n' Wild water park; the Shark Reef at the Mandalay Bay; Cirque du Soleil performances; Siegfried and Roy shows at the Mirage.

THE OTESAGA

Cooperstown, New York

Sitting in a rocker on the great curve of the verandah overlooking the lake has been a tradition for nearly a century at The Otesaga, a grand, Federal-style hostelry with 30-foot-tall white pillars and a high cupola. The imposing brick and limestone facade, gardens, and grounds front more than 700 feet of beautiful shoreline on Lake Otesaga, the famed "Glimmerglass" of James Fenimore Cooper's stories. Families return every summer to canoe on the lake, to picnic at Lakefront Park, and to watch baseball at Doubleday Field.

A recent and complete restoration added Early American–style carpeting, draperies, and upholsteries, and resurfaced antique mahogany balustrades, paneling, floors, and brass chandeliers. Museum-quality artworks line the walls. When not outdoors enjoying the many recreational venues, guests wander the heart of

the hotel, lingering in libraries and game rooms.

The guest rooms were redone, too, complete with new plumbing and climate control, fabulous new baths with roomy tubs, and fresh, floral decor. New at the resort are the resurfaced tennis courts, the outdoor heated pool, and a fitness center. Hotel guests may access the nearby Clark Sports Center, a state-of-the-art sports complex with racquetball, fitness classes, basketball, a running track, bowling, an indoor Olympic pool, and a climbing wall.

Recent renovations of the Leatherstocking Golf Course by Cupp Design has enlarged tees, improved drainage, and added a new driving range. Elevated fairways and tees give great views of the western shore of Lake Otesaga. True to the original 1909, Devereux Emmet–designed layout are numerous, steep-walled bunkers, very well-protected greens, and plenty of water hazards. Audubon International has designated Leatherstocking a Certified Audubon Cooperative Sanctuary.

Serious elevation changes and small, multilevel, difficult-to-read greens ask for a strategic short game. All of the holes play longer than they look. Reminiscent of Pebble Beach, the finishing hole doglegs left around the lake. You tee off from a tiny island in the lake and follow the dogleg to a green below the hotel verandah.

Winner of the "Teacher of the Year" award in the Northeast PGA section, Ron Philo Sr. is head instructor at the Golf School. His daughter is Laura Diaz, a top-rated player on the LPGA Tour. The Director of Golf, Dan Spooner, a former PGA player, is also available for lessons. Grass practice tees, target greens, and bunkers are among newly upgraded practice facilities.

The National Baseball Hall of Fame and Museum, a short walk or trolley ride from the hotel, is one of America's prime attractions. From the Babe and Lou Gehrig to Reggie Jackson and Cal Ripkin, the heroes of the game are honored in exhibits, interactive programs,

and special events. You can also visit the Fenimore Art Museum with its acclaimed Native American wing and the Farmers' Museum, an outdoor re-creation of rural life in 1845, with costumed docents, heritage gardens, demonstrations, and rare animal breeds.

A New Era for Bethpage Black

New York golfers and players from across the country who know of Bethpage Black Golf Course on Long Island, the top-rated course in the state, make an adventure out of obtaining tee times. They literally park their vehicles in line in the middle of the night to be at the top of the list for the first-come, first-served tee times at this public course. They are later greeted on the first tee by this large sign: WARNING: THE BLACK COURSE IS AN EXTREMELY DIFFICULT COURSE WHICH WE RECOMMEND ONLY FOR HIGHLY SKILLED GOLFERS.

Known as the "U.S. Open Doctor" for his remodels of legendary courses in preparation for the Open, Rees Jones directed the recent renovation of Bethpage Black, originally designed by A.W. Tillinghast and built in 1935. The 2002 Open was played at Bethpage Black (now 7,295 yards long), the longest course in U.S. Open history and the first ever daily-fee public course to host the tournament.

Jones said, "This was Tillinghast's last course, and although he didn't live to see it finished, I believe this was his answer to Pine Valley. This is a sandy site with his trademark mammoth bunkers, and greens elevated on natural knobs. We restored sand areas that were abandoned, and swept bunkers up to the greens on nearly every hole; they were too far away from the putting surfaces. Fairway bunkers now come into play to accommodate the modern player who drives longer. Tee boxes were pulled back, adding 350 yards to the course."

For those who are not able to get on the Black, there are four more public courses in the complex (516–249–0707).

The Otesaga
60 Lake Street
Cooperstown, NY 13326
Phone: (607) 547–9931, reservations (800) 348–6222
Fax: (607) 547–9675
Web site: www.otesaga.com
General Manager: Frank Maloney
Accommodations: 136 small- and medium-size rooms and suites with Early American–style furnishings.
Meals: Room rates include breakfast and dinner. Piano music, candlelight, and a French-American menu in the Main Dining Room. Casual meals in the mahogany-paneled Hawkeye Bar and Grill. Luncheon buffets on the Lakeside Patio. Live music and dancing in the Templeton Lounge. Lunch and snacks at the Golf House at the lake.
Facilities: Marina, fitness center, lakefront swimming pool, canoes, tennis courts, jogging and biking trails, game room.
Services and Special Programs: A free trolley runs throughout the historic village.
Rates: $$$
Golf Packages: One night standard guest room accommodations, unlimited golf, cart for one round, breakfast and dinner, and admission to three local museums. $217–$239 per person, double occupancy.
Getting There: An 80-mile drive from Albany International Airport. Private aircraft land at Cooperstown-Westville Airport and Oneonta Municipal Airport.
What's Nearby: Visit the National Baseball Hall of Fame and Museum, the Farmers' Museum, and the Fenimore Art Museum. Rent a power boat, take a lake cruise, or go lake fishing. Shop and browse the galleries in the village.

THE SAGAMORE

Appearing to float like a mirage on a private seventy-two-acre island on Lake George, adjacent to Adirondack State Park, the stately white Sagamore Hotel was built in the Victorian era. It served as a summer resort for New Yorkers and Philadelphians, and a social center for wealthy residents of the mansions along the lakeshore, known as Millionaires Row. After a $75 million restoration by new owners, the property reopened in 1985. With a splendid mountainside-and-meadow Donald Ross golf course, a major tennis complex, a new European-style spa, and myriad lakefront recreation facilities and winter sports, the Sagamore is, once again, one of America's premier vacation destinations.

Summer visitors loll on the private beach, take sightseeing cruises across the lake on a vintage yacht, and go fishing, sailing, and water skiing. In the wintertime, the golf course and the snowy woodlands are laced with cross-country ski trails. There is also ice skating, ice fishing, snowmobiling, and sledding, with shuttle service to nearby Gore Mountain for downhill skiing.

On a ridge 2 miles from the hotel, the golf course has spectacular views of Lake George and the surrounding mountains and forests. The track dips and rolls through a vast upland meadow and through stands of mature pines, brightened by the paper-whiteness of birches that turn molten gold in the fall. The golf season can run as late as November here.

Born in the Scottish highlands and apprenticed to Old Tom Morris at St. Andrews, Donald Ross planted heather imported from his native land and installed his signature "hogback" contours and plateaued, undulating greens guarded by deep, grassy hollows and bunkers. Opened in 1928, the legendary course was fully restored and reconditioned in the 1980s according to Ross's original blueprints, whereupon it won the *Golf Magazine* Silver Medal and received a *Golf Digest* ranking of fifth in the state. The fun begins on the first hole, which drops 80 feet from the tee to a fairway lined closely with tall trees. It heads back uphill to a green where balls seem to dribble off the edge; the wind will likely be in your face—club up.

The rambling, white clapboard Sagamore Hotel, built in 1883, has been lovingly restored and redecorated in luxurious, yet welcoming, English Colonial Revival–style. Even the elevators are elegant with marble floors and polished mahogany walls. Rooms are inviting, with four-poster beds, weathered barn-red armoires, and traditional nineteenth-century touches.

Individual lodges and condominiums have been added, containing charming, cozy suites with wood-burning fireplaces, dining areas, and terraces, and decorated in American-Country and Adirondack-camp style. A former carriage house, the Hermitage is now an executive retreat with ten loft suites overlooking the lake, a private garden, and dining room. Popular with families are the short-term rental, two-bedroom condominiums with fireplaces, dining rooms, and kitchens.

The hotel's glass-enclosed Veranda is the place to be for afternoon tea and for tapas, sushi, and aperitifs as the sun sets over the lake. Lunch and dinner lake cruises on *The Morgan,* a 72-foot replica nineteenth century launch, are a "must" from May through October.

Daytrippers enjoy the Adirondack Museum, where twenty exhibit buildings feature the history and art of the mountains. At Fort Ticonderoga, a restored colonial fortress, fife-and-drum performances, and cannon firings are exciting events.

The Donald Ross Legacy

America's first great golf architect, Donald J. Ross was born in Dornoch in the high-lands of Scotland in 1872. He practiced the game, built clubs, and studied course design while serving as golf pro at the Royal Dornoch Golf Club and working with Old Tom Morris at St. Andrews. He emigrated to America in 1899 for a job as groundskeeper at Oakley Country Club near Boston. He soon made his mark on the American landscape by designing three courses at Pinehurst, just as the sport began to boom in the United States. In the next four decades, he designed more than 400 courses in the eastern United States and Canada, while maintaining his skills as a professional golfer, finishing in the top ten of four U.S. Opens.

Ross's classic style combined the Scottish inclination to leave the land as it lies, with a robust, all-American desire for a good chal-lenge. His fairways are generally wide and his hogback greens are crowned, falling away into unpredictable hollows, making approach and recovery shots of the utmost importance—just as on the time-honored track at Sagamore.

Today members of the American Society of Golf Course Architects wear their red "Ross Tartan" blazers for special occasions, in honor of his legacy.

The Sagamore
110 Sagamore Road
Bolton Landing, NY 12814
Phone: (518) 644–9400, reservations (800) 358–3585
Fax: (518) 644–2851
Web site: www.thesagamore.com
General Manager: S. Lee Bowden
Accommodations: 350 rooms and suites with lake and garden views, in the updated Historic Hotel and in individual lodges and condominiums. Decor is traditional nineteenth-century in the hotel, updated Adirondack-rustic and American-Country in the lodges.
Meals: Jacket and tie are required at Trillium, the resort's four-diamond-rated, fine restaurant; on the menu are Pacific Rim and Chesapeake Bay seafood, Continental and regional dishes. Mile-long buffet tables are famous in the Sagamore Dining Room. Mister Brown's Adirondack-style pub serves up lunches and light dinners by the stone fireplace, with live entertainment in the evenings. On a hill overlooking the first tee and Lake George, the Club Grill is a cozy, English Tudor–style place serving hearty dishes from macaroni and cheese to baked beans and big steaks and chops.
Facilities: Two indoor and five outdoor tennis courts; rac-quet ball; private beach; indoor/outdoor heated swimming pool; marina with boat rentals and charters; water skiing; windsurfing; sailing; parasailing. The luxurious Sagamore Spa and Fitness Club offers health and beauty treatments, workout equipment, and classes.
Services and Special Programs: At the "Teepee Club," kids ages 3–12 are supervised at lakeside activities, games, movies, and crafts. The Teen Adventure program, for ages 13 and up, includes Frisbee golf, expeditions into town, evening "hangouts," movies and more.
Rates: $$$
Golf Packages: Classic Golf Getaway for Two includes two nights accommodations, unlimited golf for three days, cart, and shirt. $738–$938.
Getting There: A one-hour drive from Albany Interna-tional Airport and the Amtrack station; a four-hour drive from New York City and Boston.
What's Nearby: Antiques, local crafts, and folk art shop-ping in Lake George. Local history and art at the Adiron-dack Museum, the Chapman Historical Museum, and the Historical Society Museum. Fort Ticonderoga, Fort William Henry, and America's oldest race track in Saratoga Springs. Fall foliage lovers drive throughout the surrounding moun-tains and to Prospect Mountain.

PINEHURST RESORT

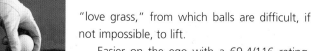

A statue of Donald Ross, the master Scottish architect of Pinehurst's first four courses, stands above the eighteenth green of Pinehurst #2. Beginning with Ross's first layout in 1907, Pinehurst has become the premier golf destination in the United States, with 144 holes of golf, a twenty-four-court tennis complex, water sports at Lake Pinehurst, and a group of lovely hotels in the historic village. The 1999 U.S. Open—won by the late Payne Stewart with a dramatic 15-foot putt—the Ryder Cup, the TOUR Championship, and a Senior Open were played here, among other golf events, and every golfer in love with the game dreams of playing Pinehurst at least once in his or her life.

Ross engineered dips, swales, 108 bunkers, and heavy breaks into the greatest achievement of his life, Pinehurst #2, which he worked on for more than thirty years. Stretching 7,252 yards, fairways are wide and flat, looking easier and playing longer than they appear. Traps, dense pine fringes, and seriously domed, false-front greens are perilous. Very fast, the greens are crowned—"turtlebacked." Regardless of pin placement, aim for the center of the green or end up in a deep collection area or in the notorious, wiry Pinehurst "love grass," from which balls are difficult, if not impossible, to lift.

Easier on the ego with a 69.4/116 rating, Pinehurst #1 is a gorgeous track asking for accuracy off the tee into densely tree-lined chutes. Aim is everything on Pinehurst #3, which rolls more than any of the tracks and is the tightest, closely bordered by trees and water.

Paying homage to the original Ross layout from 1919, Tom Fazio redesigned Pinehurst #4, retaining sloping greens. One-hundred-eighty bunkers of various sizes, many of them pot bunkers, are clustered in groups. Crowds of blooming azaleas are glorious in the springtime here.

With more water hazards than the others, Pinehurst #5 was created by Ellis Maples in 1961. His father worked with Ross for more than forty years, and that influence is reflected in the traditional Pinehurst characteristics. Framed by tall pines, like the pipes of an organ, the Cathedral Hole is postcard perfect.

In 1976 Pinehurst #6 was laid by Tom and George Fazio on a rugged site with dramatic elevation changes. Dense woods and lots of water contribute to the 73.2/132 rating.

Extensive wetlands and double doglegs are the order of the day on Pinehurst #7, a tough Rees Jones layout. Jones said, "The golf course fits very naturally, hitting from elevated tees down into the valleys and back up." With the highest slope rating of the eight tracks, this is a traditional course with small bunkers, mounds and hollows, swamps and lakes, and with a 1,700-yard difference between the front and back tees.

Pinehurst #8 was designed by Fazio in 1996 to commemorate the resort's centennial year. You play over marshes and ponds, and an old sand pit, to sloping greens with false fronts. Due to optical illusions, some bunkers that seem adjacent to the greens are twenty yards or so in front of them.

Staying at Pinehurst

Famed landscape architect Frederick Law Olmsted laid out the tree-lined streets of the Village of Pinehurst, which opened in 1895 as a health resort. Southern hospitality and a historic atmosphere holds forth today at three hotels and at rentable villas and condominiums. Since 1901 The Carolina has been the Grande Dame, with more than 200 small- and medium-size rooms and suites. Old photos and golf memorabilia create a museum atmosphere in the halls and the lounge.

The Holly Inn, a national historic landmark, is a fanciful combination of Queen Anne Revival, Arts and Crafts, and Art Nouveau with eighty-five rooms and suites, and a hand-carved Scottish bar in the Tavern. Decor has a floral theme on stenciled walls and art glass, with decorative tile and pine floors.

The sporty Manor Inn offers forty-six rooms and the sunny Pine Room, where guests read and play board games.

Adjacent to the Carolina are forty villas. Each has four guest rooms that connect to a central parlor with tufted leather sofas, traditional furnishings, and fireplaces. One-hundred-thirty-five condominiums are located on the fairways of courses #3 and #5 and on the lakeshore.

Pinehurst Golf Advantage School has a 4-to-1 student-instructor ratio. Popular programs are the Three Day Weekend, junior and women's schools, and parent/child schools. A new addition is the prestigious Dave Pelz Scoring Game School.

Pinehurst Resort
1 Carolina Vista Drive
Village of Pinehurst, NC 28374
Phone: (910) 295–6811, reservations (800) 487–4653
Fax: (910) 235–8466
Web site: www.pinehurst.com
General Manager: Clyde Smith
Accommodations: Four-diamond rated, 530 rooms, suites, villas, and condominiums.
Meals: Modified American meal plans at three hotels. American and Continental cuisine in the huge Carolina Dining Room. Seasonal New England and North Carolinian cuisine at the 1895 Room at the Holly Inn, and high tea in the lobby. Hearty meals by the fireplace or on the patio at the Scottish-style Tavern. Pub fare and sports at Mulligan's Bar and Grill. Steak and seafood at the Donald Ross Grill.
Facilities: Twenty-four Har-tru and hard-surface tennis courts with USPTA professionals, clinics, and tournament play; lawn bowling; three croquet courts; polo pitch; harness racing track; two swimming pools; Golf Caddie Hall of Fame; sailing, canoeing, fishing, and swimming at Lake Pinehurst.
Services and Special Programs: Supervised kids activities. Golf caddie service. Annual events, from live jazz and concerts to arts and wine festivals, and tennis and golf tournaments. Free shuttle around the resort.
Rates: $$$$
Golf Packages: Premier Golf Package includes two nights accommodations, dinner and breakfast daily, a round of golf per day with cart, gift, and use of tennis and fitness facilities. $1,040–$1,361 per person, double occupancy, depending on the hostelry.
Getting There: A major airline and private planes land at nearby Moore County Regional Airport. Piedmont Triad International Airport at Greensboro is 80 miles away, and Raleigh-Durham International Airport is 65 miles away. Amtrak arrives in Southern Pines.
What's Nearby: Carriage rides and antiques shopping in the village; historic walking and bike tours; visit the North Carolina Zoo; stroll college campuses and botanical gardens.

SUNRIVER RESORT

Sunriver, Oregon

The snowcapped peaks of the Cascade Range rise above sunny meadows where fifty-four holes of golf are gently laid among verdant wetlands and aspen and pine forests. Gentle may not be the word, however, that comes to mind on Robert E. Cupp and John Fought's masterpiece, Crosswater, which is 7,683 yards long and rated at a daunting 153 from the tips.

The heaths of Crosswater are reminiscent of Scottish highlands, with low stretches of golden, silver, and reddish grasses beside reedy ponds, lakes, and the arms of two rivers. The name "Crosswater" becomes obvious on carries as long as 200 yards. On the short par-4 fourth called "Left Begone," damp bogs and the Little Deschutes River, a gang of fairway bunkers, and a fast-moving green present a stern challenge. On five, you tee off over a bend in the river at two welcoming bunkers, make a long approach across 100 yards or so of streams and grasses, only to confront a long ridge dividing the front and back of the skinny, diagonal green. It's 687 yards from the gold tees on twelve, where a twenty-two-acre lake guards the left from tee to green and Mount Bachelor looms above a phalanx of pines and a tiny putting surface. In a changeable, mountain climate, shifting clouds and surrounding peaks are reflected in moving waters, where flyfishers cast their lines for rainbow and brown trout. Elk and coyote are frequent spectators, as are a variety of birds, ranging from bald eagles to ducks resting in the shallows on their annual migrations.

Sunriver's original course, the Meadows, was remod-

eled and now sports more and larger directional bunkers and fore-bunkers among groves of Ponderosa pines and along the Sun River, where otters and beavers are often seen playing their watery games among the reeds. Several elevated greens are now intriguingly two- or three-tiered, and faster than ever.

Benefiting from a recent facelift, Robert Trent Jones Jr.'s Woodlands lies in a dense, tall, lodgepole and Ponderosa pine forest. Monster drives are not required—just near-perfect accuracy to avoid deep fairway bunkers, several lakes, and some unique lava rock outcroppings.

In top tournament condition all season, the courses have hosted Shell's Wonderful World of Golf, the PGA Club Professional Championship, and the Pacific Amateur Golf Classic, among other competitions.

The allure of Sunriver is its superlative setting. Spread out in glorious meadows at 3,500 feet in elevation among thousands of evergreens at the foot of mountain ranges and the Deschutes National Forest, the resort comprises an unequaled vacationland where active families bike, hike, ski, play tennis, fish, and ride horses. You can kayak and canoe on 6 miles of calm river, or take a white-water rafting adventure. All kinds of bikes are available, from tandems to baby carriers, for 35 miles of paved trails that connect the recreation facilities (swimming complexes, tennis courts, and indoor racquet club), the shopping village, and rental houses and condos.

Pleasant places from which to watch the sun set

are the outdoor deck or seats in front of the fireplace at the Owl's Nest lounge, which has views of a vast meadow and the Sun River, its banks glowing gold and red with aspens and maples in the fall.

When snow finally blankets the fairways, get out your cross-country skis and skim across the meadows, or make the 21-mile drive to Mount Bachelor, where skiing and snowboarding lasts well into the summer—it's not uncommon to ski and golf on the same day. Easily accessible by car or by air in the wintertime, Sunriver also offers transport by horse-drawn sleigh and snowmobile.

Other Places to Play

The high grasslands and the mountains of central Oregon are blessed with glorious weather from late spring through fall. Within a short drive of Sunriver, Aspen Lakes Golf Course in the town of Sisters is an exceptional complex of three nines memorable for red sand bunkers, water carries, and views of mountain peaks (541–549–4653, www.aspenlakes.com). Nearby Tom Weiskopf and Jay Morrish integrated dramatic lava formations and rollicking terrain into elevated tees and greens at Broken Top Golf Club. Spectacular mountain views and an award-winning wine list are reasons to visit the clubhouse (541–383–8200, www.brokentop.com).

Sunriver Resort
P.O. Box 3609
Sunriver, OR 97707
Phone: (541) 593–1000, reservations (800) 801–8765
Fax: (541) 593–5458
Web site: www.sunriver-resort.com

General Manager: Scott Morris

Accommodations: Luxurious fireplace rooms with private balconies and dazzling views in the River Lodges; spacious hotel rooms and family suites in the main lodge; plus 300 privately owned condominiums and homes to rent.

Meals: Owl's Nest pub for microbrews, snacks, and bistro meals; live music on weekends. Four-star cuisine and mountain views at The Meadows. Only members and resort guests can enjoy the exceptional Pacific Northwest menu at The Grille at Crosswater, a cozy dining room on the edge of the golf course.

Facilities: There are several practice venues, from bunkers to an elaborate eighteen-hole putting course. An opulent new, full-service health and beauty spa opened in 2002. At the Nature Center and Observatory, stargazers and bird-watchers are mesmerized by the exceptional displays and the telescope.

Services and Special Programs: The Ron Seals Academy of Golf offers adult and junior classes and clinics, and half-day schools; *Golf Digest* Woman is a special three-day school. Kids are supervised in outdoor explorations and fun activities at Fort Funnigan for ages 3–10, Guided Adventures for ages 11–15, and Teen Time. For all ages a daily schedule of activities from archery to rock climbing, art, hiking, and water sports.

Rates: $$–$$$

Golf Packages: The Crosswater Experience, one night accommodations, a round of golf on Crosswater, and unlimited play on Meadows and Woodlands. $129–$179 per person, double occupancy.

Getting There: Redmond/Bend Airport is served by United Express and Horizon Air from Portland, Seattle, and San Francisco. Land your business jet or small plane on Sunriver's private, 5,500-foot paved and lighted runway.

What's Nearby: One of the largest ski resorts in the country, Mount Bachelor gets 150 to 200 inches of snow annually.

WESTIN SALISHAN LODGE AND GOLF RESORT

Gleneden Beach, Oregon

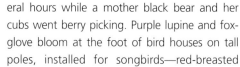

The quintessential Oregon Coast experience is accompanied by some cloudy weather, and a drop or two of rain, a climate dear to the heart of a golfer who dreams of misty Scottish links. Westin Salishan Lodge lies in a lush evergreen forest, which thrives on omnipresent moisture. The mossy visages of pines and cedars lend a certain luxuriant, primeval atmosphere to the resort and the golf course.

Westin took charge of the resort in the late 1990s, renovating the hotel and improving the golf course to the tune of $2.5 million. Closely bordered by trees and native shrubbery, the front nine fairways are wide and well bunkered with fiendishly mounded greens. Ancient cedars bearded with lichen and towering Sitka spruces stand like druids on the back nine approaching the Pacific Ocean and the shores of Siletz Bay. Links-style, windier, and liberally adorned with long, snaking traps and sod-faced pot bunkers, the finishing holes get narrow and duney, with gnarly European grass that catches and hides golf balls. Yawning downhill, the eighteenth tilts, bouncing tee shots off the fairway and into the trees. A large, tabletop green awaits, surrounded by pot bunkers.

Thickets of wild blackberries and Salal berries are favorites of birds, black-tailed deer, and the occasional small bear—one day the front nine was closed for several hours while a mother black bear and her cubs went berry picking. Purple lupine and foxglove bloom at the foot of bird houses on tall poles, installed for songbirds—red-breasted nuthatches and robins, finches, and winter wrens. In the ponds otters play on the muddy banks. Award-winning grounds superintendent, Cliff Beckman, sees his Audubon International certification for the resort's forest preserve and golf course to be "a way of thinking," an ongoing process of maintaining the natural environment and habitat without pesticides, herbicides, or fertilizers.

Antler chandeliers, crackling logs in big stone fireplaces, rustic wood beams, and forest views make the lodge a cozy retreat. Creating a comfortable environment are Native American–inspired fabrics, carved wood friezes and soft, leather sofas and armchairs, plus a library with chess sets and games. Paintings, prints, and wood carvings collected by the original resort owner are found throughout the public areas.

An eighteen-hole putting course winds around the main lodge, and there are indoor and outdoor tennis courts, half-court basketball, a complete fitness center, and all-day activities for children at the Kids Club. Across the road in the Salishan Marketplace are sixteen shops and galleries, from a deli and wine shop to fine art, jewelry, and gifts.

Rain or shine the indoor swimming pool with sheltered sun deck is a warm place to relax. Above the indoor sports facility are forest trails and sunny open areas with picnic tables and lounge chairs, where guests linger in solitude. The nature trails and running loops of the Salishan forest and beach are a primary reason to stay here—guests discover the salt marsh wildlife sanctuary, the beaver pond, the dunes, and several miles of secluded, private beach.

Some restaurant critics consider the Salishan Dining Room to be the best fine-dining venue south of Portland, and *Wine Spectator* magazine awards special recognition to the 10,000-bottle wine cellar—ask about the famous Oregon Pinots. Pacific Northwest cuisine, candlelight, and a view of Siletz Bay and the forest grounds create a romantic atmosphere. A large fireplace warms the upstairs cocktail lounge, complete with armchairs, pool tables, live music, and a deck in the treetops.

Oregon Dunes

Rocketing to the top of "Best New Courses" lists soon after they opened at the turn of the twenty-first century, the two stunning links layouts at Bandon Dunes Golf Resort are located near Coos Bay, Oregon. You walk these rugged courses (no carts allowed), you brave stiff winds and long forced carries, and you glory in the only true Scottish links-style tracks in the West. On a sandy marine terrace 100 feet above a breathtaking stretch of coastline, knobby hillocks, high dunes, deep hollows and turf-sided pot bunkers recall the first golf courses ever created. Ball-grabbing, real Scottish gorse adds to the fun. Scraped by steady ocean breezes, fairways and greens are dry and fast. *Golf Magazine* declared that only Pebble Beach and Pinehurst #2 rank ahead of Bandon Dunes. A small lodge, restaurant, and pro shop accommodate the intrepid golfers who make the pilgrimage to this remote location (888–345–6008, www.bandondunesgolf.com).

Westin Salishan Lodge and Golf Resort
7760 Highway 101 North
Gleneden Beach, OR 97388
Phone: (541) 764–2371, reservations (888) 725–4742
Fax: (541) 764–3678
Web site: www.westin.com
General Manager: Jim McGlashan
Accommodations: 205 rooms and suites with forest, golf course, or bay views and upscale lodge-style decor; all have gas fireplaces, private balconies, and original regional art.
Meals: Casual meals and buffets are taken in the Cedar Tree. The cozy Dining Room specializes in such Northwest specialties as pine nut–stuffed pork chop, duck with marionberry leek marmalade, Pacific oysters, and locally caught halibut with wild nettle pasta.
Facilities: Indoor swimming pool; weight/fitness room; saunas; whirlpool; USTA-sanctioned indoor/outdoor tennis courts; sports courts; eighteen-hole putting course and golf practice area; private beach access.
Services and Special Programs: Each room has laser printer/fax/copier/dual phone lines with data port, surge protector, ergonomic chair, and task light. Fireside massage for two is a memorable experience when rain beats on the windows. Westin Kids Club supervises games, sports, crafts, and meals. Guided nature walks.
Rates: $$$
Golf Packages: One night accommodations, unlimited golf, and breakfast. $139–$199 per person, double occupancy.
Getting There: Major carriers at Portland International Airport, a two-hour drive north. Newport Municipal Airport, 17 miles south, is serviced by Harbor Air and private jet aircraft. Smaller private aircraft are accommodated at the Siletz Bay State Airport, adjacent to the lodge.
What's Nearby: The rugged beauty of the central Oregon coast attracts beachcombers, tidepool seekers, photographers, and storm watchers. Fishing is excellent in five major rivers, their bay estuaries, and on the coast; charter companies offer fishing and whale-watching cruises. A lighthouse and the "Octopus Tree" are highlights of nearby Cape Meares State Park. Art lovers head for galleries and studios at Yachats, a charming coastal village in the Cape Perpetua Scenic Area.

NEMACOLIN WOODLANDS RESORT AND SPA
Farmington, Pennsylvania

During the nineteenth century, the remote Laurel Highlands between Maryland and Pennsylvania was a fashionable vacation retreat for the wealthy of Pittsburgh. In the 1960s a private game reserve was established in Nemacolin Woodlands, where the owner and his friends fished and hunted for silver fox, bear, and Russian white-tailed deer. Later Lakes Louise and Carol were added and Beaver Creek was developed into the excellent trout stream it is today. By 1987 a world-class resort was under construction, including the expansion of the original Tudor-style lodge. By the turn of the twenty-first century, the glamorous Château LaFayette hotel was built, and a small ski resort, an equestrian center, townhouses, a shopping center, and a second golf course, the Pete Dye–designed Mystic Rock, were added.

Inspired by classic European hotels, the Château LaFayette is a great, white, columned facade with Paladian windows. Interiors are elegant and formal, with marble floors, crystal chandeliers, American antiques, and a multimillion-dollar art collection. Guest rooms are plush, with traditional furnishings and fine jacquard and floral fabrics. Within the cozy, Tudor-style Lodge, oversized guest rooms are warm and cozy mountain-lodge style with gleaming, dark woods. In the charming half-timbered townhouses are one- and two-bedroom units with kitchens, dining and living rooms, and large patios or balconies.

The Mystic Rock golf course was laid out on a wooded site by Pete Dye. It is 6,832 yards long and accented by giant boulders, Sahara-like bunkers, and multitiered, undulating, fast greens, with long forced carries over ravines, water, and rock-strewn pastures.

The resort's original course, The Links, rambles around on very hilly terrain, with monumental rocks and water coming into play on several holes. Thick woods, high scrub, and native plants, and several lakes border the wide fairways. The mountain views are lovely.

Promoting the U.S. Kids Golf Program, the resort encourages children, ages seven to fifteen, accompanied by adults, to play nine holes on The Links course. Special tee markers shorten the yardage for youngsters.

The student-teacher ratio is 4 to 1 at the Golf Academy, which offers daily clinics, schools, the "Cure Your Slice for Life Program," the "Ready, Aim, Swing Program," and video swing analysis. Practice venues include bent-grass tees, bunkers, and greens for putting, chipping, and pitching.

At once elegant and rustic, the new spa was constructed of local materials. Traditional and specialty treatments are offered, including kurs, wraps, glows, masks, and peels; the "Neck, Back and Shoulder Massage," and, especially for athletes, the "Greek Mint Gymnasia Transformation," which uses peppermint and spearmint in a revitalizing scrub. The Paradise Pool is a huge body of water meant to look like Hawaii, with a lovely tile and ceramic border and a swim-up bar.

Outdoor Recreation Galore

Families return year after year for their summer and winter vacations at Nemacolin to enjoy the astonishing myriad of indoor and outdoor activities available on the property; from fly-fishing on Beaver Creek to canoeing and paddleboating on Lake PJ, the unique "Golf Croquet," an elaborate mini-golf course, climbing wall, beach volleyball, biking and hiking—even paintball and speedball. In the wintertime, it's sleigh and surrey rides, and downhill and Nordic skiing, snowboarding, and tubing at Mystic Mountain.

Open year-round on 140 lush acres of thick woodlands, valleys, streams, lakes, and rough pastures, the Sporting Clay Course has a commodious lodge, with restaurant, bar and pro shop. It is one of the largest and most comprehensive clay shooting complexes in the country, with thirty shooting stations and more than eighty automatic Laporte traps. N.S.C.A certified instructors are available year-round.

The Equestrian Center, with horses trained to all levels of riding, offers easy trail rides, ponies for little kids, polo exhibitions, and schooling shows.

Among the sights on resort property are more than a dozen antique cars, from a 1909 Stanley Steamer to a 1936 Cord.

Nemacolin Woodlands Resort and Spa
1001 LaFayette Drive
Farmington, PA 15437
Phone: (724) 329–8555, reservations (800) 422–2736
Fax: (724) 329–6947
Web site: www.nemacolin.com

General Manager: Ronald R. Cadrette

Accommodations: 279 luxurious rooms, suites, and townhouses, ranging in style from luxurious hotel rooms to spacious lodge rooms, and one- or two-bedroom units with kitchen, dining and living rooms, and balconies. LaFayette Club guests have a private lounge and concierge, and food and beverage presentations. Private homes are also available to rent.

Meals: Light French cuisine in a bistro setting at Lautrec in the Château, and Sunday brunch; steak, seafood, and American food menu in a casual family atmosphere at the Golden Trout; spa cuisine with an Asian flair at Seasons; hearty fare at Caddy Shack; casual pub food and antique pool tables at The Tavern; P.J.'s Ice Cream & Pizza Parlor; views of three states from the Gazebo's verandah; the Hitchin' Post Saloon; and dancing at Diamond Lil's.

Facilities: GPS golf carts, indoor golf simulator, golf academy, and golf schools; five swimming pools; four omni-turf tennis courts; croquet; climbing wall; beach volleyball courts; mini-golf; playground; bicycles; large shopping arcade; complete equestrian center with horse boarding.

Services and Special Programs: Daily classes, including yoga, Pilates, cardio exercise, water aerobics, and more. Ages 4–12 love the Kidz Klub, where they play games and try trail rides, sporting clays, climbing wall and ropes courses, swimming, and fishing; Kidz Night Out and Klub Inferno for teens, too.

Rates: $$$

Golf Packages: One night deluxe accommodations, a round of golf on The Links, golf services, and amenities. $424–$542 for two, double occupancy.

Getting There: A 70-mile drive from Pittsburgh International Airport. Private aircraft land at the resort's private airfield; ground transportation is provided.

What's Nearby: Visit Frank Lloyd Wright's Fallingwater, Fort Necessity National Battlefield, and Kentuck Knob. White-water rafting in Ohiopyle State Park. Explore a maze cave at Laurel Caverns Geological Park.

HILTON HEAD RESORTS

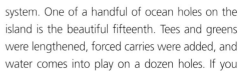

Four hundred golf holes lie on this low-country barrier island, on more than twenty courses laid out in salt marshes beneath a dense canopy of pines and moss-draped live oaks. Once you drive across the bridge onto Hilton Head, your choices include 20 miles of bike paths, fishing and swimming in the surf, and fresh- and saltwater sports and cruises. There are five major tennis complexes and the prestigious Stan Smith Tennis Academy. Choose your season wisely and make reservations well in advance, as more than two million visitors vacation here annually.

In spite of extensive "plantation" resort development, which consists of hotels, thousands of rental condominiums and villas, several shopping centers, and 250 restaurants, the natural environment is enchanting. Open savannahs and networks of lagoons and creeks are shaded by tall pines, palmettos, fragrant magnolias, and oaks. Miles of sandy beaches fringe the Intracoastal Waterway and the Atlantic, warmed year-round by the Gulf Stream.

Palmer, Nicklaus, the Joneses, two Fazios, Player, Hills, and other legendary architects have designed the famous Hilton Head golf courses. Hosting the PGA's MCI Classic Heritage of Golf and the WorldCom Classic, Harbor Town Golf Links at Sea Pines Plantation leads the list. Pete Dye engineered narrow, tree- and pine straw–bordered fairways into the low-lying, flat site, plus miniscule, firm greens, and his signature railroad ties. The lighthouse on the eighteenth hole on Calibogue Sound is one of the most recognizable landmarks in golf. You will need to hit the marks with your irons rather precisely here, as landing zones are tight and winds are steady; water appears on sixteen holes. A recent renovation rebuilt the greens, bunkers, and tee boxes, and improved drainage.

Mark McCumber redesigned the 1960s-era Ocean Course at Sea Pines Plantation in 1995, retaining the original routing beneath oak trees through the natural lagoon system. One of a handful of ocean holes on the island is the beautiful fifteenth. Tees and greens were lengthened, forced carries were added, and water comes into play on a dozen holes. If you like to fade, you will like the Ocean. Shorter and more forgiving, Sea Marsh Golf Course twists and turns through pines and oaks on the edge of the wetlands.

The first built on the island and one of three top notch tracks at Palmetto Dunes, Robert Trent Jones's design features wide fairways, big greens, and ocean views on a lagoon. The Arthur Hills course here is crisscrossed by a canal. The longest and most difficult of the three is the George Fazio course, with overhanging trees, water, and doglegs galore.

You can walk the gorgeous Arthur Hills Course at Palmetto Hall, a gently mounded beauty skirting the old Port Royal Lighthouse and overarched by established hardwoods and plenty of water. Also at Palmetto Hall, the Robert Cupp Course is unique for its sharply defined, straight-sided traps and square greens, and cart paths here are as straight as rulers. This controversial layout was computer designed.

Hilton Head Plantation has four public access courses, including two of Rees Jones's fabulous tracks, Country Club of Hilton Head and Oyster Reef.

Intimate and exclusive, The Inn at Harbour Town is a European-style hotel in the 5,000-acre Sea Pines Resort, overlooking the first tee of the Harbour Town Links. The look and feel of the place is slow and southern; gracious with porches and balconies, palms, pines, and sweeping lawns. Old World ambience is created by traditional, dark wood and fine rattan furnishings, historic artworks, and white columns, along with the cozy paneled library warmed by the fireplace. A unique and charming amenity, white-gloved, kilted butlers serve each floor.

Biking is popular on 15 miles of trails and 5 miles of hard-packed beach. Also popular is horseback riding through a 605-acre forest preserve. Canoe and

kayak rentals are available for exploring the creeks, marshes, and inlets. Motor cruises and sailboats from around the world sail into the Harbour Town Yacht Basin, which is loaded with boutique shops, galleries, restaurants, and water-sport venues.

Forrest Gump Flips for Fripp

Near the picturesque, historic town of Beaufort, Fripp Island got suddenly famous when part of the movie, *Forrest Gump,* was filmed there. The Ocean Point Golf Links at Fripp Island Resort is a breezy, target-style beauty along Fripp Inlet and the Atlantic, with a handful of forced carries and narrow fairways on flat terrain. A beautiful lagoon, home of friendly alligators, looms alongside fifteen holes that cross inlets and marshes, meandering through inland forests on the front nine and turning toward the ocean, link-like, on the back nine.

PGA star Davis Love III laid out his first design on the island, Ocean Creek Golf Club, on a pretty, windy site of tidal salt marshes and dunes. The course is situated on the banks of Hidden Lake and Old House Creek. Forced carries are on the menu, balanced by wide approaches to large greens. Deer, ospreys, cranes, and 'gators may be your companions as you navigate the network of wooden walkways and bridges that help to preserve the environment (800–832–4754, www.fripp islandresort.com).

Hilton Head Resorts
1 Lighthouse Lane
Hilton Head Island, SC 29928
Phone: (843) 785–3333, reservations (888) 807–6873
Web site: www.seapines.com
General Manager: Michael Lawrence
Accommodations: At the Inn at Harbour Town are 60 rooms, each with private balcony, armchairs, carved wood bed and Frette linens, ceiling fan, large soaking tub, refrigerator, and pantry. Villas and homes are also available in the resort.
Meals: Heritage Grill at the golf clubhouse; CQ's in Harbour Town at a restored inn for fresh seafood and game; French country house atmosphere and seafood at Charlie's L'Etoile; Kurama for sushi and steak.
Facilities: Sea Pines Golf Academy; fitness club with exercise classes; two marinas; three golf courses; beach club with water sports and live entertainment; two swimming pool complexes; twenty-three tennis courts with teaching academy.
Services and Special Programs: Twenty-four-hour butler service; a plethora of family activities, from kite making to pottery, photo tours, and teen events. Supervised programs for ages 4–12.
Rates: $$$
Golf Packages: The Ultimate 54 includes a round of golf on Harbour Town, Sea Marsh, and Ocean Courses, with cart (no accommodations). $280–$342 per person.
Getting There: Charlotte and Savannah International Airports are an hour away; the Hilton Head Airport is a 5-mile drive.
What's Nearby: Gullah heritage tours; the Coastal Discovery Museum; guided nature and history walks in the island preserves; antiques shopping and history tours in Charleston and Savannah; shopping on the island in 200 boutiques, galleries, and department stores, and three outlet malls.

KIAWAH ISLAND RESORTS
Kiawah Island, South Carolina

Fringing the barrier island of Kiawah, a 10-mile stretch of sand slopes gradually into the Atlantic, producing calm, warm surf—ideal for families who love the beach. A private, gated resort community is cleverly tucked into thousands of acres of lush maritime forest and around a vast salt marsh, a veritable wildlife sanctuary inhabited by white-tailed deer and more than 200 species of birds—including osprey, heron, egrets, ibis, pelicans, and gulls. Loggerhead turtles begin their annual egg-laying pilgrimage to the beach in May. And on the five championship golf courses on the island, the occasional alligator wiggles out of a lagoon to sun itself on a cart path.

Since the 1970s Gary Player, Tom Fazio, Jack Nicklaus, and Pete Dye have designed ninety holes of golf for Kiawah Island. Dye's Ocean Course, boasting the highest slope rating in the Carolinas (152), was host to the most dramatic Ryder Cup in history—"The War by the Shore" in 1991—and the 1997 World Cup of Golf. Ten holes are laid directly on the oceanfront, and you will view the sea and contend with steady winds on every hole. Bring your long irons for the narrow landing zones and lengthy carries over water and high grasses. With its tufted dunes and grassy lagoon, the course made its screen debut in the movie, *The Legend of Bagger Vance.* After battling the Ocean, golfers head for the absolutely stunning practice range, then to the beautiful clubhouse for restoratives.

Nicklaus designed Turtle Point in the early 1980s and then updated it in 2000 with faster, flatter greens; larger, more defined bunkers; and low-profile, wide fairways. The track winds beneath overhanging oaks, tall pines, and palmettos, and alongside lagoons, finishing with three spectacular seaside holes.

It's water, water, everywhere on Fazio's Osprey Point, where four large natural lakes and saltwater marsh guarantee watery views, and liquid hazards. Mossy oak trees and fragrant magnolias are picturesque; fairway moguls and swales make flat lies rare. One of the prettiest places to relax after a round is the plush clubhouse—cocktails on the porch watching the sun set on the lagoon, then dinner in the four-diamond-rated restaurant.

Adjoining the tidal marsh in a lovely location on the Kiawah River is Gary Player's redesigned Cougar Point, the favorite of high handicappers; five sets of tees were installed, and greens were generally doubled in size. In the lagoons, which have been reconfigured, herons stalk silently in the shallows, seeking their catches of the day.

In Hope Plantation just outside the Kiawah gate, where an indigo and cotton plantation once stood, Oak Point rambles along Haulover Creek and the river, through hardwood forests and salt marshes.

Vacationers choose from upscale hotel rooms in tropical, four-diamond-rated, Kiawah Island Inn, or from a wide variety of condominium units and privately owned rental homes. The deep, leather lounge chairs in the lobby of the inn are perfect roosts from which to contemplate the moods of the sea. Kiawah boasts one of the largest tennis centers in the country—with twenty-eight courts and a busy schedule of clinics, private lessons, and exhibitions—directed by Hall of Fame pro, Ray Barth.

The diversity of outdoor adventures is astonishing on Kiawah, from guided canoe and kayak trips to jeep tours, deep-sea fishing, sight-seeing cruises, and sailing; biking on 30 miles of paved paths; and sand volleyball, basketball, soccer, and swimming at Night Heron Park. During holiday seasons, hayrides, oyster roasts, ice-cream socials, beach bonfire parties, and live music entertain vacationers.

The Vegas of Golf: Myrtle Beach

More than one hundred golf courses are within a tee shot of Highway 17 on the coast of South Carolina, from Holden Beach to Georgetown. Called the "Grand Strand," the "Las Vegas of Golf" and the "Golf Coast," the 60-mile stretch north and south of Myrtle Beach is the place for golf. Giving the old favorite tracks some competition are the new TPC of Myrtle Beach; the dazzling designs of Dye, Norman, Fazio, and Love at Barefoot Resort; and the International World Tour Golf Links, featuring replicas of twenty-seven famous golf holes. Holding their own after all these years are the Dunes Golf and Beach Club in Myrtle Beach, Tidewater Golf Club in North Myrtle Beach, and Caledonia Golf and Fish Club at Pawleys Island. And there are more, so many more: Heritage and Litchfield Plantations; the River's Edge; Legends; Wild Wings; and Tiger's Eye, Lion's Paw, and Panther's Run at Ocean Ridge. Just remember that 11 million people visit the Myrtle Beach area every year. Choose your season wisely.

Kiawah Island Resorts
12 Kiawah Beach Drive
Kiawah Island, SC 29455
Phone: (843) 768–2121, reservations (800) 654–2924
Fax: (843) 768–9339
Web site: www.kiawahgolf.com
Managing Director: Prem Devadas
Accommodations: 150 inn rooms with lagoon, dunes, or ocean view; 580 private rental homes and condominium units with one to seven bedrooms, located in the woods, around the tennis club and pool, and near the beachfront or riverfront.
Meals: The plush Atlantic Room serves up fresh-caught seafood, lavish Sunday brunches, and sea views. The elegant Dining Room in the four-diamond-rated Osprey Point clubhouse is sumptuous with antiques and fine art; superb game and seafood are on the menu. Families like traditional Southern cooking at the Village Bistro, and inexpensive, all-American meals in the quaint West Beach Cafe.
Facilities: Five driving ranges, seven practice greens, and a top notch golf school; two tennis clubs, twenty-four Hartru and four hard-surface courts, academy with drop-in clinics, match-making, junior camps, and exhibitions (*Tennis* magazine rates this one of the top resorts in the country); at Night Heron Park: three swimming pools on the waterfront, basketball, picnic grounds, bike rentals.
Services and Special Programs: A full-time golf coordinator arranges tee times, airfares, lessons, rentals, and course condition reports. Kamp Kiawah keeps ages 3–11 busy at the beach and with crafts and games. Naturalist guides take guests on canoe trips, sea kayaking, biking, birding, and night beach walks. Teens like the late-night movies, scavenger hunts, games, dance contests, and pizza parties.
Rates: $$$
Golf Packages: One night deluxe accommodations, one round of golf, and breakfast start from $155 per person, based on four people in a four-bedroom luxury golf home, two night minimum. Three-night package includes deluxe accommodations and two rounds of golf: $233–$666 per person.
Getting There: Major airlines serve Charleston International Airport, a 35-mile drive. Private aircraft land at Charleston Executive Airport, 9 miles from Kiawah. Guests also arrive by private watercraft.
What's Nearby: On the cobblestone streets of Charleston, antiques shops, and horse-drawn carriage tours of colonial, antebellum and Victorian architecture. Charleston Tea Plantation, Medal of Honor Museum, Naval and Maritime Museum, Fort Sumter, and Drayton Hall, the only original plantation home to survive the Civil War.

WILD DUNES RESORT

Isle of Palms, South Carolina

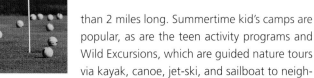

Bordered by the Atlantic and the Intracoastal Waterway, Isle of Palms is a semi-tropical barrier island off South Carolina, a short drive from historic Charleston. Unlike most of the low-country islands, this one was never cleared for sea island cotton. Until the mid-1970s, the land lay deserted, shaded by gnarled, mossy oaks and palms, and inhabited only by waterfowl in the lagoons and saltwater marshes. Scattered with feathery sea oats, massive sand dunes remain, guarding pristine beaches and lining the fairways of two Tom Fazio–designed golf courses. Loggerhead sea turtles, some weighing more than three hundred pounds, crawl out of the water to lay their eggs on the beaches. Dolphins play offshore. Boardwalks help preserve the fragile environment where herons and egrets seek their daily catch.

Nowadays Wild Dunes Resort on the island is one of the largest and most beautiful family resorts and golf destinations in the Southeast. Sport fishing, sailing, and sight-seeing cruises depart from the yacht harbor. Beachcombers stroll a wide, sandy strip more

than 2 miles long. Summertime kid's camps are popular, as are the teen activity programs and Wild Excursions, which are guided nature tours via kayak, canoe, jet-ski, and sailboat to neighboring islands. You can rent bikes for riding on the beach and on quiet back roads; take a tennis lesson or a dip in one of twenty swimming pools; go crabbing or fishing; or ride a boogie board in the surf.

The Victorian-style Boardwalk Inn reposes, grandly, a few steps from the sand. Guests line up in wicker rockers on the verandah, mesmerized by the ocean views. A boardwalk meanders to the Grand Pavilion gazebo, two oceanfront swimming pools, and the beach. A wide variety of townhouse units and privately owned cottages and homes are available to rent, and some are beachfront.

Prevailing sea breezes, endless dunes, and stretches of saltmarsh and native vegetation characterize Fazio's Wild Dunes Links. Since opening in 1980 his greens were replanted with space-age turf and several tees were added, making a top notch course into an award winner. Greens are perched on high dune ridges. Grassy hollows collect errant tee shots. On the finishing holes, hard against the sea, swirling winds and plenty of water hazards up the ante. The ancient oak in the middle of the fourteenth fairway was described by Edgar Allan Poe in his short story, "The Gold Bug," which is set on the island.

When the Harbor Course opened in 1986, *Golfweek* named it one of the best in the state. Just four years later, a complete rerouting, the addition of larger greens (the fifth is 10,000 square feet), and extensive integration of criss-crossing wetlands and lagoons transformed this short track into a true test of target golf. The duney layout borders the Intracoastal Waterway, playing from one island to another across the waters of Morgan Creek; all but one hole involves briny marshlands or freshwater streams.

Adding to the fun, Wild Dunes is one of only thirty

golf operations nationwide to offer PROLINK, the GPS in each golf cart that gives exact yardage, detailed layout of each hole, exact distances, pin placement, and tips from the resident pro.

Tennis is big, really big here on seventeen courts, supported by a staff of USPTA teaching pros; the U.S. Men's Clay Court Championships are played here. The tennis camp was named one of the "Top Five Best Kids Programs."

Summertime activities include Beach Olympics on Friday afternoons, live steel band music on weekend afternoons, jet-ski safaris, sailing tours, and a busy schedule of supervised outdoor fun.

She crab soup, crab fritters, black grouper, and Atlantic salmon are signature dishes at the elegant Sea Island Grill at the Boardwalk Inn, where the favored tables are out on the piazza overlooking the pool and tropical gardens.

Destiny

The site of the eighteenth hole of the Wild Dunes Links golf course played a big role in the Revolutionary War when Lord Cornwallis's command of two thousand soldiers landed there, planning to cross Breach Inlet to Sullivan's Island to attack Fort Moultrie from the rear. The English were met and held at bay by a force composed of six hundred North and South Carolina regulars, a company of militia, and a group of Catawba Indians. Not a single soldier crossed over to Sullivan's Island that day. It was America's first major victory in the South.

Golf course architect Tom Fazio laid eyes on the undeveloped island in the late 1970s. "I saw right away that it was an architect's dream," Fazio said. "It had all the elements you could ask for—trees, water, dunes, and an ocean coast. The routing was relatively easy because some of the holes looked like they had been there forever. The place reminded me of Pine Valley . . . an architect comes across that kind of land only once or twice in a lifetime."

Wild Dunes Resort
5757 Palm Boulevard
Isle of Palms, SC 29451
Phone: (843) 886–6000, reservations (888) 845–8926
Fax: (843) 886–2916
Web site: www.wilddunes.com
General Manager: Chris Haviland
Accommodations: 93 hotel rooms and suites; 250 two- to four-bedroom villas and three- to six-bedroom rental homes, all with equipped kitchen, washer/dryer, maid service, sundecks, cathedral ceilings, skylights, and arched windows in beautiful natural landscaping.
Meals: Hearty pub food in the wood-paneled Club Room, adjoining the Billiards Room. Seafood, steaks, and soufflés at the Sea Island Grill at the Inn. Edgar's at the Links serves regional cuisine in a casual setting, with live music in the bar. Dunes Deli and Pizzeria adjacent at the Harbor course is good for breakfast, deli lunches, and pizza. It's snacks and sandwiches, ice cream and tropical drinks at Duney's Cabana Bar and Grill at the waterfront.
Facilities: Seventeen Har-tru tennis courts; summer tennis camps; pro shop with racquet service and a full-time teaching staff; Islands Day Spa.
Services and Special Programs: A 3 to 1 player-instructor ratio and PGA Class A pro teachers give this golf school a real advantage; two-day mini-schools are popular. Kid's camps and excursions for ages 2–12.
Rates: $$$–$$$$
Golf and Spa Packages: Accommodations at the Board-walk Inn, one round of golf and breakfast: from $135–$220 per person, per night, double occupancy, two-night minimum stay. Preferred Golf Package is three nights in a two-bedroom golf villa, and two rounds of golf: from $80–$133 per person, per night, based on four golfers.
Getting There: Major airlines serve Charleston International Airport, twenty minutes from the resort. Amtrak arrives daily in North Charleston.
What's Nearby: In Charleston there are hundreds of historic buildings, the oldest museum in the country, and a line-up of antiques shops and boutiques on King Street. Take guided walking and horse-drawn carriage tours or home, garden, and plantation tours. In Mount Pleasant, Patriot's Point Maritime Museum features a WWII aircraft carrier and is the departure point for tours to historic Fort Sumter.

BARTON CREEK

Austin, Texas

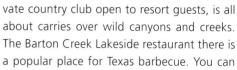

One of the largest executive conference resorts in the country, Barton Creek is also a golf mecca, with four topnotch championship courses. Fazio Foothills was named "#2 Course in Texas" and is a special favorite of President George W. Bush. Pitching and rolling across hilly terrain like a sailor on a turbulent sea, the Foothills moves in waves and hollows. When your ball disappears look for it in a rocky gully or at the bottom of a bowl lined with high grass. And, tune up your sidehill lie techniques for the steep-sided fairways. Pampas grass and prickly pear cacti sprout under the Spanish oaks and scrub pines, where a resident herd of deer hides in the shade. Silvery willows bend over an abundance of small lakes, creeks, and waterfalls. Typical of Tom Fazio's diabolical style, the 3-par third hole is a short stunner, dropping over a wide ravine onto a tabletop green between deep grass hollows and a sandy sink. Fazio declines to let up on eighteen, which is all uphill, ending in a crescendo of water cascading into a boulder-lined ravine below a high plateau where the green lies unseen until you arrive. Golfers get a break with six tee boxes on each hole, while Champions Bermuda greens put a premium on shotmaking.

Opened in 2000 and promptly named number one in the state, Fazio Canyons is laid on rolling ranchland in a beautiful Spanish oak and madrone forest, with streams and creeks on eleven holes, limestone-bedded canyons, and large greens that slope off, alarmingly so. No mega-mansions or condos distract from vistas of the surrounding hill country.

Ben Crenshaw designed the Crenshaw Cliffside with wide, gently rolling fairways in semi-links style, where you can run the ball up to the green, instead of the high lofted approach shots required on the other Barton Creek courses.

Arnold Palmer left his mark on the shores of nearby Lake Travis, where his Lakeside Course, a private country club open to resort guests, is all about carries over wild canyons and creeks. The Barton Creek Lakeside restaurant there is a popular place for Texas barbecue. You can walk all four golf courses, a pleasant experience when bluebonnets are in bloom.

Among the instructors at the Golf Academy are Chuck Cook, one of *Golf Digest*'s "Top 10 Greatest Teachers in America," and George Hannon, a "Top 10 College Golf Coach of the Century." Branches of the famous Ledbetter long-game and Pelz short-game schools are located here, too. Corporate golf school programs are popular, along with special fitness training and golf psychology classes. The pro shop has been named one of "America's Top 100 Golf Shops."

Under the umbrella of the Pinehurst Company, which owns the famous golf-oriented properties of Palmilla, the Homestead, Pinehurst, and Daufuskie Island, Barton Creek extends the high levels of personal service and special amenities that distinguish all the Pinehurst resorts. Decor in the guest rooms and the often bustling public areas is understated, masculine, and contemporary, in earth tones with leather upholstery and dark woods. A stroll throughout the labyrinthine hotel turns up a museum-like collection of historic photos, paintings, and Remington-replica cowboy sculptures.

A meeting planner's dream, Barton Creek offers the latest multimedia capability, from broadcast quality video to professional recording, special effects, lighting, and sound, with an amphitheater and event space for groups of up to 450.

Take a walk or a run around the resort on a 7-mile route, or try out the indoor track and par course. Twelve tournament-quality, outdoor lighted courts, a professional teaching staff, and pro shop appeal to tennis lovers. Guests enjoy games of pool and big screen TVs in Jim Bob's Lounge.

Dallas Stopover

Flying through Dallas? Stay a day or so to play TPC at Las Colinas, at the Four Seasons Resort. The bad news: It's under the flight path of the Dallas–Ft. Worth Airport. The good news: It's a stunner, some say the finest track in the state.

With help from Ben Crenshaw and Byron Nelson in 1983, architect Jay Morrish laid fairways open to the steady north Texas winds. A multimillion-dollar upgrade at the turn of the twenty-first century added lakes, tee boxes, and hundreds of oaks, elms and cypress trees, turning a very good course into one of the most varied, beautiful, and challenging on the PGA Tour—the Verizon Byron Nelson Classic is played here. PGA Hall of Famer Byron Nelson is often seen in the opulent clubhouse, where his memorabilia is on display; a giant bronze statue of the venerable golf great stands at the first tee.

Guests at the imposing, high-rise Four Seasons Resort may also play, one day a week, at the Cottonwood Valley Course, a pretty, private course on rolling terrain (www.fourseasons.com).

Barton Creek

8212 Barton Club Drive
Austin, TX 78735
Phone: (512) 329–4000, reservations (800) 336–6158
Fax: (512) 329–4597
Web site: www.bartoncreek.com
General Manager: James Walsh
Accommodations: For cowboys with portfolios, each of the 317 rooms and suites has plenty of elbow room: a king or two queen beds with luxurious linens, a commodious work space, a bath and a half, and private balconies with views of the countryside and golf courses. Leather, cowhide and dark woods, and cowboy- or historic-themed artworks complete the ranch-of-your-dreams feeling.
Meals: Light lunches and dinners are served up with Country Western and pop music in the Austin Grill. Besides bountiful breakfast and lunch buffets, sophisticated Southwestern-style cuisine is on the dinner menu in the Hill Country Dining Room, such as multicolored tortilla soup, blue crab dishes, and Texas-size steaks.
Facilities: A beautiful indoor lap pool lies below the Cybex fitness center. In the new European-style spa, health and beauty treatments are offered along with daily yoga, aerobics, and Pilates classes; plus, FitQuest health and fitness evaluation and personal training. Outdoor swimming pool; business center; twelve lighted tennis courts.
Services and Special Programs: Ledbetter long-game and Pelz short-game schools, corporate golf schools, plus the Barton Creek Golf Academy, offering multiday instruction with videotape analysis and on-course play. Although not a family resort, the hotel offers a child-care program and activities at the Kid's Club, with themed summer camps.
Rates: $$$
Golf Packages: The Capital of Golf package includes three nights accommodations, three rounds of golf, breakfast, and dinner. $570 per person.
Getting There: Transportation is provided from Austin Bergstrom International Airport, thirty-five minutes away. Helicopters and limousines to and from the airport and downtown Austin can be arranged.
What's Nearby: Sailing, jet skiing, and water skiing at nearby Lake Travis. At the Central Market in Austin, buy locally grown pecans, chili mixes, native brews, and salsas. Don't miss an evening on East 6th Street between Congress and Sabine—"The Strip"—which is cordoned off on weekends for revelers to stroll from restaurant to bar to nightclub in the "Live Music Capital of the World."

THE WESTIN LA CANTERA RESORT
San Antonio, Texas

On a wooded plateau at the highest point in Bexar County overlooking San Antonio, the Westin La Cantera aims to preserve the Hispanic and cowboy heritage of the original rancho that once rambled over this rugged piece of the Texas hill country. Remnants of an old quarry, massive, ivory-colored limestone walls, and boulders define the craggy landscape, creating a dramatic setting for two golf courses and the hotel, a dazzling "Texas Colonial-style" fortress and belltower built of the pale, native stone. With temperatures averaging in the mid-70s and sunny days more than 300 days a year, golf is a year-round sport.

On the hottest summer day, breezes cool golfers on the rocking and rolling terrain. The PGA Texas Open is played here on the La Cantera Golf Club course, one of the last designs of the Jay Morrish–Tom Weiskopf team. Mountain cedars, cacti, and a dense jungle of gnarled live oaks are watered by rushing streams. Many holes are fronted by creeks and wild ravines. Get out your camera on the seventh hole, which drops 80 feet above a wall of quarry stone, a large lake, a warren of sand traps, and close-up views of "The Rattler" roller-coaster at Fiesta Texas theme park. Described in the yardage booklet as "visually intimidating," the twelfth is daunting, even from the front tees: A clever series of "church pew" bunkers lies at the foot of a long, serpentine stone wall, across the fairway from a ravine. A lofted second shot is called for to stop the ball short on the green, which is guarded by two natural creeks and a beautiful, wide waterfall.

Opened in 2001, and notorious for steep terrain and stony, ball-bouncing outcroppings, dry creeks, and canyons, the Palmer Course is memorable for blind tee shots to large, fast, two- or three-tiered greens with sloping sides. The signature fourth hole is nearly all carry over a lake to a twenty-foot patch of green, fronted by a brace of waterfalls. Golfers trod to the putting surface by way of the Winnie Palmer Memorial Footbridge, dedicated by Arnie to his late wife. Bring your climbing gear for twelve, which rises to a plateau overlooking the city. If you are over this green, you are in the sand or in a cactus. Save your strength for the finishing hole, playing up, then plunging seriously downhill between a high, rocky parapet and cascades, running down to a lake then up to the huge, wavering green backed by considerable sand and more waterfalls. You may have an audience on the terrace of the Palmer clubhouse, rated by *Golf Magazine* as the "third best golf clubhouse in the world," in Southwest mission-style with a bell tower and inlaid stonework.

Awash in bluebonnets and black-eyed Susans, dense with mesquite, live oaks, and cedars, both courses provide acres of wildlife habitat, and are certified as Cooperative Sanctuaries by Audubon International.

Ironwork and heavy wooden doors, a huge fireplace, and leather sofas recreate ranch life in the hotel's great room. You can sip a margarita in Tio's Lobby Lounge or hide away in the charming little library. Golfers belly up to the bar in clubby Steinheimer's Lounge, which has a separate cigar bar, then head for steak dinners in the La Cantera Grille.

For guests desiring complete seclusion, the Casita Village in a wooded glen below the hotel fills the bill with mini-kitchens, large living rooms, carved wood furnishings and rancho artwork, fine fabrics, fireplaces, oversized tubs in marble bathrooms, pretty gardens and private patios with lovely forest views, and a swimming pool. Golf carts are provided and help you get around the sprawling resort.

Six swimming pools are laid out in a vast, landscaped terrace, comprising a sort of water theme park named "The Lost Quarry Pools." Parents like the lap pool and the adult pool. Teens head for the sports pool, while kids love the water slide and water volleyball, the Enchanted Rock Kid's Club, and the special kid's "Bubble Manicure" at the spa.

The Westin La Cantera Resort
16641 La Cantera Parkway
San Antonio, TX 78256
Phone: (210) 558–6500, reservations (800) 937–8461
Fax: (210) 558–2400
Web site: www.westinlacantera.com
General Manager: Anthony M. Cherone
Accommodations: 508 spacious rooms and suites with Southwestern-style ambience, each with private balcony, fully outfitted work spaces, and large tubs.
Meals: Elegant Southwestern cuisine in Francesca's at Sunset; indoor or outdoor casual meals at Brannon's Cafe; hearty food at the La Cantera Grille; and snacks poolside.
Facilities: Six outdoor swimming pools in terraced, garden settings, with waterfalls and cascades to mask the sound of the fun. Castle Rock Health Club has a workout center and offers health and beauty treatments, including the unique Sports Pedicure, favored by both men and women golfers. Tennis courts; two hot tubs; bicycles.
Services and Special Programs: A state-of-the-art practice center is anchored by the *Golf Digest* Academy directed by former Harvey Penick protégé, Bryan Gathright; there is junior golf too. Favored by PGA pros, the revolutionary "Mindset Academy" offers unique seminars on golf improvement. Supervised activities for ages 4–12 at the Kids Club, including nature hikes, water play, games, and craft making. Free guided tours for all ages feature nature walks, stargazing, and history-based storytelling.
Rates: $$$–$$$$
Golf Packages: Par-Tee for Two includes one night accommodations, breakfast, golf, instructional clinic, golf services, and amenities: from $419 for two, double occupancy.
Getting There: Major carriers serve San Antonio International Airport, 12 miles away. Airport transfer can be arranged.
What's Nearby: Major destinations for families are Six Flags Fiesta Texas, a large theme park adjacent to the resort; SeaWorld; and the historic Alamo. San Antonio is famous for the Riverwalk, a complex of restaurants, bars, and shops on the banks of the San Antonio River, where dinner barges and strolling mariachi bands create a party atmosphere. Pedal a bike or ride a trolley on the old Mission Trail.

A Ranch Course

Wide fairways fringed with overhanging oaks and criss-crossed by narrow creeks, the Hyatt Regency Hill Country golf course lies easy on the rolling hills of a former ranch. Imagine the country home of a flamboyant, multimillionaire Texas cattle rancher, and you get the feeling of this unique resort. Amid magnificent gardens and grounds, the white limestone hotel has pillars and balconies. Rocking chairs await the exhausted golfer on the porch under the shade trees. Kids play on a little beach and cruise around a running stream on inner tubes, while parents hide away in the idyllic adult pool area, soothed by the rush of waterfalls. Two huge fireplaces are toasty warm in the wintertime, as guests lounge on leather sofas and cowhide armchairs in the Texas-size lobby. Each of 500 rooms has a private balcony or patio, country-chic decor, and views of rolling hills or of one of the prettiest resort courses in the state.

THE EQUINOX
Manchester Village, Vermont

In the shadow of Mount Equinox, the "Green Mountain Boys" met in the Marsh Tavern in 1769 to plot their revolutionary activities. Today golfers relax in Windsor chairs by the fireside in that same tavern on the grounds of the Equinox resort. Mrs. Abraham Lincoln vacationed here in 1863. Presidents Taft, Grant, Roosevelt, and Harrison trod the marble sidewalks of Manchester Village and lingered in the hotel's elegant Federal-style lobby, a meeting place, then and now, for affluent Northeasterners.

Dressed in white, guests wield croquet mallets and tennis racquets. They fish on the pond, hike and bike in the surrounding pine and spruce forest, and browse the antiques shops and the designer outlet stores in the Colonial-era village of Manchester.

Grandly situated on the edge of the village green, between the Green and Taconic Mountain ranges at the base of Mount Equinox and a 900-acre forest preserve, the hotel is guarded by a battalion of stately white columns. Entirely renovated and updated by new owners, guest rooms and public areas are aglow with rich colors and tapestry fabrics.

Walter Travis' beloved 1927 design for the Gleneagles Golf Course languished in decline in recent decades, until 1992 when Rees Jones headed up a much-needed refurbishment and updating of the track. The original routing and the lovely, rustic Scottish flavor was carefully preserved within the spectacular mountain setting. Greens were rebuilt and expanded, bunkers reshaped, fairways elevated, and modern grasses integrated, all the while maintaining native flora

and wildlife habitat to qualify as an Audubon Society Cooperative Sanctuary. *Golf Magazine* promptly awarded the new course a Silver Medal, and *Golf for Women* named it one of the top ten women-friendly places to play.

Views of the countryside are distracting on the gentle front nine. On the fourth hole, wait to hear the bell rung by the previous foursome, before you attempt to approach down a forested chute to the green. Characteristic of the rugged back nine, the large twelfth green features a daunting circular ridge. Finishing, you turn back toward the church steeples of Main Street for two holes tilting left—one a well-bunkered dogleg, the other nearly overpowered by a huge tree.

Catering to the gentry—just like its sister resort in Scotland, the Gleneagles Hotel—the Equinox offers a Land Rover off-road driving school, a fly-fishing school, and the School of British Falconry. Many guests take the scenic 5-mile drive to the top of the mountain for dazzling views of southern Vermont and neighboring states.

Within a few miles are charming seventeenth- and eighteenth-century towns—Weston, Bennington, and others—filled with museums, antiques shops, steepled churches, and Revolutionary War monuments. Spring wildflowers and fall color in these parts are nothing short of wondrous.

The resort operates its own Cross-county Ski Touring Center with miles of village and mountain trails, and snowmobile touring on nearby U.S. Forest Service land.

Guest rooms and suites are furnished in sumptuous, traditional, Early-American style with antiques, rich fabrics, and Audubon prints. All have mountain, village, or garden views. Hearty regional cuisine, such as Yankee pot roast, mountain trout, and shepherd's pie, is served in the tavern, a cozy spot warmed by flannel wall coverings and polished wood floors. Musicians and singers hold forth into the late evening inside the tavern, and on the terrace in the summertime.

Once a boarding house and the home of Charles F. Orvis, the fly-fishing entrepreneur, the Charles Orvis Inn at the Equinox is a glorious, nineteenth-century mansion right on Main Street. It comprises nine luxurious one- and two-bedroom suites with living rooms, fireplaces, cherry-paneled kitchens with marble counters, Jacuzzi tubs, and porches with rockers—the better to watch the townspeople stroll by. Inn guests enjoy a private billiard room, a cozy bar, gardens, and a wood-paneled library.

The Doctor Pays a Call

"The Equinox resort has always been such a wonderful and important complement to Manchester, and even more now since the hotel was redone in spectacular style," said Rees Jones, the architect who directed the rebuilding of the Gleneagles Golf Course here in 1992. He said, "I believe that due to the Depression in the 1920s, Walter Travis did not have a chance to complete his original vision for Gleneagles. We tried to do that, according to his legacy."

The younger son of Robert Trent Jones Sr., Rees Jones may be best known as "The Open Doctor," for his rehabilitation of several U.S. Open venues, including Bethpage for the 2002 Open, Baltusrol (1993), Pinehurst #2 (1999), and others.

Jones said, "The site for Gleneagles was perfectly chosen, in a fine valley in this beautiful mountain setting. We added fill to some fairways for better drainage and a smoother relationship to the greens, particularly on fifteen, seventeen, and eighteen. And, many of the original bunkers were brought back and enhanced to account for today's longer hitters. Nowadays, Gleneagles is a very enjoyable golfing experience."

The Equinox
3567 Main Street
Manchester Village, VT 05254
Phone: (802) 362–4700, reservations (800) 362–4747
Fax: (802) 362–1595
Web site: www.equinoxresort.com
General Manager: Gary Thulander
Accommodations: 183 rooms and one-, two-, and three-bedroom suites in the hotel, in townhouses, and the Charles Orvis Inn; furnished with traditional pine and antiques, luxurious fabrics and fine art; with mountain, village, or garden views.
Meals: The casual Marsh Tavern serves casual meals all day and evening; lobsterfests are popular at the Dormy Grill. The Colonnade main dining room is restored to its former glory and formality, featuring contemporary American and Continental cuisine for dinner, and a popular Sunday brunch.
Facilities: The Fitness Spa offers a wide variety of health and beauty treatments, exercise classes, and weight equipment, plus a 75-foot-long, heated outdoor pool and an indoor lap pool; three plexi-cushion tennis courts with all-weather cover; paddle tennis, and volleyball.
Services and Special Programs: Learn falconry; drive a Rover off-road; flycast on the private Equinox Pond; take a guided fishing trip on local streams and ponds, and guided hikes on the Appalachian Trail. In the winter, ski and snowshoe right from the hotel, and skate on the private rink.
Rates: $$$–$$$$
Golf Packages: Green Mountain Golf Package includes two nights accommodations, unlimited golf, Equinox shirt, golf gifts, and use of the Fitness Spa. $418–$490 per person, double occupancy.
Getting There: Commercial airlines serve Rutland, Burlington, and Albany airports. Amtrak arrives in Albany. Boston is three hours away; New York City, four hours.
What's Nearby: The Vermont State Craft Center; the headquarters and stores of the outdoor outfitter, Orvis; the American Museum of Fly Fishing; Ben & Jerry's factory tours; the Bennington and the Shelbourne museums; the famous Vermont Country Store; the Vermont Teddy Bear Factory; and Hildene, Robert Todd Lincoln's Georgian revival estate. Shoot and hunt at Tinmouth Preserve; bike and hike in the Equinox Preservation Trust and around the village; take a horseback ride; rent boats, canoes, and jet skis on Lake George and Lake St. Catherine; or canoe down the Battenkill River. In the winter, ski at Bromley and Stratton Mountains.

WILLIAMSBURG INN
Williamsburg, Virginia

The re-creation of living history at Colonial Williamsburg, a pre-Revolutionary village in the Virginia woodlands, is so detailed and authentic, and so enjoyable for all ages, that every American citizen deserves a visit here, at least once in a lifetime. The surprise for golfers is that Williamsburg is more than a page from a history book. It is a major golf destination, with 126 holes of golf at three resorts.

With white-painted columns and arched windows, as dignified and imposing as a dowager duchess, the post-colonial, English Regency–style Williamsburg Inn occupies a graceful, tree-studded place of honor near the village green, and is headquarters for travelers who wish to combine sightseeing and museum-going with golf on three outstanding courses.

The Inn underwent complete and significant renovation at the turn of this century. As inviting and comfortable as those in a Virginia country house, the hotel's sixty-two guest rooms were enlarged to an average of 500 square feet, with large sitting areas and wonderful bathrooms. Each room has a photo of a famous guest, from U.S. presidents to movie stars, even Winston Churchill. French doors at the rear entry open onto a flagstone terrace shaded by tall oaks and elms, above the croquet court, lawn bowling, and the golf club.

The Golden Horseshoe Golf Club's Gold Course here was designed in 1963 by Robert Trent Jones Sr. and recently updated by his son, Rees Jones. In the spring, dogwood, cherry, wild azalea, and plum trees burst into bloom beside the fairways, which follow the dramatic ups and downs of the Tidewater landscape and ramble along the shoreline of a lake. Nowadays the track enjoys better defined targets, reconstructed bunkers, and large greens. Average players will find it more forgiving than in the past. Low handicappers says it's longer and more challenging from the tips.

With no residential development to mar the silence nor the sight of the pristine woodland setting, golfers can walk both the Gold and the Green Courses. The Green is Rees Jones's own design, a 250-acre layout with steep elevation changes atop the ridges and in the gullies, and characterized by narrow chutes lined with towering pine, cedar, and oak trees. Save your energy and an accurate tee shot for the finishing hole, where the dense forest impinges and a pond nearly surrounds the green.

Many golfers warm up on the cunning, executive-length Spotswood Course, a miniature mirror-image of the Gold Course, with holes from 100 to nearly 500 yards.

The top notch golf complexes at Kingsmill Resort and Ford's Colony are both in Williamsburg.

Living in the Eighteenth Century

Restored over a period of four decades by the John D. Rockefeller Jr. family, Colonial Williamsburg is the oldest and largest living history museum in the country. Isolated from the rest of the world by trees and meadows, the village of dozens of eighteenth-century buildings and more than a hundred glorious gardens is lost in time, poised on the eve of the American Revolution.

In a lively, true-to-history, colorful outdoor setting, denizens of the town dress in period costume and reenact daily life, from musket shooting to fife and drum playing. Firebrands read broadsides condemning the Crown. Blacksmiths and craftspeople ply their trades. Carriages clip-clop down the street, and fire brigades gallop along, calling for volunteers. Draft horses pull wagons stacked with beer barrels, and the curly locks of longwool sheep are clipped for spinning and weaving. Special demonstrations and events, such as military encampments, are scheduled throughout the year. In four authentic, charming taverns, tankards of hard cider are raised and eighteenth-century cuisine is served (800–HISTORY, www.colonialwilliamsburg.org).

Williamsburg Inn
135 East Francis Street
Williamsburg, VA 23185
Phone: (757) 229–1000, reservations (800) 361–5261
Fax: (757) 220–7096
Web site: www.colonialwilliamsburg.com
General Manager: Clyde Min
Accommodations: In the inn, 62 rooms and suites in traditional, neoclassical Regency style with reproduction art and antiques. Families favor the comfortable surroundings of 42 rooms in the Providence Hall wings, where sleeper sofas, balconies or patios, and proximity to the tennis courts are top advantages.
Meals: In the posh, four-star, Regency Room, crystal chandeliers, palm-leafed columns, and silk draperies set the scene for contemporary American regional cuisine. English tea is served in the lounge, overlooking the gardens. Both golf courses have recently renovated clubhouses with casual indoor/outdoor dining.
Facilities: Six clay and two hard surface tennis courts, and two outdoor swimming pools at the Tazewell Club Fitness Center, plus an indoor lap pool, aerobics studio, and complete workout equipment.
Services and Special Programs: Golf Digest School offers multiday sessions, spring through fall. Free golf and tennis clinics for ages 8–17. Ages 5–12 tour the historical area and play at the pool with the Colonial Kids Club.
Rates: $$$
Golf Packages: One night accommodations, breakfast, two days of unlimited golf, cart, and discounted Williamsburg passes. $238–$353 per person, per night, double occupancy, two-night minimum.
Getting There: Newport News-Williamsburg, Norfolk, and Richmond International Airports are served by major airlines. Amtrak bus connects nationwide trains with Williamsburg.
What's Nearby: Besides visiting the museums, quaint restaurants, and the many shops of Williamsburg, you can drive 8 miles to Carter's Grove to tour an eighteenth-century plantation and slave quarters, a seventeenth-century Virginia settlement, and the Winthrop Rockefeller Archaeology Museum.

THE HOMESTEAD RESORT

Hot Springs, Virginia

In the rolling foothills of the Allegheny Mountains, the Grande Dame of American mountain resorts, the Homestead, embodies pure Southern elegance, as it has since Virginia aristocracy rattled up to the imposing redbrick edifice in their horse-drawn carriages in the late 1700s. They lingered here in luxury, making frequent visits to 98-degree, crystal-clear, mineral-rich waters of the nearby Jefferson Pools at Warm Springs, renowned for their curative properties. Thomas Jefferson sojourned here for nearly a month in 1818. Financier J. Pierpont Morgan arrived in his private railroad car. Thomas Edison, the Vanderbilts, and John D. Rockefeller were also frequent visitors.

The atmosphere today remains genteel and the scene picturesque, with guests touring the grounds in antique buckboards and a fringe-topped surrey. Homestead is believed to be the longest continuously running resort in the United States.

In 1993 the Pinehurst Company began a magnificent restoration of the historic resort, returning rooms, public spaces, and grounds to their former glory. Rooms were exquisitely refurbished with traditional fabrics and furnishings, plush, patterned carpets, and floral draperies, accurately reflecting the opulent Georgian architecture.

The new European-style spa is now one of the largest and most luxurious in the Southeast, offering traditional and signature treatments such as "Mountain Laurel Soaks," "Dr. Goode's Spout Bath," and "Golfer's Glow." Naturally heated underground hot springs bubble up into the absolutely beautiful, century-old, indoor pool. Around the new outdoor pool and bathhouse are tennis courts and a lawn game area.

The Cascades, one of three championship golf courses here—each with its own clubhouse, restaurant, and pro shop—is ranked as Virginia's number one course, and some say it's the top mountain course in the United States. The William Flynn original opened in 1923, a classic track known for narrow fairways, fast greens, and the breathtaking series of waterfalls in Cascades Stream, which come into play on about half the course. The fairways are so beautifully isolated between dense forest borders that you seldom see the next foursome.

Rees Jones completed a much-needed, million-dollar redesign of Donald Ross's Old Course, including the addition of a driving range and putting green, thus bringing the 1913 design into the new millennium. Expect sidehill, uphill, and downhill lies, and very small greens. The first tee is the oldest in continuous use in the country, first played in 1892, twenty-one years before Ross made an 18-holer from the original six rustic holes.

More open and flatter than the others, with calmer stream waters on the valley floor, Lower Cascades is a Robert Trent Jones Sr. design. Not as easy as they look, these lightning fast greens have devilish slopes.

Golf great Sam Snead, who began his career at the Homestead in 1934, is a frequent visitor and a beloved friend of the resort. His memorabilia lines the hallways and he is often on hand to chat and hit a few with guests. Today's resident touring pro is Virginia native, Lanny Wadkins.

Sitting in a rocking chair on the front porch of the stately hotel, drinking in the beauty of the mountains and valley, you can contemplate fly-fishing on a four-mile-long trout stream, hiking through wildflowers beside the Cascades waterfalls, or horseback riding on pristine bridle paths. A Big Band orchestra plays for dancers in the Dining Room, while in the Players Pub, guests catch up on sports on seven screens, play darts and billiards, and dance to Top-40 tunes.

One of the most beautiful shooting facilities in the country, and host to the U.S. Open club, offers sporting clays, skeet, trap, and a rifle range. In the wintertime, skiing at a nine-run ski area, skating on an Olympic-size ice-skating rink, snowboarding, and tubing are popular.

Other Places to Play

Rees Jones has laid out 27 holes of fabulous golf on the Stoney Creek Golf Club at the Wintergreen Resort, near Hot Springs. Lake Monocan and two creeks are watery hazards on more than a dozen holes in this beautiful valley. The Devil's Knob track, at a 3,800-foot elevation in a glorious mountain setting, has wide fairways lined with magnificent maples and oaks. Both courses have clubhouses and restaurants. The resort rents more than three hundred privately owned condominiums and homes. The Wintergreen Golf Academy is located here, and a stupendous sports complex, with more than two dozen tennis courts, six swimming pools, an equestrian center, and bikes for miles of trails, including a stretch of the Appalachian Trail (800–325–2200).

The Homestead Resort
P.O. Box 2000
Hot Springs, VA 24445
Phone: (540) 839–1766, reservations (800) 838–1766
Fax: (540) 839–7670
Web site: www.thehomestead.com
General Manager: Gary Rosenberg
Accommodations: 506 rooms and suites, recently renovated, all in sumptuous, traditional Georgian-era style; some with wood-burning fireplaces and sun porches.
Meals: Meal packages are traditionally popular. In the Main Dining Room, French and American cuisine merits tableside service and a dance orchestra. In a turn-of-the-twentieth-century building, Sam Snead's Tavern, and the 1766 Grille, serve hearty pub fare and American regional dishes. The casual Casino Restaurant and Cafe Albert are good for light meals and snacks.
Facilities: Upscale shops; an equestrian center with English and Western instruction; four Har-Tru and four all-weather tennis courts and professional instruction; two outdoor pools and one large indoor pool; eight lanes of bowling; clay, skeet, trap, and rifle/pistol shooting ranges; an elegant health and beauty spa; ski resort and ski school.
Services and Special Programs: Originating at Pinehurst, the Golf Advantage School offers individual instruction and classes, with a 5 to 1 student-instructor ratio. Kid's Club for ages 3–12 with activities ranging from storytelling to crafts, hikes, fishing, tennis, sports and games. Lessons in falconry with trained falcons, hawks, and owls.
Rates: $$$–$$$$
Golf Packages: Accommodations, breakfast and dinner, and unlimited golf: $275–$364 per person, per night, double occupancy. Three-day Golf Advantage includes accommodations, all meals, unlimited golf, video analysis, and instruction: $1,050–$1,700 per person, double occupancy.
Getting There: Ninety minutes from Roanoke Regional Airport, served by major airlines; shuttle and limousine service available. Private aircraft arrive at Bath County Airport, 17 miles away. Amtrak trains at Clifton Forge.
What's Nearby: One hundred miles of hiking and biking trails, and the historic Warm Springs Pools, 5 miles from the hotel.

KINGSMILL RESORT
Williamsburg, Virginia

Draped gracefully along the banks of the wide James River, 3 miles from the historic streets of Colonial Williamsburg, Kingsmill Resort is a plantation-style complex of condominium-style villas, four superior golf courses, and a rambling sports center, making this a top vacation destination for active families.

Developed by one of the Anheuser-Busch companies, the four-star, four-diamond property is host to the PGA Tour's Michelob Championship, which is played on the rolling hills of the River Course, one of Pete Dye's masterworks. A renovation in 1998 added denser rough and firmer, faster, quite elevated greens,

earning a 137 slope. Large and guarded by legions of bunkers, greens are as rippled and as swift as the river itself. Deep, unplayable ravines and wooded chasms criss-cross the track, a gracious Southern beauty shaded with weeping willows and ancient oaks. Always one for devilish surprises, Dye has a 300-yard-long sand trap awaiting you. Bordering the river, where Curtis Strange's "navy" anchors during the tournament, the seventeenth hole is a Revolutionary War and Civil War historical site.

High handicappers head for the Plantation Course, which Arnold Palmer and Ed Seay laid on the site of an original 1736 plantation, among historical buildings and artifacts. Although fairways are wide and forgiving, accurate irons are called for on the sidehill lies, the water on eight holes, and the tiered, wavery greens. Alongside the second hole are fragments of the original plantation mansion and attendant buildings.

Newest at the resort, less varied in terrain but no less challenging than the River Course, is the Woods Course, which lies in a lovely, secluded, pine and hardwood forest setting. Designed by Tom Clark and Curtis Strange, Kingsmill's resident touring professional and U.S. Open winner, the Woods is a parkland track with wide fairways and the ubiquitous, brambly gullies, Virginia countryside.

Bray Links may be the most elaborate and beautiful par-3 course in the country, with holes from 58 to 109 yards. On the riverside, this is a natural looking, swaled, and mounded-links layout with an island green. The greens are regulation size and as perfectly maintained as on the championship courses.

Two-hour mini-schools are popular at the Golf Academy, as is the short-game school, the "Slicer's Only" school, the Ladies School, and the Power School, all with a 5 to 1 student-teacher ratio. Outdoor and new indoor, weatherproof practice facilities are exceptional.

At the new Spa and Sports Club are indoor and

outdoor swimming pools, racquetball, squash, and aerobics classes. Anchoring the clay tennis court complex is a sizable, newly renovated tennis clubhouse. After a day of golf, guests head to the spa for sports massage, for the "Kingsmill Sugar Scrub," or the seaweed "Peppermint Twist."

Throughout the lovely, forested, and landscaped grounds, well-appointed accommodations feature reproduction, Colonial-style furnishings with fine draperies and linens. Be sure to take the self-guided walking tour past seasonally blooming flower beds, specimen trees, and native plantings.

Other Places to Play

The Golden Horseshoe courses and the Kingsmill complex, both at Williamsburg, get so much deserved attention that Ford's Colony may go unnoticed by some traveling golfers. The extraordinary variety of terrain characterizes the pretty clutch of fifty-four holes of golf at Ford's Colony. On Marsh Hawk, the greens are wildly undulating. On Blackheath, greens are large and flattish, with big landing areas; a large reservoir and other water hazards come prominently into play on thirteen holes. Tall pines give the Blue Heron Course a real Pinehurst look. In fact the architect of all three Ford's tracks is Dan Maples, a Pinehurst resident whose father and grandfather worked with Donald Ross, the Scottish genius of Pinehurst (757–258–4130, www.FordsColony.com).

Kingsmill Resort
1010 Kingsmill Road
Williamsburg, VA 23185
Phone: (757) 253–1703, reservations (800) 832–5665
Fax: (757) 253–8237
Web site: www.kingsmill.com
General Manager: Joseph A. Durante III
Accommodations: 400 guest rooms and one-, two-, and three-bedroom suites overlooking fairways, the river, or the tennis center; with kitchens, living and dining areas, fireplaces, and outdoor decks.
Meals: Jackets required in the riverside Bray Dining Room for contemporary cuisine and regional seafood. Hearty meals at Eagles' at the Golf Club at the eighteenth green of the River Course. A fun, casual atmosphere, bistro food, and pizza at Regattas' Cafe. Try Moody's Tavern for cozy fireplaces, billiards, live entertainment, and light meals.
Facilities: Fifteen clay tennis courts, match-making, professional instruction, and exceptional practice facilities; ninety-one-slip marina accessible to the James River and the Intracoastal Waterway; indoor and outdoor pools; two racquetball courts, Cybex and Keiser circuit training equipment, cardio-stations, and classes in the health club.
Services and Special Programs: Kingsmill Kampers program for ages 5–12, with golf, tennis, games, and crafts. Resident junior golf and tennis camps. Weekly calendar of outdoor activities for all ages in the summertime.
Rates: $$$
Golf Packages: Unlimited Golf includes accommodations, unlimited golf and cart on all the courses, use of practice facilities, and par-3 course: $220–$330 per golfer, per night, double occupancy. Golf and Spa Package includes a forty-five-minute golf lesson, a fifty-minute sports massage, and a hydrating or gentleman's manicure: $160. Family packages include admission to nearby theme parks.
Getting There: International airports include Richmond, Norfolk, and Newport News/Williamsburg; Amtrak railroad service to Williamsburg.
What's Nearby: Transportation is provided to the European-style villages, rides and exhibits at Busch Gardens, and to Colonial Williamsburg. Also visit Water Country USA, the historic villages of Jamestown and Yorktown, the College of William and Mary, and the Abby Aldrich Rockefeller Folk Art Center. Fishing in the James River for croaker, trout, flounder, and rock fish.

RESORT SEMIAHMOO
Blaine, Washington

At the tip of a mile-long, sandy peninsula jutting into Puget Sound, near the Canadian border just south of Vancouver, British Columbia, Semiahmoo is surrounded by more than a thousand acres of pristine wildlife preserve and is the state's largest, full-service destination resort. A new owner invested millions in a complete renovation and expansion of the property, resulting in service, style, and amenities taking a giant step upward, and membership in the prestigious group of Preferred Hotels and Resorts being granted. Two championship golf courses make this an important stop for golfers visiting the Northwest.

On the narrow finger between Semiahmoo Bay and Drayton Harbor, 5 miles of beaches are fine for clam digging and beachcombing. A naturalist leads kayak trips to see seals and other wildlife around the bay, while bicyclers and in-line skaters ply the paved trails. Nature seekers wander the shore, along with bald eagles, blue herons, kingfishers, and a host of other birds.

Free concerts are frequently held in glorious outdoor venues at the resort, and sometimes indoors by the fireplace. Guest rooms are warm and sleek, Northwest-cottage style, with pine and stone accents, fire-

places, patios or balconies with mountain or bay views, and windows that open to the salt air.

The new Spa by the Sea is a thalassotherapy center offering traditional and exotic treatments. Men go for the "Executive," which involves exfoliation to soothe skin conditions and razor burn; a face, neck, and hand massage; and hydrating masque. The "Sports Massage" reduces soreness and lactic acid build up and increases flexibility.

Golf for Women magazine calls Semiahmoo Golf Club one of the Top Women-Friendly Courses. An Arnold Palmer design and an Audubon Cooperative Sanctuary, the track lies in a tall, lovely cedar and fir forest, 7,005 yards from the tips. Ponds and lakes are rimmed with wildflowers and stone retaining walls. Fairways are wide and greens are relatively large and cleverly contoured.

A masterpiece of Canadian designer Graham Cooke, the Loomis Trail Golf Club has water on every hole, smooth, fast greens, and the second highest slope rating in Washington State. Superior drainage makes play enjoyable all year long. Several elevated tees have views of open fairways and medium-size, flattish greens.

A former PGA pro, Jeff Coston directs the Golf Academy, offering lessons and clinics with video and high-tech swing analysis in a new indoor heated training center.

Mountain Views, Sidehill Lies

A short ferry ride or drive from the Puget Sound town of Winslow, Port Ludlow Golf Club is a stunner surrounded by snowcapped Mount Rainier, the Olympic Mountains, and the Seattle skyline. Robert Muir Graves designed three nines—Tides, Trail, and Timber—on very hilly, forested terrain. Practice your uphill and downhill shots, and be prepared for doglegs and blind shots, fast greens, narrow fairways, and small landing zones. Port Ludlow is consistently considered to be the toughest in the state (360–437–0637).

Resort Semiahmoo
9565 Semiahmoo Parkway
Blaine, WA 98230–9326
Phone: (360) 318–2000, reservations (800) 770–7992
Web site: www.semiahmoo.com
General Manager: Tom Waithe
Accommodations: Four-diamond rated, 198 rooms and suites in soft earth-tone colors, with plush sheepskin mattress padding and feather pillows, fireplaces, private balconies or patios, and original artworks.
Meals: Fresh Northwest Pacific seafood and steaks at Star, with a bay view. Fried oyster sandwiches and more hearty fare at Packers Bar and Grill. Great Blue Heron Bar and Grill features smoked chicken quesadilla, homemade soups, a bistro menu, and microbrews. Sandwiches, salads, and snacks to eat at the Gift Shop Cafe or take out to the beach.
Facilities: Two golf clubhouses with pro shops and restaurants, driving range, and putting and chipping greens; two indoor and two outdoor tennis courts; indoor/outdoor pool; racquetball; indoor running track; fitness center; books, games, and playing cards in the library; 300-slip, full-service marina.
Services and Special Programs: Dogs are welcome for a fee. Guided nature walks and kayak tours; frequent free concerts; guitar sing-alongs and bonfires on the beach; Semiahmoo Kids Kamp for ages 12 months to 12 years. Borrow fishing poles, beach buckets and toys, soccer balls and basketballs, horseshoes, and croquet equipment.
Rates: $$–$$$
Golf Packages: Best of the West includes overnight accommodations, continental breakfast, a round of golf and cart. $199–379 for two, double occupancy.
Getting There: A two-hour drive from Seattle International Airport, a one-hour drive from Vancouver, B.C. Bellingham Airport is twenty minutes away.
What's Nearby: Scenic seaside touring on world famous Chuckanut Drive. Explore White Rock, a charming community of sandy beaches, shops, and lively waterfront activities. Shopping, gallery hopping, and sightseeing in turn-of-the-century-era Fairhaven; kayaking and sailing in the bay; deep-sea fishing; whale watching; sightseeing in the Dutch village of Lynden.

THE GREENBRIER

White Sulphur Springs, West Virginia

Golf legend Sam Snead was the long-time resident pro here at one of the most impressive and largest destination resorts in the South. Two-story, paned windows and Georgian columns grace the colossal, white, wedding cake of a hotel, surrounded by 6,500 acres of gardens and woodlands, and the Allegheny Mountains. Decorated by world-famous interior designers Dorothy Draper and Carleton Varney, a series of lobbies, sitting rooms, and the guest rooms are formal and elegant, with crystal chandeliers, gilt mirrors, marble fireplaces, vibrant floral wall coverings and draperies, antique furnishings, and historic paintings. Horse-drawn carriages glide around the grounds while guests, all in white, play croquet and take guided tours of the glorious gardens and historic sites. It's no wonder that guests receive a booklet detailing the dress code for various venues and activities.

Seventeen hundred staff members, many of whom are second- and third-generation at the resort, consider themselves "ladies and gentlemen serving ladies and gentlemen."

Millions were invested in a recent major renovation and expansion, restoring this National Historic Monument to the apex of perfection in lodging, dining, and impeccable personal service, with three golf courses, a new golf academy, and a variety of activities including horseback riding, tennis, falconry, fishing, and French cooking lessons—more than fifty activities in all.

Opened in 1913 for seekers of health and restoration in the natural White Sulphur Springs mineral baths, the spa was expanded and renovated in 2001 and continues to focus on hydrotherapy, with European-style signature treatments.

Jack Nicklaus updated and expanded the 1924 Greenbrier Golf Course for the 1977 and 1979 Ryder Cup Matches. Heavily wooded with terraced greens and plenty of water, the course calls for accurate iron play.

One of the early masters, Charles Blair MacDonald, laid out the Old White Course in 1913 on rolling terrain, in Scottish style with plenty of pitch and run, and some forced carries onto contoured and sloping greens. In 1956 President Dwight D. Eisenhower shot a 93 on the Old White, a few months after his heart attack.

A brilliant and much-needed 1999 redesign of the Meadows Course by Robert Cupp added 500 yards, reshaped bunkers, and moved tee boxes, giving this lovely, lakeside track new life. This is a beauty with a meandering stream and views of Whiterock Mountain framed by the Midland gap, hundreds of spruces, oaks, maples, willows, and birches, and blooming dogwood and cherry trees.

Golf teaching techniques at the Sam Snead Golf Academy, which opened in 1999, are based on Snead's theories and those of the John Jacobs Golf Group. New millennium facilities include video swing analysis, covered hitting bays, and several practice greens, offering daily clinics and private lessons.

America's First Organized Golf Club

Oakhurst Links at White Sulphur Springs offers a unique experience for golfers on a lovely, short course that was originally laid out in 1884 by a group of Scottish, English, and American gentlemen. This was the first organized golf club in the country and founded the oldest known tournament, the Oakhurst Challenge Medal.

The course languished for decades until the early 1990s, when local legend, Sam Snead, encouraged the owners, the Keller family, to restore it for public play. Architect Bob Cupp joined in the effort, restoring Oakhurst to its nineteenth-century condition and 2,235-yard length—-the game was originally played with "gutta percha" balls, when a drive of 150 or 160 yards was considered admirable. A flock of thirty-five sheep roam the gently rolling forestlands, helping to keep the fairways "mowed."

Leave your cavity-back irons, titanium drivers, and your tees in your vehicle, as golf at Oakhurst is played with replica, nineteenth-century, long-nose hickory-shafted clubs and gutta-percha balls hit from sand tees. The equipment is made in St. Andrews, Scotland, and in England, exclusively for Oakhurst Links, and is included in your green fee. At the charming farmhouse museum and clubhouse, you get instruction on the use of the equipment and the art of forming a sand tee.

Oakhurst Links is open for play and museum visits from May 1 through October 31, and by special appointment (304–536–1884, www.oakhurstlinks.com).

The Greenbrier
300 West Main Street
White Sulphur Springs, WV 24986
Phone: (304) 536–1110, reservations (800) 453–4858
Fax: (304) 536–7854
Web site: www.greenbrier.com
General Manager: Ted J. Kleisner
Accommodations: Five-diamond rated, 739 rooms, suites, and estate houses, with traditional furnishings, floral fabrics, fine bedding, sitting areas; some four-poster beds and fireplaces; all include breakfast and dinner.
Meals: Continental and classic American cuisine and a formal atmosphere in the Main Dining Room; hearty, wood-fired specialties from the open kitchen at the Golf Club; Draper's Cafe for breakfast, lunch, and desserts; dinner with a wine motif at the intimate Tavern Room; cocktails, snacks, and dancing at the refined Old White Club and contemporary Slammin' Sammy's.
Facilities: Indoor and outdoor tennis courts; indoor and outdoor swimming pools; full-service health and beauty spa and salon; upscale shopping arcade; the Greenbrier Clinic offers diagnostic services and evaluation; trap and skeet shooting; bowling; horseback riding.
Services and Special Programs: Golf caddie services; La Varenne French-cooking school; Land Rover driving school; falconry academy. Supervised children's activities, from games and crafts to golf and tennis instruction.
Rates: $$$$
Golf Packages: Deluxe Package includes unlimited golf and cart, one night accommodations, breakfast, dinner, golf clinic, and golf services. $262–$463 per person, double occupancy.
Getting There: Major carriers service Yeager Airport in Charleston, a one-and-a-half hour drive away, and Roanoke Regional Airport. Private aircraft land at Greenbrier Valley Airport in Lewisburg, a fifteen-minute drive. Amtrak trains arrive at the circa 1925 station here.
What's Nearby: At Tamarack, daily demonstrations of West Virginia arts, crafts, music and foods, with theatrical and musical programs throughout the year. White-water rafting, skiing, fishing, and exploring historic towns.

THE AMERICAN CLUB
Kohler, Wisconsin

At the peak of his career at the end of the twentieth century, Pete Dye created a monument to his design sensibilities and expertise with two championship golf courses at Whistling Straits and two at Blackwolf Run—all seventy-two holes within the rugged, northwoods setting of the American Club resort.

Host venue for the 2004 PGA Championship, the Straits Course is Dye's vision of traditional British Isles links, laid with massive dunes and native grasses along the banks of Lake Michigan and high above on the bluffs. Just as in Ireland and Scotland, you walk this track—along with the resident flock of long-wool, Scottish Blackface sheep—and you are glad that caddies are required on the rising and falling hills and dales formed by ancient glacial moraines. Golfers confront armies of bunkers, narrow fairways with raggedy rough, and heaving greens as unpredictable as the winds off the lake.

Awash in rolling dunes, the Irish Course seems as isolated and lonely as if beside the Irish Sea. Grassy, mountainous piles of sand and four natural streams bisect the fairways, contributing to a hefty 146 slope rating from the back tees. The track opened in 2000 to high acclaim and numerous awards.

Anchoring Whistling Straits is the coziest clubhouse of all time, an immense, slate-roofed, stone-faced Irish farmhouse with hewn oak timbers and five stone fire-places to warm the restaurant, pro shop, bar, and men's locker room. Wool plaids and leather clothe the armchairs and plush sofas, wherein golfers rest from their labors and contemplate, through the mullioned windows, the ninth and eighteenth greens and Lake Michigan, beyond.

Blackwolf Run comprises Meadow Valleys and the River Course, river and woodland layouts of exceptional wildness and beauty. The front nine of Meadow Valleys is breezy, with open meadows and high prairie grasses between rocky gullies and a dense hardwood forest. The curvy arms of the Sheboygan River come into play on the finishing holes. Liquid hazards and glassy greens, and Dye's signature railroad tie bunkers and Sahara-size traps, are prominent on the River Course, which follows the Sheboygan on fourteen holes.

With steep, green and purple slate roofs and dormers, the redbrick, Tudor-style hotel, built in 1918, has the look of an old manor house in the English countryside. Hardwood paneling and oak trim are background for sumptuous American-country decor in guest rooms and suites. Each hotel room is adorned with memorabilia relating to a famous American, while elegant Baker and McGuire furniture and floral fabrics set the tone in the new wing. In the Carriage House is one of the country's largest collections of original horse and carriage artwork. Big whirlpool tubs in every room in

the resort are welcome retreats of comfort.

Among charming surprises on the grounds is the antique solarium, shipped from England and now standing in one of the four courtyard gardens as a cafe for snacks, ice cream, and pastries. A tribute to the hotel's ethnic heritage, eighteenth-century Dutch ceramics and artifacts from other northern European cultures decorate six rooms of the Immigrant Restaurant and Winery; the European-style wine cellar is a snug spot in which to taste rare vintages.

One of the glories of the resort is River Wildlife, a private 500-acre wilderness preserve enjoyed by hunting parties and horseback riders, and cross-country skiers on 20 miles of groomed trails; you can canoe the river and fish for trout and salmon. Secluded within the preserve is a cozy log cabin restaurant with a stone fireplace and weathered pine interior, where wild game, wild mushroom soup, and cherry brie bread pudding are specialties.

The World of Kohler

Dating back well over a century, the Kohler Company owns about 25 percent of the plumbing-products business in the United States. On and nearby the grounds of the resort are fascinating Kohler-related tours and museums. At the Design Center, many-hued toilets and bathtubs, space-age showers, and whirlpool tubs big enough for a foursome are fun to see, along with fine furniture, tile and stone vignettes, and historical displays of antique plumbing. The three-hour tour of the Kohler Company plant is also popular.

Waelderhaus, "The house in the woods," replicates an Austrian home in the Bregenzerwald of the late 1800s, with antique furnishings, carvings and woodcuts, and iron and pewter artwork.

You can tour picturesque and entirely unique Kohler Village, one of the earliest planned garden communities in America, and the Kohler Arts Center, dedicated to contemporary visual and performing arts, where a summer theater program and Sunday afternoon folk dance performances are held.

The American Club
1111 West Riverside Drive
Kohler, WI 53044
Phone: (920) 457–4446, reservations (800) 344–2838
Fax: (920) 457–0299
Web site: www.destinationkohler.com

General Manager: Jim Beley

Accommodations: 236 spacious rooms and suites in American-country style, all with whirlpool tubs and special showers; some with super-size tubs, saunas, skylights, and private patios. Lavish baths are showcases for gleaming Kohler fixtures.

Meals: Leaded glass windows and antique chandeliers gleam in the Wisconsin Room; outdoor dining terraces are favored in the summertime. Kohler beef at the Immigrant Restaurant, and a world-class wine list; American and Irish fare at the Whistling Straits Clubhouse—Dublin beef stew, cornmeal-crusted walleye; casual indoor and outdoor family meals at the Jumpin' Jacks Cafe on Wood Lake; a pub atmosphere at the Horse and Plow.

Facilities: At the Sports Core is a fitness club offering indoor/outdoor tennis operated by a full-time staff of Burwash International pros; racquetball; private beach; two indoor swimming pools; 2-mile running path; and classes from kick boxing to spinning and Tai Chi. The Waters Spa features traditional health and beauty treatments, pool with waterfall, and unique hydro-therapies such as the Tsunami. Swimming and water sports on Wood Lake, and many shops and galleries at Woodlake Kohler.

Services and Special Programs: Supervised child care for ages 18 months to 7 years. Sporting clay and trap shooting; guided hunting for upland game birds and waterfowl.

Rates: $$$–$$$$

Golf Packages: Three nights deluxe accommodations, six rounds of golf with complimentary additional golf based on availability, half-hour golf lesson, one-hour golf clinic, caddie fees, and extras. $1,860–$2,060 for two people.

Getting There: An hour's drive from General Mitchell International Airport in Milwaukee and two-and-a-half hours from O'Hare International Airport, both served by major airlines.

What's Nearby: River Wildlife wilderness preserve; 20-mile, paved Old Plant Road Recreational Trail for biking and hiking; sport fishing in Lake Michigan; fly-fishing in the Sheboygan River; Road America, a world-famous natural road-racing track.

THE FAIRMONT BANFF SPRINGS

Banff, Alberta, Canada

Early mountaineers discovered hot springs in a spectacular valley in the Canadian Rockies. As word spread, people made arduous treks to the medicinal waters, and in the 1880s, the Canadian Pacific Railroad built the Banff Springs Hotel, one in a chain of luxury hostelries along the railway line through the Rocky and Selkirk Mountains. A baronial, Scottish-style castle at the confluence of the Bow and the Spray Rivers overlooking the Bow Valley, Banff was the grandest of all. Now a National Historic Site and a big tourist attraction, the massive hotel recently received a $100 million refurbishment, including the addition of a beautiful indoor saltwater pool and Jacuzzi, and an outdoor pool with a terrace overlooking the valley. Most rooms have stunning views of the river valley and the mountains, where constantly changing skies are mesmerizing, from dramatic cloud buildups to thundershowers, brilliant sun to mist, all in the same day.

The resort-wide renovation included a luxurious grand lobby and shopping arcade; a new clubhouse and pro shop; expansion of small guest rooms into suites and parlors; and the redecorating of restaurants. Sweeping stairways; carved beamed ceilings; baronial chandeliers; high, paned windows; massive columns; and European manor-house-style furnishings, including huge stone fireplaces and richly colored fabrics and wall coverings, create a castlelike atmosphere.

Now 7,074 yards long, the routing of the golf course has been changed, somewhat, to accommodate today's longer hitters and to restore master architect Stanley Thompson's original 1924 vision. The slope is now 142, with a 74.4 course rating. In a gorgeous, pine, fir, and aspen forest and valley setting alongside the river, the track is thickly bordered with high grasses, stately Queen Anne's lace, purple lupine and mountain aster, wild iris, and other wildflowers. As many as fifty elk at a time cruise the course.

Waves of uptilted, steep, flashed sandtraps, and abundant mounding are typical Thompson features. Fairways are flattish and it is advisable to stay on them, as high grasses, scrub, dense woods, and the rushing Bow River are major hazards. Approaches are often backdropped by massive granite walls.

Golfers often hold up the game on the fourth hole, called "Devil's Cauldron," one of the most dramatic par-3's in golf—*Golf Magazine* named it one of the best eighteen holes in the world. The tee is perched high on a granite shelf above a crystal clear lake and beautiful wetlands, with a phalanx of tall pines. The elevated green sits in a natural bowl or "cauldron" just over the lake, 170 yards away and guarded by five "devilish" bunkers.

Save some of your film for sixteen, from a tabletop green high above the fast-moving river, which is rimmed with grassy, rocky banks.

Below the hotel is a lovely walking path that meanders along the river, past a rumbling cascade and into town, where touristy shops and galleries await.

The new 12-million-dollar spa is elegant, with fabulous views, cascading waterfall massage pools, mineral pool, and sun terraces. Traditional and exotic treatments from thalassotherapy to kurs and Turkish scrubs are offered.

Other Places to Play

The Canadian Rockies surround you, crystalline glaciers cascade nearly to the highway, and lakes and rivers sparkle all along the four-hour drive from Banff to Jasper. At the Fairmont Jasper Park Lodge is a lovely, rugged golf course designed by Stanley Thompson. It meanders through aspen groves, around gigantic boulders, and along the edge of azure Lac Beauvert, surrounded by mountains and pure wilderness. Bear, elk, and coyote play on the fairways while golfers contend with elevated tees and huge, undulating greens, devilishly sloping off at the sides (780–852-3301, www.jasperparklodge.com). Like an upscale summer camp, the lodge has a Great Room with vintage sofas and armchairs, writing tables, rocking chairs, fireplaces, and views of what seems like half of the Canadian Rockies.

Between Banff and Calgary in a pristine, undeveloped, densely forested valley lie thirty-six holes of the Kananaskis Country Golf Course, a Robert Trent Jones Sr. creation beneath the dramatic cliff faces of Mt. Kidd and Mt. Lorette. The Kananaskis River, its streams, and creeks crisscross the absolutely beautiful track. Fine, white sand fills 136 traps, with water on twenty holes (403-591-7154).

The Fairmont Banff Springs
P.O. Box 960
Banff, Alberta T0L 0C0
Canada
Phone: (403) 762-2211, reservations (800) 441-1414
Fax: (403) 762-4447
Web site: www.banffsprings.com
General Manager: David Bayne
Accommodations: 770 rooms and suites vary greatly in size. Most are spacious and charming, with fabulous views of the surrounding mountains; Scottish Highland decor and elegant traditional furnishings, English floral fabrics, and plaids; some rooms have fireplaces.
Meals: Among seventeen food and beverage venues are the pubby, Bavarian-style Waldhaus, the Scottish-style Banffshire Club, and the Bow Valley Grill. Elaborate tea service in the Rundle Room; sushi at Samurai; Italian fare at Castello; prime rib, planked salmon, and bison at the Alhambra.
Facilities: Golf Academy; business center; elaborate, full-service spa and fitness center; salon; indoor saltwater swimming pool and outdoor pool; Heritage Hall, a museum of the West; cross-country skiing, with downhill nearby.
Services and Special Programs: Interpretive hikes and climbing trips, yoga and exercise classes, and guided walks.
Rates: $$$–$$$$
Golf and Spa Packages: Ultimate Golf Retreat includes deluxe accommodations, three meals, spa admission, a round of golf, golf clinic, and club rental: from $724 for two, per night, double occupancy.
Getting There: One-and-a half hours west of Calgary on the Trans-Canada Highway.
What's Nearby: Take a gondola ride to a mountaintop for Rocky Mountain views, and often, to see grizzly bears, elk, and bighorn sheep. Tour spectacular Banff and Jasper National Parks. Loll in naturally heated outdoor mineral water pools at Sulphur Mountain. Ride on huge "snow coaches" in the Columbia Icefields, halfway between Banff and Jasper.

FAIRMONT CHÂTEAU WHISTLER

Whistler, British Columbia, Canada

The golfing season on the four championship courses at Whistler Resort, in southwestern British Columbia, runs from May through the middle of October. Magenta and blue lupine line the fairways in spring, while alders blaze red and aspens are golden against the dark firs in the fall. On rugged terraces at the base of the glacier-capped Coast Mountains, the Château Whistler Golf Club— designed by Robert Trent Jones Jr.—sits on tilting, high-altitude terrain studded with monumental granite outcroppings. Cascading across the course are three glacier-fed streams, spawning grounds for rainbow trout and kokanee salmon. Black bears gorge on wild berries in the summertime, while coyotes and deer stand their ground on the edges of the forest. Golfers in the know bring their binoculars and cameras for the daily pageant of golden eagles, swooping osprey, and resident pileated woodpeckers.

GPS on the carts comes in handy for managing elevation changes of more than 400 feet and for judging sightings over and around towering, ancient Douglas firs. A slope of 142 and course rating of 72.8 are mitigated by four sets of tees and generous landing zones.

At the edge of the European-style village of Whistler, the massive Château Whistler hotel is a castlelike dawn-colored edifice surrounded by mountain peaks. It is the first large, luxury resort built in western Canada in a century.

The hotel's Mallard Terrace is one of the world's greatest places to bask in the sun and enjoy a tremendous view of snowcapped peaks and forest-covered slopes. Stone columns, a museum-like collection of Canadiana, vibrantly colored Mennonite rugs, a giant

stone fireplace and overstuffed armchairs and sofas in the soaring Great Hall create a cozy environment from which to watch the spectacular outdoor scene.

With annual snowfall of 30 feet and thousands of acres of skiable terrain on Blackcomb and Whistler Mountains, Whistler Resort earns the title "Number 1 Ski Resort in North America" nearly every year. Annual events in the charming, pedestrian-only village range from all-summer, live street entertainment to World Beat Weekend, the First Nations Festival, and Jazz and Blues Weekend, as well as numerous wintertime fests. An exhilarating recreational and sight-seeing activity is taking the gondola up the mountain for summertime hiking and picnicking in alpine meadows, and having Sunday brunch with a view at the Roundhouse Lodge.

B.C. Golf Trio

Three more outstanding golf courses are accessible to Whistler Resort guests. The only Nicklaus design that bears his name, Nicklaus North Golf Course is the highest-rated golf resort in Western Canada. Whistler's famous "River of Golden Dreams" meanders through the fairways, while feisty Fitzsimmons Creek creates havoc for golfers on the eighteenth hole, where it fronts the green along with a huge cottonwood tree. Lightly laid on a rugged, densely forested site on the shores of glacial Green Lake, the Audubon Society Certified track is habitat for black bears, wood ducks, osprey, and bald eagles (800–386–9898, www.nicklausnorth.com).

A recent renovation brings the Arnold Palmer–designed Whistler Golf Club to top standards. The layout features nine lakes, two lovely, winding creeks, and gorgeous mountain views (800–376–1777, www.whistlergolf.com).

A Robert Cupp original at the foot of Mount Currie, Big Sky Golf and Country Club is a stunner, and relatively flat with plenty of reed-bordered lakes and ponds. The golf academy here has excellent practice facilities for two- and three-day schools (800–668–7900, www.bigskygolf.com)

Fairmont Château Whistler
4599 Château Boulevard
Whistler, British Columbia V0N 1B4
Canada
Phone: (604) 938–8000, reservations (800) 441–1414
Fax: (604) 938–2291
Web site: www.fairmont.com
General Manager: David Roberts
Accommodations: 558 rooms and suites in a twelve-story hotel, with country manor-style, traditional furnishings, down-filled duvets, and quilts. Entree Gold accommodations have fireplaces, Jacuzzi tubs, complimentary food and beverages, private lounge, and special services.
Meals: Sophisticated Pacific Coast cuisine, elegant dinners, and buffet brunches are served at the Wildflower restaurant. Dine casually indoors or on the patio, and watch the open kitchen, at Portobello. Settle into a wing chair for light meals by the double-sided, stone fireplace in the Mallard Bar.
Facilities: Three tennis courts; indoor-outdoor swimming pool and lap pool with underwater sound; full-service health and beauty spa with unique Ayurvedic steam cabinets and European skin care program; fitness center.
Services and Special Programs: Golf instruction from top CGA teaching pros.
Rates: $$$$
Golf Packages: Four Course Package includes four nights deluxe accommodations, one dinner, and a round of golf at one of the four Whistler courses: from $1,516–$2,156 per person, double occupancy. Total Summer Adventure includes accommodation, three meals a day, unlimited activities such as golf, horseback riding, fishing, rafting and spa services, from $574 per person, per night, double occupancy.
Getting There: A two-hour drive on the Sea to Sky Highway from Vancouver International Airport, with motorcoach and van service; or a three-hour, scenic trip on B.C. Rail. Public transit throughout Whistler Village and the valley. Private floatplanes land at the Nicklaus North Golf Course.
What's Nearby: Downhill and cross-country skiing; ice-skating; mountain biking and hiking; horseback riding; fishing and boating in five lakes; river rafting; jet boating and backcountry explorations; ATV tours. Walk to shopping, restaurants, and nightclubs in Whistler Village.

FAIRMONT LE CHÂTEAU MONTEBELLO
Montebello, Quebec, Canada

In a glorious woodland wilderness on the north shore of the Ottawa River between Montréal and Ottawa, Château Montebello was built in 1930 to resemble a grand hotel in the Swiss Alps. Formerly a private club whose members included prime ministers and foreign dignitaries, Montebello was sold to Canadian Pacific Hotels in 1970 and transformed into a luxurious, rustic hostelry.

The monumental red cedar lodge, the heart of the sprawling resort, is one of the largest and most beautiful log buildings in Canada. A soaring, three-story lobby is anchored solidly by a six-sided stone fireplace and huge log beams and columns, with open log balconies and sweeping stairways. Guest rooms are warm and cozy with gleaming wood furnishings and fine fabrics, and have bay windows overlooking greenswards, gardens, lakes, streams, and forests. Rooms in the main lodge are

romantic hideaways. At the ends of the hallways, with alcoved sitting areas, Premier Rooms accommodate six people, or more on sofabeds.

Among dozens of summertime activities available at this popular family destination resort are canoeing, kayaking, cycling, clay shooting, river and lake fishing, hiking, horseback riding, boating, ATV touring, Petanque, squash, and sailing. A gigantic indoor swimming pool and indoor tennis and squash courts are warm retreats on cool days and in the wintertime when Nordic skiing and snow sports are the big attractions. You can explore the extensive snowmobile circuit on your own or with a guide, take a horse-drawn sleigh ride, go dogsledding, or learn to curl and ice fish.

Accessible to hotel guests, nearby Fairmont Kenauk comprises 100 square miles of forests and seventy lakes and beaver ponds dotted with secluded vacation cot-

tages. Family-size cabins have fireplaces, screened-in porches, and private docks and boats. Both properties are wildlife preserves where animals and birds are often sighted, from loons, herons, and grouse to moose, deer, coyote, mink, and muskrat. Fishing is good for rainbow and speckled trout and bass.

Designed by Stanley Thompson in 1930 and hewn from granite outcroppings on the lower slopes of Westcott Mountain, the golf course winds in a series of sheltered, narrow fairways through a mature oak and maple forest, and is well watered by the Ottawa River. Elevated tees give lovely views of the surrounding Laurentians. The mountainside site involves dramatic elevation changes and vertical drops to tilting greens.

The course's classic design takes full advantage of magnificent natural settings and is what makes the Montebello layout such a beauty. Thompson, one of the Scottish masters, became famous for the Banff Springs and Jasper Park courses in the Canadian Rockies. His ability to route a course and his signature large, flared bunkers remain much in evidence. A 1991 redesign installed new fairway bunkers and lengthened the course.

The Devil and the Giant

North of Montréal, another Fairmont resort, Château Mont Tremblant, is a golfer's destination with two championship courses. Michael Hurdzan's design, Le Diablo, reposes in a beautiful red pine forest. Unusual in Canada, beach-size, red-sand bunkers line the bent grass fairways.

Fifty-two white sand bunkers adorn Thomas McBroom's new design, Le Géant, bordered by the beautiful Diable River and Lac Tremblant. This is a classic track with wide, undulating fairways on hillside plateaus menaced with huge native stone ledges and massive fairway bunkers (800–461-8711, www.tremblant.ca).

The new Tremblant Golf Academy offers a variety of programs, including "All for One and One for All" family instruction, the "Gold Escape" for seniors, and "Elle Golf" for women.

Fairmont Le Château Montebello
392, rue Notre Dame
Montebello, Quebec J0V 1L0
Canada
Phone: (819) 423–6341, reservations (800) 441–1414
Fax: (819) 423–5511
Web site: www.fairmont.com
General Manager: Werner Sapp
Accommodations: 211 rooms and suites in four wings, each with bay windows and garden, river, or mountain and forest views; thirteen secluded, lakeside chalets at Kenauk.
Meals: Elegant regional cuisine, period decor, and a river view in the main dining room at Aux Chantignoles; American plan or a la carte buffet breakfasts and lunches, barbecues, dinners, and Sunday brunches; light meals at Le Seigneurie Bistro Bar.
Facilities: The Ultima Spa offers European-style health and beauty treatments and a fitness center. Indoor and outdoor tennis and squash courts; indoor and outdoor swimming pools; business center; four curling rinks; snowmobile and cross-country trails.
Services and Special Programs: Club Monte welcomes kids ages 3–12 for daycare and films, crafts, outdoor activities, and meals. Guided nature hikes in the Kenauk forestlands. Small pets are permitted. A variety of sports equipment and boats can be rented.
Rates: $$$
Golf Packages: One night accommodations, dinner, buffet breakfast, a round of golf and cart, gift, and discount at pro shop. $252–$281 per person, double occupancy.
Getting There: A sixty-minute drive from Ottawa International Airport and seventy-five minutes from Montreal International Airport.
What's Nearby: Walking trails to spectacular Plaissance Falls; canoeing and picnicking at nearby Whitefish Lake; a drive through Omega Park to see wild bison, bear, boar, and red deer.

FOUR SEASONS RESORT PUNTA MITA

Nayarit, Mexico

On a wild and rugged point at the northern end of Bahia Banderas, fringed by white sand beaches and backed by the dramatic Western Sierra Madre Mountains, Punta Mita is a secluded, 3,000-acre retreat a half-hour's drive from Puerto Vallarta. As for the interior decor, imagine the contemporary seaside villa of a Mexican multimillionaire.

A zero-edge swimming pool appears to drop into the sea, where migrating whales, schools of dolphins, and manta rays are commonly seen from throughout the resort. Scuba diving and snorkeling on the coral reef and surfing are popular sports offshore of the resort's twin beaches. Guest rooms and suites are in tile-roofed, Mexican-style casitas: spacious and luxuriously decorated as vacation homes, each has a very private garden terrace or balcony. You can choose the contents of your custom bar setup and soak for hours in a deep tub. Typical of the international hotel chain, Four Seasons's standard of personal service and guest room amenities are unparalleled. For example, when the sun is high, tennis players are cooled by iced towels and misters, and enjoy the services of ball boys.

Only resort guests and club members play on the Jack Nicklaus–designed golf course, a coastal masterpiece blooming with tropical flowers and shaded by palms, with eight ocean-side holes. Bermuda grass greens were designed to USGA standards. Wide fairways and five sets of tees make it possible for everyone to manage the constant sea breezes and well-protected greens with narrow approaches. The golf course's resident crocodile, Brock, observes, objectively, from his home in the lake. Also, practice facilities are excellent here, including a forty-station, double-sided driving range, two putting areas and bunkers, and a chipping green.

The impressive stone clubhouse is a breezy getaway, where the Tail of the Whale restaurant and seafront terrace bar are shady beneath a thatched roof.

The hotel provides transportation to Puerto Vallarta for boutique and gallery browsing, and for strolling the *malecon,* the waterfront promenade, where tourists and locals hob-nob.

The executive chef meets with local fisherman on the beach several times a week, choosing the fresh catch right from the boats. Fish, octopus, shrimp, and lobster are featured at the Ceviche Bar, a quaint garden patio where guests enjoy table-side, custom-prepared, marinated seafood. Tequila tastings are held weekly, and you can arrange a romantic, private dinner under the stars on the beach or at "The Rock," a grassy knoll overlooking the ocean.

Apuane Spa offers traditional and exotic treatments, such as a massage using tequila, sage oil, and Mexican healing techniques. Men like the "Man for All Seasons Facial," designed to neutralize the effects of sun, stress, sports, and harsh abrasives. Couples retire to double spa rooms with whirlpool tubs and private garden patios. Relax in the spa lounge with current American newspapers, table games, and fresh juices.

The fascinating Cultural Center is a comfortable, open-air library and resource center for exploring the cultural, environmental, and historic treasures of Punta Mita and the bay region, focusing on Huichol Indians.

The Tiger, the Bear, and Tom

Midway around the curve of Bahia Banderas, the Golf Club of Vista Vallarta is built on rolling terrain in the foothills of the Sierra Madre Mountain range above Puerto Vallarta. The 7,057-yard, Jack Nicklaus signature course is gently sloped, rambling across valleys and dry arroyos in a dense native forest of palms and giant ficus, and liberally watered by natural creeks.

Opened in 2002 the Tom Weiskopf–designed track at Vista Vallarta strides boldly through wild, deep ravines, through jungly vegetation, and past rippling creeks (52–322–290–0030, www. vistavallartagolf.com).

Also new in 2002 El Tigre Golf Course in the Paradise Village development, ten minutes from the airport, was designed by Robert von Hagge and is managed by the top notch company, Troon Golf. Expect more than 120 sandy sites on this links layout—steep, sod-sided pot bunkers, shallow beach bunkers, and desertlike waste areas. Greens are medium-size, some bulkheaded, and the five tee boxes come in handy with water hazards on twelve holes, and with the 74.5 rating and 133 slope. The eighteenth hole is 621 yards from the back tees with water along the entire fairway and a giant waste bunker completely surrounding the green, a demanding conclusion to the 7,239-yard course (800–995–5714, www.paradisemexico.com).

Four Seasons Resort Punta Mita
Bahia de Banderas
Nayarit, Mexico 63734
Phone: 52–329–291–6000, reservations (800) 332–3442
Fax: 52–329–291–6060
Web site: www.fourseasons.com/puntamita/vacations
General Manager: Ricardo Acevedo
Accommodations: Five-diamond rated, 140 rooms and one-, two-, or three-bedroom suites in Mexican-style casitas with marble floors, dark-wood shutters, sofas and armchairs, and balcony or terrace with full or partial ocean view; most with private plunge pool. Oversize bathrooms with deep tubs. Suites have outdoor showers, living and dining rooms, and powder rooms.
Meals: Nuevo Latino cuisine at Aramara, a fine dining restaurant with a beautiful garden terrace, and cocktail lounge with live music. Under a palapa roof, the casual cafe, Ketsi, serves theme buffets, light Continental dishes, and seafood. Box lunches are available.
Facilities: Early arrival and late departure lounge; two Hartru and two artificial grass tennis courts, with clinics and socials; nonmotorized water vehicles, water sports equipment, and toys; full-service spa and fitness center; PGA golf teaching professionals.
Services and Special Programs: Childproofed rooms on request. Kids for All Seasons supervised activities and child care, with a wading pool and play patio.
Rates: $$$$
Golf Packages: One night luxury accommodations, unlimited golf, breakfast, two golf shirts, two fifty-minute massages, and golf clinic; use of golf practice facilities, tennis courts, and nonmotorized watersports. $420–$900 per room, single or double occupancy.
Getting There: Thirty minutes from Puerto Vallarta International Airport, with private transportation available.
What's Nearby: Shopping and sightseeing in Puerto Vallarta; sailing; deep-sea fishing.

GRAND BAY HOTEL ISLA NAVIDAD

Isla Navidad, Mexico

On the western "Gold Coast" of Mexico between Acapulco and Puerto Vallarta, Isla Navidad is a tropical peninsula fringed by the blue Pacific and the lovely, protected Bahia Navidad. Terraced down a hillside above the bay and a yacht marina, the resort has the look of a luxurious Mexican colonial estate. There is a feeling of seclusion among blooming gardens, fountains, and thousands of coconut palms and fruit trees.

Twenty-seven holes of Robert Von Hagge–designed golf—the Ocean, the Lagoon, and the Mountain courses—are grand complements to a plethora of recreation, from boating and deep-sea sport fishing to tennis; swimming and water sports in the protected bay; and long, long beach walks. Among three swimming pools is a lagoon-type pool connected by water-

slides. A favorite adventure is taking the water taxi to the charming village of Barra de Navidad for arts and crafts shopping.

Rooms and suites look onto the ocean, the lagoon, and the mountains. Unlike most Mexican resorts where interiors are done up in vibrant primary colors and contemporary furnishings, guest spaces here are elegant and traditional, in subtle golden and off-white fabrics and tile floors, accented by fancy, Spanish-style wrought iron and fine, original artworks.

The Isla Navidad Country Club is one of only two in Mexico to win *Golf Magazine*'s Gold Medal Award. On the three parkland-style nines, elevated tees and greens provide spectacular views of the sea and a freshwater lagoon, where the mangroves are habitat for hundreds of tropical birds. You will encounter huge putting surfaces and deep lakes, ponds, or the lagoon on twenty-three holes. Some tees and greens were built in sand dunes, and extensive sandy waste areas follow the fairways. With several holes directly along the coastline or above it, ocean breezes are a major factor.

Golfers relax in the sprawling, colonial-style clubhouse, a cacophony of red-rile roofs, archways, and open verandahs. The nineteenth hole is well-stocked with Cuban cigars and literally hundreds of brands of tequila, while the armchairs are deep and wide (ask about the in-house master cigar maker). You can take a sauna, take a Turkish bath, get a massage, and work out in the gym here too.

Hedonists head for the spa for "Consienta a sus Pies," a treatment combining reflexology and Swedish massage of the feet. Sesame seeds, honey, and lime is used to scrub and smooth the skin in the "Thai Exfoliation."

Remote, Romantic Tamarindo

It is possible that more shots are taken with cameras than with golf clubs at El Tamarindo Golf Resort, a lush and lovely track carved from dense native rain forest on rocky cliffs above an idyllic stretch of coastline. The small, remote, romantic hotel here on Dorada Beach has just twenty-eight palapa-roofed casitas with hammocks and private plunge pools (877–278–8018, www.ghmmexico.com).

Golfers often find themselves nearly alone on the golf holes—each of which seems isolated from the others—either surrounded by a canopy of gorgeous, gigantic blooming trees and shrubs or perched above the crashing surf. One of the world's greatest halfway houses between the nines serves Mexican beer, margaritas, and *ceviche*. Do not be surprised if tee times are unnecessary, as few golfers are in the know about this stunningly beautiful and challenging course.

Grand Bay Hotel Isla Navidad
Circuito de los Marinos S/N
Fraccionamiento Isla Navidad
Manzanillo, Colima, Mexico 28830
Phone: 52–335–55050, reservations (800) 996–3426
Fax: 52–335–56070
Web site: www.wyndhammexicohotels.com
General Manager: Rolando Miravette
Accommodations: Five-diamond, five-star rated, 200 rooms and suites with private balconies, luxurious baths, sitting areas. Golf course villas are 7,532 to 13,372 square feet, three to four bedrooms; each with swimming pool, complete privacy, and elegant interiors.
Meals: An intimate, romantic atmosphere is found at Antonio's, serving Continental and regional Mexican cuisine. Casual and lively, the Grand Cafe specializes in international buffets and a stunning ocean view. Poolside in a garden setting, La Plazuela has a presentation kitchen.
Facilities: Three swimming pools; three artificial grass tennis courts; 200-slip marina; full-service spa and fitness center; golf practice range, lessons, and clinics.
Services and Special Programs: Supervised Kid's Club for ages 4–10.
Rates: $$$$
Golf Packages: Three nights deluxe accommodations, breakfast daily, and twenty-seven holes of golf daily. $1,905 for two, double occupancy.
Getting There: A twenty-five-minute drive from Manzanillo's Playa de Oro International Airport.
What's Nearby: The hotel will arrange deep-sea fishing cruises for marlin, sailfish, tuna, Mahi-Mahi, tarpon, and snook. Set off on a horseback ride on the beach, or an ATV or jeep expedition. Shop for arts and crafts in the nearby village of Barra de Navidad and in nearby Manzanillo.

MELIÁ CABO REAL BEACH AND GOLF RESORT

San Jose del Cabo, Baja California Sur, Mexico

In the 19-mile corridor between the Mexican village of San Jose del Cabo and the tourist town of Cabo San Lucas are more than a dozen upscale resorts and hotels, and seven golf courses along the gorgeous coastline of the Cape Baja peninsula. Above a protected cove and Playa Bedito, within the Cabo Real development, the Meliá Cabo Real Resort is an organized jumble of terra-cotta-colored cubes topped by a unique glass and onyx pyramid dome. The resort recently underwent a million-dollar expansion of its open-air, hacienda-style buildings, making it the largest hostelry in the state of Baja. The cobblestoned grounds are filled with cacti, palms, and blooming tropical flowers and trees cooled by fountains and waterfalls, ponds and swimming pools, leading the eye ultimately to the main attractions—a perfectly white beach and the cerulean waters of Mar de Cortez. This is a lively place, with music in the lobby bar, a beach bar, and a swim-up pool bar. You can walk on the sand for miles in either direction, and the water-sports center will arrange deep-sea fishing and scuba diving, both superb in these waters.

Surrounding the resort is the Robert Trent Jones Jr.–designed Cabo Real Golf Course, a series of green islands in a fearsome desert landscape of huge cardon cacti, ball-snatching arroyos, and rocky outcroppings, with views of the sea from every hole, and three holes on the oceanfront. Site of the PGA Senior Slam, and with a challenging 73.8 rating and 135 slope, the track ascends on narrow fairways into mountainous territory and valleys for six holes, then winds back down; the fifth drops 200 feet. A spectacular view of the course is provided from the fifteenth tee above the crashing surf. Five sets of tees provide fairness for high handicappers contending with rolling fairways and unpredictable sea breezes.

Adjacent to Cabo Real is Los Cabo's newest golf course, and the third on the Cape by Jack Nicklaus, the

El Dorado Golf Course. This course has five oceanfront holes, four lakes, and an intimidating slope of 143. Both nines run inland through vast, saguaro-studded gulches up into the rugged foothills of the Sierra de la Laguna, returning to the sea. Get out your camera for the third, in a picturesque box canyon. The ninth and eighteenth run right along the beach. The El Dorado clubhouse and restaurant sit on a spectacular, clifftop site above the ocean.

Cape of the Sun

An average daily temperature of 75 degrees and 300 plus days of pure sunshine make the master-planned community of Cabo del Sol an idyllic location for two hotels, nearly two thousand residential units, and what some consider to be the two top golf courses in Baja.

The Desert Course is Tom Weiskopf's target-style inland layout with panoramic sea views from nearly every hole; 7,100 yards of immense, sandy waste areas; natural river washes; and rock outcroppings. Lakes, a waterfall, and a stream add to the beauty and the task of maneuvering along the roller-coaster terrain. Generous landing zones and a lack of forced carries are balanced by several blind shots and hidden gullies, and an abundance of tall cardon cacti.

Along a mile of coastline, Jack Nicklaus's Ocean Course has been named the "Pebble Beach of Baja," a glorious union of mountain, desert, and sea, with seven oceanfront holes and three of the finest finishing holes in golf. Sea breezes, sand-surrounded, undulating fairways on low, rocky, surf-splashed cliffs are reminiscent of the Monterey Peninsula—except for the giant cacti. A small par-4, sixteen heads downhill, directly to a large green on a rocky plateau, the approach shots silhouetted against the blue Pacific. On seventeen, you drive 178 yards from a clifftop over a cove to a rocky parapet surrounded by churning water. The stunning eighteenth is as married to the natural land- and seascape as the last hole at Pebble.

Meliá Cabo Real Beach and Golf Resort
Carretera Transpeninsular Km. 19.5
San Jose del Cabo
Baja California Sur, Mexico 23400
Phone: 52–624–14–40000, reservations (800) 336–3542
Fax: 52–624–14–40101
Web site: www.meliacaboreal.solmelia.com
General Manager: David Cayuela
Accommodations: Recently renovated, five-diamond, five-star-rated, 302 spacious rooms and suites, each with private balcony and ocean view. Decor is upscale, brightly colored, contemporary Mexican style with marble, wood, and wicker accents, and carved folk art paneling. Also, luxury accommodations at Meliá Los Cabos All-Suites Oceanfront Spa and Golf Resort.
Meals: La Terraza is open-air, featuring live music and fine Mexican and Continental cuisine. At poolside, La Palapa serves up casual fare and ocean views. The El Quetzal Coffee Shop specializes in seafood.
Facilities: Two tennis courts; huge swimming pool; two secluded beaches; water-sports center with deep-sea fishing, scuba diving, parasailing, wind surfing, and beach volleyball; fitness center and beauty spa; salon; water aerobics; fifty-passenger catamaran for guest use.
Services and Special Programs: Guests have access to the Desert and Ocean course at Cabo del Sol. Supervised children's activities. Complimentary shuttle to Cabo San Lucas and to a sister hotel, the Melia Los Cabos.
Rates: $$$
Golf Packages: Three nights ocean view room, daily American or buffet breakfast, and a round of golf at both the Cabo Real and El Dorado courses. $478–$655 for two.
Getting There: Fifteen minutes from San Jose del Cabo International Airport.
What's Nearby: Deep-sea fishing and whale-watching tours depart from the hotel's beach. Horseback riding and ATV rides in the desert; sight-seeing tours and shopping in Cabo San Lucas; accessible by water taxi is the secluded beach, Playa del Amor, near El Arco, the natural arch at Land's End.

PALMILLA RESORT AND GOLF CLUB

Baja California Sur, Mexico

On the southernmost tip of the Baja Peninsula between San Jose del Cabo and Cabo San Lucas, more than a dozen upscale resorts are located on the dramatic coastline of the Sea of Cortés. Gray whales are winter visitors every year, swimming south from the icy Bering Sea in Alaska to the warm, protected bays of Baja, and arriving in December, about when the "Snow Birds" begin to arrive from chilly climes, golf clubs in hand.

The Palmilla Hotel, one of the exclusive Pinehurst Company Resorts (including Pinehurst and the Homestead) is a luxurious retreat high on a bluff above one of the loveliest bays in Mexico and a secluded white sand beach. The compound of whitewashed buildings with red-tile roofs is surrounded by thousands of palm trees in tropical gardens, with bubbling fountains and bougainvillea-draped loggias. Swimming is idyllic in the infinity pool, which seems to flow right into the sea. Snorkeling and diving is excellent in the crystal-clear waters.

Palmilla has one of the longest established and largest deep-sea fishing fleets on the Sea of Cortés—31-foot fishing boats and 25-foot *parangas* manned by top captains and crews. Anglers come from all over the world to ply the waters of the Sea of Cortés for marlin, sailfish, dolphin, tuna, and other large species. The scuba diving headquarters here is also one of the best in Baja.

A recent multimillion-dollar expansion added oceanfront suites and a new beachfront swimming pool and health

club, all elaborately landscaped and gracefully integrated into the original property, which features classic Mexican architecture and an old-world atmosphere. With hand-crafted Mexican furnishings, a valuable collection of art and tiles, and several open-air restaurants and bars, the hotel is a tourist attraction in itself.

The Jack Nicklaus Signature Palmilla Golf Course lies along the rocky coastline and in the foothills of the Sierra de la Laguna, the mountain barrier looming above the Sea of Cortés. About his first design for Latin America, Nicklaus said, "I let the surroundings shape the holes . . . to avoid disrupting the natural setting as much as possible."

In the striking desert and mountain landscape, with respect for the dramatic elevation changes and a distractingly beautiful shoreline, he deftly arranged Palmilla's three nines, placing fairways, greens, and tee boxes between mature cacti and oak, pine, and piñon woodlands, with forced carries over deep ravines, and giving nearly every hole a sea view. On the Mountain nine from a slightly elevated tee, the golfer is faced with a steep drop off to a canyon in front and a sandy arroyo along the right side of and fronting the green, which is surrounded by wild desert. On the Ocean nine, the sea sparkles cerulean behind a battalion of century-old Cardon cacti and *torote* trees, and every putt breaks toward the water. Nearly 7,000 yards long, with a 144 rating, the course has five sets of tees.

The scorecard reads, "Please be careful of desert vegetation as contact with it could cause injury." The iguanas and the roadrunners ignore the warning, while golfers dodge cactus spines.

A margarita on the oceanfront terrace followed by dinner on the verandah of the La Paloma restaurant is a romantic, even idyllic, experience as the sun fades into a star-sparkled, blue-black sky. Palmilla's Friday fiesta buffets are legendary, with mariachi bands playing and every kind of fresh fish imaginable—ceviche, ahi, sashimi, and tartare, fish tacos, and your own freshly caught Dorado or tuna, which the hotel chefs will prepare to your order.

Perfect Climate, Private Golf

Baja, California, a long peninsula separated from mainland Mexico, receives only 10 inches of rain annually, and averages 85 degrees in the summertime and 72 degrees in winter. The starkly beautiful landscape is comparable to the deserts of Arizona and Southern California, where golf courses number in the hundreds.

Washing the entire eastern shore of Baja are the reflective, blue-green waters of the Sea of Cortés, a mecca for trophy marlin fishermen. The sea remains at a constant temperature between 70 and 75 degrees and teems with semitropical wildlife, an unequaled environment for snorkeling, scuba diving, and swimming.

Many visitors fall in love with the climate, the beauty of the land and sea, and the relaxed lifestyle—not to mention the golf—along the developed stretch of coastline between San Jose del Cabo and Cabo San Lucas. Some decide to build or buy second homes on the "Los Cabos" corridor. New villas are rising at Querencia, where the first private golf course on Los Cabos was built in a gated community between Palmilla and Costa Azul (www.loscabosquerencia.com).

Palmilla Resort and Golf Club
Apartado Postal 52
San Jose del Cabo
Baja California Sur, Mexico 23400
Phone: 52–414–67000, reservations (877) 4–PALMILLA
Fax: 52–414–67001
Web site: www.palmillaresort.com
General Manager: Christopher Bush
Accommodations: 24 spacious rooms and 92 suites in hacienda-style, white, stucco buildings with red-tile roofs, gleaming tile floors, private balconies or patios with panoramic ocean views, sitting areas, and commodious baths. Complimentary Continental breakfast.
Meals: Regional Mexican and Continental cuisine at La Paloma; light meals and snacks at El Jardin, poolside, and at Bar Neptuna, with views of the crashing surf.
Facilities: Two lighted tennis courts; swimming pool; volleyball; putting green; equipment available for scuba diving, kayaking, and snorkeling off the private beach, library; regulation croquet court.
Services and Special Programs: Arrangements can be made for a variety of fishing and desert exploration expeditions.
Rates: $$$
Golf Packages: Unlimited Golf Package includes three nights in an oceanfront, junior suite, with Continental breakfast, and unlimited golf and cart. $1,535 for two.
Getting There: Twenty minutes to the Los Cabos International Airport, serviced by major airlines; hotel shuttle is available.
What's Nearby: Horseback riding; four-wheel-drive treks into the mountains and the desert; whale-watching and sunset cruises; shopping and nightclubbing in San Jose del Cabo and Cabo San Lucas.

WESTIN REGINA GOLF AND BEACH RESORT LOS CABOS

San Jose del Cabo, Mexico

Where the Sea of Cortés meets the Pacific Ocean at Land's End, this resort stands boldly at the water's edge, an architectural masterpiece of contemporary design in vibrant red sandstone and vivid raspberry, pumpkin, and sunflower colors, dramatic against the stark desert and the dazzling azure waters. From a distance, the colors of the buildings melt right into the landscape. Above the surf-lapped beach, blazing sunsets and pale dawns reflect in seven free-form swimming pools, while hundreds of palms are silhouetted against the sky.

The lobby is an open gallery of inlaid stone and glasswork, Mexican sculptures, and terra-cotta pottery. Hand-crafted furnishings and original art enlivens oceanfront guest rooms, each with a private balcony.

The resort will book tee times in advance for all seven of the Los Cabos golf courses. The nearest course to Cabo San Lucas, the Cabo San Lucas Country Club, is a 7,220-yard Roy Dye design on relatively flat terrain with a 75.4 rating and 138 slope, small greens, and tight fairways. Views of Land's End, San Lucas Bay, and the Sea of Cortés are dazzling backdrops for the challenge of the course. Several lakes are hazards on ten holes, and elevation changes range to 300 feet up and down the hillsides, which are adorned with platoons of *palo blanco* and elephant trees, cardon cacti, and bougainvillea. The 610-yard seventh is Baja's longest hole, a double dogleg around a lake. If desert-style, target golf gets your goat, take a two-hour clinic or a two-day school at the excellent Golf Academy.

Besides golf, deep-sea sportfishing—for trophy marlin, sailfish, tuna, wahoo, dorado, and roosterfish—is the big attraction in Baja. While October through May is the best time for golf, hot summers are the best time for hooking blue marlin. April through mid-July is good for catching the large reef fish: grouper and pargo, amberjack and yellowtail.

Scuba divers find the warm, clear waters a delight, and encounter sea lions, giant manta rays, hammerhead sharks, moray eels, and tropical fish. Jacques Cousteau called the Sea of Cortés, "The World's Aquarium."

One advantage to staying at an established resort is for its long-time relationships with the best fishing fleets (the safest and most modern) and the top scuba diving companies. The Westin Regina will make all of your arrangements in advance for sportfishing charters—from fast cruisers to "pangas," which are 22-foot skiffs.

Public and Private

Built by the Mexican government, which maintains top-notch conditions, the nine-hole San Jose del Cabo Municipal Golf Course is perfect for intermediate and beginning golfers and is a great value. You get some ocean views—and a lot of condo views—without the ball grabbing, prickly cacti, narrow fairways, and desert wilderness that you find at the resort courses (52–142–0905).

The Cape's only private course, the Querencia Golf Club, is a Tom Fazio layout with wide fairways that meander 7,070 yards over rocky hillsides and across canyons. The track lies well above the ocean, with panoramic views. Elevation changes are to be reckoned with, as are the cacti, hundreds of palms, dry gullies, and barrancas. The beautiful green on the fourth hole hangs over the sea. There is also a nine-hole Fazio-designed short course and a state of the art practice facility (888–346–6188, www.loscabosquerencia.com).

Westin Regina Golf and Beach Resort Los Cabos
Carretera Transpeninsular KM 22.5
San Jose Del Cabo
Baja California Sur, Mexico 23400
Phone: 52–624–1429–000, reservations (800) 937–8461
Fax: 52–624–1429–050
Web site: www.westin.com
General Manager: Michele McShane
Accommodations: 243 rooms and suites in nine-story towers with private balconies, ocean views, and Westin's signature "Heavenly Beds." Rooms have vibrantly colored, contemporary furnishings and large baths; some rooms have sitting areas. Royal Beach Club guests have a private lounge with daily food and beverage presentations.
Meals: Arrecifes offers sophisticated Mexican flavors and a Continental menu, overlooking the sea; traditional Mexican and international cuisine at La Cascada; El Set and La Playa feature lighter fare, poolside or at the beach; at La Cantina, drinks, snacks, and big-screen TV, sports memorabilia, and table games.
Facilities: Business center; two tennis courts; aerobics studio and fitness center; full-service spa; 1.8-mile private, sandy beach.
Services and Special Programs: Supervised Westin Kid's Club, for toddlers through teens, includes crafts, games, swimming, outdoor play, movies, and meals; with special services and amenities for infants. Concierge makes arrangements for sailing, scuba diving, deep-sea fishing, windsurfing, and jet skiing. Guests have access to five championship golf courses nearby.
Rates: $$$–$$$$
Golf Packages: None available.
Getting There: Fifteen miles from San Jose del Cabo International Airport; transportation available.
What's Nearby: Hiking, hunting, four-wheel-drive, and horseback riding expeditions into the Baja desert; shopping and nightclubbing in San Jose del Cabo and Cabo San Lucas. A six-block area of Cabo San Lucas is crowded with lively restaurants and bars like The Giggling Marlin and Squid Roe. The rock group Van Halen owns the dance club, Cabo Wabo.

EUROPE

DOLCE CHANTILLY

Chantilly, France

A mere half-hour drive from Paris are six beautiful golf courses, open to the public, and one of the country's most important tourist attractions, the fourteenth century Château de Chantilly. Near the charming, historic country town of Chantilly, the Dolce Hotel was completely renovated and expanded in the "Ile-de-France" style, creating a perfect base for a golfing vacation. Step out the door onto Golf Chantilly, an inland links course in fairly flat, open parkland with sandy subsoil and routed through the dense and lovely woods of the Condé Forest. Overhanging, long-established trees and plenty of water are balanced by generous fairways. A traditional "Jardins à la Française" design by Nelson and Huau, the 6,756-yard track is decorated with elegant landscaping and gardens. Floating balls are fun to use on the driving range.

The hotel will arrange tee times for you at several nearby golf clubs, including prestigious Golf de Chantilly, often rated number one in France and host of several French Opens and European championships. These thirty-six holes opened in 1909 and were designed by Englishman Tom Simpson, famous for Cruden Bay, Senlis, and his revisions of Muirfield and Ballybunion. No water comes into play—just high, punishing rough, well-protected, sloping greens, and deep gullies and bunkers. The Chantilly Forest lines the fairways.

The historic country town of Chantilly and the surrounding region are renowned for Chantilly lace and for thoroughbred horse racing on one of the most beautiful turf tracks in Europe. The Prix du Jockey-Club and Prix de Diane-Hermes races occur in June.

Adjacent to the Dolce Hotel in the Chantilly Forest, surrounded by a dramatic moat, the fairy-tale castle of Château de Chantilly rises from the confluence of the Seine and Oise Rivers. Andre Le Notre, of Versailles

fame, designed the spectacular gardens in 1663. Second only to the Louvre in its collection of Renaissance paintings, Musée Condé here houses the second largest private art collection in France, including works of Botticelli, Raphael, Poussin, Delacroix, and Giotto. The great Musée Vivant du Cheval, stables of the Princes of Condé, comprise an eighteenth-century architectural masterpiece. You can take a tethered, or nontethered, hot air balloon ride to glide above breathtaking views of the châteaux, the countryside, and Paris in the distance.

Under new ownership by an upscale hotel chain, Dolce Chantilly caters to vacationing golfers, providing freshly redecorated, contemporary-design guest rooms and suites; excellent on-site restaurants; and expert concierges who will arrange golf outings at the top-notch nearby clubs.

Other Places to Play

In the quaint village of Baillet-en-France, the Paris International Golf Club is a Jack Nicklaus signature design, host of the French Ladies Open (33–5–34–69–90–00). In typical Nicklaus style, long par-4s and turf-sided bunkers, and well-protected greens with narrow approaches are on the menu. Herons and more beautiful birds and ducks inhabit the lake, ponds, and creeks. The dramatic, seventeenth-century-style Le Château clubhouse contains a handful of nice guest suites. You will definitely be asked to show your handicap card.

In springtime bluebells blanket the meadows around the Château de Raray Golf Club: three loops of nine holes in a mature forest, with a gorgeous old château for a clubhouse containing museum-quality artworks (03–44–54–70–61). Six of the par-4s are over 400 yards. There is also a less demanding, nine-hole "Blue" course.

Designed by John Jacobs for Japanese owners, Apremont Golf Club lies on relatively flat, sandy, wooded land, meandering 7,038 yards through the Chantilly forest (03–44–25–61–11). A flawless, manicured look is reminiscent of Japanese-style gardens; and the Japanese food here is superb.

Dolce Chantilly
Route d'Apremont, Vineuil-St-Firmin
60500 Chantilly, France
Phone: 33–03–44–58–47–77
Fax: 33–03–44–58–50–28
Web site: www.dolce.com/chantilly
General Manager: Philippe Attia
Accommodations: Four-star rated, 202 rooms and suites with terraces or balconies overlooking the forest or golf course. Furnishings and decor are sleek and contemporary, with luxurious, pale-toned fabrics.
Meals: The Carmontelle serves gourmet French and Continental cuisine in an elegant dining room and on the rotunda overlooking the course. Sumptuous luncheon buffets are popular at L'Etoile. Le Swing in the clubhouse serves buffet lunches and light snacks.
Facilities: Large indoor swimming pool, heated outdoor pool, new fitness center, sauna, badminton, volleyball, boules, jogging trail, table tennis, tennis courts, billiards, mountain bikes, croquet, and business center.
Services and Special Programs: Tee times arranged at nearby courses; golf caddie service.
Rates: $$$
Golf Packages: Golf and Gastronomic Weekend includes one night accommodations, buffet breakfast, a round of golf, gourmet dinner, and drinks. 165 Euros ($167 U.S. dollars) per person, double occupancy.
Getting There: A thirty-minute drive from Roissy Charles de Gaulle International Airport; forty-five minutes from Orly International Airport; rail from Paris to Chantilly.
What's Nearby: You can walk to Château de Chantilly and Musée Condé, or take an electric boat ride in the moat or on the Grand Canal. Charming shops and restaurants are in Chantilly, as well as the Living Horse Museum. Attend a polo match at the Polo Club. Visit the Roman village of Senlis, known for the spectacular cathedral built in 1153, cobbled streets and fortified walls, and a typical French market.

DOLCE FRÉGATE

Saint Cyr-sur-Mer, France

On a wooded, hilly site with wide views of the Mediterranean, this small, boutique hotel in the south of France is tucked between the charming, seaside, vacation villages of Saint Cyr sur Mer and Bandol. Estate wines and olive oils are produced on the property from hundreds of acres of vineyards and groves. Walking trails meander the countryside, fragrant with wild herbs and lavender.

Along with golf on one of the most popular and prettiest courses in Provence, you can combine expeditions to nearby ateliers, wineries, beaches, and world-famous restaurants. Search for the best bouillabaisse in nearby harbor towns; become an expert on Grasse perfumes; paint the same landscape as Cézanne and visit a museum of his works; sunbathe on rocky beaches; or, just stay put at Frégate by one of four swimming pools.

The sunny, low-rise resort complex resembles a traditional Provençal village with stone walls and tile roofs. The resort's own wine label, Château Romanin, is available in the restaurants, which feature regional specialties such as truffles, ratatouille, and grilled seafood, all infused with the legendary Provençal herbs. The salad bar is a colorful collage of French lentils; fruits and vegetables; fresh, marinated mozzarella; local olives; and juicy Marseilles figs.

Stunning, endless views of the Mediterranean are a given on the Frégate Golf Club, designed by American Ronald Fream on slanting, tilting, rolling foothills of the Esterel mountain range. The course is imperiled

by rugged, rust-colored limestone outcroppings, grass-sided bunkers, and steady winds. Five sets of tees are set on stone terrace walls, while vivaciously blooming flower beds are postcard perfect. The weather is clear and mild in spring and fall; summers are sizzling.

Do yourself a favor and take a cart for steep terrain, and practice sidehill lies. Narrow fairways are bordered by tall pines, junipers, vineyards and olive groves, and scrubby rough. Save some energy for the finishing hole, a doozy, with a series of cascading lakes and a 240-yard carry from the back tees.

Guests have access to the practice facilities at the Frégate Golf Academy—a driving range and two putting surfaces, and "La Fregalon," an FFG-certified, nine-hole executive pitch-and-putt course.

Other Places to Play

Wild thyme and rosemary, grapevines and olive trees, and fields of lavender are beautiful backdrops for golf on the French Riviera. On a mountainous site between Aix-en-Provence and Avignon, Seve Ballesteros created his first course in France, Pont Royal Golf Club, a tree-lined, well-watered layout with unique cliff-top holes played over deep gorges (33–04–90–57–40–79, pont royal@aol.com).

Gary Player's first course in France is Golf de Taulane in the foothills of the French Alps an hour's drive from Cannes and anchored by the glorious, eighteenth century, golden-toned, Château de Taulane hotel. The signature hole features a fountain in a small lake with a circular bunker surrounding a lone pine (33–04–93–60–31–30, www.chateautaulane.com).

Near the small medieval town of Mougins, where Picasso lived his later years, the Cannes-Mougins Country Club is a stop on the PGA European Tour (33–04–93–75–79–13, golf.opio.valbonne@wanadoo.fr). Part of the lovely, parkland track is on the former hunting estate of a nobleman. The picturesque clubhouse was once a seventeenth-century olive mill.

Dolce Frégate
Route de Bandol
83270 Saint Cyr-sur-Mer, France
Phone: 33–494–293–939, reservations (800) 993–6523
Fax: 33–494–293–940
Web site: www.dolce.com/fregate
General Manager: Giovanni Donati
Accommodations: Four-star rated, 133 rooms and suites, each with private, sea view balcony or terrace, large baths, and sitting areas; decorated with traditional Provençal fabrics and artworks.
Meals: The formal Mas des Vignes restaurant serves fine French regional cuisine indoors and on terraces and patios. The casual, brasserie style La Restanque is a grille and rotisserie, with outdoor seating. Le Gazebo offers quick poolside dining. The golf clubhouse specializes in hearty sandwiches and salads.
Facilities: Indoor and outdoor swimming pools; fitness center; one hard surface and two clay tennis courts, lessons; biking; hiking; cross-country ski trails.
Services and Special Programs: Spa services; aerobics classes; supervised kid's club.
Rates: $$$
Golf Packages: Golfeur Package includes deluxe accommodations, buffet breakfast, "nature" dinner, and a round of golf; from 183–207 Euros ($181–$204 U.S. dollars) per person, double occupancy.
Getting There: Forty-five minutes to Marseilles International Airport, and twenty minutes to Toulon Airport.
What's Nearby: The Provençal road system can be confusing; for expeditions into the countryside, ask the concierge to book a driver for you. Visit the mountain villages of Le Catellet and La Cadiere d'Azur, and Atelier Paul Cézanne in Aix-en-Provence. Fishing, sailing, and cruising on the coastline.

ROYAL PARC EVIAN

Evian-les-Bains, France

Opened in 1904 and 1922 in ravishing wooded parkland on the south bank of Lake Leman, the Royal Golf Club Evian was completely redesigned in 1990 by American architect Cabell B. Robinson. Hilly fairways overlook Lake Geneva and the nearby peaks of the Memises and Dent d'Oche Mountains below the French Alps. Tight fairways lead to narrow approaches and firm, raised greens that predictably slope towards the lake. Deep, grassy bunkers and abundant white sand fairway bunkers, several lakes and ponds, and thousands of overhanging trees make the 6,674 yards seem longer. The course is a veritable botanical garden, with more than five hundred well-established trees, including massive chestnuts, creating a thick curtain of foliage.

In addition to a comprehensive choice of lessons and clinics for all ages, the golf school offers five-day "On the Course" training for advanced players, consisting of two hours of daily practice and four hours on the course with the instructor. Covered and uncovered practice ranges with mirrors, two putting greens, and bunkers are available to all golfers.

Après golf, players head for the Chalet du Golf to relax with a drink by the fireplace in red leather armchairs and to dig into a buffet of locally produced and hearty Savoyard dishes, smoked meats, and cheeses. These foods can also be enjoyed on the deck under the century-old linden tree.

Within an exclusive enclosure of glorious gardens, centenarian trees, ponds and fountains, the Royal Parc Evian resort comprises the Hotel Royal, the Hotel Ermitage, and the Casino of Evian. There are also vari-

ous outdoor sports venues such as an archery range, tennis and horse-riding centers, swimming pools, and more. As pure white and multilayered as a wedding cake—a Belle Epoque masterpiece of columns, frescoes, and rotundas—the Hotel Royal is as splendiferous today as when it opened in 1909 in honor of King Edward VII. From the fancifully decorated, vaulted ceilings and Provincial prints of the grand lounge, to huge, carved stone fireplaces and lavish silver service in the elegant restaurants, the Hotel Royal is something to behold. Walls are painted with trees and gardens with flowing waterfalls. Custom-built furnishings are of rosewood, mahogany, and exotic lemon.

Opened two years earlier, the Hotel Ermitage is a sweet cross between an English cottage and a Savoyard chalet. It is a charming, intimate inn with big, soft armchairs, a cozy fireplace in the "Birdie" bar, and very private, luxurious guest rooms with flowered fabrics, and painted and carved wood accents.

The Better Living Institute and the Form and Relaxation centers offer comprehensive programs of mind/body, health, and beauty treatments and consultations, including Thai massage, yoga, wraps, scrubs, "Royal Energization," "Sports," "45-Plus Plan," and other encounters; plus indoor and outdoor pools.

When tired of golf, gourmet food, wine, and health treatments, guests hike, mountain bike, and horseback ride in the foothills of the Alps. They also canoe, go boating or four-wheeling, fish, water ski, and sail on the lakes. In the wintertime you can cross-country ski right from the door, or go downhill and

heli-skiing nearby. Some guests risk it all at American and European games at the rococo, domed casino, where the restaurants and discotheque are worth a visit.

Teske at Evian

Australian Rachel Teske is one of the top LPGA players and winner of the Evian Masters LPGA Tour event in 2001. The $2.1-million purse is the second richest in women's golf, after the U.S. Open (www.evianmasters.com).

Ms. Teske said, "The Royal Club Evian is an unbelievable course to play. Not only is the course challenging, but the views from practically every hole on the golf course are unbelievable! So, whether you're concentrating on your golf, or the magnificent views of the surrounding area, you will thoroughly enjoy your time in the area.

"Evian is one of the most picturesque courses I have played. My favorite hole is the par-3 second hole. It is a short downhill that overlooks Lake Geneva. There is no room for error, so make sure you take one or two clubs less, to safely hit the middle of the green. And, enjoy the view!"

Royal Parc Evian
Rive Sud du Lac de Genève
74500 Evian-les-Bains
BP 8–74501 Evian-les-Bains Cedex, France
Phone: 33 (0) 4–50–26–85–11, reservations 33 (0) 4–50–26–85–00
Fax: 33 (0) 4–50–75–61–00
Web site: www.royalparcevian.com
General Manager: Roger Mercier
Accommodations: 154 elaborately decorated rooms and suites in the Hotel Royal, most with private balconies and sitting areas; 91 sumptuous, comfortable rooms and suites in the Hotel Ermitage, with private balconies or terraces.
Meals: Among eight restaurants at the resort Le Cafe Royal is formal, in a Belle Epoque setting under domed ceilings; rotisserie, grill, and buffet at La Veranda; local cuisine in a warm, casual atmosphere at Le Gourmandin; in the casino, dinners at Le Baccara, and late nights at the bar-brassierie, Le Liberte; light and healthy fare at Le Jardin des Lys; Scottish-style pub food at Au Bureau.
Facilities: Three "green set" tennis courts, one synthetic grass court and one indoor court; zero-edge swimming pool and indoor pools; fitness center and classes; oxygen track; archery; shooting; French bowls; squash; climbing wall.
Services and Special Programs: The Children's Club for ages 2–11, with swimming, meals, playground, games, computers, and sports; and the Fun Club, for ages 12–18. Special annual presentations, tournaments, concerts, cooking and painting classes, and festivals with renowned scientists, artists, musicians, chefs, and "Women of Taste." Pets allowed.
Rates: $$$$
Golf Packages: Golf Passion Break includes two nights accommodations, a round of golf and cart daily, buffet breakfast and lunch or dinner daily, and golf amenities. 592–662 Euros ($585–$654 U.S. dollars) per person, double occupancy.
Getting There: A forty-five-minute drive from Geneva Cointrin International Airport, and 360 miles from Paris. Thirty-five minutes by boat from Lausanne. Private helipad.
What's Nearby: Cruise on the resort's 13-meter sailing boat, *Soleil*. Take guided day trips to the medieval village of Yvoire, the Château de Chillon in Montreux, and the abbeys in Abondance and Saint Maurice, or visit Geneva, Lausanne, or Chamonix.

ADARE MANOR HOTEL AND GOLF RESORT
Adare, Ireland

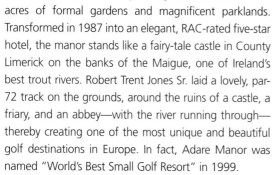

Built as the family seat of the Earls of Dunraven in 1832, Adare Manor is a Gothic-style master-piece of towers, turrets, and ornamental stonework surrounded by nearly a thousand acres of formal gardens and magnificent parklands. Transformed in 1987 into an elegant, RAC-rated five-star hotel, the manor stands like a fairy-tale castle in County Limerick on the banks of the Maigue, one of Ireland's best trout rivers. Robert Trent Jones Sr. laid a lovely, par-72 track on the grounds, around the ruins of a castle, a friary, and an abbey—with the river running through—thereby creating one of the most unique and beautiful golf destinations in Europe. In fact, Adare Manor was named "World's Best Small Golf Resort" in 1999.

Formal gardens, which were planted in the 1850s, are shaded by towering Cedars of Lebanon and beeches, monkey puzzle, cork, and cherry trees, which burst into spring bloom. Fifty-two chimneys can be counted on the rooftops, and seventy-five fireplaces inside, along with nearly four hundred glass windows framed by fancifully carved stone arches and bays. Stone gargoyles peer into the grand, high-ceilinged interior spaces. Inspired by the Hall of Mirrors in Versailles and lined with seventeenth-century Flemish choir stalls, the Minstrel's Gallery is 132 feet long and 26 feet high, decorated with valuable tapestries and carved wood furnishings.

When not playing golf, guests mount up for horse-back riding, and engage in shooting, salmon and trout fishing, cycling, and archery.

Opened in 1995 the Adare Golf Club meanders 7,138 yards through idyllic countryside, with three lakes on the front nine and the omnipresent river alongside and across the finishing holes. Well-bunkered putting surfaces are characteristically fast with fiendish slopes. Fairways are lined with legions of tall, overhanging, mature trees and freshened by dependably breezy conditions.

The eighteenth hole is a stunner. From the tee the fairway extends straight out in front of you with the manor house in the distance. On your left the River Maigue runs along the entire length while a cluster of giant cottonwood trees on the right marks a distance of 200 yards to the green. As you approach the elevated green comes into view across the river, nestled between a dense grove of evergreens and a historic Cedar of Lebanon. The manor house is a picturesque backdrop for the green and the parterre wall, marked by two giant magnolia trees. The entrance to the huge, undulating putting surface is over a stone bridge, a replica of the Halfpenny Bridge in Dublin.

Lady Dunraven's apartment (guest room number 203) has elaborately carved stone decoration and beautiful wood craftsmanship, with a fireplace and a sweeping view of the river. Although not every room is as luscious as Lady Dunraven's, there are one-of-a-kind fireplaces in many rooms, exquisite dark wood furnishings, and rich velvet, silk, and brocade fabrics and drapes. Most accommodations look onto serene gardens and parklands.

Some of the memorable moments of a stay at Adare Manor are candlelight dinners, cordials in the library, afternoon "cream" teas, and sing-alongs in the Tack Room pub. On a cloudy day, enjoy a swim in the warm, indoor pool or a good read by the fire.

The hotel is within walking and biking distance of the quaint village of Adare, where visitors explore the narrow lanes and photograph the beautiful stonework of the Trinitarian Abbey, sweet, thatched cottages, and the antiques shops on Main Street. A ramble around the estate turns up fragments of Desmond Castle, an interesting example of feudal architecture composed of a keep, curtain walls, great halls, the kitchen, bakery, and stable.

Après golf, guests head for the new spa, head-quartered in a charming old stone cottage. The

"Golfers Elixir" includes soothing hydrotherapy and the "Well Being Back Massage" focuses entirely on the back and shoulders to relieve aching muscles. Women love the "Exotic Enriching Milk Bath" and the healing and energizing effects of the "Detox Ocean Bath," a seawater therapy combined with juniper, lemon, and sea fennel and sea buckthorn essential oils.

Other Places to Play

Some of the top courses in the west and southwest of Ireland are within a short drive, including the legendary Ballybunion, Lahinch, Tralee, Killarney, and Old Head of Kinsale. In a tiny ancient village above a mile-long beach on Doughmore Bay lies a notable, new links layout masterminded by Aussie great, Greg Norman—Doonbeg Golf Club, where skinny, rocky fairways slither between the ocean breakers and monstrously high dunes (www.doonbeggolfclub.com).

On an ancient royal site with a castle ruin and an eighteenth-century lighthouse, picturesque Old Head Golf Links near the harbor town of Kinsale in County Cork lies on a rocky promontory 300 feet above the Atlantic. Luckily, power carts are allowed—the better to battle the wind, rain, and fog on the treeless headlands and the battalions of rocks and boulders framing a wild coastal landscape. The *Lusitania* was sunk offshore in 1915 by a German U-boat, resulting in America's entering World War I.

Adare Manor Hotel and Golf Resort
Adare, Limerick, Ireland
Phone: 353-61-396566, reservations (800) 462-3273
Fax: 353-61-396124
Web site: www.adaremanor.com
General Manager: Ferghal Purcell
Accommodations: 138 rooms and suites, including 63 manor house rooms, 11 clubhouse rooms, and 25 new, two- and four-bedroom garden townhouses. Townhouses each have a private entrance, kitchen, dining room, den, washer and dryer, and a full bath for every bedroom.
Meals: The elegant dining room serves Continental cuisine with an Irish flair. The golf clubhouse serves breakfast, lunch, and dinner. The Tack Room is good for pub lunches and hearty dinners.
Facilities: Indoor swimming pool; heath and beauty treatments, complete exercise equipment, and sauna in the new spa; equestrian center offers horseback riding on the estate.
Special Programs: Guided fly-fishing and clay-pigeon shooting.
Rates: $$$–$$$$
Golf Packages: Three nights accommodations, three breakfasts, two dinners, two rounds of golf, and special amenities: $623–$1,175 Euros ($615–$1,161 U.S. dollars) per person, double occupancy. Townhome Packages include two nights accommodations, breakfast, one dinner, and one round of golf: $305–360 Euros ($301–$356 U.S. dollars) per person, based on four-person occupancy.
Getting There: Shannon International Airport is a thirty-minute taxi ride; or, you can land your helicopter at the estate.
What's Nearby: Shop and sightsee in the village; visit the Heritage Center. Within a short drive are Bunratty Castle and Folk Park, the Burren and Cliffs of Moher, Blarney Castle and the Dingle Peninsula, the Ring of Kerry, and the Lakes of Killarney. Top-notch shopping is in Limerick City, 11 miles to the north.

THE KILDARE HOTEL AND GOLF CLUB

Straffan, Ireland

After the Anglo-Norman invasion of Ireland in about 550 A.D., Straffan House was granted to an ancestor of the Dukes of Leinster and confirmed by Richard the Lionheart's brother, who later became King John of England. A series of titled families took ownership throughout the centuries, including the Bartons, winery owners in Bordeaux who redesigned the house to be a French château. The estate was purchased in the 1980s by a developer, gloriously renovated, and opened as a luxury resort hotel in 1991, whereupon it was promptly awarded the first and only five-red-star rating in Ireland.

Like a scene in a Constable painting, the pure-white mansion is set in an idyllic 330-acre estate in County Kildare woodland, bordered by the River Liffey and surrounded by the parkland golf course. Planted in the nineteenth century, oaks, limes, and beeches are magnificent backdrops for plantings on the banks of the river and a glorious formal, walled garden. Bicycles are a pleasant way to tour the extensive grounds.

The light of wood fires in the Georgian fireplaces reflects in the Waterford crystal chandeliers of the rooms and suites. Over the stately English, hand-printed wallpaper hang an important collection of paintings by Jack Yeats, the Irish poet's brother. Reproduction Chippendale furniture and commodious baths, some with whirlpool tubs, complete the sumptuous decor.

At a championship length of 7,159 yards, the Arnold Palmer/Ed Seay–designed golf course will be the site of the 2006 Ryder Cup. Extraordinary, considering the youth of the course, the club has already hosted the Irish PGA Championship, the Irish Open, and the European Open.

The river and fourteen lakes come into play on most holes, with cleverly contoured greens inclined toward the water. Grassy hummocks abound, and unique beach bunkers run right into the lakes. The seventh is a 608-yard, daunting challenge, with double doglegs, encroaching gorse, an obstacle course of wide, flat, bunkers, and plenty of dense rough. Players trod a century-old iron bridge to reach the green perched on a little island between two streams. The 380-yard, par-4 eighth is routed all along the river to a small green, sloped perfectly to roll your ball into the water. Across the river on a stretch of pastureland, a new Palmer course will open in 2003.

Non-golfing guests take the half-hour drive into Dublin for theater and shopping, or stroll the lanes of the tiny, picturesque village of Straffan. You can also fish for salmon, trout, and pike, with the expert assistance of a ghillie (a fishing guide), on a private mile of the River Liffey and on three private lakes on the estate. Clay target shooting is popular, as well as driven game shoots.

Do not be surprised to see a European Tour pro or two practicing beside you on the driving range and out on the golf course, enjoying this American-style layout—some say it is Palmer and Seay's very best.

McGinley at K Club

A member of the World Cup of Golf team and the European Ryder Cup Team, Paul McGinley won the 2001 Irish PGA on the European Tour. The Tournament Professional of the K Club, he said, "Although very demanding, golfers of all abilities will . . . find the course a pleasure to play because of its beautiful setting. There are splashes of yellow gorse everywhere, huge chestnut trees and plenty of water features, with the magnificent hotel at the centre. Among the six or seven showpiece holes, the seventh and sixteenth are generally regarded as the best. I particularly like the seventeenth, but maybe that is because I helped to design the new back tee!

"Designed by the great Arnold Palmer, the K Club has been home to a leading European Tour event, the Smurfit European Open, since 1995, and it is certainly a whole different ball game played under tournament conditions and from the very back sticks. Certainly, my performances in the event have not matched my enjoyment of the course but I hope to rectify that in the coming years!"

The Kildare Hotel and Golf Club
At Straffan
County Kildare, Ireland
Phone: 353–1–6017200, reservations (800) 323–7500
Fax: 353–1–6017299
Web site: www.kclub.ie
General Manager: Ray Carroll
Accommodations: 69 rooms and suites; deluxe rooms are larger with gardens and/or river views. Garden and fountain suites have two bedrooms, two baths, lounge/dining areas, and small kitchens.
Meals: Jacket and tie are required after 7:00 P.M. in the elegant dining room, the Byerly Turk, where French cuisine is served along with Irish regional specialties. In the Legends Restaurant in the opulent golf clubhouse, the menu is Continental and the atmosphere relaxed at lunch but formal at dinner. Barbecues and picnics take place at the Island Inish Mor.
Facilities: Two indoor tennis courts; squash; a state-of-the-art fitness venue and gymnasium; indoor swimming pool; archery range; croquet court; and complete health and beauty spa services.
Services and Special Programs: Driven game shoots in season; transportation to nearby horseback riding, fishing on a private mile of the River Liffey and in three private lakes, with equipment provided.
Rates: $$$$
Golf Packages: Two nights deluxe accommodations, full Irish Breakfast daily, and two rounds of golf: from 615 to 660 Euros ($607–$652 U.S. dollars) per person, double occupancy.
Getting There: Thirty-minute drive from Dublin International Airport; limousine service and use of the estate's helipad is available.
What's Nearby: Kildare is world famous for breeding thoroughbred racehorses (see them at the Curragh racecourse and the National Stud Farm, a few minutes away). Visit Castletown House, the Japanese Gardens, the Steam Museum, and the Butterfly Farm in Straffan. Shopping, restaurants, museums, and events are in the capital city of Dublin—the hotel will arrange chauffeur and/or guide for you.

PORTMARNOCK HOTEL AND GOLF LINKS

Portmarnock, County Dublin, Ireland

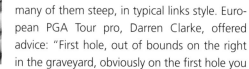

The Prince of Wales, later King Edward VII, often visited the Jameson family at their estate, St. Marnock's House, on a peninsula jutting into the Irish Sea, not far from Dublin City. On his last visit in 1907, he unveiled a plaque commemorating the marriage between two great whiskey distilling families, Jameson and Haig. You can find the plaque in the garden of the ancestral home, which is now the luxurious Portmarnock Hotel, opened in 1995. The twelfth-century church of the local saint, St. Marnock, overlooks the property while two emerald-green islands, Lambay and Ireland's Eye, float offshore.

The Jameson's original, century-old nine-hole golf course is now part of the hotel's Bernhard Langer–designed Golf Links, opened in 1996. It is separated from the Irish Sea by sand dunes and a wide beach where local residents walk their dogs within view of Dublin harbor. Site of several Irish Opens and the 1991 Walker Cup, and the only PGA European Tour course in Ireland, the Links begins on flatlands, weaving through dunes and marram grass hummocks, the ubiquitous Irish gorse bush, and ninety-eight bunkers,

many of them steep, in typical links style. European PGA Tour pro, Darren Clarke, offered advice: "First hole, out of bounds on the right in the graveyard, obviously on the first hole you don't want to go visiting in there." Nor do you want to visit in the creek that crosses the fairway.

A five-minute drive south along the coast brings you to twenty-seven holes of the Portmarnock Golf Club, one of the oldest clubs in the country and what some consider to be Ireland's best links course. This course is windy, always windy, with ocean on three sides, and pocked with deep bunkers. Twisting through impenetrable fescue and marram grass rough, fairways are narrow and mounded, with few flat lies. One of eighteen signature holes, right at the water's edge with prevailing headwinds, the fifteenth shoots from an elevated tee over a long, gorsy patch to the green below, menaced by three pot bunkers, hedges, grasses, and a ravine named "The Valley of Sin." Just head for the sea and pray you blow back.

Sir Peter Allen gleefully describes the colors: "White water to the west, blue sea and sky, the rough a pale

khaki color, the fairways the light green of an olive, the watered greens the colour of emeralds, picked out by black-and-white posts topped by scarlet flags. What a wonderful place to play the best of games."

Unlike in Scotland, where some golfers are intimidated by the staid attitudes and dour visages at the legendary golf clubs, the locals in Ireland are friendly, welcoming, and humorous. The clear, sunny days of spring are the best for golf.

Archery, air rifle shooting, and lolling by the swimming pool are some of the activities available on the grounds, along with fishing nearby. There are also practice fields for football and rugby, and you can rent quad bikes. A welcome retreat after a blustery day on the links, the new health and beauty spa offers traditional treatments, steam, sauna, and gym.

A ten-minute drive or a bracing walk away on the coastal path, the seaside village of Malahide makes a nice day trip; go there to visit Malahide Castle, circa 1185, and to shop for local crafts. The glories of Dublin are 11 miles north.

Other Places to Play

Within thirty minutes of Portmarnock are such venerable golf courses as the K Club, Baltray, the Island, Royal Dublin (established in 1889), Druids Glen, Powerscourt, the European Club, and Rathsallagh.

Opened in 1991 the Jack Nicklaus–designed Mount Juliet in County Kilkenny hosted the Irish Open in the mid-1990s. The beautiful inland track rambles through the woodlands by the River Nore, and water comes into play on six holes. Ireland's only David Leadbetter Golf Academy and a unique eighteen-hole putting course make this a major destination for golfers.

A stay at 200-year-old Mount Juliet House is a step back in time. A massive Georgian-era manor house set in a 1,500-acre estate, this is a charming, quite luxurious hotel that attracts golfers, equestrians, shootists, and salmon fishermen (011–353–567–3000, www.mountjuliet.ie).

Portmarnock Hotel and Golf Links
Strand Road, Portmarnock
County Dublin, Ireland
Phone: 353–1–846–0611, reservations (800) 457–4000
Fax: 353–1–846–2442
Web site: www.portmarnock.com
General Manager: Shane Cookman
Accommodations: 103 rooms and suites of small and medium size, each with a view of the sea or the golf course, some with large bay windows or balconies. Decor and furnishings are traditional and sumptuous. Room rates includes full Irish breakfast.
Meals: Bistro food at the contemporary-style Links Restaurant and bar at the golf clubhouse; award-winning Continental cuisine at Osborne Restaurant, with occasional ethnic evenings featuring Italian, French, and barbecue; formal tea and light fare in the Cocktail Foyer.
Facilities: Full-service fitness center and spa, business center.
Services and Special Programs: Golf caddie service.
Rates: $$$
Golf Packages: Links Golfer Package includes two nights accommodations, full Irish breakfast daily, and a round of golf. 228–316 Euros ($225–$312 U.S. dollars) per person, double occupancy.
Getting There: A fifteen-minute drive from Dublin International Airport (taxi available); helipad on site.
What's Nearby: Browse the craft center in Portmarnock village and in the closeby hamlets of Howth and Malahide. In Dublin City, visit Dublin Castle, St. Patrick's Cathedral, Trinity College, and charming Temple Bar, plus museums, art galleries, nightlife, and great shopping.

PALAZZO ARZAGA HOTEL SPA
AND GOLF RESORT

Brescia, Italy

If luxe could kill, all of the Palazzo Argaza guests would drop dead. And this has likely been true since the fifteenth century, when the former monastery was transformed into a magnificent *palazzo*. Lucky for golfers vacationing in Italy, Arzaga was opened in 1999 as a privately owned, five-star hotel and spa in a thousand acres of oak and chestnut forest and rolling countryside in the foothills of the Alps, a short distance from Lake Garda. Beside a lovely, twelfth-century chapel, the hotel is graced throughout with original, restored wall frescoes and painted ceilings, stone fireplaces, stunning antiques, and historic artworks in interconnecting salons—music and reading rooms, restaurants, galleries, and lounges.

Decorated in eighteenth-century Venetian or nine-teenth-century Lombardy style, suites and guest rooms are surrounded by formal gardens and an inner court-yard, an old orchard, the terrace, and the golf courses. Avid golfers stay in newer, equally commodious, Italian country-style clubhouse lodgings.

The Jack Nicklaus II and Gary Player Design companies each inte-grated their golf-course layouts into the gentle terrain. They wrapped fair-ways and greens around gorgeous, mature woods, and native vegetation bordering several lakes and ponds. The uniquely mild climate allows golf to be played throughout the year.

In true Nicklaus style multileveled and often sloped greens are convinc-ingly protected by batteries of deep bunkers and narrow approaches. Five lakes are wildlife habitats and beautiful hazards.

The nine-hole Player Course,

soon to be expanded to eighteen, is enhanced by the clear-and-present danger of a dense hardwood forest and several lakes. The par-4 third is short and difficult, with three deep fair-way bunkers with 90 degree vertical faces, fronting a wide green guarded by a large trap. One of the longest par-5s in Europe, the 610-yard fourth hole asks for a drive to right-center to avoid a yawning fair-way bunker. Multitiered, elevated putting surfaces on peninsulas and fronted by water and trees are harbin-gers of the remaining back nine to come.

A top attraction at Arzaga is the Golf Academy, the first Teaching and Learning Centre of the PGA of Europe in Italy. Private and clinic instruction is offered to amateurs, to juniors, and to professional golfers under the direction of Donato DiPonziano, named "Golf Pro of the Year" in 1995, and developer of the PGA's advanced training program. Among the excel-lent practice venues are covered and heated tee areas.

Sailing, canoeing, and windsurfing on Lake Garda are popular, as well as cycling about the estate and on idyllic country roads. After a day of golf or water-sports, sightseeing in Mantova, and seeking Shakespeare in Verona, a nap on the sleek sun terrace by the swimming pool comes easy.

In collaboration with the world-famous Terme di Saturnia in Tuscany, Arzaga's Saturnia Wellness Centre features traditional beauty treatments and state-of-the-art health evaluation and therapies, such as bio-peeling, anti-aging facials, shiatsu, massage, and body toning. The center also fea-tures a beautiful indoor, heated mineral pool for lap swimming. Guests enjoy the golfers' warm-up exercises and sports massages.

Nowhere in Italy is there a more enchanting terrace for a pre-dinner aperitif than at the Arzaga, while the sun settles into the surrounding Lombardy countryside; particularly, when aperitifs are followed by dinner in Sala Moretto, where candlelight and firelight flicker on the vaulted ceilings and the bucolic tapestries. Diners enjoy some of the finest classic Italian and international cuisine served in the region. In the original centuries-old cellar of the *palazzo,* La Taverna is a charming, barrel-ceilinged hideaway for romantic dinners. Breakfast is served in the antiques-filled gallery and on the inner courtyard.

Fairway Cruising

Golfers often wonder if vacation cruises are too confining for their active lifestyles. Catering to links lovers, the luxury line Silversea Cruises, offers "Silver Links" sailing itineraries that include pro-escorted golfing excursions to top clubs in the Mediterranean. Among the stops on various cruises are Garlenda, Carthage, Frégate, Son Vida, Montecastillo and the legendary Valderrama. Onboard a PGA pro gives clinics and private lessons using golf cages, video-computer technology, contests, and demonstrations, with new Callaway clubs available (800–774–9996, www.silversea.com).

Arzaga and several more golf courses in Northern Italy are on the cruise arranged by Kalos Golf, a company that arranges upscale golf trips by yacht and riverboat in Europe. In addition to six rounds of golf, passengers hobnob with golf celebs and teachers onboard, and enjoy matches with their companions. The British Isles two-week itinerary includes Royal County Down, Portmarnock, Celtic Manor, Royal Saint David's, and other seaside courses. San Roque Club, Valderrama, and Sotogrande are among the highlights of the Iberian Peninsula sail on the magnificent sailing ship, the *Sea Cloud II* (www.kalosgolf.com).

Palazzo Arzaga Hotel Spa and Golf Resort

25080 Carzago di Calvagese della Riviera
Brescia, Italy
Phone: 39–030–680–600, reservations (800) 323–7500
Fax: 39–030–680–6270
Web site: www.palazzoarzaga.com
General Manager: Giampaolo Burratin
Accommodations: 84 rooms in the mansion are in a variety of sizes and styles; all are commodious and elegant with antiques, Italian marble baths, and sumptuous upholstery fabrics, draperies, and bed linens; high-tech amenities for business travelers. Some rooms have original fifteenth-century frescoes and king size beds. Rooms near the historic chapel and in the "golf residence" are decorated in Italian country style.
Meals: Exquisite Italian and Continental cuisine at Il Moretto restaurant; intimate dinners in La Taverna; breakfast in the light-filled gallery and in the courtyard; buffet lunches and dinners at the golf clubhouse.
Facilities: Marked nature trails for walking and biking; a jogging track; two Har-tru tennis courts; horseback riding and stables; an elegant Gianfranco Ferre boutique; the Saturnia Wellness Centre; a European PGA-certified golf academy with superior practice facilities, high-tech analysis, covered and heated practice areas, and two putting greens; indoor and outdoor swimming pools.
Services and Special Programs: Outdoor yoga and tai-chi instruction. Children ages 2–6 are cared for and entertained at the "Mini Club" by an Italian, English, and German-speaking staff. Junior Golf Academy.
Rates: $$$$
Golf Packages: The three-night Golf Vacation includes deluxe accommodations, two rounds of golf, one spa treatment, buffet breakfasts, and two dinners. 659–744 Euros ($651–$735 U.S. dollars) per person, double occupancy.
Getting There: Driving time from Venice is two hours; ninety minutes from Milan Linate and Milan Malpensa Airports; thirty minutes from Verona; the railroad station is at Garda.
What's Nearby: A short drive to art, history, and archaeological museums, and sightseeing in Verona, Milan, Mantova, Cremona, and Brescia; the House of Stradivari; Verona's opera season; the ancient Roman town of Santa Giulia; botanical gardens, abbeys, and parks. A few minutes away on Lake Garda are watersports and lakeside activities, such as boat tours, canoeing, windsurfing, and sailing.

CARNOUSTIE HOTEL GOLF RESORT AND SPA

Carnoustie, Scotland

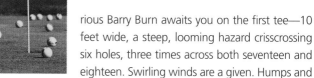

In the 1500s the links of Carnoustie on the northeast coast of Scotland were laid out by Old Tom Morris (later by James Braid), and built by hand among the fescue, the broom, the sea grass hummocks, and the gorse. This is the second oldest course in Scotland after St. Andrews, which is just across the Tay Estuary, a forty-minute drive away. Carnoustie has hosted several British Opens, the first in 1931 and the most recent in 1999, won by Paul Lawrie.

The 128th Open was controversial, with many players complaining that the course was too tough, the fairways too narrow, and the rough punishing. Add typical Carnoustie winds and the average score on the first day was 78. Lawrie battled Justin Leonard and Jean Van de Velde in a playoff to become the first home-based Scot to take the Open in 106 years.

On the Carnoustie Championship Course, the noto-rious Barry Burn awaits you on the first tee—10 feet wide, a steep, looming hazard crisscrossing six holes, three times across both seventeen and eighteen. Swirling winds are a given. Humps and hollows parade down the narrow corridors of fairways between high sand dunes. Requiring long, straight shots on every hole, and 7,368 yards from the back tees, the course does not run out and back in typical links fashion. Each hole heads in a different direction, making it difficult to judge the wind. The stroke-saver booklet describes one green." The steadily sloped green is guarded at the front by the mean little Jockie's Burn, to the left by a cavernous bunker and to the right by the sort of vegetation that has probably not yet found its way into a naturalist's handbook."

Fairways are tight and rumpled on the Burnside Course, fringed by dense heather and gorse, and menaced by devilishly located, deep pot bunkers—a

true links test. Greens are small and sloping, and hard to hold in dry, wind-strafed conditions. Barry Burn makes its appearance here too.

With each hole named for a famous battle, Buddon Links Course is closest to the sea. It is shorter with just one par-5, and less demanding than the others.

As at most Scottish clubs, proof of handicap must be shown; the minimum for men is 28, for ladies 36.

Opened in time for the 1999 Open, with views over Carnoustie Bay and the North Sea and overlooking the first and finishing holes of the Championship Course, the luxury hotel is a warm and elegant refuge from the coastal climate. Rooms and suites, each with a view of the sea, the golf course, or the town, are furnished with locally crafted pieces and imported ceramics. From "Sports Massage" to the "Golfers Luxury Tonic," health and beauty treatments are on the menu at the Spa Club, which has a large indoor swimming pool, sauna, steam room, and whirlpool.

Muirfield and Nicklaus

More than 200 courses are within two hours of Carnoustie, including St. Andrews, Kingsbarns, Muirfield, Gleneagles, Royal Aberdeen, Cruden Bay, Monifieth, and other famous clubs.

Jack Nicklaus was nineteen years old when he played Muirfield Golf Links for the first time as a member of the 1959 Walker Cup Team. He won his first British Open at Muirfield, and named his own course in Ohio after the East Lothian track. Seven more Opens were hosted here, the latest in 2002.

On Tuesday and Thursday, with a handicap of 18 or less (24 or less for women), you can play Muirfield (01620–842293). No trees or water come into play on this seaside course. Unlike other Scottish links, all hazards are visible; in fact, you can see the entire course from the clubhouse. Long, snarled grass grabs and keeps balls. Bunkers are strategic (to say the least), turf-faced, and as deep as 6 feet.

Carnoustie Hotel Golf Resort and Spa
Links Parade
Carnoustie DD7 7JE, Scotland
Phone: 44–1241–411999, reservations (800) 322–2403
Fax: 44–1241–411998
Web site: www.carnoustie-hotel.com
General Manager: Jerry Foster
Accommodations: Four-star rated, 75 rooms and suites with golf, ocean, or park view; deluxe amenities; traditional furnishings and plush fabrics; and sitting areas.
Meals: Continental and Mediterranean cuisine with Scottish specialties at the Dalhousie Restaurant; hearty pub food in Calder's Bar, Brassiere, and Terrace, from a char-grilled steak sandwich to fresh fish and salads.
Facilities: Full-service spa, indoor swimming pool, fitness center.
Services and Special Programs: Golf caddies, preferred tee times.
Rates: $$$
Golf Packages: One night accommodations, dinner, breakfast, a round of golf on Championship and Buddon. 116–155 Euros ($115–$153 U.S. dollars) per person, double occupancy.
Getting There: International flights arrive at Glasgow, an hour and forty-five minutes away; domestic flights at Edinburgh, an hour-and-a-half drive. Private aircraft land at Dundee City Airport. Chauffeured transport is available.
What's Nearby: Guided or independent walks in the Angus Glens. Take the train into Edinburgh for shopping and sightseeing. Tour Caithness Glass Factory, Blair Castle, and Glamis Castle. Spend the day at St. Andrews visiting the castle, the British Golf Museum, the University grounds, and browse the antiques shops.

THE GLENEAGLES HOTEL

Auchterarder, Scotland

Among the moors and the heather in the foothills of the Scottish highlands lies a parkland golf course of legendary form and beauty. In a dreamlike setting between the emerald Ochil Hills, the looming Trossachs and the rugged Glendevon rift, the King's course meanders, anchored by the premier resort hotel and sport center in the country. The castlelike edifice was built in the Roaring Twenties and remains one of the grandest country hotels in the world.

Golfers come for three renowned golf courses, the unparalleled practice facilities, and the golf academy. Equestrians bring their horses to one of Europe's largest centers for riding lessons and shows. Fly-fishers cast for salmon on private "beats" on the River Tay and for trout in the lochs of the Gleneagles estate. Located here are the famed Jackie Stewart Shooting and Fishing School, and the British School of Falconry.

Designed by five-time British Open champ, James Braid, and opened at the end of World War I, the King's Course twists and roils through birches and pines, burnished golden gorse and purple heather bordering fairways of springy moorland turf. The generally large greens are easy to hit, not so easy to putt. Rising to 600 feet in elevation, views are stunning, and breezes blow steadily. Generously festooned with deep, turf-lined pot bunkers and American-style traps, each hole has a sweet name, such as "Blink Bonnie," "Kittle Kink," "Denty Den"—and "Het Girdle," where the tabletop green is reached way, way up a wild, gorsy slope and guarded by a battalion of giant bunkers.

The Queen's Course winds around Loch-an-Erie in a nook of hills, where grouse, deer, and pheasant share the landscape. Playing longer than it looks, the track is often strafed by prevailing winds, requiring a club-up on most holes to reach elevated greens over gaping gullies and long stretches of native grasses.

Jack Nicklaus's 7,081-yard creation, the PGA Centenary Course, was opened in the late 1980s. It is the first in the country with paved cart paths (as throughout most of Scotland, no carts are allowed on the King's and Queen's Courses). "Wester Greenwells" is the skinny second hole along the loch. The fifth, "Crookit Cratur," snakes toward a narrow entry to the large, undulating green, while number eight, "Sidlin' Brows," uncoils into a rising and falling fairway between elevated traps, dropping to a seriously two-tiered green bordered by turf-sided bunkers.

The Wee Course is a par-3, nine-holer on moorland, where children and high handicappers practice and have fun; and there is also a pitch-and-putt course.

Hotel guests loll in the indoor pool, the lap pool, the solarium, and the Turkish bath. And even nonriders enjoy the indoor and outdoor Equestrian Centre arenas where some of Europe's most beautiful horses perform and are exercised. Classes are offered in polo, dressage, English and Western riding, and carriage driving. You can also take an off-road driving lesson in the

Perthshire hills in a Land Rover. Your child can learn to drive in a quarter-size Rover on a specially built course.

Dress is quite formal at this five-star rated hostelry. Gentlemen wear jackets and ties, and ladies turn out for dinner in designer frocks. From kilted doormen to eager caddies, personal service is superb and your every wish is satisfied: Just ask for a tour of the countryside in a chauffeured Rolls Royce or a plate of hot scones in your room—you've got it.

Public spaces and guest rooms are luxuriant with dark wood furnishings, classic artworks, regal brocades and lively chintzes, marble baths, and gilt mirrors.

Gleneagles is the site of the annual Scottish Open and has been selected as the venue for the fortieth Ryder Cup in 2014, when the resort will celebrate its ninetieth anniversary.

The Royal Golfer

Crossing the Firth of Forth over the magnificent circa-1880 Forth Railway Bridge, the Royal Scotsman chugs through the Kingdom of Fife and along the coastline through Burntisland and Kirkcaldy. Afternoon tea is served promptly at 4:00 P.M. while the luxurious passenger train crosses the Tay Bridge into Dundee.

Like a country house on wheels, the Royal Scotsman is one of the world's most famous trains, a vestige from the romantic age of railway travel. Just thirty-six passengers are accommodated on golfing tours of Scotland, and on a variety of other itineraries. Lounging in Edwardian splendor on plaid sofas and deep armchairs in the salon while the hills and lakes of the highlands roll by, golfers rest between golf outings to Carnoustie, Royal Dornoch, Nairn, and Gleneagles—truly, some of the most celebrated and beautiful golf courses ever built.

Along the way passengers debark for private tours of the Dunrobin, Glamis, and Ballindalloch Castles; the Glenmorangie Distillery; and for cashmere shopping at Johnstons Woolen Mill (www.royalscotsman.com).

The Gleneagles Hotel
Auchterarder, Perthshire PH3 1NF
Scotland
Phone: 017–64–662231, reservations (866) 881–9525
Fax: 017–64–662134
Web site: www.gleneagles.com
General Manager: Patrick Elsmie
Accommodations: 234 spacious rooms and suites vary in size; most have countryside or garden views; some are newly renovated with contemporary decor and large baths. Sumptuous furnishings, elegant bedding and upholstery fabrics, sitting areas, and work stations with Internet connection.
Meals: Andrew Fairlie, one of the United Kingdom's culinary elite, heads the French kitchen at Andrew Fairlie at Gleneagles, an opulent dining room. The Strathearn Restaurant was named one of the world's best hotel restaurants, serving classic Continental fare. The Club Restaurant features Mediterranean and California cuisine. With the ambience of an ocean liner, The Bar is the place for light lunches, afternoon tea, and snacks. A golfer's buffet is popular at the new Dormly Clubhouse Restaurant and Bar.
Facilities: Two indoor swimming pools; weight and workout venues; fitness classes—from aerobics to boxercise; a full-service health and beauty spa (golfing gentlemen like the "Laird's Remedy" aromatherapy massage); upscale shopping arcade; tennis on four all-weather courts and one grass court; croquet, petanque, and lawn bowling; complimentary bikes; walking and running trails on 850 acres.
Services and Special Programs: The Golf Academy has the newest video analysis equipment and top-notch instructors.
Rates: $$$$
Golf Packages: One night accommodations in a Classic room, breakfast, dinner, and golf: 638 Euros ($630 U.S. dollars) for two. Perthshire Paradise includes one night accommodations, unlimited access to all sporting activities, three meals, and spa treatments: 411–588 Euros ($406–$581 U.S. dollars) per person, double occupancy.
Getting There: International flights arrive at Glasgow Prestwick International Airport and domestic flights arrive at Edinburgh International Airport, both less than an hour's drive away. Chauffeured transport is available, and your helicopter can land here. The Gleneagles Railroad Station is a few minutes away.
What's Nearby: In Scotland's capital city, visit Edinburgh Castle, art galleries, museums, and theaters. The Edinburgh International Festival in August is Europe's largest celebration of music and dance. See stately homes, Blair and Drummond Castles, Scone Palace, the Bell's national heather collection at Perth, and Lake of Menteith. Tour malt whiskey distilleries or tramp in the Grampian Mountains and the Cairngorms.

OLD COURSE HOTEL GOLF RESORT AND SPA

St. Andrews, Scotland

Every golfer dreams of a pilgrimage to St. Andrews, the birthplace of the game and the site of the oldest and most revered golf course in the world—the Old Course. From Old Tom Morris to Tom Watson and Tiger Woods, for more than six centuries and in twenty-six British Opens, players have battled the elements on this formidable, true links land—against bracing winds off the North Sea; in rain and swirling mists; through prickly, knee-high gorse; across rolling dunes; and into grassy hollows. You will find no waterfalls or railroad ties, and no palm trees—no trees at all—just low mounds and long stretches of scruffy, natural heathers, and brooms; shockingly deep pot bunkers; and mammoth double greens, each with two flags, swept dry and hard by the nearly unceasing breath of the sea. Practice your knock-down shots, pitch-and-runs, and long, long putts; stay low at all costs.

If you are fortunate enough to snag a tee time on the Old, come early to experience the look and the palpable spirit of the place. Shoulder to shoulder the picturesque buildings of the ancient town create a backdrop unlike any other in golfdom. Expect an audience on the first tee—a crowd of sightseers, townspeople, caddies, and golfers is omnipresent. All are rapt as the starter calls, "Gentlemen, hit away." A decent drive earns applause; an errant one gets sympathetic sighs. As you step across the hallowed stones of Swilican Bridge on the finishing hole, look up to see the venerable members of the Royal and Ancient, with single malt whiskeys in hand, peering out the bay windows of their clubhouse.

The Old Course and four more are owned by the town of St. Andrews; the hotel opened the Duke's Course in 1995. Tee times on the Old are hard to come by and must be booked months, even up to two years, in advance. A stellar alternative, with first-come-first-served access, is the New Course, built in 1895. It is easily as beautiful and demanding as the Old, and longer and tighter. Expect blowing sand and stunning sea views on the Jubilee Course, circa 1897.

Designed by five-time British Open champ, Peter Thomson, the Duke's Course is the first and only parkland course at St. Andrews, and, at 7,271 yards, is the longest inland track in Scotland. High handicappers favor the Strathtyrum Course, a par-69, 5,094-yard beauty. The Kingsbarns Course, opened in 2000, is the only links course in St. Andrews built in this century. The Eden Course is a 1914 Alister Mackenzie original. The nine-hole Balgrove is primarily for beginners and children.

In time for the 2000 British Open, the Old Course Hotel completed a multimillion-dollar refurbishment of the five-star property, opening a new spa and opulent new rooms and suites. Overlooking the notorious seventeenth hole, the new wing has shatterproof glass windows. The Golf Practice Centre has the latest video equipment and Daiwa rental clubs. Five miles from the hotel is the largest indoor practice facility in Europe, the Scottish Golf Centre.

Call well ahead to arrange the golf experience of a lifetime; and to book river and loch fishing trips; horseback riding and sight-seeing tours in the idyllic countryside, and tours to Edinburgh, an easy day trip.

The Road Hole Grill is the best place from which to watch the golf action on nearly the entire Old Course, and to enjoy sea views while digging into hearty Scottish salmon and roasted meats. International cuisine, from sushi to tapas, is served in the Sands, a contemporary-style brasserie. After a blustery day outdoors, golfers and caddies warm their toes and swallow pints of ale by the open hearth in the cozy pub, the Jigger Inn, built in 1850. The Road Hole Bar stocks at least one malt whiskey from every Scottish distillery; perhaps David Duval hoisted one of these after his unfortunate experience in the "Road Hole" bunker on the last day of the Millennium Open, which Tiger Woods won by eight strokes.

Tee Times on the Old Course

To obtain a guaranteed tee time on the Old Course, it is necessary to place a reservation with the St. Andrews Links Trust many months, even two years or more, in advance. For information on this rather complicated procedure, go to www.standrews.org.uk/courses; pre-paid green fees are nonrefundable. To bypass the reservation process, look into packages that include accommodations and tee times, such as those offered by "Old Course Experience," at www.oldcourse-experience.com.

About half of all starting times are put into a daily lottery drawn for the next day's play. You can either telephone or apply in person at the reservations office (44–1334–466666). The Old Course Hotel golf steward will do this for guests. Single golfers actually have the best chance of snagging a slot by checking in with the starter early in the morning. Keep in mind that golfers must have a handicap card or certificate (minimum 24 for men, 36 for ladies) and proof of identity.

Old Course Hotel Golf Resort and Spa
St. Andrews, Kingdom of Fife KY16 9SP
Scotland
Phone: 011–44–1334–474371, reservations (800) 223–6800
Fax: 011–44–1334–477668
Web site: www.oldcoursehotel.co.uk
General Manager: Jonathan Stapleton
Accommodations: 146 rooms and suites with elegant ochre, taupe, and terra-cotta interiors; some have fireplaces; most have private balconies overlooking the links, the sea, or the town. Decor is either classic traditional with tapestry fabrics and chintzes, or sleek contemporary. Phones with data ports, wide-screen TV, and spacious marble baths are among the deluxe amenities. Large suites feature large dining areas, large viewing balconies, fireplaces, and Jacuzzis for two.
Meals: The open kitchen in the Road Hole Grill serves up Scottish meats, fish, and game. The Sands caters to an international clientele with a seafood bar and a bistro menu. The elegant Duke's Clubhouse offers grills and traditional roasts, salads, breakfast sandwiches, and buffets. Pubby snacks, small meals, and drinks are served at the Jigger Inn.
Facilities: The Spa features a sizable, indoor lap pool, a solarium, saunas and steam, and a gym; traditional beauty and health treatments include a "Golfer's Massage."
Services and Special Programs: Dogs are welcomed with special doggie treats and amenities.
Rates: $$$$
Golf Packages: The Golf Indulgence Break includes a two-night stay, two breakfasts, one dinner, use of the spa, thirty-six holes of golf, and gift pack: from 430 Euros ($425 U.S. dollars) per person, double occupancy. Warm up with the Improver's Golf package, which includes one hour lesson on links golf, nine holes of play with a PGA pro on the Duke's Course, and gift pack: from 410 Euros ($405 U.S. dollars) per person, double occupancy.
Getting There: Major carriers serve Edinburgh Airport, an hour away, and Glasgow Airport, a two-hour drive from the resort. Hourly rail service from London Kings Cross to Leuchars Station, nearby. Helipad and chauffeured transportation available.
What's Nearby: Visit the British Golf Museum, the St. Andrews Museum, and the St. Andrews Sea Life Centre. In Edinburgh stroll about Scotland's oldest university, Old Town, and the dramatic ruins of Edinburgh Castle; shop in lovely galleries and antiques shops. Take a drive along the rugged coastline to stately homes and tiny fishing villages; the hotel will arrange guided tours.

WESTIN TURNBERRY RESORT

Ayrshire, Scotland

The Arran Mountains loom above the Irish Sea and the Firth of Clyde on Scotland's southwest Ayrshire coast. In knee-high grasses and heather on billowing terrain, the Alisa Course at Turnberry is said to be the most beautiful of all British Open courses. In World Wars I and II, concrete was laid on the fairways, transforming them into runways for RAF planes. In 1951 the course reopened with a glorious redesign by Mackenzie Ross in time to host the 106th British Open.

As the Scots say, "If there's nae wind, it's nae golf." Never was that more true than during the first cold and blustery day of the 1986 Open when no player scored under par. Greg Norman managed to post a 63 in the second round and won. Tom Watson bested the field in 1977, while Nick Price eagled a 50-foot putt on seventeen to win in 1994.

The ancient lighthouse and the haunting ruins of King Robert the Bruce's Castle, dating to the four-teenth century, are among the most legendary of golf course settings. Unlike most, rather flat links layouts, Alisa sports very large, duney mounds and oceans of undulations, creating a number of blind shots. The brisk breeze will be at your back on the way out, and in your face on the return. The tenth is a monster, a 452-yard dogleg left bordering the sea and imperiled by a monumental bunker with a domed piece of turf in the middle. Another famous hole, "Wee Burn" calls for a carry of 250 yards to a green that is surrounded by Wilson's Burn. Make the green or watch your ball slide

away into the creek; long-handled ball retrievers are thoughtfully provided.

The former Arran Course, now the Kintyre Course, was redesigned by Donald Steel in grand links-land style, reopening in 2001. From elevated tees, views of the Isle of Arran, the Mull of Kintyre, the lighthouse, and Alisa Craig are magnificent. Varying greatly in elevation, pocked with deep pot bunkers, and wiry with gorse, fairways are mounded and rolled like the folds of a blanket. Greens were redefined, bunkers were added, and tees were expanded, moved back, and raised.

A stellar attraction at Turnberry is the new Colin Montgomerie Links Golf Academy, with programs ranging from "Monty's Fundamentals Review" to "The Full Monty," conducted by PGA pros and focusing, for the most part, on links-style play. State-of-the-art facilities include indoor and outdoor teaching venues, computerized videos, simulators, and swing analyzers; covered bays with spectacular views; the Cairngorms putting course; a driving range; and comprehensive short game area. Parts of the old Arran Course were salvaged to create the new, nine-hole Arran Academy Course. All in all, this comprises one of Europe's most complete golf schools.

The imposing, country estate–style, Westin hotel, built in 1915, gleams with white siding and a red-tiled roof high on a hill above the Firth of Clyde and Alisa Craig, the steep-sided dome of granite towering from the sea. Public rooms are grand, paneled in oak, and are enhanced by antique, golf-related art. Reading rooms and lounges are formal yet cozy with fireplaces and leather sofas. Every evening a Highland bagpiper trods the grounds, his eerie strain heralding the setting sun.

Many original guest rooms were renovated and updated, and are now complete with Westin's signature "Heavenly Beds." The spa was expanded and now offers a wide variety of treatments, including the "Jet Lag Reviver Massage," the "Holistic Stressbuster" and the "Life Saving Back Massage."

Guests make their pilgrimages into the ancient town of Ayrshire to visit the cottage birthplace of Robert Burns, the National Bard of Scotland, who spent his early years here. Also in "Ayr" are a miniature railway, a boating pond, shops, and galleries.

Scottish weather as it may be, this part of the coastline is warmed by the Gulf Stream, prompting the hotel to offer a guarantee: If you cannot play after 10:30 A.M. due to snow or frost, you will receive a complimentary night's bed, breakfast, and dinner.

Scottish Links

More golf courses are clustered on Scotland's west coast than anywhere in Europe, and there are several eminently playable clubs within a short drive of Turnberry. For many visiting golfers, Royal Troon tops the list when it comes to true Scottish-links style and beauty, with a long and venerable history and a terrific clubhouse to boot (44–1292–311555). The track was first played in 1878 and hosted the British Open seven times.

A parade of challenging, narrow, windy seaside holes leads to the famous "Postage Stamp," a brief skirmish with what may be the tiniest green in golf. Tiger Woods triple bogied it in 1997. The back nine heads away from the coast into sandy hills, and unfortunately, into the noise of Prestwick Airport. Take time to browse the absolutely fabulous pro shop, and have lunch—isolated from club members, but nice, nonetheless.

Westin Turnberry Resort
Ayrshire, KA26 9LT
Scotland
Phone: 44–1655–331000, reservations (800) 325–3535
Fax: 44–1655–331706
Web site: www.turnberry.co.uk
General Manager: Stewart Selbie
Accommodations: Five-star-rated, 221 rooms, suites, lodges, and cottages overlooking the golf courses and coastline; large bathrooms with whirlpool tubs, elegant Edwardian-style furnishings, and sumptuous draperies, upholsteries, and linens. New cottages have six or eight bedrooms and living rooms.
Meals: French cuisine and classic Scottish dishes, with oceanviews, in the elegant Turnberry Restaurant; light Mediterranean fare at the Terrace Brasserie above the spa; hearty food at the Tappie Toorie Grill in the golf clubhouse; high tea in the lounge.
Facilities: Twenty-meter, heated indoor pool; two indoor tennis courts; squash courts; billiards room; full-service spa and salon; business center. Activity Centre offers trout fishing, clay target shooting, archery, falconry, four-wheel-driving, quad biking, mountain biking, and horseback riding.
Services and Special Programs: Golf caddie service; cooking school; supervised activities at the Westin Kids Club.
Rates: $$$$
Golf Packages: Great Golf Break includes two nights accommodations, breakfast, two dinners, a ninety-minute Monty Links lesson, use of practice facilities, and a round of golf on each course: from £650–£1,250 ($997–$1,918 U.S. dollars) per person, double occupancy.
Getting There: Resort is 55 miles from Glasgow International Airport; chauffeur-driven sedans, limousines, and vans available. Helipad on-site.
What's Nearby: Culzean Castle is five minutes away. Visit the Isle of Arran and Glengoyne Distillery. Walk in Glentrool Forest, shop for Scottish knitwear in Ayrshire, and visit Burns Cottage.

THE SAN ROQUE CLUB

San Roque, Spain

Impenetrable walls of well-established trees, numerous water hazards, and steady winds off the Mediterranean are a few of the challenges that bring Spanish golf greats, Ballesteros, Olazabal, and their European PGA colleagues to the "Golden Triangle" to practice. Near the tip of the Iberian peninsula above the busy, seaside vacationland of the Costa del Sol, the San Roque Club comprises one of the arms of the Golden Triangle of Spanish golf—nearby are Valderrama and Sotogrande, the two other golden arms.

San Roque was once the domain of the Domecq family's sherry dynasty. In the late 1980s the estate and acres of boulder-strewn, hilly, cork oak forest and grounds were transformed into a rambling resort and golf course. Now headquarters of the European PGA, the club has hosted Ryder Cup teams and is the site of the Player's Championship. Golfers tee off over lakes, rushing streams, and wild ravines toward knee-deep bunkers and sharply inclined fairways. The front nine winds through shady oak woods in a mountain set-

ting. The back is laid across rolling hills while the closing holes move around the lakes.

A feather in the cap of the resort is the Seve Ballesteros Natural Golf School, founded by the charismatic, beloved Spanish golfer who won two Masters and three British Opens, among other majors. A golf instructor for more than thirty years, Seve's brother, Vicente, and a PGA pro staff, teach the distinctive Ballesteros style, focusing on touch and the short game. As Northern European touring pros and teams come here to train in the wintertime, the practice facilities are exceptional and the clubhouse and locker rooms luxurious.

High above sunny Mediterranean beaches in the foothills of the Sierra Bermeja, the intimacy, the understated elegance, and the rich trappings of a Spanish hacienda remain. Massive, carved wooden doors lead to arched loggias and quiet garden courtyards. The suites, some of which have dining areas and kitchens, are more like country villas than hotel rooms, with their private patios lush with blooming tropical flowers and trees. The public areas of the resort, some with cozy reading nooks and fireplaces, are decorated with light woods and white marble. Fountains, winding pathways, palms, ancient oaks, and a large pool courtyard create an oasis of calm.

One of the finest in Europe, the equestrian center is run by British Horse Society–qualified instructors. You can take private or group riding lessons, or just enjoy a picnic ride through the Andalusian countryside or ride on the beach.

A resort shuttle whisks sun-seekers to a private Beach Club at Alcaidesa, just five minutes away. You can swim, tan, or hide in a cabana or under an umbrella, and have light meals and drinks at La Hacienda restaurant. Champagne and caviar on a sunset cruise on the Ancaster sailing yacht can be a romantic experience. Shoppers hop aboard the *Sun Seeker* yacht to shop up the coast at Puerto Banus or for picnic expeditions to Tarifa.

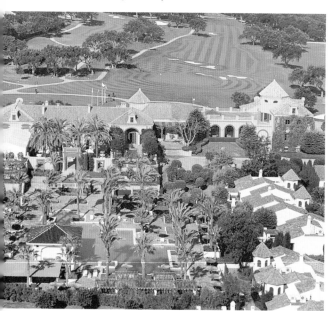

Golfing in Spain

In the 1970s Robert Trent Jones Sr. made a dramatic mark on Spain by designing seven courses on the Costa del Sol and the Costa Brava—including the incomparable Valderama and Sotogrande—a move that set off a blizzard of new golf courses and resorts through the end of the century. Mijas Golf Club near Malaga has two Jones Sr. tracks surrounding the French operated Hotel Byblos Andaluz, a Moorish-style palace of towers, archways, fountains, and reflecting pools, with an elaborate spa.

In a climate mild and sunny more than three hundred days a year, millions of orange and olive trees thrive on the hillsides and along the fairways in the "Valley of Golf" near Marbella, where Seve Ballesteros designed Los Arqueros. Two courses at La Cala Golf and Country Club were designed by American Cabell B. Robinson. Fulfilling the desires of Europeans who want more than just golf during their winter vacations, the valley developments have squash and tennis courts, indoor and outdoor swimming pools, and commodious clubhouses and restaurants.

The best time to play in southern Spain is in winter, early spring, and late fall. In midsummer, temperatures climb to more than 100 degrees and tourists crowd the hotels and the golf courses. Guests at San Roque Club have the great advantage of accessibility to preferred rates and sought-after tee times at Valderrama, Sotogrande, Alcaidesa, Almendara, La Quinta, and Los Naranjos, some of the finest courses in the region.

The San Roque Club
C.N.340. Km.127, 11360 San Roque
Cádiz, Spain
Phone: 34–956–613030, reservations (800) 323–7500
Fax: 34–956–613012
Web site: www.sanroqueclub.com
General Manager: Carlos Braun
Accommodations: 50 spacious rooms and 50 suites in tile-roofed, hacienda-style buildings surrounded by tropical gardens; some have dining areas and kitchens. Folk art and traditional art and artifacts are colorful accents for the casually elegant furnishings.
Meals: Traditional Spanish cuisine and international specialties are served in the elegant Bolero restaurant. Kama Kura is southern Spain's only Japanese restaurant, serving sushi in serene, elegant surroundings or on the terrace. Hearty meals and snacks are offered at the golf clubhouse restaurant.
Facilities: Seve Ballesteros Natural Golf School with PGA pros, extensive pitching and chipping areas, and covered driving range with twenty-eight bays; two eighteen-hole and one nine-hole putting green; GPS carts; heated lagoon swimming pool; jogging and bike trails; beach club; tennis court; equestrian center.
Services and Special Programs: Weekly programs of Spanish and Japanese cookery lessons, sherry tasting, and Flamenco dancing. Cruises on a private sailing yacht and hunting parties can be arranged. For ages 3–15, multilingual, supervised swimming, art, cooking, nature walks, cart driving, Spanish lessons, and horse feeding.
Rates: $$$–$$$$
Golf Packages: "Great Golf in Andalucia" includes four nights accommodations, daily breakfast, one dinner, two rounds of golf on-site and one at Sotogrande, and golf services (one round of golf may be exchanged for a golf lesson).1,007 Euros ($995 U.S. dollars) per person, double occupancy.
Getting There: Gibraltar Airport is a twenty-minute drive on the hotel shuttle; Malaga Airport is ninety minutes away.
What's Nearby: Guided or independent day trips to Tangiers, the Alhambra Palace and historic sites in Granada, the mosque at Cordoba, and the "white town" of Ronda; sherry tasting and horse shows in Jerez; the sights of Seville; sailing and water sports at the Sotogrande Marina.

WESTIN LA QUINTA GOLF RESORT

Marbella, Malaga, Spain

Andaluz, or Andalusia as it is known in English, was the heart of Moorish Spain, bounded to the east and south by the Mediterranean and the Atlantic. During the era of sailing ships, Andalusia was Spain's southern highway to the outside world. Nowadays along the coastline from Malaga to Gibraltar, the Costa del Sol is nonstop high-rise hotels, tourist towns, swimming pools, and sunny beaches—a vacationland to which Europeans flock in the wintertime, escaping the harsh northern climes.

More than forty golf courses along the same coast comprise the "Costa del Golf," and they are the top courses in the country. Ten minutes from Marbella the beautiful new Westin La Quinta and the La Quinta Golf Course and Golf Academy are an exclusive haven away from the traffic and congestion, yet under the same, sunny Spanish skies.

Majestic white columns frame the grand, white staircase in the palm-bedecked lobby of the new resort hotel. The architectural influence of the Moorish era is evident in the high, arched windows, bubbling fountains, reflecting pools, and gardens and courtyards landscaped with bougainvillea and citrus trees. Guest rooms and public areas capture the soul of Mediterranean-Andalusian style with warm tones, rugged wood beams and bright, hand-painted ceramic tiles.

Listening to soft guitars and passionate flamenco music, diners linger under the palms on the terrace at the Restaurante La Dorada Los Arcos, enjoying the fragrance of the gardens, a rocky stream, and the dramatic views of the valley and the illuminated swimming pool.

Cool tile floors lead to private balconies in the guest rooms, decorated simply and elegantly in contemporary Spanish style with wide, shuttered doors open to the subtropical climate and golf course views. Westin's signature "Heavenly Beds" are pure white bliss, with pillowtop mattresses, down comforters, and a clutch of plush pillows.

The great wall of the Sierra Bermeja protects the golf course from northern winds, so that even winter months are quite mild. Palm trees and cork oaks line the rather narrow fairways of twenty-seven holes which roam up and down the shifting, hillside terrain. Huge, shallow fairway bunkers, dependably elevated tees, and a considerable number of liquid hazards add to the fun, along with mountain, valley, and ocean views. The track was designed by Antonio Garcia Garrido and Manuel Pinero, former Ryder Cup player and current Director of Golf.

The Golf Academy offers splendid facilities, including two practice ranges, a chipping zone, and greens for pitching, bunkers, and putting. Video analysis is part of the high-tech approach to private lessons and clinics. Northern European pros train here, and it is the official base of the German PGA.

The whole of the Sierra Blanca Valley is within view of the shady terrace of the clubhouse, where golfers relax at La Quinta Restaurant. Fresh seafood and Mediterranean cuisine are featured on the menu.

Ladies are required to show proof of a 30 minimum handicap, and for gentlemen, a 24.

Other Places to Play

Among the several golf courses accessible to guests of the Westin La Quinta is Monte Mayor Club de Golf, reached by a scenic drive up a mountainside to an isolated, pristine valley at a 1,200-foot elevation. Like a green apparition floating dreamily below the ruins of an eleventh century Moorish fortress, Monte Mayor is a quiet, wild place, dotted with old farmhouses and fragrant with wild sage. Local white marble was quarried for the bridges and walls, and crushed to pave the cart paths. A cart is a must to navigate the steep terrain, and accurate driving is a must over ravines and winding streams to elevated greens.

The westernmost course on the Costa del Sol, Alcaidesa Links Golf Course rambles up and down along the Mediterranean, offering wide views of the sea, the Rock of Gibraltar, and the coast of North Africa. Designed by Peter Alliss and built in 1992, the track was a daunting challenge, perhaps too daunting, for most golfers until a recent renovation that widened the fairways somewhat, rebuilt the tenth and eleventh holes, and took the rampant slopes out of the greens. Now the links-golf experience, in the mild, sunny climate of Southern Europe, is delightful (www.alcaidesa.com).

Westin La Quinta Golf Resort
Urbanizacion La Quinta, Nueva Andalucia
Marbella, Malaga, Spain 29660
Phone: 34–952–762000, reservations (800) 937–8461
Fax: 34–952–762020
Web site: www.westin.com
General Manager: Jordi E. Tarrida
Accommodations: 172 rooms and suites with private balconies, writing desks, dark-wood shutters, ceiling fans, and "Heavenly Beds."
Meals: Indoors or on the terrace, Spanish regional and Continental cuisine is served at Los Arcos. Snacks and drinks are offered by the fireplace in the Aljama Bar. The Kaede Japanese Restaurant is decorated in exquisite minimalist style, serving *teppan-yaki* cuisine and sushi. Hearty lunches are enjoyed on the golf clubhouse terrace at La Quinta Restaurant.
Facilities: Two swimming pools; children's pool; full-service health and beauty spa with sauna and Turkish bath; paddle tennis.
Services and Special Programs: Shuttle to beach club at Puerto Banús; tee times and arranged transportation to nearby golf clubs, including Los Naranjos, Las Brisas, Los Arqueros.
Rates: $$$
Golf Packages: None available.
Getting There: Thirty-five minutes from Malaga International Airport, serving major airlines.
What's Nearby: Shopping, beaches, and nightlife in Puerto Banús and Marbella; day trips to the ancient walled town of Ronda; catamaran or ferry cruises to Northern Africa; two-hour drive from the historic cities of Cordoba, Sevilla, and Granada.

CARIBBEAN ISLANDS & THE BAHAMAS

OCEAN CLUB
Paradise Island, Nassau, Bahamas

At the eastern end of Paradise Island just across the bridge from Nassau, a formerly private jet-set hideaway is now a secluded retreat for those desiring faultless personal service in an unequaled tropical setting. Built in the 1930s the colonial-style mansion was purchased in the 1960s by Huntington Hartford II, who added a twelfth-century French cloister and glorious Versailles-style gardens. After a $100 million restoration, today's Ocean Club is a posh compound along a stretch of pearly white sand beach, complete with a new Tom Weiskopf championship golf course.

Based on Louis XIV's famous gardens, a half-mile of terraces rises in gentle levels of greenery and floral displays past classical marble and bronze statuary. From the picturesque cloister on the hilltop, guests linger over the view of what has been called the most beautiful beach in the Caribbean. Throughout the small resort, the sound of the foamy surf shields guests from the outside world. At the foot of the terraces, the flower-filled pool terrace is a serene hideaway.

Dark cherry floors gleam in the oversize guest rooms. Carved mahogany beds are heaped with down pillows and bolsters. Jumbo tubs are embellished with mosaics. Wide plantation-shuttered doors open to spacious private balconies or terraces where chaise lounges await the tuckered golfer. Hammocks drift beneath tall palms on greenswards above the cerulean sea.

Breakfast starts the day on the beachfront deck, with rolling waves near your feet. Evenings are breezy at the beach bar, a marble masterpiece illuminated by oil lanterns, and a romantic setting for a "goombay smash" or a "yellowbird" rum drink. Candlelight glows in the sultry night at the sleek, Manhattan-style restaurant, Dune, for which renowned New York chef, Jean-Georges Vongerichte, developed a French-Asian and Bahamian menu. Peekyboo crab salad, lobster in coconut curry sauce, and the molten, Volharona chocolate dessert are favorites. An ensemble plays nightly in the formal Courtyard Terrace, where American regional food fuses with classic French.

Weiskopf's new links-style Ocean Club Golf Course is a 7,123-yard beauty vigorously brushed by trade winds. It is a rather flat, sandy, well-watered track, nearly surrounded by the pellucid Atlantic and fed by lagoons and ponds within. Generous fairways and five sets of tees mitigate the unpredictability of the winds and the abundance of water hazards. The sixth hole, "Breakwater," follows the beach from tee to green with a phalanx of palms. Bring a camera for the panoramic vista of the entire course and miles of azure ocean and Nassau Harbor from the twelfth hole, "Spyglass"; the tee shot requires a carry over wetlands that are habitat for sea turtles and shorebirds. The seventeenth plays right along Snorkelers Cove and one of the loveliest beaches in the Bahamas.

Marine Life and Watery Fun

Guests at the Ocean Club have full privileges at nearby Atlantis, a flamboyant, showstopper of a resort with a thousand rooms, thirty-eight restaurants, bars, and lounges; a spectacular casino; a haute-couture shopping arcade; and The Dig, the largest outdoor aquarium in the world. In millions of gallons of seawater are rare reef and pelagic fish, the only manta ray and hammerhead shark in captivity, other sharks, and colorful tropical fish—thousands of marine animals in entertaining, theme-park-style settings. Children are in kid heaven at eleven swimming complexes, where they can play in the waterfalls, cruise the snorkeling lagoon, and scoot down the six-story-tall replica of a Mayan temple complete with five water slides. Adults enjoy the sensation of walking into the ocean in the zero-entry River Pool (www.Atlantis.com).

Managed by the top-notch American company, Troon Golf, the course is anchored by a parrot-yellow clubhouse with a breezy dining terrace, where movie stars and moguls get together for the Michael Jordan Celebrity Invitational in September. For the annual Office Depot Father/Son Challenge at the Ocean Club, the messieurs Nicklaus, Trevino, Watson, Player, Floyd, Weiskopf, and Kite assemble for friendly competition. Another frequent denizen of the club is South African golf superstar, Ernie Els, who is the resident pro.

Ocean Club
P.O. Box N-4777
Paradise Island
Nassau, Bahamas
Phone: (242) 363–2501, reservations (800) 321–3000
Fax: (242) 363–2424
Web site: www.oceanclub.com
General Manager: Russell Miller
Accommodations: Five-star rated, 108 spacious rooms and suites, with private oceanfront balconies or terraces in two-story buildings; and two-bedroom villas with private, oceanview patios. Blooming orchids and tropical plants, Frette linens, massive mahogany beds, plantation-style furnishings, oversize, mosaic-tile and marble tubs, steam showers, and European amenities.
Meals: French-Asian and Bahamian cuisine at Dune; classic French and American regional cuisine in the elegant Courtyard Terrace; casual open-air meals and snacks poolside at the Clubhouse Grill.
Facilities: Full-service, Ocean Club Spa by Mandara, with Balinese-style spa villas and private suites, and Indonesian-inspired treatments, nine Har-Tru tennis courts, teaching staff, and pro shop; fitness center; large, freshwater swimming pool.
Services and Special Programs: Personal, twenty-four-hour butler; thrice-daily maid service; beach attendants; complimentary bicycles; Aquacat sailing, kayaks, and snorkeling equipment available.
Rates: $$$$
Golf Packages: None available.
Getting There: Luxury car transport from Nassau International Airport, a forty-minute drive.
What's Nearby: Deep-sea fishing, scuba diving, windsurfing, and sailing; nightlife; the casino, shopping, and sightseeing at Atlantis.

OUR LUCAYA BEACH AND GOLF RESORT

Freeport, Grand Bahama Island

The sand is so pearly-white, the water so electric blue green, the waving palms so green, and the banana boats so banana yellow, Our Lucaya is the postcard-perfect beach resort. Guests arrive at the lemon-colored Manor House, amble through the British-Colonial style lobby and enter the tropics. Sprawling is the word for the complex of three resorts in one, joined by palm-studded lawns and gardens, and a great curve of beach. Anchored by a long, white high-rise hotel is the Breaker's Cay central courtyard, with a gigantic, serpentine swimming pool, a disappearing edge pool, and Hammerhead's beach bar. Also here is an Asian-inspired alfresco cafe, the lively "Prop Club" nightclub and sports bar, and a greensward for dance lessons and other group activities.

The Reef Village is family oriented, with a huge, landscaped swimming pool, a waterslide, outdoor bar and grill, a headquarters for water sports, Camp Lucaya for kids, and 1950s-style Barracudas, a primary-colored, fun restaurant.

The Lanai Suites—all opening onto lawns and beachfront— and the Lighthouse Pointe rooms are in a low-rise enclave in a quiet, pretty setting. This is the location of choice for guests who crave romance and privacy. The disappearing edge pool here seems to merge with the sea, and a long lap pool and adults-only Jacuzzi complete the picture.

In the midst of a dozen themed restaurants and lounges, Churchill's Chop House is formal and traditional, with chandeliers and white-coated waiters. Cigar smokers retire to the Havana Cay Cigar Bar, while a jazz singer holds forth at the grand piano in the Manor House. A trio plays nightly at Portobello, a romantic Italian restaurant, where the lounge and the terrace are lovely for cocktails. A cross between Rangoon 1930, an Egyptian marketplace, and an African safari, Willy Broadleaf's puts on mile-long buffets for diners who sit in tented booths under oil lanterns, or at booths with ocean views.

Hotel shuttles transport golfers to the nearby Lucayan Course, where fairways are generally tight and densely lined by magnificent woods of pine, eucalyptus, and flame-red blooming poinciana, a junglelike canopy over impenetrable, low shrubs and grasses. You have the feeling of isolation, seldom catching sight of other foursomes. More than seventy soft-sand bunkers guard elevated greens and wiry Bermuda grass fairways. Steady trade winds add to the fun, making this a perfect site for the Caribbean Open, which is played here in February.

Although you can't see the ocean, sea breezes are definitely a factor on the wide-open fairways and mostly large, flat greens of the brand new, links-style, Robert Trent Jones Jr.–designed Reef Course. It may look easy, but you would do well to bring extra balls for the lakes and ponds on thirteen holes, and the dense undergrowth beneath the trees. The Senior PGA tour played their Senior Slam on the Reef.

Tiger Woods's longtime teacher, Butch Harmon, recently opened a golf school adjacent to the Lucayan Course. Liberally adorned with images of the world's best golfer, practice bays feature the highest of high-tech, four-camera swing analysis. Golfers who have difficulty booking Harmon's only other school, at Rio Secco Golf Club in Las Vegas, are signing up for the one-day short game and three-day instructional packages here.

After golf water sports are on the menu, from snorkeling and kayaking to jet skiing and sailing, right off the Lucaya beach. Or the full-service Senses Spa offers luxurious rain massages and algae baths; traditional health and beauty treatments; healthy meals and drinks in the spa cafe; and a workout venue with an ocean view.

New Again on Grand Bahama

As part of a dramatic renovation and expansion in 2001, the Royal Oasis Golf Resort and Casino on Grand Bahama Island called in the Fazio Design Group for a much-needed upgrade of their Ruby and Emerald golf courses. Aging tropical beauties, both tracks are now longer and better defined for twenty-first-century golfers, with bunkers both strategically and visually reshaped. Greens were enlarged and planted with space-age turf. The two hotel towers are also entirely brand new, inside and out. Additions to the resort include a million-gallon "sand pool" with water slides and waterfalls (800–545–1300, www.gbvac.com).

Our Lucaya Beach and Golf Resort
Freeport, Grand Bahama Island
Phone: (242) 373–1333, reservations (877) 772–6471
Fax: (242) 373–8804
Web site: www.ourlucaya.com
General Manager: Eric Waldburger
Accommodations: 1,350 spacious, sleek, Art-Deco-style rooms and suites in bright sky blues and lime greens, with blond maple furnishings. Most rooms in the central high-rise and the smaller Reef Village, Lanai Suites, and Light-house Pointe buildings have ocean views, and all have private balconies or patios. Suites have microwaves, refrigerators, wet bars, living rooms, and double size-balconies.
Meals: Among a dozen restaurants and food outlets are: a kid-friendly menu and family-size booths at Barracudas; elegant, traditional Continental cuisine and steaks at Churchill's; fresh pastries, desserts, and breads made by a French chef for bountiful buffets at Willy Broadleaf's; Asian cuisine at China Beach.
Facilities: Artificial grass, hard court, grass, and clay tennis courts; sand volleyball; basketball.
Services and Special Programs: The Marine Explorer's Club teaches ocean and marine experiences to all ages. Activities include party cruises, boat tours, deep sea and bone fishing, sea kayak nature tours, and dolphin adventures. Camp Lucaya keeps kids up to age 12 busy with games and native crafts, with their own sandy beach, play structures and wading pool; snorkeling lessons, too. Child-care is available for infants.
Rates: $$$
Golf Packages: One night accommodations, breakfast, and unlimited golf is $312 for two. Golf school three-day package incudes four nights accommodations, three days of instruction including play, lunches, and personalized video: $2,600 per person.
Getting There: A thirty-five-minute flight from Miami, major airlines arrive at Grand Bahama International Airport, a fifteen-minute drive from the resort.
What's Nearby: Duty-free shopping at the Port Lucaya Marketplace across the street. Snorkeling and diving on Deadman's Reef, at uninhabited Lightbourne Cay—accessible only by boat—and at shipwrecks, including the USS *Adirondack*, a 125-year-old American warship.

SANDY LANE HOTEL AND GOLF CLUB

St. James, Barbados

Despite more than thirty years of independence from Great Britain, Barbados enjoys a charming British ambience, and no less at Sandy Lane. Formerly a privately owned retreat for international celebrities and European royalty, Sandy Lane was transformed at the turn of the twentieth century into a classical estate reminiscent of colonial Barbados, with accommodations to rival the most luxurious in the Caribbean. Completing the exquisite resort are a thousand-foot-long crescent of sugar-white sand beach, gorgeous mahogany trees and tropical gardens, a truly magnificent spa, and two golf courses designed by one of the masters, Tom Fazio.

The ivory-toned, Palladian-style, coral-stone villa is the heart of the resort. It is surrounded by refreshing water features, fountains and falls, sweeping, grand staircases, and shady, intimate courtyards. The staff moves discretely in a network of underground tunnels.

Plantation-style armchairs and sofas rest on Italian marble floors in the guest rooms, which are complete with massive, carved mahogany beds piled with pillows and sumptuous bedding, and private verandahs ornamented with white wrought iron. Bedside controls adjust the flat-screen TV, lights, air, and drapes. Personalized full bars, blooming orchids and tropical flowers, heated mirrors, and stereo speakers in the bathroom are just a few of the thoughtful amenities.

Your personal, twenty-four-hour butler puts your mind at ease from the moment of your arrival by Bentley from the airport. He will help to arrange a helicopter tour, a submarine cruise, or an island-hop on a catamaran. He will escort your child to the Treehouse Club, press your dancing clothes at one in the morning, and book your caddy and your tee times for the Country Club and the Old Nine.

Tom Fazio built playability into the new Country Club Course, laying out a stern test for low handicappers from the tips, while providing an enjoyable experience for the average golfer on the forward tees. Hiding cart paths with mounds and vegetation, he focused on the stunning ocean view, winding the track 7,060 yards around five lakes, towering coral boulders, and what seems like an endless series of gullies. Some of the gullies are inhabited by Bajan green monkeys, who appear when least expected.

Fazio took into account the constant trade winds, which cool the tropical atmosphere and come into play on most holes, making the generous fairways more difficult than they appear. The clever golfer aims away from the target and allows the wind to bring the ball back to the landing zones. Just when you think you have this course figured out, seriously sloped greens may add to your score. Putting surfaces are large, and well protected by

equally large bunkers. (Fazio's newest design for Sandy Lane, the "Green Monkey," is another championship course in the works.)

Built in the 1960s and recently updated to contemporary standards, the Old Nine was one of the first resort courses in the Caribbean, The lush, landscaped track winds between sea pines and palms through the resort and past the mansions of the estate. High handicappers and beginners enjoy the lack of water hazards; scratch golfers love to walk it, as a warm-up for the Fazio.

The brand-new monumental golf clubhouse is an architectural masterpiece of coral and limestone blocks, breezy archways and terraces, and gleaming mahogany embellishments, with a gourmet restaurant, lounge, and pro shop.

Waterfalls cascade across the rotunda of the three-level, domed spa, dropping into a huge, free-form swimming pool fringed by gardens and palms. Each unique treatment suite features private bathrooms, showers, elegant marble and wood decor, and gardens or hydrotherapy pools—very intimate settings for health and beauty therapies. Underwater massage is a favored treatment, along with the jet blitz, and a post-sauna ice cave. Yoga, Tai-Chi, and Pilates sessions are also offered. Nothing is more reviving than the "Jet Lag Reviver Massage" and calypso aerobics.

Other Places to Play

Just 21 miles long and 14 miles wide, Barbados is easy to navigate. Golfers willing to leave the grandeur of Sandy Lane will find a plethora of golf adventures. The island's first daily-fee public course, the Barbados Golf Club at Christchurch opened at the beginning of this century in tournament condition, hosting the 2000 Caribbean Open. It will soon host a 2003 PGA Senior Tour event (www.barbadosgolf.com). A cross between a parkland and a links layout, it is strafed by trade winds, and menaced by white coral waste bunkers and umbrella-like, mature trees. On the signature fifteenth, a massive, bearded fig tree stands guard, its aerial roots reaching out for errant balls.

A Robert Trent Jones Jr. design, the Royal Westmoreland Golf and Country Club is the gem in a $400 million residential and resort development on the Platinum Coast, on the western shore of Barbados (www.royal-west moreland.com). Twenty-seven holes ramble through a former quarry and sugar cane plantation, requiring perfect club selection and dead aim over stony gorges. On the fifteenth tee is a plaque, with Jones's words: MAY THE WIND BE AT YOUR BACK AND YOUR SHOT-MAKING SKILLS TESTED WHEN YOU PLAY THIS CHALLENGING HOLE.

Sandy Lane Hotel and Golf Club
St. James, Barbados, West Indies
Phone: (246) 444–2000, reservations (800) 444–2001
Fax: (246) 444–2222
Web site: www.sandylane.com
General Manager: Colm Hannon
Accommodations: 112 luxurious rooms and suites, averaging 900 square feet, with private balconies or patios, sitting and dressing areas, wonderful sea views, sumptuous linens, fine fabrics, and artwork.
Meals: Fancifully painted ceiling and murals in the Monkey Bar; haute French cuisine at L'Acajou, on a terrace above the sea; organic ingredients and regional cuisine at Bajan Blue on the beach; healthy fare at the Spa Cafe.
Facilities: GPS carts, two-sided driving range, and caddy service; nine hard surface and grass tennis courts, teaching pro, matching, and lessons; upscale boutiques; full-service health and beauty spa; nonmotorized water sports are complimentary.
Services and Special Programs: From toddler to age 12, kids play at the Treehouse Club; art, games, and expeditions are featured. Teens go to the Den for pool, computers, parties, sports clinics, and water sports. Kids have their own chef.
Rates: $$$$
Golf Packages: None available.
Getting There: Thirty-five minutes from Grantley Adams International Airport, with transportation by luxury car.
What's Nearby: Shopping and sightseeing in the capital, Bridgetown; scenic expeditions to Holetown for antiques shopping, or to St. Nicholas Abbey, a Jacobean mansion from the 1600s. In Belleplain, buy glazed Bajan pottery.

CASA DE CAMPO
La Romana, Dominican Republic

Casa de Campo means "country home." This 7,000-acre resort on the southeast coast of the Dominican Republic is hardly a country place. Rather, it is a dream of a tropical beachfront destination with two Pete Dye golf courses, and world-renowned equestrian and tennis centers.

Since 1999, more than one hundred million dollars was invested in new and renovated accommodations and restaurants, an international airport, a marina and yacht club, and a third golf course.

Enveloped in blooming gardens of bougainvillea, fuchsia, alamanda, and hibiscus, freshly decorated guest accommodations have private balconies, which overlook the golf courses and the tennis complex. Gleaming tile floors and dark mahogany furnishings are accented by tropical-color fabrics and artwork. Wide, shuttered doors open to the mild Caribbean climate. For longer stays, the tennis and golf villas are elegant hideaways with private garden patios, swimming pools, personal butlers, and special services. The waters off the private Minitas Beach are translucent and calm, perfect for swimming, snorkeling, kayaking, and every kind of water sport.

Hewn by hand from dry coral reefs along the spectacular shoreline and through acres of dense jungle, the Teeth of the Dog has retained the title "Number One Golf Course in the Caribbean" since its opening more than three decades ago. Pete Dye designed seven holes so near the sea that you will feel the mist, hear the surf, and definitely contend with steady winds and balls bouncing off the rocks. Seemingly endless sandy waste areas are ball collectors, as are Dye's ubiquitous pot bunkers.

Dye's trademark mounds and hollows seem to whirl and swell like the ocean itself. On the seventh hole, a 224-yard carry over a jagged shoreline finds no safe landing zone, save the green. Expect relief on the eighth when you tee off from a peninsula washed with refreshing sea spray. Number twelve asks for a 200-yard drive over the airport runway. Golfers bide their time when a jet lands.

Meandering up into the green hills through guinea grass and cactus, and back to the coastline, the Links Course is a rolling layout with extremely difficult, small greens. Even with five holes along the ocean, you get less wind than the Dog, and tighter, undulating fairways. Hiring a caddy is a good idea for help reading these greens. A massive waste bunker looms on the sixteenth—the green drops right off into the rocks and the sea.

Pete and Alice Dye are designing a new course for a stunning location—on a bluff above the Chavón River, wrapped around the quaint village of Altos de Chavón.

Sports Galore

A golf cart is the way to explore the many sports venues at Casa de Campo—everything ranging from polo, shooting, and tennis, to fishing and myriad water sports.

A world renowned polo champion and an Indian Prince, Maharajah Jabar Singh founded the equestrian center, where polo ponies and riding horses are bred and trained. Resort guests may take Western or English riding, dressage, and polo lessons, and sign on for guided trail rides along the river and on the beach. From late fall through the spring, international polo teams practice and compete on the beautiful playing fields here.

Two thirty-one-foot sport fishing boats take guests on deep sea expeditions, often returning with huge tuna and kingfish, and trophy sailfish and marlin. Freshwater fishermen cast for snook on the river. Daytrippers cruise and sail on catamarans, small sailboats, and yachts to Catalina and Saona Islands.

Shaped like the Eiffel Tower, one of the tallest sporting clay towers in the world stands above the 245-acre, state-of-the-art Shooting Center. Beginners and children are welcome to take lessons.

Named the "Wimbledon of the Caribbean," La Terraza Tennis Center has thirteen Har-Tru courts in a lovely, garden setting on the hillside. Decked out in crisp white outfits are a platoon of ball boys and more than a dozen instructors and teaching pros.

Casa de Campo

P.O. Box 140
La Romana, Dominican Republic
Phone: (305) 856–5405, reservations (800) 877–3643
Fax: (305) 858–4677
Web site: www.casadecampo.cc

General Manager: AnaLisa Brache

Accommodations: 300 hotel rooms and suites in one- and two-story clusters surrounded by gardens; luxury rooms are spacious and elegant with mahogany furnishings and fine fabrics, private terraces, new bathrooms, and plantation-style touches. 150 spacious villas are on the golf course and tennis complex. Excel Club villas have private gardens, swimming pools, maids and butlers, private lounge and concierge, special amenities and services.

Meals: Ten restaurants, seven lounges, and three night-clubs with live and recorded music; traditional Dominican and Continental cuisine at El Patio; steak and seafood at Tropicana by the pool; light meals and tropical drinks at El Pescador on the beach; American-style breakfasts and lunches at Lago Grill, served on the terrace with sea and golf-course views. On the menu at the new Safari Club Restaurant is exotic game, as well as tamer fare.

Facilities: Large driving range, short game practice area, clinics, and private lessons; huge main swimming pool, lap pool, children's pool, and additional swimming pools at the villas; at the brand new Marina and Yacht Club, 183 boat slips, shopping, and restaurants; tennis, shooting, and equestrian centers.

Services and Special Programs: Kids 'n Casa for ages 3–6, with beach play, treasure hunts, art, and games; kids ages 7–12 are in the Tween Program, with tennis, horseback riding, nature walks, and more. Teens 13–18 like Que Pasa 'n Casa where they hang out with their friends. For all ages, beach Olympics, golf cart rallies, organized games, and daily activities.

Rates: $$$

Golf Packages: Completely Golf includes one night accommodations; breakfast, lunch, and dinner; unlimited cocktails and drinks; one round on the Links and one on Teeth of the Dog per day; shared cart; and unlimited horseback riding, tennis, and nonmotorized water sports; from $275–$510 per person, double occupancy.

Getting There: Direct flights on major airlines to Las Americas International Airport in Santo Domingo, an hour away, and to La Romana/Casa de Campo International Airport, a ten-minute drive from the resort.

What's Nearby: Day trips to the capital city of Santo Domingo for shopping and museums; kayaking on the Chavón River; cruising to the resort's private island; shopping and sightseeing at Altos de Chavón, the sixteenth-century replica artisan's village.

PUNTA CANA RESORT AND CLUB

Punta Cana Beach, Higuey, Dominican Republic

Resorts are sprouting up on the Coconut Coast on the northeastern side of the Dominican Republic where rain forest–covered peaks rise abruptly from the turquoise waters of the Caribbean Sea. Sprawled along 3 miles of white-sand beach fringed with thousands of palms, Punta Cana is a destination resort surrounded by a junglelike nature preserve.

Couturier Oscar de la Renta, one of the co-developers, was the interior designer for the golf villas. His pure white walls, fabrics, and floor coverings are a pristine background for plantation-style furnishings of gleaming, dark mahogany. De la Renta also built himself a mansion here, as did Julio Iglesias and Mikhail Baryshnikov. Glamorous visitors from all over the world sail into the full-service Punta Cana marina in yachts up to 70 feet long.

Within flourishing, tropical gardens are a variety of accommodations, from hotel rooms at the beach to two- and three-bedroom villas at the tennis complex, and recently remodeled deluxe rooms and golf villas on the golf course.

Equipment and instruction for many of the watersports and outdoor recreation are free of charge, from kayaking and snorkeling to golf clinics, pedal boats, sailing, tennis, and windsurfing. Daily beach games, sports competitions, and entertainment are part of the fun. Evenings are lively with a different show each night, a dance band playing merengue and other Latin music, and guitar and piano in the lounges. La Proa Discotheque is open until the wee hours.

The White Sands golf course, a dazzler, is a vivid mélange of verdant vegetation and snow-white beach bunkers. The architect is P.B. Dye, son of Pete Dye, who designed the famous Teeth of the Dog course at Casa de Campo on this island. In a nod to his dad, perhaps, the son integrates dozens of pot bunkers into the 7,152-yard layout and uses sections of palm trees as retaining walls, instead of the railroad

ties that are a Pete Dye tradition. Fairways are planted with Seashore Paspalum, a revolutionary, new hybrid grass that is irrigated with seawater. Fast growing and vibrant emerald green, the turf seems to be a success.

Fourteen holes are within sight of the ocean and four play right on the breezy seafront. Vast, sandy waste bunkers are scattered abundantly around the track, along with hundreds of coconut palms and several lakes. The seventh hole is a dogleg left playing directly into the trade winds, with a high carry over palm trees toward twenty-one pot bunkers arrayed in front of a small, elevated green. Dye calls this area "Hecklebirnie" and says, "You don't want to be short here."

P.B. Dye is designing a second championship layout for Punta Cana along a rocky stretch of shoreline. One spectacular hole will play over a cove with sheer cliffs and a blowhole.

Winter temperatures at Punta Cana average about 80 degrees while summers are six or eight degrees warmer. Water temperatures range between 75 and 85 degrees, perfect for swimming in the crystalline waters. Scuba divers find the coral reefs offshore to be a fascinating habitat for a wide variety of marine life. The reefs are located at the point where the Atlantic and Caribbean come together in the deepwater Mona Passage between this island and Puerto Rico. Within the golf course is a freshwater cavern, Laguna Pepe, where adventurous divers explore a cathedral-like chamber nearly 200 feet wide and 70 feet high, and filled with light.

Above the resort on the picturesque Chavón River, Altos de Chavón is the replication of a sixteenth-century artisans' village of workshops, galleries, restaurants, shops, and a wonderful museum of Taino Indian art and artifacts. A wander through the cobblestone streets and stone buildings will turn up artists at work, bubbling fountains, a beautiful stone church, and stupendous views of the valley and the distant Caribbean.

Other Places to Play

The twenty-seven-hole course of the Cocotal Golf and Country Club, opened in 1999, was designed by Spanish golf great José Gancedo at the Sol Meliá Resort a short drive away. Although surrounded by a residential development, the track is a pleasant, windswept layout with several lakes, hundreds of coconut palms, and some oceanfront holes. The new Golf Academy is the winter training home of the PGA of Germany. The huge resort is worth a visit to see the spectacular Italian marble, reflecting pools, gardens, fountains, and outdoor statuary (www.solmelia.com).

Punta Cana Resort and Club
Punta Cana Beach, Higuey
Dominican Republic
Phone: (809) 959–2262, reservations (888) 442–2262
Fax: (809) 687–8745
Web site: www.puntacana.com
General Manager: Andres Pichardo
Accommodations: 432 spacious hotel rooms in three-story buildings at the beach, decorated in bright Caribbean colors, each with two queens or doubles and private balcony or terrace. Two-level, contemporary-motif villas have living/dining rooms, kitchens, lush gardens, and Jacuzzis.
Meals: Nouvelle Caribbean cuisine and sea views at elegant La Cana; bountiful buffets at La Tortuga; grilled fresh seafood, sandwiches, and salads at La Choza at the beach and marina; Franco's Pizzeria and Mamma Venezia for fine Italian food; La Yola, on the water at the marina, for seafood and pasta. At Altos de Chavón: antipasto at La Piazetta; Mexican food and mariachis at El Sombrero; pizza at Cafe del Sol; French cuisine with a Caribbean flair at Casa del Rio.
Facilities: Full-service marina for vessels up to 70 feet; horseback riding; complimentary sailing, windsurfing, water skiing, kayaking, golf clinics, pedal boats, fitness classes, tennis, and snorkeling.
Services and Special Programs: Children's Carrousel program for ages 4–12, with boat rides, horseback riding, games, and art; PADI Gold Palm scuba dive center with daily dive trips and instruction.
Rates: $$$$
Golf packages: Titanium Golf Package includes three nights in seaside accommodations; breakfast, lunch, and dinner daily; unlimited golf; golf lesson; airport transport; gifts; and extras. $985 per person, double occupancy.
Getting There: Transportation is complimentary from the world's first privately owned international airport, Punta Cana International, five minutes away; served by major airlines with direct flights.
What's Nearby: Guided tours of the Punta Cana Ecological Reserve and the Cornell University Biodiversity Laboratory.

RITZ-CARLTON GOLF AND SPA RESORT, ROSE HALL

St. James, Jamaica

One of Jamaica's legends tells of the "White Witch" of Rose Hall, the beautiful nineteenth-century mistress of a sugar plantation who cast black magic spells and murdered three successive husbands. Locals say that Annee Palmer still haunts the Rose Hall Great House, a grandly restored museum filled with furnishings and artifacts of her era. Annee's house is now surrounded by impressive vacation villas and the White Witch Golf Course, a Robert von Hagge/Rick Baril design that is the jewel of the new Ritz-Carlton Rose Hall resort in Montego Bay.

Soon after opening in 2000, the White Witch hosted Shell's Wonderful World of Golf, and sultry fairways rolling through the velvet-green hills became instantly world famous. Views of the Caribbean from most parts of the track soften the challenge of its mountainous, rocky terrain carved from limestone ridges 1,000 feet above the shoreline and caressed by steady trade winds. Your caddy, called a golf concierge, chases balls in the dense vegetation and offers advice on how to manage the dramatic elevation changes and forced carries over crashing surf and wild gorges to peninsula greens. Five tees are a help;

even seven tees on the tenth hole, where you hit over a valley onto a daunting, plateaued fairway. Rugged coral and sandstone outcroppings shore up the greens and tees, and delineate the fairways that tumble down the mountainside.

Von Hagge said, "The course is alluringly dangerous and unpredictable. Just as her personality might shift without warning, so do the winds shift from morning to night, turning a six-iron shot in the morning into a five-wood late in the day."

Majestic above a pure-white sandy beach and a cerulean swimming lagoon, the Ritz exemplifies Old World charm and personal service. Inspired by British colonial times, the architecture of the main pavilion and guest wings—ivory stucco with peach-colored roofs—recalls gracious plantation homes. Interiors are vibrant with Caribbean colors of fuchsia, gold, and turquoise, with arched windows and doorways, vaulted ceilings, and tall, formal columns.

Daytime temperatures along the coast remain near constant at 80 to 86 degrees, making seasons virtually nonexistent. Sea grape trees and an explosion of blooming tropical plants fill the lush grounds. Scuba diving and snorkeling are idyllic on the reef. Following an afternoon of riding a jet ski or a Wave Runner at the Beach Club, a soothing sugarcane facial or a "Yam Festival" revitalizer at the new spa can be the perfect ending to a guest's day. West Indies decor and a spicy scent set the spa scene, where mind/body fitness activities are offered, including "Blue Mountain Sunrise Yoga" and the "Cayman Sunset Stretch," both on the beach.

If the White Witch proves to be a daunting test, perhaps you should leave a few flowers on Annee Palmer's grave amid the copperwood trees at Rose Hall; she may grant you a few more birdies. If not, settle in on Cohoba's sea-front lobby terrace for rum tasting and a cigar. The resident "rummier" will offer sips of some one-hundred-fifty different rums.

Vintage Jones

Adjacent to the Ritz is the elegant Half Moon Resort—its mature Robert Trent Jones Sr. layout was built in the 1960s. The long, narrow, windy track is a 7,119-yard amble of wide, rolling fairways with more than one hundred bunkers and water on seven holes. The lovely trees and flowers, and the sight of the sea on nearly every hole, makes this a pleasant getaway. Also at the resort are the David Leadbetter Golf Academy, accommodations in golf-course villas, fifty-four swimming pools, and a mile-long, sandy beach (www.halfmoon.com.jm).

Ritz-Carlton Golf and Spa Resort, Rose Hall
1 Ritz-Carlton Drive
Rose Hall, St. James
Jamaica, West Indies
Phone: (876) 953–2800, reservations (800) 241–3333
Fax: (876) 953–2501
Web site: www.ritzcarlton.com
General Manager: Doug Brooks
Accommodations: Five-star rated, 427 rooms and suites with private, covered balconies; European-style amenities; Frette linens; pastel hues and original floral prints; plantation-style mahogany beds and elegant rattan furnishings; sitting areas; and plush, spacious baths.
Meals: Buffets, Continental cuisine, healthy fare, and live entertainment at Horizon's Restaurant; Jamaican/Asian specialties and jazz at Jasmine's; hearty golfer's fare and panoramic views at the White Witch Club House; American and Caribbean food poolside at Mango's, plus chef's demonstrations and live entertainment.
Facilities: Full-service spa and fitness center; tennis center; nonmotorized water sports at the private beach; motorized water sports at the Rose Hall Beach Club five minutes away, including jet skis and Wave Runners.
Services and Special Programs: Ritz Club Floor guests enjoy a private lounge and personal concierge, complimentary food and beverage presentations, and special services. For ages 5–12, Ritz Kids provides supervised crafts, water sports, beach games, and nature tours. Technology butler and twenty-four-hour secretarial services are available. Enjoy dinner concerts for two aboard a moonlit catamaran.
Rates: $$$$
Golf Packages: Deluxe accommodations, a round of golf for one and cart, golf caddy service, and golf services. $275–$520 per room, per night.
Getting There: Luxury coach or limousine available from or to the Donald Sangster International Airport, a fifteen-minute drive away; served by major airlines.
What's Nearby: Explore the restored, eighteenth-century Rose Hall Great House museum, built of native coralstone. See magnificent Dunns River Falls. Take the hotel shuttle to Montego Bay for shopping, sightseeing, and restaurants, or to the Half Moon Shopping Village. Enjoy guided horseback rides in the mountains and along the beach. Go rafting on the Martha Brae River.

WYNDHAM ROSE HALL RESORT
AND COUNTRY CLUB

Montego Bay, Jamaica

A remarkable quartet of golf courses around Montego Bay—the new Three Palms and White Witch Courses (both von Hagge designs) and the recently updated, legendary Tryall and Half Moon tracks—has transformed Jamaica into a compelling golf destination.

Presiding over a curve of white sandy beach, with the spectacular Three Palms Ocean Course snuggled up beside it, the Wyndham Hotel at Rose Hall Resort was renovated in its entirety, with lovely results. Accommodations are tranquil retreats, decorated in tropical pastels with textured walls, vibrant handmade tiles, and wicker furnishings. From private balconies on the West Wing, you can view the Caribbean, the golf course, Rose Hall's Great House, and the mist-shrouded Blue Mountains. From the East Wing, you can see lively Sugar Mills Falls and sunrises over the ocean.

Among the multimillion-dollar enhancements is the giant water theme park, Sugar Mills Falls, the first of its kind in Jamaica. Waterfalls cascade over rock formations into three terraced pools and lagoons. Kids have their own pool, while adults can linger at the swim-up bar. Everyone takes a turn on the 280-foot-long water slide.

Built in the 1970s the Three Palms Ocean Course was completely remade by world-renowned architects Robert von Hagge and Rick Baril and reopened in 2001. Von Hagge and Baril directed the replacing of greens and tee boxes, and the rebuilding of fairways and cart paths. They lengthened and rerouted most of the course and updated irrigation. Formerly called the Ocean Course, it was already memorable for spectacular views and tropical beauty. Several holes are now more difficult and additional ocean-view holes were added.

Along the sea the front nine is generally flat and dependably windy, with some peninsula greens hanging over the crashing surf. Mountainous, roller-coaster-like terrain takes over on the back nine, winding up and down through the green hills and valleys of Rose Hall Resort, with putting surfaces and

tees bolstered by native stone walls. "Dead and Gone," "Caribbean Ghost," and "The Ruins" are a few of the quaint names bestowed on each hole. The fifteenth, "Mountain Falls," sports a 75-foot drop over a jungle to the tee, which is backed by a waterfall. This picturesque scene was used in the James Bond film *Live and Let Die.*

Seventeen begins with a panoramic sea view, then descends to a wide fairway that heads to a pristine valley and the ghostly ruins of an eighteenth-century aqueduct. Scattered throughout the track are several historic gravestones, monuments, and above-ground tombs from plantation days.

When golf loses appeal, guests head for the water park, climb onboard a yellow tube, and float the lazy river. As the stars come out, the night glows brightly inside the resort's casino, and in the nightclubs in nearby Montego Bay.

Tryall Golf Better Than Ever

Nearly half of the tee shots are played from nicely elevated tee boxes, providing birds'-eye views of the turquoise Caribbean Sea from the Tryall Golf Club, just west of Montego Bay. Site of the Johnnie Walker World Championship, Tryall has a long history of excellent golfing. A comprehensive renovation of the track in 2001 included all traps and bunkers, which are now redefined, reshaped, and filled with sparkling white sand. The hilly layout winds through diverse terrain, past lily ponds, an eighteenth-century waterwheel, thousands of coconut palms, and blooming shrubs, down to a mile-and-a-half shoreline.

Extensive changes were also made to the driving ranges and practice greens and bunkers. Privately owned, upscale rental villas and suites at the Georgian Great House are headquarters for guests who come for the golf, the water sports, and the award-winning tennis complex (www.tryallclub.com).

Wyndham Rose Hall Resort and Country Club
P.O. Box 999
Montego Bay
Jamaica, West Indies
Phone: (876) 953–2650, reservations (800) 996–3426
Fax: (876) 953–2617
Web site: www.wyndam.com
General Manager: Craig Martin
Accommodations: Four-diamond rated, 488 rooms and suites in two seven-story towers, each with private balcony or terrace, and ocean or mountain view.
Meals: Among five restaurants: Ambrosia Restaurant serves Mediterranean cuisine on a romantic verandah; northern Italian food at the contemporary Luna Di Mare; buffets and nightly entertainment at the Terrace; casual meals at the Cafe.
Facilities: Business center; tennis complex; beach club with complimentary equipment for snorkeling, windsurfing, kayaking, and sailing; sports bar, swim-up bar, lobby terrace lounge; fitness center; elaborate water park.
Services and Special Programs: Supervised Kids Retreat for ages 4–12. Shuttle to Montego Bay and Dunn's River Falls.
Rates: $$$
Golf Packages: All-Inclusive Golf Package includes luxury accommodations, unlimited golf, all meals and beverages (not including liquor or wine or champagne by the bottle), one golf clinic per package, and special amenities. $432–$504 per room, double occupancy.
Getting There: Fifteen minutes from Montego Bay and Sangster International Airports, both served by major airlines.
What's Nearby: Horseback riding, parasailing, water skiing, scuba diving, glass-bottom boat tours, and shopping in Montego Bay.

FOUR SEASONS RESORT NEVIS

Nevis, West Indies

Lush rain forests blanket the slopes of cloud-kissed Mount Nevis, which dominates the tiny island of Nevis, one of the Leeward Islands in the West Indies. Just 36 square miles, Nevis lies in the path of cooling northeast tradewinds and enjoys average daytime temperatures of 78 to 86 degrees. Once a playground for wealthy, eighteenth-century British plantation owners, the island remains a quiet retreat. At the foot of the velvety-green mountain, the Four Seasons Resort is nestled in palm trees and tropical flower gardens on one of the world's most beautiful beaches. Guests fly into St. Kitts and are ferried on a private launch to the resort, where they are greeted by a reception line of smiling staff.

Following a yearlong renovation after Hurricane Lenny in 1999, the resort reopened with a fresh face. There are now two new, lagoonlike infinity-edge pools rimmed with palms and blooming bougainvillea, vivid pink hibiscus, blue morning glory vines, tea roses, and banana, mango, and papaya trees. A new poolside restaurant and beach bar, and a shaded bocce court were also added.

Guests have complimentary use of nonmotorized water-sports equipment for snorkeling, scuba diving, windsurfing, and sailing. Idyllic 4-mile-long Pinney's Beach is protected by massive rock breakwaters. The water here is calm and translucent, great for swimming.

The heart of the place is the airy, high-ceilinged great house, comfy with British khaki–striped armchairs and sofas; traditional, English-style, dark wood furnishings; and ceiling fans. Rooms and suites, the largest in the Caribbean, are in a cluster of two-story, beachfront, plantation-style cottages with quaint gingerbread trim. Fine fabrics in Caribbean colors, classic mahogany beds and shutters, wrought iron accents, and wicker furniture add warmth to the accommodations, with cool stone tile floors.

Candles and torches are lit at sunset, when guests amble to the Ocean Terrace for steel-band music and local entertainment. A hideaway for enjoying a tot of rum, a cigar, and a good read, the mahogany-paneled Library is an intimate bar lined with bookshelves and often visited by tiny birds, such as bananaquits and jewel-toned hummingbirds.

Popular with adventurous guests are the guided hiking and walking tours: the Bush Medicine Walk, the

Monkey Excursion into the jungle, a Historic Charlestown tour, and a village walk.

Refilled with imported, white sand, seventy-two bunkers have been redefined on the Robert Trent Jones Jr. course, which winds up Nevis Peak on narrow fairways lined with dense, jungle vegetation, then undulates its way back down to the beach. The farther up you go, the cooler, mistier, and windier it is. Keep in mind that putts roll either swiftly downhill away from the mountain, or sluggishly uphill toward it. Cuban cigars and chilled towels are among the treats served by the refreshment cart.

Black-faced vervet monkeys, wild donkeys, goats, and vibrantly colored birds and butterflies are commonly sighted on the course. The signature fifteenth hole, 450 feet above sea level with dazzling sea views, asks for a 240-yard carry from the back tee across a deep ravine; most golfers save their mulligan for this attempt. On the sixteenth and seventeenth, which are crossed by the island road, watch for enterprising citizens selling golf balls scavenged from the impenetrable rough.

The finishing hole rockets to within 20 yards of the sea, the green perched above a stone wall over the crashing surf.

St. Kitts

Two miles across the channel, a thirty-minute boat ride from Nevis, the sister island of St. Kitts makes a nice day-trip destination for sightseeing, water sports, and golf. Snorkeling and scuba diving off the endless coral reefs is unequaled in the Caribbean.

Five-time British Open Champion, Peter Thompson, laid the Royal St. Kitts Golf Course on a beautiful, rather flat, oceanfront peninsula near Frigate Bay. The front nine ambles along the Atlantic, and the back nine is on the Caribbean. Both are quite breezy and more difficult than they seem, with thousands of palm trees and water on twelve holes.

Four Seasons Resort Nevis
P.O. Box 565
Pinney's Beach, Charlestown
Nevis, West Indies
Phone: (869) 469–1111, reservations (800) 332–3442
Fax: (869) 469–1040
Web site: www.fourseasons.com/nevis
General Manager: Robert Whitfield
Accommodations: Five-diamond rated, 196 rooms and suites in plantation-style decor, with large balconies or patios, sea or golf course views; separate sitting areas, colorful dhurrie rugs, huge bathrooms, and soaking tubs. Also large, duplex-style villas and elegant estate homes are available to rent.
Meals: Casual buffets and meals in the open-air, sea-front Grill Room; a stone fireplace, wood-plank floors, hurricane lamps, and international cuisine in the Dining Room; exciting Caribbean fare at the Cabana on the pool deck; weekly poolside West Indian buffets with live music.
Facilities: Golf practice range, putting, and chipping greens; Peter Burwash International tennis complex with four clay and six all-weather courts, clinics and lessons, PBI instructors, and pro shop; young adult entertainment center; new high-tech business center; fitness center; spa services; salon; English-style horseback riding.
Services and Special Programs: Complimentary, supervised Kids for All Seasons for ages 3–9, offering bike tours, rain-forest hikes, kayaking, swimming, and snorkeling. For all ages, organized beach games, volleyball, croquet, and golf competitions. Exercise classes and daily guided walks. NAUI and PADI scuba instruction and guided dives.
Rates: $$$$
Golf Packages: Seven nights luxury accommodations; breakfast, dinner, and unlimited golf daily; complimentary golf clinics; two half-hour private lessons; and extras. $3,505–$7,455 for two.
Getting There: A two-hour flight from Miami to St. Kitts, with transfer by private launch. Private aircraft land at Nevis Airport.
What's Nearby: The tiny, nineteenth-century town of Charleston; plantation tours; yacht, powerboat, and fishing charters; kayak tours to a sheltered cove and along the coast to Pelican Point.

HYATT REGENCY CERROMAR BEACH

Dorado, Puerto Rico

Side-by-side on the same luxuriant property on Puerto Rico's north coast are two Hyatt resorts, the Cerromar Beach and the Dorado Beach. Recent renovations to both hotels and all four golf courses, plus a gorgeous new golf clubhouse and a new spa, have created a vacation destination unequaled in the Caribbean. Guests happily get lost in the sprawling grounds, wandering in lush rain forest among waterfalls and blooming gardens. Tropical birds can be found among the palms and the fruit trees. More than two hundred varieties of orchids are on display.

At the Cerromar Beach, the world's longest freshwater swimming pool meanders 1,776 feet, with a lively current, fourteen waterfalls, water slides, and walkways and bridges. Water sports are the main attraction in the calm lagoon, as well as offshore from the sheltered beaches and the reef. The resort offers the only certified windsurfing program in Puerto Rico—you are guaranteed to be flying over the water

within ninety minutes. Take a ride on a Hobie Cat, and learn to ocean kayak, scuba dive, or sail a Sunfish. Float around the River Pool on a raft or take a swim in the brand new Olympic-size swimming pool.

Guest rooms have been completely renovated and feature bright tropical colors and dramatic ocean views from private balconies.

In the 1970s Robert Trent Jones Sr. integrated ninety-five bunkers into the links-style North Course along with his massive greens and signature "runway" tees, some of which reach out a hundred yards or more. With big mountain and ocean views, and rather flat terrain, most of the holes run east-west and are densely bordered by mature palms and native trees. Cameras come out on the seventh, which plays into the prevailing wind toward a sea of blooming flowers and the ocean itself.

On the rolling South Course, prevailing northeast winds and water hazards are the main challenges, with

ponds, streams, or lagoons on all but five holes. The Raymond Floyd Group did a complete renovation of the North, the South, and the Hyatt Dorado Beach Courses.

A "yoga-ssage" and a "De-Stress Aromatherapy Cocoon Wrap" await the tired resort guest at the new Spa del Sol. Getting into shape here is almost painless, as it is likely to be on the outdoor aerobics deck and on the cardio-theater equipment, where you can watch videos while working out. Children have their own yoga classes.

Daytime temperatures remain around 80 degrees on the island, year-round. Trade winds cool the evenings at the new, high-tech, Vegas-style discotheque, Bacchus, where wine and spirits, salsa and rock are on the menu. Perhaps the prettiest in the Caribbean, the casino offers live music and a bright new Copacabana-style atmosphere.

RTJ Classics at Dorado Beach

Opened in 1966 the East and West Courses at the Hyatt Dorado Beach Resort were renovated and a beautiful Spanish-style clubhouse was built at the end of the twentieth century. Fairways, bunkers, and greens were restored according to Robert Trent Jones Sr.'s original vision. Exotic landscaping and water features were added to the hundreds of existing coconut and citrus trees, and tropical rain forest.

The sight and sound of crashing surf serves as a backdrop to most of the holes on the 7,005-yard East Course. The holes run in different directions, bringing the unpredictable Atlantic trade winds into play on the generous fairways. The infamous thirteenth is 540 yards to a double dogleg and over two ponds to a large, elevated, undulating green—typical of most of the greens on the East.

Improved overall conditions resulting in a higher level of difficulty were completed in time for the Senior PGA Tour's Match Play Challenge (www.hyatt.com/puerto_rico).

Hyatt Regency Cerromar Beach
Highway 693
Dorado, Puerto Rico 00646
Phone: (787) 796–1234, reservations (800) 554–9288
Fax: (787) 796–4647
Web site: www.cerromarbeach.hyatt.com
General Manager: Tom Netting
Accommodations: 506 rooms and suites, most with private balconies or garden patios with views of the beachfront, in elegant seven-story buildings. Regency Club guests enjoy special services.
Meals: With a garden and waterfall backdrop, big steaks, seafood, and Caribbean cuisine at The Steak Company; luscious buffets at the three-level outdoor Swan Cafe, with ocean and garden views; in a garden setting, Zen Garden serves elegant pan-Asian cuisine and sushi.
Facilities: Full-service business center; casino with live entertainment; Spa del Sol Health and Beauty Center with meditation room, fitness club, outdoor aerobics deck, and juice bar; fourteen-court Peter Burwash tennis center with full-time pros; jogging and bicycling trails; water sports equipment.
Services and Special Programs: Resort guests have reciprocal privileges at the Hyatt Dorado Beach; access by free shuttle. Camp Hyatt, for ages 3–12, offers Spanish lessons, snorkeling, cultural crafts, beach activities, and meals.
Rates: $$$$
Golf Packages: Three nights garden-view room, daily round of golf and shared cart (unlimited golf April 15–November 30), twice weekly golf clinic, airport transfers, golf services, and gifts. $606–$965 per person, double occupancy.
Getting There: Forty-five minutes to Luis Muñoz Marìn International Airport.
What's Nearby: Go deep sea fishing on the *Great Lady,* a 53-foot Hatteras yacht. Shop and sightsee in historic San Juan, a scenic 22-mile drive away. Explore Camuy Caverns, tour and taste at the Bacardi Rum Distillery, or scan the heavens at the Arecibo Observatory.

WESTIN RIO MAR BEACH RESORT
AND GOLF CLUB
Rio Grande, Puerto Rico

Five-hundred-year-old stone fortresses, cobblestone streets, a tropical climate and championship golf make the United States commonwealth of Puerto Rico a popular vacation destination. Pineapples, piña coladas, and Chi Chi Rodriguez come to mind. Most everyone speaks English, no passport is required, the currency is the American dollar, and the average year-round temperature is 82 degrees. On the northeast shoreline near gorgeous beaches, a newly updated, vintage Fazio brothers course and a new Greg Norman course are main attractions at the brand-new Westin Rio Mar.

The seven-story, manor house-style hotel at Puerto Rico's first new resort in more than a decade lies on a mile-long, palm-fringed beach adjacent to El Yunque National Forest. Breezy archways and loggias, open to the sea air, lead to lush gardens and guest rooms warm with natural woods, Italian tile, and tropical-themed fabrics. Westin's signature "Heavenly Bed"—with a pillowtop mattress, down comforter, and a pile

of pillows—is a welcome retreat after a day of golf in the Caribbean sun, tapas and cocktails in Boleros, and dancing to a live Caribbean band in the Lobby Lounge.

Wide fairways, multitiered, elevated greens, and acres of sand define the Ocean Course, a Tom and George Fazio design from the mid-1970s that was entirely reconditioned in 1996. A misty mountain backdrop hangs above the well-established track, one of the most beautiful in the islands. Almond and Flamboyan trees, Royal and coconut palms, and tropical flowers make this a garden for golf. Watch for the giant iguanas on number four, and keep your irons low in the steady sea winds.

Greg Norman saved his first design effort in the Caribbean for the 7,004-yard River Course, opened in 1996. On gently rolling terrain, the track sports a formidable 135 slope and 74.5 course rating; GPS helps with course management. The beautiful Mameyes River and a creek run riot across several holes, while serene wet-

lands require forced carries on more than half the layout. Nearly eighty shallow bunkers—some turf-sided—and large, elevated greens are enhanced by blooming Reine del Floral trees and hundreds of coconut palms.

Among the wide choice of outdoor activities are the clinics and private lessons at the Peter Burwash Tennis Center; parasailing; and enjoying the water on Wave Runners, and jet skis, Windsurfers, kayaks, Hobie Cats, Lasers, and Sunfish. Swimmers and sunbathers head for three beachfront swimming pools, the golden sand beach, and the translucent waters around a nearby island sandbar. You can take a cruise on luxury catamarans and yachts, or go deep-sea fishing and scuba diving. On the longest reef in the Caribbean, diving and snorkeling are superb. Ask about the short day sail to the small, deserted islands of Icacos, Palominito, Lobos, and Palominos, where guests step off the boat into shallow water and spend the day beachcombing, snorkeling, diving, swimming, and digging into a bountiful lunch buffet.

Le Spa is a popular place at the end of the day for golfers and divers with aching muscles. The "Antistress Back Treatment" and the "Stimulating Leg Treatment" are among signature treatments for athletes.

Golf on St. Croix

Golf Magazine gave the Carambola Golf Course a gold medal and the LPGA plays the annual Konica USVI Classic here (809–778–0797). Just a short flight from San Juan to St. Croix in the U.S. Virgin Islands, and a fifteen-minute drive from the airport, bring you to this great track designed by Robert Trent Jones Sr. in the 1960s. At the edge of a rain forest, the course winds and rolls through a deep, verdant valley liberally watered with spring-fed lakes. Ninety-four bunkers are brilliant against the tropical foliage. Quaint, red-roofed villas on a stunning white sand beach at the Carambola Beach Resort are the best places to stay—just remember to drive on the left (877–258–2786).

Westin Rio Mar Beach Resort and Golf Club
6000 Rio Mar Boulevard
Rio Grande, Puerto Rico 00745–6100
Phone: (787) 888–6000, reservations (888) 627–8556
Fax: (787) 888–6600
Web site: www.westinriomar.com
Managing Director: Reinhard Werthner
Accommodations: Four-diamond rated, 694 rooms and suites with private balconies and terraces in seven-story, Caribbean-style buildings, with ocean or forest views; one-, two-, and three-bedroom oceanfront villas with kitchens. Royal Beach Club level merits complimentary food service, personalized concierge, and special services and amenities.
Meals: Among a dozen restaurants and lounges: Shimas Asian Bistro and Sushi Bar; four-diamond-rated, northern Italian cuisine at Palio; Tex-Mex at Cactus Jack's; nouvelle cuisine at the Grille Room; casual dining at three-story, oceanfront Marbella; seafood at the elegant Ocean Club.
Facilities: Full-service spa and salon; thirteen Har-tru tennis courts with professional instruction, clinics, and pro shop; three beachfront swimming pools; casino; shopping arcade; jogging trail; on-site PADI dive training.
Services and Special Programs: Camp Iguana for kids ages 4 to 12 offers crafts, games, meals, tennis and golf clinics, sailing, beach activities, and more. Fitness training and evaluations for golf and tennis players.
Rates: $$$–$$$$
Golf Packages: Unlimited Golf includes three nights accommodations, unlimited golf and cart, daily continental breakfast, golf services and gifts, and airport transfer. $1,100–$2,450 per couple, double occupancy.
Getting There: Nineteen miles from the Luis Muñoz Marín International Airport; scheduled shuttle and/or limousine transportation.
What's Nearby: The El Yunque Caribbean National Forest is filled with waterfalls, rain forest greenery, birdlife, and swimming holes. Enjoy deep-sea fishing for marlin and sailfish; sunset cruises, sailing, and boating day trips to the Bahamas; horseback riding from Hacienda Carabalí to the lowlands of Rio Mar and to a river where riders can sunbathe and swim.

WYNDHAM EL CONQUISTADOR RESORT

Fajardo, Puerto Rico

The farthest east of the Greater Antilles islands, Puerto Rico enjoys temperatures in the lower-70s in the wintertime, and in the mid-80s with high humidity in the summer. High season runs from mid-November until the end of March, when vacationers flock here to swim and dive in the warm, crystalline waters, and to explore Spanish colonial towns and lush rain forests.

On the northeasternmost tip of the island, in green splendor on a clifftop peninsula above the confluence of the Caribbean and the Atlantic Oceans, El Conquistador offers a wide variety of vacation options, from golfing on a championship course that rambles around in the hills, to pampering in the new Golden Door Spa, or water sports on the resort's private Palomino Island.

The choices are endless—windsurfing, Hobie Cat and Laser sailing, pedal bikes, Wave Runners, banana boat rides, glass-bottom boat tours, and snorkeling. Kayakers paddle their way to a nearby uninhabited island for romantic, private swims and picnics. Mountain goats and giant iguanas are among the sights for horseback riders who trod the trails at Palomino Ranch and into the surf at the beach. Yachts from around the world cruise into the marina.

Guest accommodations are Caribbean-pink or white-stucco buildings with red-tile roofs, luxuriant with flora, and located in separate, charming villages. Las Brisas and La Vista are at the heart of the resort. Reached by funicular, Las Olas is tucked dramatically into the cliffside, while La Marina lies at the waterfront overlooking the fishing port and yacht harbor. Las Casitas Village is an exclusive, luxury hotel with five-diamond-rated personal service and larger accommodations. Throughout, the traditional,

Spanish colonial influence lives on in the Moorish-Mediterranean–style garden courtyards, the many water features, and bougainvillea-draped archways and trellises.

As emerald green as Ireland, the golf course is a 1994 Arthur Hills redesign of a Robert von Hagge original. The upgrade defined bunkers, added tee boxes, and toughened up the greens, which are now mostly elevated and difficult to hold. The 6,662-yard track roils and heaves up and down the hillsides, with elevation changes of up to 200 feet on a single hole. Views of the gorgeous El Yunque Rain Forest and the sea are part of the reward. Beginning with a bang on number one, "The Ledge," you drive down a sweeping dogleg right to a narrow fairway, and, avoiding the namesake ledge on the right, move on to a deep green lying 30 feet below. Named "The Postage Stamp," nine runs uphill past a pond, into the wind, to a minuscule green. A pond borders the length of the eighteenth to a double green backed by a waterfall. Sidehill lies are the order of the day.

At the three-level Golden Door Spa, women golfers go for the "Pineapple Polish," an antioxidant body scrub, while the "Tub, Scrub, and Rub" is popular with men. The spa offers personal, golf-specific training and lower back exercises, as well as after-sun therapy. Smoothies and juices are refreshing on the sea-view terrace.

You can take a complimentary gaming lesson by the pool in the afternoon, then play at the casino into the early hours. Latin rhythms are lively for dancing at Casablanca's, a Moroccan-themed nightclub. Drakes Cigar Bar is a mellow sanctuary for a quiet read and billiards.

Rees Jones in the Tropics

Rees Jones designed the newest track on the island, the Flamboyan Course at Palmas del Mar Country Club, around the eastern end of the island at Humacao. Fortunately you can play your second shot from the beach on the thirteenth hole. Gary Player laid out the Palm Course among the coconut palms here three decades ago. It's still lovely with sea views from elevated tees (787–285–2211).

Wyndham El Conquistador
1000 Conquistador Avenue
Fajardo, Puerto Rico 00738
Phone: (787) 863–1000, reservations (800) 996–3426
Fax: (787) 863–6500
Web site: www.wyndham.com

General Manager: Rob Gunthneris
Accommodations: 918 guest rooms and 109 suites in the Grand Hotel, at cliffside Las Olas Village, and at La Marina Village on the waterfront. Spanish-style La Casitas Village is a separate, five-star hotel above the resort, offering ninety one-, two-, and three-bedroom casitas with kitchens, butler service, and special amenities.

Meals: Among thirteen restaurants and cafes; casual meals at Las Brisas Terrace; legendary Seafood Sunday brunch at Isabela's; teppanyaki, Chinese food, and sushi at Blossom's; northern Italian cuisine at Otello's; nouvelle Caribbean cuisine at Cassave; a French menu at Le Bistro.

Facilities: Full-service Golden Door Spa and salon with twenty-five treatment rooms, classes, fitness center, and Wellness Center; casino; two shopping arcades; seven tennis courts, instruction, and pro shop; six outdoor swimming pools; 55-slip marina.

Services and Special Programs: Water taxi to a private island is available. Camp Coqui keeps kids from toddlers to teens busy with nature hikes, games, snorkeling, water sports, and educational activities. Gifts for guests on arrival. Daily pool and beach activities and games for all ages. For families, cooking, games, and campfires.

Rates: $$$–$$$$

Golf Packages: Great Golf includes three nights deluxe ocean-view accommodations, unlimited golf and cart, complimentary golf clinic daily, breakfast buffet daily, golf services and gifts, and airport transfers. $695–$1,065 per person, double occupancy.

Getting There: Major airlines service Luis Muñoz Marín International Airport in San Juan, a one-hour drive away. Private aircraft land at Fajardo Airport, 10 miles away.

What's Nearby: Hiking, picnicking, and wildlife viewing at El Yunque Caribbean National Forest, a tropical rain forest, and at Las Cabezas de San Juan Nature Preserve; shopping, gallery hopping, and sightseeing in historic Old San Juan and on St. Thomas.

AFRICA

SUN CITY RESORT

Sun City, South Africa

Often called the "Kingdom of Pleasure," the flamboyant, truly spectacular vacation complex at Sun City in the Pilanesberg region just north of Johannesburg comprises five hotels, two golf courses, the largest water park on the continent, a large lake for water sports, casinos, live entertainment venues, and vast botanical gardens and forests—all surrounded by wild and mountainous African bushveld and a national park.

Footpaths thread through the Lost City jungle and gardens, with more than a million exotic plants, trees, and flowering shrubs, including the largest baobabs ever transplanted. Within the lush, botanical wonderland are waterfalls and cascades, rivers and wetlands.

The Valley of the Waves is a fabulous, gigantic water park with an artificial beach and tidal waves, water slides, a lazy river, swimming pools, and waterfalls.

Dominating the horizon, the Palace of the Lost City luxury hotel is a fantastical vision of soaring towers and domes, wildlife carvings, outstretched cranes, and life-size elephants—and these are just on the exterior. Bubbling streams, the Cheetah Fountain, guardian leopards, and elephant columns create an impressive entryway leading to a three-story rotunda with wood and marble carvings, inlaid floors, a grand staircase made of rock crystal and bronze, and more dazzling wildlife-related decorations. A simulated volcano erupts in the Tusk Lounge, just a taste of the theme-park-style entertainments throughout the resort. Rooms and suites are quite spacious, each fancifully furnished in wildlife and nature themes.

A little less showy the Sun City Hotel is built around a tropical atrium and is surrounded by the Gary Player

Country Club Golf Course. Site of the annual Nedbank Million Dollar Golf Challenge and other golf events, the Player course is a beautiful bushveld layout in the crater of an extinct volcano. More than 7,600 yards long, it may be the longest ever built and is one of Africa's most difficult—*Golf Digest South Africa* calls it the country's best. As flashy and unique as the resort itself, the course seems to swirl with swales and mounds on narrow kikuya grass fairways. Tall grass, thorn trees, short, sticky kikuya, and stones greet you in the rough. Clover-shaped greens are slick and sloping. The terrain is rather flat, with a large lake, stone walls, and walkways, and well-established, overhanging trees inhabited by more than three hundred species of birds.

Another Gary Player masterpiece, the Lost City Golf Course is about rocky outcroppings and enormous waste bunkers, wild gullies, cacti, and many water features. Front-nine fairways are generous to large, flattish greens. Elevated tees and narrow fairways on the back nine are terraced downhill on a mountainside into the bushveld. The thirteenth green is shaped like the African continent and surrounded by bunkers of different colors of sand. Golfers are discouraged from retrieving their balls from the crocodile pool, home of several dozen of the observant creatures.

A pleasant spot for an after-golf "sundowner," the recently renovated clubhouse is done up in "Zimbabwe Ruins" style, with heavy timbers, leather sofas, and green Italian marble accents. The ultimate reward for the golfer, however, is at the new spa—the "Golfers Delight" is a five-hour indulgence including facial, massage, hydrotherapy, manicure, pedicure, and hair treatment.

Sun Country Golf

The Wild Coast Sun Country Club, the only Robert Trent Jones Jr. design in South Africa, is cut through ravines, and across waterfalls and the Umtamvuna River. It has dramatic changes in elevation, and great views of the Indian Ocean and the Transkeian countryside. Brisk winds add to the challenge. The Wild Coast Sun resort hotel lies right on the beach (www.suninternational.com).

Another Gary Player original, Fish River Sun Country Club at Port Elizabeth on the southeast side of the country lies in overgrown natural vegetation and rugged sand dunes along the Indian Ocean coastline, a cross between links and parkland. Expect to cross Old Woman's River twice, by raft, and contend with pot bunkers and constant prevailing sea winds. The charming, Polynesian-style, country hotel, the Fish River Sun, is one of South Africa's most pleasant hostelries (www.suninternational.com).

Sun City Resort
P.O. Box 2
Sun City, South Africa
Phone: 011–27–14–557–1000, reservations (800) 223–6800
Fax: (954) 713–2071
Web site: www.sun-international.com
General Manager: Peter Birchall
Accommodations: 338 luxurious, large rooms and suites with sitting areas, carved armoires, lounge chairs, and wildlife-themed furnishings and decor.
Meals: Cascades, a river, an elephant fountain, and live music create the backdrop for international cuisine at the Crystal Court; northern Italian cuisine overlooking the Grand Pool at Villa de Palazzo; casual meals and barbecues at the Pool Restaurant; hors d'oeuvres and piano music in the spectacular Tusk Lounge; and several other restaurants throughout the resort.
Facilities: Full-service spa and fitness center; Titleist Golf Academy; live theater shows, movie theaters, discos, and casinos; three squash courts; twelve tennis courts; jogging tracks; lawn bowling; jet-skiing, water-skiing, and parasailing on the private lake.
Services and Special Programs: Supervised play at Kamp Kwena for ages 2–12. Guided game drives in the national park.
Rates: $$$
Golf Packages: None available.
Getting There: Johannesburg International Airport is 187 kilometers away; major airlines also service Pilanesberg Airport, a ten-minute drive away, with hotel transport available.
What's Nearby: Elephants, rhinos, lions, and antelope are among the animals sighted on game drives in the adjacent Pilanesberg National Park. Enjoy hot-air balloon flights, horseback riding, and a plethora of water sports.

PACIFIC RIM

HYATT REGENCY SANCTUARY COVE
Hope Island, Queensland, Australia

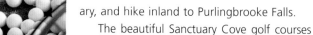

Reigning like a dowager queen over a secluded bay on the spectacular Gold Coast, the Great House is a gleaming white, homestead-style manse riding high above terraced gardens, towering gum trees, pines and palms, fountains and reflecting pools. Traditional 1940s-era and rattan furnishings create a luxurious, lodge feeling. Simple elegance is attained with lacquered wood floors, floral carpets, stone fireplaces, and vaulted ceilings. In the dry, warm, coastal climate, guests linger on the white sand beach which fringes a saltwater lagoon pool. Dressed all in white, lawn bowlers strike their poses, while yachts from around the world cruise into the marina.

The Hyatt is within Sanctuary Cove, a large, multifaceted resort located where the picturesque Coomera River flows into the Broadwater. The resort is complete with a large marina, a golf academy, two championship courses, a lively schedule of free events and entertainments, and a casino—all near miles of Gold Coast beaches. Daytrippers explore nearby Lamington National Park, the Koala Sanctu-

ary, and hike inland to Purlingbrooke Falls.

The beautiful Sanctuary Cove golf courses are the only courses in Australia to receive Audubon Cooperative Sanctuary status. Open to resort guests and members only, the Pines is the country's only Arnold Palmer design, recently updated and vastly improved. Among other hazards, golfers dodge the resident wallabies that roam freely, often lazing in the bunkers. With a 76 course rating, and 7,349 yards long, this is one of the country's toughest layouts. A pine forest impinges on the fairways, and the winds, from breezes to gusts, are a major factor on most holes. On the par-5 eleventh, you drive into a chute between fairway bunkers and the pines, avoiding water running down the right side and across the front of the undulating green. Expect an acre of sand on the sixteenth, a lake carry on the dogleg seventeenth, and water from tee to green on the finishing hole.

Fred Bolton laid out the Palms, a public course that was also renovated recently, adding new bent grass greens and reconstructed bunkers. Wear your

wind shirt for this track, too, and carry your ball retriever for the numerous lakes and water hazards. Gorgeous old cabbage palms and narrow greens add to the beauty and the challenge.

Among a variety of schools, clinics, and lessons available at the Sanctuary Cove Golf Academy is the popular "Half Day Improver Workshop," comprising two hours of off-course instruction, computer and video analysis, and a nine-hole playing lesson on The Palms.

Gold Coast Links

New owners of the Hope Island Resort on the Gold Coast have updated and improved a beautiful Peter Thomson–Mike Wolveridge design in a gorgeous wetlands setting. (Thomson is a five time British Open winner.) The Links at Hope Island, 7,064 yards long, is a true Scottish-links layout with pot bunkers, plenty of water, undulating fairways, mounded tussocks, and native grasses. Not Scottish, but magnificent, are the massive fig trees. Expect water carries, bump and run, and prevailing winds. Mediterranean-style villas on the golf course are available to rent (61–7–5530–9000, www.hir.com.au).

Hyatt Regency Sanctuary Cove
Manor Circle, Casey Road
Hope Island, Queensland 4212, Australia
Phone: 61–7–5530–1234, reservations (800) 233–1234
Fax: 61–7–5577–8234
Web site: www.sanctuarycove.hyatt.com
General Manager: Kim Powley
Accommodations: Five-star rated, 247 rooms and suites in low-rise clusters. Each is quite spacious, in Aussie-lodge style, and furnished with sleigh-style beds; timber and marble accents; a wall of shutters on a private balcony with views of the marina, the golf course, or the lagoon; a king or two doubles; deep tubs; walk-in closets; sitting areas; and work station. Regency Club guests have a private lounge, and complimentary breakfast and light refreshments.
Meals: Prime meats and seafood are prepared in the wood-fired exhibition kitchen at the Fireplace Restaurant, where a soaring, timber-framed ceiling and two-story fireplace create warmth and comfort. Daily specialties in a casual atmosphere, indoors or on the terrace, and Sunday seafood lunch with live jazz, at the Cove Cafe. Sunday tea buffet in the Verandah Bar.
Facilities: Sanctuary Cove Golf Academy Recreation Club with fitness equipment, lap pool, exercise classes, sauna, and spa, health and beauty treatments; salon; nine tennis courts with plexicushion, Supergrass, and rebound ace surfaces; tennis coaching and clinics; lawn bowling; business center; full-service, 330-berth marina.
Services and Special Programs: Supervised play for ages 4–12 at Camp Hyatt. Free shuttle bus transportation to nearby theme parks and attractions.
Rates: $$$
Golf Packages: The Sanctuary Cove includes one night accommodations, breakfast, use of the recreation club, and a round of golf on the Palms (you may substitute a golf lesson, a massage, or meals for the round of golf): from $165 per person, double occupancy.
Getting There: Forty minutes from Coolangatta Airport and from Brisbane International Airport, with limousine, shuttle bus, and taxi available; helipad on-site.
What's Nearby: Take a brewery tour or a day cruise, walk to Marine Village for shopping in eighty boutiques, or try your luck at Conrad Jupiter's Casino. Treat the kids to Dreamworld, Warner Brothers Movie World, or Sea World theme parks.

AMANUSA

Nusa Dua, Bali, Indonesia

The clouds and the changing sky are mirrored in the water shining in rice-paddy terraces that descend the hillsides of southern Bali. Beneath ancient banyan trees in a tropical garden, Amanusa is a very private, very exclusive enclave of thatch-roofed, Thai-style villas above the Indian Ocean. The heavy scent of tuberose floods the colonnaded, golden marble–floor foyer, where a massive teak-wood sculpture depicts scenes from the Ramayana, a Hindu legend. From here you can see the Bali Golf and Country Club, the southern coastline, and a rim of misty, green mountains. The warm, humid climate is most pleasant from June through September; humidity is highest in the rainy season, November through March.

The Shangri-la-like setting has a timeless atmosphere. Guest suites are hidden behind mossy stone walls. Each has a private courtyard; four-poster bed; mahogany and teak furnishings; sunken, marble-tiled tubs; outdoor showers; and reflection ponds. Some have private plunge pools. Suites also have oversize, canopied daybeds on balconies, and bay-window sofas, from which to contemplate the idyllic landscape.

A wide, blue swimming pool is lined with peach-colored bougainvillea-draped arbors and lush pale-pink and white frangipani. The Beach Club is just a few minutes away by car or resort bicycle, where "bales," or cabanas, are shady hideaways with plush mattresses and cushions, and pots of frangipani water to wash away the sand. Snorkeling and diving is superb on the coral reef; you can walk to it at low tide. Beach barbecues are popular, complete with flickering torches and Balinese flags lining the path that leads to candlelit tables. Swimming is safe in the protected lagoon, and surfing is very good on the nearby Nusa Dua reef.

Wide ocean and countryside views from the Terrace restaurant set the tone for Asian specialties, while the Restaurant features Italian cuisine in a garden courtyard. One of the pleasures of Thai cuisine is the

luscious fruit, ranging from tiny, sweet bananas and papayas, to huge jack-fruit, snake fruit, hairy rambutans, and mangosteens.

Guests get preferred tee times and transportation to the Bali Golf and Country Club nearby, one of the loveliest and most challenging courses in Asia. It was designed by Robin Nelson and Rodney Wright in the early l990s. The front nine, in a dense rain forest, is hilly and fairways seem to roll with all the movement of the ocean. The back nine drops towards the beach in an endless series of sprawling, sandy bunkers dotted with coconut palms. The narrow dogleg-left sixteenth hole is a veritable Sahara of sand bordering the fairway from tee to green. Cascades of bougainvillea frame gorgeous ocean views and the occasional water buffalo reminds golfers they are playing in a pristine environment. Nick Faldo set a course record of 64 here during the Dunhill Masters tournament.

At the beautiful, Thai-style clubhouse are a driving range, putting and chipping greens, a pro shop, restaurant and bar, swimming pool, and spa. The golf club is within a congested, elaborately landscaped development of hotels, restaurants, and boutiques in the Nusa Dua resort district, where tourists gather on Kuta Beach.

Bali High

Within an extinct volcanic crater near Bedugul, Bali Handara Kosaido Country Club is a Thomson, Wolverage, and Perret creation in Bali's northern mountains, a two-hour drive from Amanusa. The oldest course on the island, and the longest at 7,024 yards, this may also be the most scenic, with panoramic views of glimmering Lake Byuan and the surrounding valleys. The course is criss-crossed by a rushing stream. One advantage is the wonderfully cool weather at 4,000 feet in elevation. Green fees include the services of a caddie. There is also a pro shop, driving range, spa, sauna, and a clubhouse restaurant serving local, Western, and Japanese cuisine (62–361–262–531, www.99bali.com/golf/handara).

Amanusa
P.O. Box 33
Nusa Dua 80363
Bali, Indonesia
Phone: 62–361–772–333, reservations 62–361–771–267
Fax: 62–361–772–335
Web site: www.amanusa.com
General Manager: Dan Reid
Accommodations: 35 very private, thatch-roofed suites in garden settings, with marble floors, contemporary mahogany furnishings, private patios, luxurious amenities, and superb personal service.
Meals: Exquisite Asian food at the Terrace; fine Italian cuisine at the Restaurant; light fare poolside.
Facilities: Two hard-surface tennis courts, with ball boys; library specializing in Indonesian books; antiques gallery and boutique.
Services and Special Programs: Salon services and seaside or in-room massage; cooking classes; yacht, sailboat, and catamaran charters, and personalized island tours can be arranged.
Rates: $$$$
Golf Packages: None available.
Getting There: A limousine will pick you up at Bali's International Airport, a twenty-minute drive.
What's Nearby: The hotel will pack picnic lunches and arrange tours of rural villages and rice terraces; Denpasar, the island capital; and the "the six temples of the heavens." The ancient Luhur Uluwatu temple on the tip of a peninsula at the south end of the island lies above the sea on a magnificent stone outcropping. A car and driver are a good idea in the wild and crazy Balinese traffic.

LE MERIDIEN NIRWANA GOLF AND SPA RESORT

Tabanan, Bali, Indonesia

On the southwest coast of Bali, the entrance road to this serene resort drifts through vivid green, water-filled rice terraces, some of which are actually part of the Greg Norman–designed golf course. Arriving in the open air lobby, guests are irresistibly drawn to the balcony above the crashing surf of the Indian Ocean and the unforgettable sight of the multiroofed, Pura Tanah Lot, a dreamlike temple on a rocky islet. Balinese wood carving decorates the soaring peak of the "alang-alang" thatched roof of the main building. Along with vibrantly colored art-works and temples, impressive stone reliefs depict ancient Hindu tales, creating a mystical, calming atmosphere. Throughout the grounds are riots of blooming tropical trees and flowers, waterfalls, lotus ponds, and interlinked, beachfront swimming pools.

One of the most spectacular courses in Asia, the Nirwana Bali Golf Club drops gracefully down to a clifftop. It is 6,805 yards of tropical beauty with wonderful sea views, devilish sea breezes, and a backdrop of dramatic, volcanic mountains. Freshwater creeks, wetlands and

rice terraces, and thousands of palms border the fairways and the hodgepodge of big bunkers. Carries are over high, green grasses; over some deep valleys, and, occasionally, over the beach or the ocean.

A 214-yard par-3, the seventh carries from clifftop to clifftop across a blue, blue bay. Twelve is a great short hole along a ridge studded with Balinese temples and a river to the right. Aim your downhill second shot to the island green perched on a stone ledge. If your ball lands in one of the ten Hindu shrines on the track, you can pick it out and drop without a penalty.

Club up on fourteen, "The Shark," in a headwind, to make it across the beach to the cliff-top green.

In addition to rooms, suites, and villas in the hotel complex are a plethora of homes and townhouses to rent. Le Meridien's guest rooms and Executive Suites are oversize and done up in sleek, understated, contemporary Balinese style with lovely, Batik fabrics and original artworks. Villas have individual plunge pools, butler service, outdoor living pavilions, and showers, and lush tropical gardens, each quiet and screened completely for privacy.

Ladies on the Links

As at most resort courses in Asia, the caddies at Le Meridien Nirwana are well-trained, young women and men who are invariably charming and helpful. Their personal service ranges from marking and cleaning balls to wading into the rice paddies, searching for your lost balls.

It is not unusual on some courses for each golfer in a foursome to have several caddies: one to tote clubs; one to carry an umbrella for sun and rain, or to carry a chair, water, and a mobile phone; and one to serve as forecaddie. This parade of people is a new experience for many traveling golfers and may be unsettling. Just enjoy those sweet dispositions, all the personal assistance, and local knowledge, and you may well play the best round of your life.

The words for thank you are *selamat tinggal!*

Le Meridien Nirwana Golf and Spa Resort
P.O. Box 158
Kediri, Tabanan 82171
Bali, Indonesia
Phone: 62–361–815–900, reservations (800) 300–9147
Fax: 62–361–815–901
Web site: www.lemeridien-bali.com

General Manager: Mark Griffiths

Accommodations: Five-star rated, 278 rooms and suites in low-rise, traditional Balinese-style buildings, with views of the ocean, gardens, or golf course. Decor is spare and sophisticated, using locally produced fabrics, artworks, and furnishings. Surrounding the hotel are rentable luxury villas, timeshare suites, resort homes, and townhouses.

Meals: Asian specialties and Dutch-style *rijstaffel* at Nirwana Restaurant, accompanied by traditional *gamelan* music; Continental and regional menus, and sunset buffets at Cendana, served indoors or on the terrace; at the Pool Grill, snacks and light meals during the day, and Mediterranean cuisine, seafood, candlelight, and live jazz at night; at the Nautilus Fun Pub, snacks, darts, billiards, live music, karaoke, and sports broadcasts; high tea and appetizers in the Lobby Lounge.

Facilities: Five swimming pools and a 54-meter-long water slide; tennis courts and teaching pro; squash courts; a restaurant and pro shop at the golf clubhouse.

Services and Special Programs: Penguin Club, a supervised daily program for toddlers to teens, includes beach and pool play, games, and meals.

Rates: $$$–$$$$

Golf Packages: Simply Golf Package includes three nights luxurious accommodations, two rounds of golf with caddie and cart, airport transfers, and full buffet breakfast daily: from $270 per person, double occupancy.

Getting There: Just forty-five minutes from Ngurah Rai (Denpasar) International Airport.

What's Nearby: Shopping for folk art in the artists' town of Ubud, for wood carvings in Mas, and for silver and goldsmithing in Celuk; complimentary hotel shuttle to Ubud and Kuta for sightseeing. The hotel will arrange outdoor recreation in Kintamani and Bedugal, including white-water rafting, elephant trekking, hiking, and four-wheel driving.

AMANPURI

Pansea Beach, Phuket, Thailand

On the island of Phuket in the gentle, crystalline Andaman Sea, off the southern coast of Thailand, Amanpuri is set apart from the hubbub of tourism. Resting on a green headland in a grove of tall coconut palms above the curve of sugar-white Pansea Beach, the serene resort, built of local granite and hardwoods with high pitched roofs, resembles a clutch of Thai temples. A glimmering, midnight-blue swimming pool, lily ponds, and a stone terrace define a dramatic central courtyard where traditional Thai music is performed in the evenings. A sweeping stairway shaded with palms descends gracefully to the beach below. The pool is lighted and an impromptu sunset bar is set up nightly above the waterfront. With bamboo torches lit in the sand and underwater lamps glowing in the sea, beach barbecues are romantic occasions.

Forty guest pavilions are positioned for privacy. Some have sea views, all have outdoor *salas* and sundecks. Adjacent to the resort among the palms are thirty privately owned, oceanfront villas with private pools and live-in staff.

A Chinese sailing junk, speedboats, and an Italian luxury motor cruiser are among the more than twenty vessels in the resort's fleet. They are used to sail along the coastline and to the nearby islands for sightseeing, scuba diving, snorkeling, and fishing. You can also water ski, windsurf, and sail a Hobie Cat from the beach.

Four beautiful golf courses are within a thirty-minute drive. The resort owns a corporate membership at the very private Blue Canyon Golf and Country Club, comprising two of the top courses in Southeast Asia and the best in Thailand. The Canyon Course is laid in rugged hills across two wooded valleys and a ridge, tumbling downhill along a series of pristine freshwater lakes. Well-established trees narrow the rolling fairways down to landing zones and approaches requiring precise iron play. On hot, humid days—nearly every day—five refreshment kiosks on the course and a second caddie to carry a shade umbrella are appreciated. The back nine is defined by deep, water-filled canyons. Tiger Woods won the 1998 Johnnie Walker Classic here, coming from seven back on Sunday to beat Ernie Els in a thrilling playoff.

Newer and a little longer, the Lakes Course is a combination of a rubber plantation and more deep gorges, with gentler, wider fairways, water on seventeen holes, and gargantuan greens. The clubhouse has a spa and two restaurants serving excellent Thai, Western, and Japanese food.

Orange-robed Buddhist monks walk the winding roads, which are lined with pineapple and coconut plantations and often decorated with elaborate flower and fruit offerings. Water buffalo are picturesque silhouettes in the rice paddies. Golfers from around the world find themselves in a tropical paradise.

Other Places to Play

Five top-notch golf courses are within an hour's drive from Amanpuri. The Thai Muang Beach Golf Club is the only one that runs directly along the seaside. Backed by mountains and low, forested hills, this Pete Dye–design is a links-style track of 7,026 yards, with deep, undulating bunkers and Dye's trademark railroad ties shoring up the tees, greens, and traps. A handful of forced water carries adds to the fun (66–76–571–533).

Just ten minutes from Amanpuri, the Banyan Tree Golf Club in secluded Bang Tao Bay is laid in a valley of blooming trees and flowers, surrounded by wooded hills and coconut trees on an old plantation, with plenty of water hazards (66–76–324–350).

On rolling foothills around a large lagoon, the Phuket Country Club starts with six undulating, grassy holes, then flattens into a garden area, and finishes in a rain forest, with elevated tees.

The nine-hole Country Club Course here asks for water carries over every hole. At the clubhouse is a swimming pool, spa, and restaurant serving good Thai cuisine (66–76–321–038, www.phuketcountryclub.com).

Amanpuri
P.O. Box 196
Phuket 83000, Thailand
Phone: 66–76–324–333, reservations 66–76–324–333
Fax: 66–76–324–100
Web site: www.amanresorts.com
General Manager: Ferdinand Wortelboer
Accommodations: Forty spacious pavilions, each with private garden terrace, some with sea views. Decor is contemporary Thai with art and antiques. Baths and dressing areas are large. Thirty privately owned, oceanfront villas are available to rent, each with a pool, two to six bedrooms, live-in maid, and cook.
Meals: The casual Terrace specializes in Thai and European cuisine, alfresco; the Restaurant serves Italian food; the Bar offers poolside drinks and snacks.
Facilities: Six tennis courts and teaching pro; freshwater, chlorine-free swimming pool; upscale boutique selling Asian jewelry, artifacts, and gifts; full-service spa and salon; on the beach, a fitness center with personal trainers; library stocked with 1,000 volumes, novels, travel guides, art books, and CDs.
Services and Special Programs: Dive yachts and PADI-accredited program for advanced or novice divers.
Rates: $$$$
Golf Packages: None available.
Getting There: Limousines are complimentary for the half-hour drive from Phuket International Airport.
What's Nearby: The concierge will arrange a car and driver for day trips to more than thirty Buddhist temples in the countryside, to deserted beaches, and to Khao Phra Thaew National Park. Phuket town is fun for shopping in the central market and dining. Divers take overnight cruises to the Similan Islands.

CENTRAL AMERICA

MELIÁ PLAYA CONCHAL ALL-SUITES BEACH AND GOLF RESORT

Santa Cruz, Costa Rica

When someone says, *"Pura vida!"* to you in Costa Rica, they mean, "I wish you the good life!" And the best of the good life is lived at Playa Conchal, located on Costa Rica's relatively undeveloped, northwest Pacific coast and situ-ated on 2,400 lushly landscaped acres surrounded by hills, valleys, volcanoes, and views of the Gulf of Papagayo. Designed by a renowned Spanish architect, the secluded, self-contained resort resembles a quaint village. Fountains and lakes are refreshing in the tropical sun, while footpaths take you through botanical gardens. The interior of the open-air reception area mirrors the ecological spirit of the resort with the use of volcanic stone walls and uninterrupted vistas of the stunning environs. Made of pink-white, crushed seashells, the idyllic 1.5-mile beach is fringed with palms. Right on the curve of the beautiful bay, a complex of low-rise, tile-roofed, Spanish-colonial–style buildings house the elegant, very large guest suites.

Ecotourists come to see wildlife in the glorious rain-forest parks—Santa Rosa, Rincon de la Vieja Volcano, Barra Honda, and Palo Verde. Those who love sportfishing cast for trophy-size sailfish, marlin, swordfish, and tuna. Surfers flock here for the big waves. Golfers spend their time on Garra de León, the "Lion's Paw."

Garra de León is a new course designed by Robert Trent Jones Jr. He chose a scenic route through dry forest on hilly land studded with huge trees. Fairways are wide, greens are large, and side-hill lies are many. Ravines seem to career back and forth across the track. Lagoons, lakes, and prevailing winds complicate matters, contributing to the 74.2 course rating and 134 slope. Thirteen bunkers and a large body of water up the ante on the seventh hole. The 100-foot drop from the back tees on twelve is distracting; mind the dense forest bordering the dogleg right. Wetlands menace the sixteenth green, 80 yards out, with pounding surf as a backdrop; bring your binoculars to see the birdlife on the small island. Crocodiles occasionally make their presence felt on this hole, too.

Moaning like banshees in the early morning, bands of howler monkeys scamper across the tree-tops, occasionally alighting on the fairways. Maintaining superb wildlife and environmental standards, Garra de León is the first Latin American course to receive Audubon Cooperative Sanctuary designation.

The best time of year to golf in Costa Rica is late-December to mid-April. Hot afternoons are best spent in Central America's largest free-form swimming pool, at the swim-up bar, or floating in the cerulean waters off Playa Conchal. Jet skiing, sailing, sea kayaking, windsurfing, and snorkeling are popular water sports. Evenings are lively at the casino and disco bar.

Other Places to Play

One of the longest established and most famous courses in Latin America, the Cariari Country Club opened in 1974 on the outskirts of the capital city San José (011–506–293–3211, extension 133). It makes a nice stop on the way to the Pacific coast. George Fazio designed narrow fairways lined by towering pine trees at a refreshingly cool 4,000 feet above sea level. The lush, green terrain undulates like an ocean, playing longer than 6,590 yards. If your ball flies into the dense rough, leave it for the giant lizards, monkeys, and snakes; and consider hiring a caddie for those blind shots. Stay at the Herradura Hotel (800–245–8420) or the adjacent Meliá Cariari Golf Resort (800–336–3542).

A new championship course at Tamarindo, about twenty minutes from Playa Conchal, is a Ron Garl design. Rancho las Colinas Golf and Country Club ambles over hill and dale and around a small mountain (011–506–383–3759). Thirteen is the signature hole, where you traverse a creek and head uphill to an elevated green with a menacing rock face.

Meliá Playa Conchal All-Suites Beach and Golf Resort
Playa Conchal, Santa Cruz
Guanacaste, Costa Rica
Phone: (506) 654–4123, reservations (800) 336–3542
Fax: (506) 654–4181
Web site: www.solmelia.com
General Manager: Richard Pfeifer
Accommodations: 308 suites in 39 two-story villas, each with a spacious private terrace and a balcony, elegant living room area, air-conditioning, and lavish baths.
Meals: Eleven restaurants and bars, including buffet-style Mitra; Italian cuisine at Faisanella; grilled seafood and steak poolside at La Caracola; Caribbean food in a hillside setting at Astrea; and Spanish tapas at Cauri.
Facilities: Travel agency; car rental; mini-market; four lighted tennis courts; fully equipped health club with aerobics classes; volleyball, basketball, table tennis, bicycles, and water sports equipment.
Services and Special Programs: Twenty-four-hour medical services; multilingual staff; extensive activities and entertainment program for adults and children; live shows each night.
Rates: $$$
Golf Packages: Two nights accommodations in a villa suite, two lunches, unlimited golf and cart, gift, and golf services. $689 for two, double occupancy.
Getting There: Fifteen minutes from Tamarindo Airport and forty-five minutes from Guanacaste International Airport in Liberia, with shuttle service. The capital city of San José is forty-five minutes away by plane.
What's Nearby: The concierge will arrange day trips to Volcan Rincon de la Vieja, and to the nearby resort towns of Flamingo and Tamarindo; scuba diving; deep-sea fishing; horseback riding; rain-forest tours; and river rafting.

ABOUT THE AUTHOR

KAREN MISURACA is a golf, travel, and outdoor writer whose golf-related articles have appeared in *Golfweek, Alaska Airlines Magazine, Global Golfer,* and other magazines and newspapers. She is the author of six regional guidebooks and lives in Sonoma, California. When traveling around the world on assignments, Karen plays golf with her partner, Michael Capp.